T0382920

Sustainable Green Development and Manufacturing Performance through Modern Production Techniques

Sustainable Green Development and Manufacturing Performance through Modern Production Techniques

Chandan Deep Singh

Harleen Kaur

CRC Press
Taylor & Francis Group
Boca Raton London New York

CRC Press is an imprint of the
Taylor & Francis Group, an **informa** business

First edition published 2022
by CRC Press
6000 Broken Sound Parkway NW, Suite 300, Boca Raton, FL 33487-2742

and by CRC Press
2 Park Square, Milton Park, Abingdon, Oxon, OX14 4RN

© 2022 Chandan Deep Singh and Harleen Kaur

CRC Press is an imprint of Taylor & Francis Group, LLC

Library of Congress Cataloging-in-Publication Data
Names: Singh, Chandan Deep, author. | Kaur, Harleen, author.
Title: Sustainable green development and manufacturing performance through
    modern production techniques / Chandan Deep Singh, Harleen Kaur.
Description: First edition. | Boca Raton, FL : CRC Press, 2022. | Includes
    bibliographical references and index.
Identifiers: LCCN 2021030341 (print) | LCCN 2021030342 (ebook) | ISBN
    9781032038834 (hbk) | ISBN 9781032038858 (pbk) | ISBN 9781003189510 (ebk)
Subjects: LCSH: Lean manufacturing. | Manufacturing
    processes--Environmental aspects. | Sustainable engineering.
Classification: LCC TS155.7 .S56 2022 (print) | LCC TS155.7 (ebook) | DDC 658.408--dc23
LC record available at https://lccn.loc.gov/2021030341
LC ebook record available at https://lccn.loc.gov/2021030342

ISBN: 978-1-032-03883-4 (hbk)
ISBN: 978-1-032-03885-8 (pbk)
ISBN: 978-1-003-18951-0 (ebk)

DOI: 10.1201/9781003189510

Typeset in Times
by SPi Technologies India Pvt Ltd (Straive)

Contents

Preface

Today, most of the production strategies are influenced by quality, cost, delivery, innovation, and responsiveness. Firms have traditionally pursued these goals through adoption of production practices, such as simultaneous engineering, increasing efficiency through elimination of defects, setup reduction etc., and worker empowerment. Recent developments in industry suggest another way of achieving excellence in production, that is, industry regulators and professional bodies must encourage innovation in a broad range of high-tech production facilities with environment in mind. Success of the industry depends upon production facilities and the competitive advantage that the industry gains because of better quality and reliability. This advantage leads to increase in the sales and the creation of a sound customer base for greater market share, which eventually leads to more profit, growth and expansion.

A firm's processes must possess operating advantages in the form of competitive priorities to outperform its competitors. The operating advantage of the industry is assessed, evaluated, and measured along the parameters of cost, quality, time, design, flexibility, etc. The present research attempts to come up to the expectations of industrialists, policy makers, academicians by evaluating the impact of production facilities, upon which the success of the industry depends. In this research high priority risk factors of industry are taken up so as to provide a suitable qualitative model based on these.

Taking into account the literature survey, the need of the present study arose because impact of sustainable green development through advanced manufacturing and maintenance techniques in manufacturing performance of manufacturing industry has not been yet addressed. For this purpose, the present study has been designed to investigate and suggest the parameters that contribute to the success of manufacturing industry. Moreover, this topic is need of the hour as it involves environment. For this purpose, the present study is so designed to investigate the sustainable green development initiatives that contribute to the performance of the industry. Based on the risks involved in the industry suitable model will be developed based on sustainable green development which will go a long way in serving industries as well as academicians.

To summarize, this research makes a significant contribution in the direction of sustainable green development through advanced manufacturing and maintenance techniques. However, this study helps to overcome the limitations that were encountered with the most methodological sound techniques. This study will encourage other researchers to engage into more research regarding sustainable development, green engineering, advanced manufacturing and maintenance while hoping that such efforts will enhance the performance of organisations, its managers and customers with regard to common advantages and benefits. In the end, a final model has been developed for sustainable green initiatives through advanced manufacturing and maintenance techniques. This model has been developed based on the validation of selected input factors by using various qualitative and quantitative techniques.

Author's Biography

Dr. Chandan Deep Singh has been working as assistant professor in the Department of Mechanical Engineering, Punjabi University, Patiala, Punjab (India) since 2011. He completed his Ph.D. in November 2016 from the same institution. His M.Tech. (Manufacturing Systems Engineering) is from Sant Longowal Institute of Engineering and Technology, Longowal, Sangrur, Punjab (India), completed in 2011. He completed B.Tech. in Mechanical Engineering in 2009 from Giani Zail Singh College of Engineering and Technology, Bathinda, Punjab (India). He scored 94.8 percentile in GATE examination in 2010. He has published 56 books (2 books including his PhD thesis have been published by Taylor & Francis) and guided 57 students for M.Tech. thesis. He has published more than 80 papers in various *scopus/SCI* indexed and other peer reviewed international journals and 16 papers in international conferences. To add to it, 10 papers have been accepted and 5 papers are under review in *scopus/SCI* indexed international journals and 2 papers have been accepted in international conferences. Further, a book, as an editor, is accepted by Wiley-Scrivener Publisher. Presently, 3 M. Tech. and 8 Ph. D. students are working under his guidance. Further, 2 chapters in book have been published by Taylor & Francis in their initiative SDGO and 1 chapter has been published in Springer series and 2 chapters have been accepted for publication in HICO 2021 under Wiley-Scrivener publications and 1 chapter is accepted for publication in *Factories of the Future*, book to be published in 2022 under Wiley-Scrivener publications. Lastly, he is working on 4 industry-sponsored projects.

Dr. Harleen Kaur has been working as Manager (HR) at DELBREC Industries, Pvt. Ltd., Chandigarh. Earlier, she served as Assistant Professor of Management in Asra Institute of Advanced Studies, Bhawanigarh until Sept 2019. Until 2013, she worked as HR (Executive) at International Farm Fresh Products (India), Ltd., Channo (Bhawanigarh). She completed her Ph.D. in 2019 from Punjabi University, Patiala. She completed her MBA in HR from RIMT, Mandi Gobindgarh in 2011. She has published more than 10 research papers in various international journals and conferences along with 19 books with international publishers (her PhD thesis has been published as a book by Taylor & Francis). To add to it, 3 papers have been accepted in *scopus* indexed international journals. Further, a book, as an editor is accepted in Wiley-Scrivener Publisher. Lately, 2 more chapters have been accepted for publication in HICO 2021 under Wiley-Scrivener publications and 1 chapter is accepted for publication in Factories of the Future book to be published in 2022 under Wiley-Scrivener publications. Lastly, she is working on 1 industry sponsored project.

1 Sustainable Development

1.1 INTRODUCTION

Nowadays, manufacturing firms are all facing increasing pressure to become greener and more environmentally friendly. Therefore, they have had to review or instigate changes in their manufacturing processes to able to cope with the community and concerned government. The modern sustainability and environmental factors are considered important topics for strategic business, management, manufacturing and decision when developing a new product. Manufacturing firms therefore often develop sustainable programmes with the objective of "greening" their own products and processes and reducing the impacts of their activities on the environment. The main aim of green manufacturing and sustainability is to minimize the environmental damage due to the manufacturing firms. In this chapter, the significance of sustainable development, green engineering, advanced manufacturing and maintenance techniques, competency, and their function in manufacturing performance are discussed.

The manufacturing sector plays a significant role in the economy of almost every country in the world, and certainly in all the developed countries. In 1990, India and China had similar gross domestic product (GDP) per capita. After that, driven by its manufacturing sector, China's economy has grown faster than India's and its GDP per capita on a PPP basis is 90% higher than India's Gross domestic product per capita. To attain higher rates of monetary growth, India immediately needs to strengthen its own manufacturing sector. The Indian economy is firmly on the path of stable growth; even throughout the last decade when other countries have been in the grip of a massive slowdown, India continued to enjoy a comfortable economic position. The growth in the manufacturing sector is dependent on the investment climate. The structural reforms since 1990 have made some progress, and despite current setbacks, it is generally recognized that the reform process in India can't be reversed, and sooner or later these reforms will be executed. Nevertheless, the long-term competitive capability of Indian industries depends on their manufacture efficiency.

Manufacturing efficiency is dependent on the ability to develop, import and adapt for new-age technologies, amongst other factors. India has made significant progress in various spheres of science and technology over the last few years, and takes pride in having a strong network of science and technology organizations, skilled manpower and an inventive knowledge base. Considering the rapid pace of globalization, fast-depleting material resources, and increasing competitiveness among different nations, a need to protect intellectual property and strengthening of technology base have become an important issue. While India's technical talent is recognized worldwide, there have been serious institutional gaps in promoting industry research methodology and interaction with various institutes.

The structural transformation of the Indian economy over the last three decades had been spectacular, mainly due to the growth of its services segment, which now reports for about 50% of the GDP. However, the rapid growth in the service sector, which is attaining maturity, before the growth in the manufacturing industry is not a strong indication. An information-based financial system cannot be maintained in the long run unless it is adequately supported by a growing manufacturing financial system. Furthermore, a service financial system cannot persist to thrive on a long-term basis in a country where over 80% of the population is educated below the middle-school level.

Some sectors, such as information technology and pharmaceuticals, compete globally, employing perhaps 2% of the population and bringing wealth to various parts of India. At the same time, around 60% of the population remains dependent upon the Agricultural segment, distribution less than one-quarter of India's GDP. Without reforms, agriculture will continue to suffer from prevalent under-employment, low wages and depend on the monsoon. This will result in continued urban immigration, but without the expansion of an industrial segment this will lead to a rise of unemployment in many cities. The growth of this pattern is unsustainable.

It is estimated that India needs to create 8–9 million new jobs every year, besides agriculture, to stay at its current unemployment level of 7%. Manufacturing jobs are ideal for workers, transitioning them out of agriculture as service jobs require a high level of education and expertise. The revitalization of the manufacturing segment can create close to 2.6 million new jobs every year. With the removal of all quantitative restrictions on imports and the falling import tariffs under the world trade organization regime, it becomes a bigger concern for the Indian industry to improvise its competitive edge.

Indian manufacturing industries have always been pushed from the protected environment of the licence-permit-quota regime to an uncertain environment of liberalization, privatization and globalization, which provides intense Global competition. Indian industries quite often follow an opportunistic approach with respect to growth as opposed to the capability-driven approach and paid very little strategic attention to their shop floors in the last few decades. Now, gradually Indian manufacturing industries have started re-organizing themselves, driven by their Global competition.

Facilities departments are under tremendous pressure to quickly provide more information, and at a lower cost to the company. At the same time, many companies have reduced staff to a bare minimum. Maintenance professionals are presented with more difficult challenges today than ever before. The biggest obstacle of all confronting maintenance professionals is being forced to do more with fewer resources. Maintenance departments must deliver superior service, comply with regulatory requirements and provided detail financial accountably all within the confines of limited and/or reduce budgets. In order to meet these challenges, maintenance professionals are arming themselves with economical computerized maintenance management systems. In recent years flexible, dependable and economical computerized maintenance management systems have become available to help fight the never-ending struggle to operate and maintain the built environment.

1.2 SUSTAINABILITY

A large and growing number of manufacturers are realizing substantial financial and environmental benefits from sustainable business practices. Sustainable manufacturing is the creation of manufactured products through economically-sound processes that minimize negative environmental impacts while conserving energy and natural resources. Sustainable manufacturing also enhances employee, community and product safety. A growing number of companies are treating sustainability as an important objective in their strategy and operations to increase growth and global competitiveness. This trend has reached well beyond the small niche of those who traditionally positioned themselves as green, and now includes many prominent businesses across many different industry sectors. In many cases, these efforts are having significant results. There are a number of reasons why companies are pursuing sustainability:

- Increase operational efficiency by reducing costs and waste
- Respond to or reach new customers and increase competitive advantage
- Protect and strengthen brand and reputation and build public trust
- Build long-term business viability and success
- Respond to regulatory constraints and opportunities

Sustainable engineering is the process of designing or operating systems such that they use energy and resources sustainably, in other words, at a rate that does not compromise the natural environment, or the ability of future generations to meet their own needs. Sustainable development meets the needs of the present without compromising the ability of future generations to achieve their own needs.

As customer demands are changing rapidly in terms of sophistication of products and services they require, organizations need to become more responsive to customer and market needs. In fact, the integrated management of product-related information through the entire product lifecycle – known as product lifecycle management (PLM) – is a key element for companies in creating sustainable value. Thus, in order to proactively respond to these new demands, managers require up-to-date and accurate performance information on its business. This performance information needs to be integrated and accessible to support the monitoring and the improvement of the performance of an organization and its business processes. Thus, a performance measurement system (PMS) is a vital part of a company's managerial system. The PMS of an organization can be defined as a set of indicators used to quantify the efficiency and/or the effectiveness of their actions.

1.3 SUSTAINABLE DEVELOPMENT

Sustainable development is the organizing principle for meeting human development goals while simultaneously sustaining the ability of natural systems to provide the natural resources and ecosystem services based upon which the economy and society depend. The desired result is a state of society where living conditions and resources are used to continue to meet human needs without undermining the integrity and stability of the natural system. Sustainable development can be defined as development that meets the needs of the present without compromising the ability of future generations to meet their own needs.

While the modern concept of sustainable development is derived mostly from the 1987 Brundtland Report, it is also rooted in earlier ideas about sustainable forest management and twentieth-century environmental concerns. As the concept developed, it has shifted its focus more towards the economic development, social development and environmental protection for future generations. It has been suggested that the term 'sustainability' should be viewed as humanity's target goal of human-ecosystem equilibrium, while 'sustainable development' refers to the holistic approach and temporal processes that lead us to the end point of sustainability. Modern economies are endeavouring to reconcile ambitious economic development and obligations of preserving natural resources and ecosystems, as the two are usually seen as of conflicting nature. Instead of holding climate change commitments and other sustainability measures as a remedy to economic development, turning and leveraging them into market opportunities will do greater good. The economic development brought by such organized principles and practices in an economy is called Managed Sustainable Development (MSD). The concept of sustainable development has been, and still is, subject to criticism, including the question of what is to be sustained. It has been argued that there is no such thing as a sustainable use of a non-renewable resource, since any positive rate of exploitation will eventually lead to the exhaustion of earth's finite stock; this perspective renders the Industrial Revolution as a whole unsustainable.

After the Brundtland Commission first introduced the concept of sustainable development, a growing number of national and international organizations, governments, communities and companies are embracing sustainability. In this way, companies are facing tough challenges to succeed in a global competitive market especially to address this issue of sustainability. It has inspired many researchers and practitioners to search for ways to use tools for measuring and evaluating their progress. In this context, sustainability indicators have emerged as one widely accepted tool. Therefore, an increasing number of voluntary initiatives and companies have begun developing and using sustainability indicators. Such indicators might be used to improve a company's public image and thus create a competitive advantage through product/service differentiation. As a result, companies around the world have recognized the need to respond appropriately to the sustainable development challenge and, consequently, many have changed their business activities in product development. This increasing upsurge of incorporation of sustainability in the processes to all phases of a product's life resulted into the need of assessment of its performance.

In the current competitive and regulated landscape, manufacturing enterprises struggle to improve their performances, encompassing environmental as well as economic objectives, towards sustainable manufacturing and the future Eco-factories. Experts and scholars have developed more and more indicators, usually referred to as Key Performance Indicators (KPIs), as a means for steering and controlling the complex factory systems, characterized by dynamic interdependencies among different subsystems and external variables. The present study proposes a synthetic framework to bring back hundreds of environmental and economic KPIs to a few sound intuitive categories, in order to reduce duplications, recuperate meaningfulness and consciousness, facilitate inter and intra-organizational benchmarking. The approach, based on input/output modelling of physical flows (products, materials, energy, emissions, etc.) in manufacturing systems, can be used at different hierarchical levels in the plant and in different factory lifecycle phases (design, operations and re-design). The application of the framework is demonstrated on an extensive review of performance indicators gathered in industrial cases and in the literature.

Sustainability indicators have emerged as a key element in a market where customers are interested in the environmental impacts of the products they consume. Companies are trying to incorporate them into their Performance Measurement Systems (PMS). However, there is little information available to managers to guide them on the incorporation. Hence, this paper presents the results of an action research carried out to improve the PMS of a Brazilian consumer goods company with the incorporation of sustainability indicators. The findings illustrate that is possible to incorporate them into the PMS as long as there are stakeholders interested in establishing strategic objectives for sustainability.

The cement industries are facing challenges to implement sustainable manufacturing into their products and processes. Cement manufacturing has remarked as an intensive consumer of natural raw materials, fossil fuels, energy, and a major source of multiple pollutants. Thus, evaluating the sustainable manufacturing in this industry is become a necessity. This paper proposes a set of Key Performance Indicators (KPIs) for evaluating the sustainable manufacturing believed to be appropriate to the cement industry based on the triple bottom line of sustainability. The Analytical Hierarchy Process (AHP) method is applied to prioritize the performance indicators by summarizing the opinions of experts. It is hoped that the proposed KPIs enables and assists the cement industry to achieve the higher performance in sustainable manufacturing and so as to increase the competitiveness (Figure 1.1).

Over the past decade, several articles on corporate performance measurement system (PMS) related to sustainability have been published in a wide variety of journals.

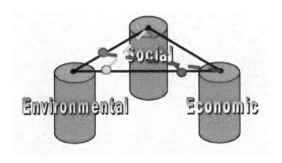 

FIGURE 1.1 Parameters of sustainable development.

A robust PMS can help decision makers overcome the challenges of corporate sustainability by helping them to better understand their current situation and their desired end state. The majority of researches on indicators have focused on design of sets of corporate sustainability indicators. However, despite several contributions, many corporations still struggle to develop, implement, use, and improve PMS.

Green manufacturing and eco innovation impact the sustainability performance. The study investigated the data collected from 53 manufacturing firms from the automotive, chemistry and electronic sectors in Turkey. The collected data was tested using regression analysis to verify the hypothetical relationships of the study. The results of the regression analysis concludes that green manufacturing application have a positive effect on social performance and environmental performance. The results also show that the eco innovation has a significant positive impact on sustainability performance.

Sustainability indicators were incorporated into a performance measurement system. This work presented the results of an action research carried out to improve the performance measurement system of a Brazilian consumer goods company with the incorporation of sustainability indicators. The results says that it is possible to incorporate the sustainability indicators in performance measurement system as long as there are stakeholders interested in establishing strategic objectives for sustainability (Figure 1.2).

Key performance indicators for evaluating the sustainable manufacturing believed to be appropriate with the cement industry based on the triple bottom line of sustainability have been presented. The results show the existing performance levels of the company and provide the suggestions to company to improve their sustainable manufacturing performances (Amrina and Vilci, 2015).

Sustainable environmental manufacturing practice (SEMP) influences firm performance. The survey was done from 103 manufacturing firms from Malaysia which were analyzed using smart PLS. The results show a significant relationship between SEMP and environmental performance but could not find an evidence of a significant relationship between SEMP and financial and operational performance. This implies

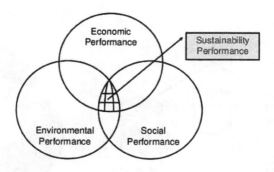

FIGURE 1.2   Three-dimensional indicators of sustainability performance.

that SEMP is yet to be considered as a strategic resource in achieving competitive advantage and better firm performance among manufacturing companies. The research tends to investigate the effect of firm size on the relationship between sustainable manufacturing drivers and firm performance. Data was collected from manufacturing firms from Malaysia and analyzed by SEM-AMOS. The results shows that firm size moderates with the relationship the market forces and leadership with firm performance. The results also indicates that the larger firms will experience a higher rate of firm performance as having advantage of firm size as compared to small firms.

Sustainability and environmental stewardship will be increasingly important considerations in manufacturing and design in future and are likely to influence the main priorities for advancing manufacturing operations and technologies. Designers and manufacturing decision makers who adopt a sustainability culture within companies are more likely to be successful in enhancing their design and manufacturing. The results also concluded that more extensive research and collaboration is needed to improve understanding of sustainability in manufacturing and design and to enhance applications of sustainability (Rosen and Kishawy, 2012) (Figure 1.3).

Sustainable manufacturing practices (SMP) and innovation have an impact on economic performance. The research reported in this paper aims to analyze the effect of SMP on economic sustainability (ES) and the mediated effect of SMP on ES through innovation performance (IP). Using survey data collected from 150 Malaysian manufacturers, this paper empirically examines the relationships that exist among SMP (internal and external SMP), IP (product, process, organizational and marketing), and ES. Adopting PLS-SEM technique, the study found that internal SMP has a positive effect on ES and process innovation partially mediates this internal SMP-ES link. Surprisingly, although the relationship between external SMP and ES is not significant, incorporating product and process innovations into this link have changed the significance of the relationship. In general, the results have empirically proven the role of SMP and IP in influencing the economic performance.

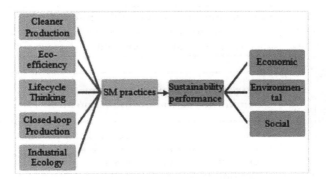

FIGURE 1.3 Conceptual model of achieving sustainability performance through implementation of SM practices.

In manufacturing, development of green technologies (from process and tooling to the entire enterprise) is one way to ensure that the future manufacturing systems are sustainable. For this purpose the innovation in advanced manufacturing is needed. The basic requirements of green technology are discussed in this paper along with methods and tools to ensure that they are effectively applied, and their impacts are measured (David, 2014).

Green engineering design is an important aspect for lifecycle assessment tool. The article begins with a brief case of historical paths of early aspects of sustainability starting from a regulatory perspective. The case is made that the adoption of programmes that safeguard human health and ecological systems was primarily due to a series of disastrous incidents and then regulations were enacted. This cycle of steps needs to change to proactive use of sustainable and green engineering. Adoption of many of the sustainable technologies in this encyclopaedia as well as educational programmes in sustainability should be implemented (Figure 1.4).

FIGURE 1.4   The evolution of SM concepts and practices.

Sustainability assessment tools have applications in manufacturing. This paper aims to review the state of the art associated with the latter, synthesizing and analyzing the applicability of the different approaches with their practical applicability in real-world manufacturing. Based on review of research trends within sustainability assessment, the author identified a list of tools addressing three pillars of sustainability which all can be applied on company level.

Sustainable manufacturing is the need of the hour and future of industries depends on it. It deals with objectives of design, its functions, competitiveness, profitability and productivity. It is likely that in future sustainability and other environmental practices will have many considerations in manufacturing and designs and have influence on main priorities for advancing manufacturing operations and technologies. Designers, manufacturers and decision makers who need to practice and establish a sustainability culture in industries will surely remain successful in their fields as these are key requirements of today and future. Also extensive research and group work is needed to enhance and improve understanding of sustainability in manufacturing and its applications.

A framework in formulating a sustainable manufacturing strategy which is grounded on sustainability without disregarding the internal and external competitive functions of manufacturing. The proposed framework attempts to integrate classical theories on manufacturing strategy and the current demands on sustainable manufacturing in an attempt to formulate a sustainable manufacturing strategy that describes two distinct functions of manufacturing – competitiveness and sustainability (Lanndon and Omela, 2015).

Various assessment methods have been applied to review the sustainability performance of palm oil production in Malaysia. The paper reviews how the stakeholders define the sustainable palm oil and effectiveness of existing sustainability evaluation through tools, standards and legislative requirements to identify gaps and barriers to achieve environmental, economic and social objectives of sustainable palm oil production (Biswas et al., 2015).

Value creation can be achieved through sustainable manufacturing. The paper presents major business imperatives and the strategic capabilities required to enable value creation through the sustainable manufacturing identified based on extensive engagement with business leaders and industry professionals as well as academic experts and government agency representatives. This paper also presents a future vision for sustainable products, processes and systems that can be derived from such capabilities.

Sustainability performance indicators have an impact on manufacturing in large companies. This article investigates sustainability in the performance measurement systems of Swedish manufacturing companies. It builds on a previous study that documents relatively few direct environmental indicators at shop floor level, which raises questions about possible indirect links between existing indicators and the environment that could be used to improve the environmental aspect of company´s sustainability ambitions. A method for identifying and categorizing indirect links to sustainability issues was defined and used. The results suggest that at shop floor level 90% of the indicators have at least an indirect relation to one or more of the sustainability dimensions economy, environment and social, of which 26% are at least indirectly related to the environmental dimension. Despite the many indirect connections, participating companies perceive a need to improve sustainability indicators and some ideas are suggested (Zackrisson et al., 2017).

There are various enablers and barriers of sustainable manufacturing. The author tends to present the opinions of various researchers around the globe and industry professionals on the important enablers and barriers and to analyze them using statistical techniques to highlight the differences in opinions for strategic implementation of sustainable manufacturing. As per results based on the survey there seems to be huge difference in line of operation of researchers and industry professionals with regard to sustainable manufacturing. However, both the groups need to collaborate in order to work together to strengthen the enablers and diminish the barriers.

Distributed manufacturing systems (DMS) are currently discussed in science as a possible approach for the realization of sustainable manufacturing. This paper gives an overview of trends towards distributed manufacturing systems as well as reasons and arguments why Distributed Manufacturing Systems are appropriate concepts for more sustainable manufacturing.

The expected impact of the 'global drivers' (such as population demographics, food security; energy security; community security and safety) and the role of sustainability engineering in mitigating the potential effects of these global drivers. The message of the paper was that sustainability requires a significant input from ergonomics and human factors, but whereas the profession needs some expansion in its thinking in order to make this contribution.

Sustainable design-centred manufacturing (SDM) creates competitive advantages for future new product development. In this study the author defines the major indicators of social sustainability for development of SDM and proposes a balanced scorecard method to evaluate the weighting factors among the three pillars and the indicators used to assess each pillar. The algorithm for the analysis is based on structural equation modelling (SEM). A case, using the manufacturing data for poly lactic acid (PLA), is developed. The results can be adapted to evaluate the performance of outcomes for new product development utilizing SDM.

The new method uses the principles from existing methods, VSM, DES, and LCA. SMM takes a goal-oriented approach, a principle that is known in LCA (ISO 14040 2006). Choosing the right indicators according to the goal, and setting the system boundaries are essential steps for SMM. The challenge of the goal-oriented approach is that comparing different systems may be problematic because the assessment does not use the same indicators.

Environmental issues affect the manufacturing sector and explains how taking action on sustainability can help mitigate perennial business challenges. It also outlines a sustainable design methodology that can assist in lowering the environmental impact of any part, quickly and cost-effectively, with the help of advanced design software tools.

The lifecycle energy analysis sheds light on the importance of considering use phase while evaluating the energy saving potential of remanufacturing appliances upon reaching end-of-life. A total lifecycle perspective, remanufacturing is a net-energy-expending end-of-life option. The economic assessments indicate that if the cost of reuse/remanufacturing is minimal compared to the purchase cost, then appliance remanufacturing may provide an economic incentive for consumers. Our retrospective approach demonstrates the criticality to study macroscopic factors such as technological improvements, policy impacts, economic incentives in order to draw insights about energy and economic saving potential of appliance remanufacturing.

A framework included the indicators buffer, measurement process, and performance evolution on the basis of bottom line. Bottom line takes into account ecological and social performance in addition to financial performance. Carbon emission and energy use indicators are taken into consideration. Sustainability measurement is limited to machining operations only.

An exergy is defined as the potential of a system to cause change as it achieves equilibrium with its environment. When the environment is used as heat reservoir, exergy is the energy that is available to be used. Although exergy contains more information regarding energy losses to the environment, it is the use of energy during production that should be computed and then reduced for individual parts or component. Study focused on the industrial sector as a whole and not able to measure the environmental impact of a company.

Indicators of sustainable production are categorized into social, economic and environmental indicators on the basis of available data and commonly measured aspects of production including materials use, energy use, water consumption, parts, waste, and air emissions. Study is mainly focused on the environmental aspect of production system. A methodology has been developed for measuring sustainability indicators and a strategic set of matrices for assessing the sustainability level of a company has also been provided. The choice of the sustainability indicator for a company is left to the user. The user has to consider each indicator separately for its implementation in a company. The use of indicator is company specific. If an indicator is effective for one company it may not be effective for the other. Thus, the variation in selection of the indicators hinders in comparing the two companies on the basis of sustainability. The proposed indicators have not been implemented on any process or company.

A composite sustainable development index depicts performance of companies along all the three dimensions of sustainability – economic, environmental, and societal. In the first part of the paper, the procedure of calculating the index that would enable comparisons of companies in specific sector regarding sustainability performance is presented. However, the emphasis of the paper is on the second part, where the effectiveness of the proposed model is illustrated with a case study in which two companies from specific sector are compared regarding their sustainability performance.

Lifecycle assessment tool is used to quantify the environmental impacts from the energy inputs. In addition to this, solid waste and air emissions from the production of energy and on-site air emissions from the burning of fossil fuel, outputs have also been included within the scope of the study. A science based mathematical relations have been used for the determination of energy use, waste and air emissions from the process information (Singh et al., 2012).

Interaction between lean manufacturing practices environmental management (e.g., environmental management practices and environmental performance) and business performance outcomes (e.g., market and financial performance) has been carried out. This investigation representation near lean manufacturing as an essential ancestor of environmental management practices.

Adaptive lean judgement gives a valuable way to direct the lean implementation process. Using the web-based programme, a judgement model is produced adaptively for each user to estimate the existing position of the system, identify the imperative goal for development, and classify the suitable tools and procedure for developing action plans.

Plant size, unionization and plant age, matters with regard to implementation of lean practices, even though not all characteristics, are subject to the same level. Synergistic package of lean practices alongside emerges to make significant payment to prepared concert over and above the small but major effects of context.

There are some issues, playing the key roles in the collapse of lean implementation practices like: lack of an exact foundation for lean manufacturing and its connected alteration process, lack of accurately known requirements and reasons for transform, opposition to change etc. They projected a self-evident model as the form of FR-DP-PV relationships that provide a scientific model for concepts, principles and methodologies of lean manufacturing and thereby alleviating many obtainable achievement limitations. The proposed hierarchical arrangement illuminates the interrelationships of concepts, principles, and methodologies in the best way.

Lean principles and techniques have been functional in a broad range of association, from make-to-stock to engineer-to-order industries, and even in distinctive service sectors, such as healthcare. In order to apply lean principles in various areas, variants were urbanized of well-known method, such as Kanban, Kaizen, SMED, and 5-S. They suggested to stimulate research labours that added advance lean production in manufacturing and service industries. Application of lean production principles in engineer-to-order industries and manufacturing services emerge to best till sheathing after, because numerous of the conventional techniques cannot be applied directly in their processes.

A hybrid simulation approach is employed using Microsoft Excel to model the Manufacturing Resource Planning (MRPII) function, while Pro Model simulation software is used for the advancement and operation of the mould production surroundings. Microsoft Visual Basic is used to create a connection between systems for schedule dissemination and inventory updates. 5-S methodology of lean manufacturing solves the problems of ceramic industry. They implement 5-S methodology in storage departments and the result is 13.91% sq. ft. space saving.

The estimated impacts of their training programme on sales revenues are statistically insignificant, but value-added profits are economically strong and significant. By contrast, those business owners who received other business training in the past had significantly greater sales revenues, but their added value and profits are not significantly different from the averages. These results support hypothesis that KAIZEN training boosts value added and profits by reducing wasted materials and activities.

Implemented the 5-S methodology in laboratories of university engineering school by surveying the industries which have 5-S methodology, results to become these labs to industrial labs, adapting the conditions of security. The 5-S methodology application in university organizations provides a basis to create an organization culture and start working with continuous improvement criteria. This applies both in the processes related to the students learning, and in teaching and non-teaching activities. The new culture has resulted in an improvement of the working environment and an increase in the motivation of the staff involved.

A discrete simulation event is an event in which various improvements are done at interval or precise time. After implementation of kaizen, discrete simulation event technique is applied. Kaizen and discrete simulation event are parallel implemented. Reduction in the lead time accommodates more deliveries per year. Various improvements in cell synthesis culture (i.e., adoption of platform technology, information sharing). The main area of Kaizen approach is protein purification. The impact of Kaizen was 110 in 10 months in pre-Kaizen period and 114 in 8 months in post Kaizen period. The various enterprises of the cluster zone are called off to join the training. A baseline survey was conducted of two industries. The total impact of training after a 3-year programme is calculated by statistical analysis and impact score is calculated.

A cross culture idea Kaizen is adopted by Chinese but workers don't feel good as it is a cross culture idea. A three-stage principle Activator Behaviour Consequence in which first the mind of worker is changed to adopt the new technology by providing them new charts. The behaviour towards kaizen is tested and the result has been made by ANOVA test by statistical analysis. Because Kaizen is sensitive methodology the behaviour towards this approach is changed. 5-S factors have an impact on SME's through visualize area of small-scale industries. The area was identified surveys, performance measures and implementation of 5-S was carried out. The result shows the effect on importance of organization's climate and risks are decreased.

The effectiveness of the kaizen approach and its application to wood products industry was studied. A survey and interview were conducted with staff member of each company and developed a tool to measure the effectiveness of kaizen events. By statistically, the motivators related to cost, quality and barriers related to time, money, management were viewed. The effect of management commitment on organization of work teams in benefits of implement Kaizen in industrial enterprise's during planning stages. 200 questionnaires were applied to 68 companies distributed in Mexico and least partial squares technology is used for structural equations to conclude the impacts of profit and positive impact of success factor of Kaizen and 5-S. 5-S is a simple approach to small scale manufacturing organization for becoming productive and more efficient. Four data collection methods have been used to ensure right implementation of 5-S. Tool searching time for shop floor has been reduced from 30 to 5 minutes. 5-S audit score has been increased from 7 (week 1) to 55 (week 20).

Kaizen techniques in assembly line workshops in India was implemented at different levels of manufacturing and assembly. The factors as distribution, marketing was motivated so that problems like shortage of supply are solved. The result of implementation was to lower the overall cost and to boost the quality. The main focus is on multi-skilling of labour rather than number of labours. By industry engineering tools, the skill level points are collected (125 points). The level of workmanship is checked. The result was the worker's skill level is increased and the load on the supervisor is decreased (Singh et al., 2014).

The main objective is to reduce abnormality in organization by using process parameters communication as to increase information, ergonomics as machine control, by correcting waste of motion and time, by planning material handling techniques, the performance is obtained. This implementation decreased the searching time by 6–8 minutes and saved cost of blades by 1200–3600/month. Also quality users are improved (Singh et al., 2015). The main objective is to upgrade the standards of enterprises by applying Kaizen in medium scale units. By analyzing the process parameters as production efficiency, production cost, turnover capacity etc. the production was improved from 200 axle per shift to 210 axle per shift, by reducing the number of operations by 15. The conclusion was that there is the effect by enhance the customer satisfaction level on medium enterprises. A list of drawbacks of Kaizen with Indian philosophies was prepared. They concluded that Kaizen merged with Indian scriptures is very effective and efficient (Singh et al., 2014). By defining target from top to lower management they used Supplier Kaizen approach to implement the lean manufacturing technology. There was a big improvement in results as lead time (50%), production floor space (42%), WIP stock (37%).

Cross-sectional analyses of the performance results reveal that distinctions in Six Sigma impacts across producing and service companies are negligible. Interestingly, we realize that the performance impact of Six Sigma adoption negatively correlates to the firm's quality system maturity (indicated by previous ISO 9000 certification). Further analyses of producing and service corporations reveals that advantages of Six Sigma significantly correlate to intensity in producing of any product from raw material, and with financial performance before adoption in services. We discuss the implications of these techniques for observe and for future analysis. Study provides solid support for the hypothesis that Six Sigma adoption tends to manufacture important abnormal advantages to firm profit. These benefits seem to be persistent over factors associated with an "effective" Six Sigma programme, including motivation, fit with culture of industry or firm, and conformance to programme structure.

The study is based on the current manufacturing operation line of an Air Cleaner. The employment of the novel storage system provided benefits to the production line by eliminating waste of redundant motion and the waiting time when reloading the product. By presenting the GFR system in the assembly line, the existing material handling activities can be improved. Good storage system is vital for real material handling system to attain on-time delivery and develop efficacy.

Further study is recommended to carry out simulation of the GFR system in order to identify the smooth flow of poly-boxes by adjusting the inclination angle of the rack. The results attained from the computer simulation were equated to the prevailing performance of the line. Inventory level has been able to be declined by 74% while space deployment reduced by 18.18%. Besides, before and after implementation of GFR was compared to check whether the manufacturing performance had enhanced or not. However, additional study is recommended for simulating the GFR system to recognize the even flow of poly-boxes by altering the inclination angle of the rack. In addition, a detailed examination on the material supervisor in terms of path taken on the assemblage line cycle time, responsibilities and job proficiency can also be inspected.

On successfully implementing the ideas, it can be seen that there is incessant and precise flow of resources at the correct time and in the correct quantity. An equilibrium must be upheld by using Kanban system, where it comprises of two containers containing components alongside with the cards called as Kanban cards representing the maximum quantity of resources to be ordered after scanning the bar code on it, the main tenacity of scanning is, as the constituents are getting consumed the barcode is scanned by the one in the material branch which behaves as a signal which acts as assigning an order to the supplier.

The data was collected from three diverse countries and three dissimilar industries. JIT production was introduced by Japanese firms and for long time it was viewed as a Japanese production philosophy. Though JIT production have been widely accepted by western manufacturer and they assume that the level of JIT implementation and development still higher in Japan. In augmentation to this, JIT production was started by Toyota and many researchers often call it as Toyota production system. Later, JIT was accepted by many automobile companies in order to attain Toyota's high quality and low-cost cars. They expect that the implementation of JIT production is still higher in automotive industry than electronics or machinery.

The nature of JIT production is that it necessitates everyone's involvement and input in order to reassure smooth operations. Cooperation and coordination amongst employees, progressions, and tasks are of vital prominence for JIT success. In addition, Supply chain management is the pivotal point in JIT atmosphere and disappointment in appropriately managing suppliers. Moreover, customers will essentially obstruct JIT production. This infers that supplementary responsibilities will be endured by managers and workers. These new responsibilities comprise everyone's responsibility for quality control and precautionary maintenance, multi-functional employees, recommendations for incessant improvements and contribution in small groups for solving problems.

Technology also shows a significant role in JIT atmosphere to ensure that time-tables always meet and set up times are condensed to the lowest potential. Progressive and innovative technology will also improve the competitive nature of the firm and novel product development. Consequently, the paper proposed that well-developed and interconnected manufacturing strategy companywide will subsidize to the level of JIT enlargement and implementation. The efficacy of JIT production is anticipated to be greater in an organization with a distinct manufacturing strategy Manufacturing strategy is likely to include all the issues debated above and will assist as a perfect roadmap so that everybody in the plant is predictable to recognize that the business strategy is erected upon the manufacturing competences and that he or she is playing a central tactical role in the application of JIT production. Manufacturing strategy varies from human resource management practices linked with JIT; it slightly high-points the planned role of the manufacturing which is anticipated to lead the complete business approach in JIT atmosphere.

For the other three elements of manufacturing strategy – achievement of functional integration, manufacturing-business strategy linkage, and proprietary equipment – significant differences were not found among these countries. Based on study, the following conclusions are drawn.

First, country and industry alone clarified a substantial portion (15.2%) of disparity in JIT application level. This variance was mainly enlightened by the industry, and analysis did not expose substantial differences among the three countries-Japan, USA, and Italy in the level of JIT application. As for industry, the results presented that the automotive industry has greater levels of JIT application and expressively differs from electronics and machinery industries.

Second, country and industry alone elucidated an irrelevant portion (9.1%) of variation in JIT performance level. The results expose that automobile industry has upper levels of JIT performance than electronics industry.

Third, this study specified that manufacturing strategy basics have a positive and substantial impact on JIT application and improvement level. This offers guidance for managers allowing for or attempting employment of JIT production. The results recommend that manufacturing strategy is a significant substructure for JIT and must be involved to the traditional infrastructure practices usually associated with JIT production. The results showed that some manufacturing strategy elements are more implemented in Japan than USA and Italy (Anticipation of New Technologies, Communication of Manufacturing Strategy, and Formal Strategic Planning). The results also indicated that the impact of manufacturing strategy elements on JIT production is higher in Japan than USA and Italy. The results showed that though the application of four manufacturing strategy elements is meaningfully higher in the automotive industry than the other two industries, the impact of manufacturing strategy essentials on JIT production is alike in the three industries except for the communication of manufacturing strategy where the influence is considerably less in the machinery industry than automobile.

Fourth, the investigation presented that all the manufacturing strategy basics, except for Communication of Manufacturing Strategy, have a constructive and substantial impact on JIT performance. This discovery provides supplementary support to former research demonstrating that JIT performance does not trust purely on JIT practices, but on the plant's structure. The results presented that manufacturing strategy elements are an imperative infrastructure for JIT success.

The results also specified that the influence of some industrialized strategy rudiments on JIT performance is higher in Japan among nations and automotive industry among industries. The constraint of study is that only three developed countries were encompassed and about half of the sample plants are world-class, consequently the consequences may present some prejudice and restriction of range. Also, in addition, JIT performance was measured comparative to competitors, not to performance preceding JIT introduction.

Related research must be commenced for less developed countries. Also, further research is needed with a greater sample and supplementary industries so that casual modelling practices of investigation could be functional. Finally, additional research is desirable to explore how manufacturing strategy affects other operational practices and employee contribution. In this universal competitiveness, seller should be able to meet his manufacturer desires and capable to satisfy his demands.

1. Every part of the product should be identified, and common trust should be recognized between seller and the manufacturer.
2. The portions which are being delivered by the seller should have least flaws in order to provide quality and JIT distribution to the customers.
3. Size of Inventory should be condensed in order to diminish the cost.
4. Waiting time should be decreased. Pull system should be reformed in its place of Push system.
5. Seller should have coordination with their associated department.
6. There should be no communication barrier between seller and producer.

7. Mutual strategy should be approved to tackle with unstable business atmosphere which results in lessening of stock transportation, motion and processing waste.
8. Both seller and producer should emphasis on end buyer wants.

More opportunities for exploring further deeply into the associations between JIT supply, JIT production and performance lie in the application of different research practices and methods that could assist as well as supplement the outcomes observed in this research. The hypotheses in this paper have been verified using statistics from the third round of the High-Performance Manufacturing (HPM) project. Data were collected by the international team of scholars working in different academies. They comprise responses from manufacturing plants functioning in the mechanical, electronics and transportation equipment sectors and situated in different nations: Finland, USA, Japan, Germany, Sweden, Italy, and Austria. These countries were involved because they comprise a mix of high performance and old-style manufacturing plants in the particular trades, while providing variety of national cultural and economic characteristics. Within the study group, for every country, a group of scholars and a person in charge of plant selection process and data collection were recognized. The author was the part of the Italian HPM research team. Four multi-item constructs were considered in this paper, referred to as JIT production (JIT pro), JIT supply (JIT sup), efficiency (EFF) and delivery (DEL).

Further, forthcoming studies could put some additional light on connections between JIT supply and JIT manufacturing by further probing some results evolving from this research. The influence of JIT manufacturing on delivery performance could even be negative. According to the experts questioned, this outcome is noteworthy, but deserves further investigation, since author calculated that underneath the JIT supply threshold value of 21.00, the minimal effect of JIT production is not statistically substantial.

Conservative management accounting system can inspire performance that is uneven with a just-in-time manufacturing thinking. Management accounting should care just–in–time manufacturing by observing, recognizing and co-operating to decision makers any suspension, fault and left-over in the system. Modern management accounting system are now assigning greater importance on providing data on supplier dependability, set-up times throughput cycle times, fraction of deliveries that can be time and defect rates.

JIT manufacturing systems end in the formation of production cubicles that are devoted to the manufacturing of a particular product or a family of alike products, several of the support undertakings can be straight outlined dedicated cells. Therefore, a high percentage of charges can be right allocated to products. Hence the advantages from applying ABC product will be lower in JIT organization.

1.4 COMPETITION AND CONSOLIDATION IN MANUFACTURING

Competitiveness pertains to the ability and performance of a firm, sub-sector or country to sell and supply goods and services in a given market, in relation to the ability and performance of other firms, sub-sectors or countries in the same market. The term may also be applied to markets, where it is used to refer to the extent to which the market structure may be regarded as perfectly competitive. This usage has nothing to do with the extent to which individual firms are "competitive".

Competitive advantage seeks to address some of the criticisms of comparative advantage. Michael Porter proposed the theory in 1985. Porter emphasizes productivity growth as the focus of national strategies. Competitive advantage rests on the notion that cheap labour is ubiquitous and natural resources are not necessary for a good economy. The other theory, comparative advantage, can lead countries to specialize in exporting primary goods and raw materials that trap countries in low-wage economies due to terms of trade. Competitive advantage attempts to correct for this issue by stressing maximizing scale economies in goods and services that garner premium prices. Competitive advantage occurs when an organization acquires or develops an attribute or combination of attributes that allows it to outperform its competitors. These attributes can include access to natural resources, such as high-grade ores or inexpensive power, or access to highly trained and skilled personnel human resources. New technologies such as robotics and information technology can provide competitive advantage, whether as a part of the product itself, as an advantage to the making of the product, or as a competitive aid in the business process (for example, better identification and understanding of customers).

The term "competitive advantage" refers to the ability gained through attributes and resources to perform at a higher level than others in the same industry or market. The study of such advantage has attracted profound research interest due to contemporary issues regarding superior performance levels of firms in the present competitive market conditions. "A firm is said to have a competitive advantage when it is implementing a value creating strategy not simultaneously being implemented by any current or potential player". Successfully implemented strategies will lift a firm to superior performance by facilitating the firm with competitive advantage to outperform current or potential players. To gain competitive advantage a business strategy of a firm manipulates the various resources over which it has direct control, and these resources have the ability to generate competitive advantage. Superior performance outcomes and superiority in production resources reflects competitive advantage.

Above writings signify competitive advantage as the ability to stay ahead of present or potential competition, thus superior performance reached through competitive advantage will ensure market leadership. They provide the understanding that resources held by a firm and the business strategy will have a profound impact on generating competitive advantage. Powell views business strategy as the tool that manipulates the resources and create competitive advantage, hence, viable business strategy may not be adequate unless it possesses control over unique resources that has the ability to create such a unique advantage. Summarizing the viewpoints, competitive advantage is a key determinant of superior performance, and it will ensure survival and prominent placing in the market. Superior performance being the ultimate desired goal of a firm, competitive advantage becomes the foundation highlighting the significant importance to develop same.

Risk management is the process of identification, analysis and either acceptance or mitigation of uncertainty in investment decision-making. Essentially, risk management occurs anytime an investor or fund manager analyses and attempts to quantify the potential for losses in an investment and then takes the appropriate action (or inaction) given their investment objectives and risk tolerance. Inadequate risk management can result in severe consequences for companies as well as individuals. For example, the recession that began in 2008 was largely caused by the loose credit risk management of financial firms. Risk management is a two-step process – determining what risks exist in an investment and then handling those risks in a way best-suited to your investment objectives. Risk management occurs everywhere in the financial world. It occurs when an investor buys low-risk government bonds over more risky corporate debt, when a fund manager hedges their currency exposure with currency derivatives and when a bank performs a credit check on an individual before issuing them a personal line of credit.

Risk management should:

- create value – resources expended to mitigate risk should be less than the consequence of inaction, the gain should exceed the pain;
- be an integral part of organizational processes;
- be part of decision-making process;
- explicitly address uncertainty and assumptions;
- be systematic and structured;
- be based on the best available information;
- be tailor able;
- Take human factors into account.
- be transparent and inclusive;
- be dynamic, iterative and responsive to change;
- be capable of continual improvement and enhancement; and
- be continually or periodically re-assessed.

1.5   RAW MATERIAL

Industrial production depends upon the trade in raw materials such as metals, minerals and natural resources. Prices and qualities of these materials are strongly influenced by the global demand but also by the policies in the countries that produce such raw material. Raw material is the essential part of any of the manufacturing firms. An organization cannot operate without the presence of the raw material. When we want to start a manufacturing firm, we generally check that the basic material from which a good product is manufactured required for the production is how easily can be available and the quantity of the material available for the starting of manufacturing firm.

Use this function to check whether material components in networks are available on the requirements date. If the requirements are not covered on the requirements date, the system determines the date on which they can be covered. Each material, whose availability you want to check, must be assigned a checking group on the

MRP detail screen in its material master. The checking group combines materials whose availability is checked at the same time. You can, for instance, group materials according to the material type or the MRP type. Since purchase order and purchase requisitions are irrelevant to internally produced materials, you can assign such materials to checking groups whose check scope does not include these MRP elements. There are four basic reasons for keeping an inventory:

1. Time: The time lags present in the supply chain, from supplier to user at every stage, requires that you maintain certain amounts of inventory to use in this lead time. However, in practice, inventory is to be maintained for consumption during "variations in lead time". Lead time itself can be addressed by ordering that many days in advance.
2. Uncertainty: Inventories are maintained as buffers to meet uncertainties in demand, supply and movements of goods.
3. Economies of scale: Ideal conditions of "one unit at a time at a place where a user needs it, when he needs it" principle tends to incur lots of costs in terms of logistics. So, bulk buying, movement and storing brings in economies of scale; thus inventory.
4. Appreciation in value: In some situations, some stock gains the required value when it is kept for some time to allow it to reach the desired standard for consumption, or for production. For example, beer in the brewing industry.

A procedure whereby a company gradually builds up a holding of shares in a company it wishes to takeover in the future.

Warehousing is necessary due to the following reasons.

- Seasonal Production: You know that agricultural commodities are harvested during certain seasons, but their consumption or use takes place throughout the year Therefore, there is a need for proper storage or warehousing for these commodities, from where they can be supplied as and when required.
- Seasonal Demand: There are certain goods, which are demanded seasonally, like woollen garments in winters or umbrellas in the rainy season. The production of these goods takes place throughout the year to meet the seasonal demand. So there is a need to store these goods in a warehouse to make them available at the time of need.
- Large-scale Production: In case of manufactured goods, now-a-days production takes place to meet the existing as well as future demand of the products. Manufacturers also produce goods in huge quantity to enjoy the benefits of large-scale production, which is more economical. So the finished products, which are produced on a large scale, need to be stored properly till they are cleared by sales.
- Quick Supply: Both industrial as well as agricultural goods are produced at some specific places but consumed throughout the country. Therefore, it is essential to stock these goods near the place of consumption, so that without making any delay these goods are made available to the consumers at the time of their need.

- Continuous Production: Continuous production of goods in factories requires adequate supply of raw materials. So there is a need to keep sufficient quantity of stock of raw material in the warehouse to ensure continuous production.
- Price Stabilization: To maintain a reasonable level of the price of the goods in the market there is a need to keep sufficient stock in the warehouses. Scarcity in supply of goods may increase their price in the market. Again, excess production and supply may also lead to fall in prices of the product by maintaining a balance of supply of goods, warehousing leads to price stabilization.

Customer needs are changing day by day. To meet these changes it is the responsibility at the design phase to make necessary changes. Product design is the process of creating a new product to be sold by a business to its customers. A very broad concept, it is essentially the efficient and effective generation and development of ideas through a process that leads to new products. In a systematic approach, product designers conceptualize and evaluate ideas, turning them into tangible inventions and products. The product designer's role is to combine art, science, and technology to create new products that other people can use. Their evolving role has been facilitated by digital tools that now allow designers to communicate, visualize, analyse and actually produce tangible ideas in a way that would have taken greater manpower in the past. Product design is dependent on idea generation. Idea for any new product or changes in existing one may be achieved by:

a. Innovation
   Innovation is the development of new values through solutions that meet new requirements, inarticulate needs, or old customer and market needs in value adding new ways. This is accomplished through more effective products, processes, services, technologies, or ideas that are readily available to markets, governments, and society. Innovation differs from invention in that innovation refers to the use of a better and, as a result, novel idea or method, whereas invention refers more directly to the creation of the idea or method itself.

   Innovation differs from improvement in that innovation refers to the notion of doing something different rather than doing the same thing better. In the organizational context, innovation may be linked to positive changes in efficiency, productivity, quality, competitiveness, market share, and others. However, research findings highlight the complementary role of organizational culture in enabling organizations to translate innovative activity into tangible performance improvements.

b. Creativity
   Creativity can be defined as the tendency to produce or recognize ideas, possibilities or alternatives that may be useful in solving difficulties and communicating. Creativity is the ability to think up and design new inventions, produce works of art, solve problems in new ways, or develop an idea based on an original, novel, or unconventional approach. Ability to produce something new through imaginative skill, whether a new solution to a problem, or a new artistic object or form.

The term generally refers to a richness of ideas and originality of thinking. Psychological studies of highly creative people have shown that many have a strong interest in apparent disorder, contradiction, and imbalance, which seem to be perceived as challenges. Such individuals may possess an exceptionally deep, broad, and flexible awareness of themselves. Studies also show that intelligence has little correlation with creativity; thus, a highly intelligent person may not be very creative, such as a genius or gifted child.

c. Invention

Invention is often a creative process. An open and curious mind allows an inventor to see beyond what is known. Thames and Hudson saw that a new possibility, connection, or relationship can spark an invention. Inventive thinking frequently involves combining concepts or elements from different realms that would not normally be put together. Sometimes inventors disregard the boundaries between distinctly separate territories or fields. Several concepts may be considered when thinking about invention.

d. Evolution

Evolution is a process of gradual, progressive change and development, as in a social or economic structure with the passage of time. a process in which something passes by degrees to a different stage (especially a more advanced or mature stage); "the development of his ideas took many years"; "the evolution of Greek civilization"; "the slow development of her skill as a writer. It is important to understand these various definitions relative to each other and to show that accepting evolution as defined in the sciences does not commit one to accepting another form, as proposed by theology or philosophy. In particular it is important to realize that, contrary to many non-scientific uses of the term, evolution is neither a progressive process modern theory does not make it inevitable that the latest is the best nor can we expect to be able to predict the next step in evolution.

The clients to whom a business sells products and services. The customer base is a relatively broad number of customers, with a smaller section of the base being comprised of repeat customers.

The customer base is the group of customers and/or consumers that a business serves. In the most situations, a large part of this group is made up of repeat customers with a high ratio of purchase over time. These customers are the main source of consumer spending. In many cases, the customer base is considered the business's target market, where customer behaviours are well understood through market research or past experience. All actions the company takes would be through consideration of its customer base.

"Market share is the percentage of a market accounted for by a specific entity". In a survey of nearly 200 senior marketing managers, 67% responded that they found the "dollar market share" metric very useful, while 61% found "unit market share" very useful.

Marketers need to be able to translate sales targets into market share because this will demonstrate whether forecasts are to be attained by growing with the market or by capturing share from competitors. The latter will almost always be more difficult to achieve. Market share is closely monitored for signs of change in the competitive landscape, and it frequently drives strategic or tactical action.

Increasing market share is one of the most important objectives of business. The main advantage of using market share as a measure of business performance is that it is less dependent upon macro environmental variables such as the state of the economy or changes in tax policy. However, increasing market share may be dangerous for makers of fungible hazardous products, particularly products sold into the United States market, where they may be subject to market share liability.

Market share is a key indicator of market competitiveness – that is, how well a firm is doing against its competitors.

> This metric, supplemented by changes in sales revenue, helps managers evaluate both primary and selective demand in their market. That is, it enables them to judge not only total market growth or decline but also trends in customers' selections among competitors. Generally, sales growth resulting from primary demand (total market growth) is less costly and more profitable than that achieved by capturing share from competitors. Conversely, losses in market share can signal serious long-term problems that require strategic adjustments. Firms with market shares below a certain level may not be viable. Similarly, within a firm's product line, market share trends for individual products are considered early indicators of future opportunities or problems.

Research has also shown that market share is a desired asset among competing firms. Experts, however, discourage making market share an objective and criterion upon which to base economic policies. The aforementioned usage of market share as a basis for gauging the performance of competing firms has fostered a system in which firms make decisions with regard to their operation with careful consideration of the impact of each decision on the market share of their competitors.

It is generally necessary to commission market research (generally desk/secondary research) to determine. Sometimes, though, one can use primary research to estimate the total market size and a company's market share.

The percentage of an industry or market's total sales that is earned by a particular company over a specified time period. Market share is calculated by taking the company's sales over the period and dividing it by the total sales of the industry over the same period. This metric is used to give a general idea of the size of a company to its market and its competitors.

Investors look at market share increases and decreases carefully because they can be a sign of the relative competitiveness of the company's products or services. As the total market for a product or service grows, a company that is maintaining its market share is growing revenues at the same rate as the total market. A company that is growing its market share will be growing its revenues faster than its competitors.

Market share increases can allow a company to achieve greater scale in its operations and improve profitability. Companies are always looking to expand their share of the market, in addition to trying to grow the size of the total market by appealing to larger demographics, lowering prices, or through advertising. This calculation is sometimes done over specific countries such as Canada market share or US market share.

Investors can obtain market share data from various independent sources (such as trade groups and regulatory bodies), and often from the company itself, although some industries are harder to measure with accuracy than others.

1.6 ERGONOMICS

The goal of organizational ergonomics is the attainment of a fully harmonized work system that ensures employee job satisfaction and commitment. It also includes the study of technology's consequences on human relationships, processes, and institutions. Typical interventions include:

- Involving workers in identifying and resolving ergonomic issues. This is also known as participatory ergonomics.
- Improving total system processes, such as manufacturing value streams and managerial processes.
- Successfully installing safety as an integral part of the organizational culture.

The organizationally ergonomic workplace adheres to the balance model. All systems interact, and any change in one system impacts the other elements. If all elements are not designed to work in confluence, safety, productivity, efficiency, and quality can all suffer. Furthermore, attaining balance realizes cost savings or avoidance. Therefore under the balance model, every effort is made to anticipate and minimize the impact of changes. Factors that tend to impede balance can be individual or organization-wide:

- A worker lacks the skills or knowledge base to complete tasks effectively and efficiently.
- Employees disagree with management practices.
- The organization is harming the environment.
- Outside factors influence the work environment.

The organizational ergonomist will identify and remedy elements or factors that prevent the attainment of balance.

The most widespread application for organizational ergonomics is in the introduction and integration of new technology into the workplace. As companies implement new technologies, they must consider several factors of those tools:

- Functions
- Capabilities
- Capacities
- User-friendliness
- Integration

Presently, sustainability issues have become a critical factor of competition and firm performance among manufacturers. Thus, it compels many manufacturing firms to include sustainable environmental practices in their strategies and operations (Amrina and Yusof, 2011). However, authors on environmental practices affirmed that the concerns of firms about environmental issues are not only about their environmental values, but also about the economic success and performance of their organizations (Henri and Journeault, 2008). A firm may initiate environmental practices either as an ethical behaviour (Bansal and Roth, 2000) or as a critical factor in achieving competitive advantage and better firm performance (Schoenherr and Talluri, 2012).

As posited by the natural resource-based view (NRBV) theory, organizations can achieve competitive advantages and better firm performance by incorporating sustainable environmental manufacturing practices (Hart, 1995). The NRBV lays emphasis on the firm's resources, capabilities and the management of the firm's strategic action as influencing the relationship between SEMP and firm performance. Thus, the natural environment within which firm operates can enhance better performance if it is strategically managed. The emphasis on NRBV has encouraged researchers to identify the link between firms' sustainable environmental practices and performance. Literatures have found that firms that implement sustainable environmental practices will gain better plant efficiency (Schoenherr and Talluri, 2012).

The manufacturing companies, now a days are in a tough situation where they are to handle the vast demand across the various segments of the market while making judicious use of natural resources which are depleting at an alarming rate. Moreover, this increased manufacturing activity has contributed to the problems like global warming, and environment degradation. These problems further lead to the health and social problems in the society. The government agencies are enforcing tough regulations to resolve these problems. So the manufacturing industry could not sustain long if some solution is not found at the earliest.

The solution to these above-mentioned problems have been found in the sustainable manufacturing. The concept of sustainable manufacturing emerged at the United Nations Conference on Environment and Development in 1992 and is a key component of sustainable development, which balances three principal requirements: the social, economic and environmental. Sustainable manufacturing is defined as the creation of manufactured parts through processes that are non-polluting, conserve energy and natural resources, and are economically sound and safe for employees, communities, and consumers. (http://www.nacfam.org).

If the manufacturing companies want to achieve the objectives of sustainable manufacturing, then they must minimize all kinds of wastes as well as the use of natural resources, raw materials and energy. This goal requires a fundamental re-think in the design of a part to take account of all stages of a part's lifecycle, and a shift in manufacturing processes from cleaning technologies to clean technologies, which reduce the actual level of emissions produced as well as the energy and other resources used during processing. A set of necessary conditions that firms must fulfil in order to manufacture a sustainable part includes:

- Reducing the use of materials and energy in manufacturing of parts.
- Minimization or avoidance of waste.

- Reuse and recycling parts.
- Disposing of non-recyclable parts or production waste in an environmentally acceptable way.
- Planning of parts which are easy to repair, adaptable, durable and with longer lifetime.
- Minimization of transportation needs.
- Cleaner production technologies and procedures throughout the part lifecycle
- Improving a process technology.
- Research and development in environmentally sound technologies.
- Consideration of the social role played.

Before the necessary conditions for sustainable manufacturing are applied, one must be familiar with the method to measure sustainability. The sustainability of a part could be measured by performing the lifecycle analysis of a part. Lifecycle Analysis is a technique for assessing all the inputs and outputs of a part, process, or service (lifecycle inventory, here after LCI); assessing the associated wastes, human health and ecological burdens (impact assessment); and interpreting and communicating the results of the assessment throughout the lifecycle of the parts or processes under review.

Lifecycle of a typical part is shown in Figure 1.5. Lifecycle of a part starts with the extraction of the raw material. Then the manufacturing of the part is carried out. The part is then packed and shipped to the customer. The part is used by the customer for specified time and finally it is disposed of or recycled.

Industrial sectors such as the pulp and paper sector, chemical industries, and the metal industries, are a step ahead in improving their environmental performance.

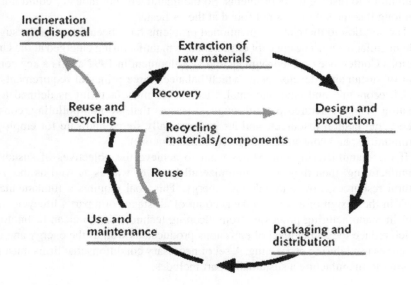

FIGURE 1.5   Lifecycle of a part [Labour Cost Control, 2011].

However, a large number of studies have been conducted on metal industries with focus on primary and secondary metals industry. Only a few studies have been reported for the metal casting industry.

1.7 LEAN MANUFACTURING

Lean Manufacturing is defined as efficient approach to identifying and eliminating waste (non–value add activities) through regular improvement flowing the product in the pull of the customer in reach of perfection. Lean manufacturing is often simply "lean", is a systematic method for the leave out of waste ("Muda") within a manufacturing system. Lean also takes into account waste created through overwhelm ("Muri") and waste created through imperfection in workloads ("Mura"). Working from the angle of the client who consumes a product, "value" is any action or process that a customer wants to pay for.

> To solve the problem of waste, Lean Manufacturing has number of tools at its disposal. These include continuous process improvement the '5 Ways' and mistake-proofing. Thus it can be seen as taking a very similar approach to other improvement procedure.

Principles

Lean principles at Toyota evolved out of their Toyota Production System (TSP). There are number of principles, but we will assemble our work into four broad categories: investigate the elimination of waste, search improved quality, search for increased product flow, and search out reduced cost. By eliminating wasted resources from any manufacturing or production system, we can instantly increase that system's productivity. If we increase productivity while reducing the resource inputs into the system, we decrease costs, which are passed along to the customer in terms of lower prices, resulting the increase in market share which increase benefit in long-term. It is driving strategy of all Japanese manufacturers which clasp lean principles.

Wastes in Lean Manufacturing

The object of Lean Manufacturing is the reduction of waste in every site of production including customer relations, product design, supplier networks, and factory management. Its aim is to incorporate less human effort, less inventory, less time in production, and less space to become highly responsive to customer demand while producing top quality products in a very advanced and accurate method. Imperatively, a "waste" is any product for which the customer is not wanting to pay. Typically the types of waste considered in a lean manufacturing system include:

1. **Overproduction**

   To produce more than demanded or produce it before it is needed. It is visible as storage of material. It is the result of producing to extra products. Overproduction means making more than is required by the next process, making earlier than is required by the next process, or making faster than is required by the next process. Causes for overproduction waste include:

- Just-in-case logic.
- Abuse of automatic machine control.
- Zagged programme.
- Unstable workload.
- Large process system.
- Unnecessary investigation.

2. **Waiting**

In traditional manufacturing processes, when one part of the manufacturing phase is completed there is usually a waiting period before the next phase can be continued. With Lean Manufacturing the waiting time (Waiting Waste) for a product is narrowed down to a much shorter period, or eliminated completely. The main aim is to increase the employment/capability of the worker instead of increasing the usage of the machines. Causes of waiting waste include:

- Unstable workload.
- random arrangement.
- Large process system times.
- abuse of automatic machine control.
- Unlevelled arrangements.
- Difficult feature troubles.

3. **Inventory or Work in Process (WIP)**

This is material between activity due to long portion manufacturing or methods with long cycle times. Causes of excess inventory include:

- Save the company from careless and instantaneous problems.
- Compound multiplicity.
- Unlevelled arrangement.
- Low retail prediction.
- Unstable workload.
- Unfaithful shipments by suppliers.
- Poor communications.

4. **Processing waste**

It should be reduced by asking why a definite procedure step is required and why an individual product is manufactured. All waste processing steps should be reduced. Causes for processing waste include:

- Product can be changed without any change in process.
- Just-in-case logic.
- True consumer requirements are endless.
- Over processing to put up stopping time.
- Poor transmission.
- Unwanted authorization.
- Unnecessary copies/more information.

5. **Transportation**

   This does not add any value to the product. Rather than developing the transportation, it should be decreased or reduced (e.g., forming cells). Causes of transportation waste include:

   - Low quality plant design.
   - Poor responsibility of the process flow for manufacturing.
   - Big batch sizes, lengthy lead times, and huge storage areas.

6. **Motion**

   Motion of the machines, transport and workers (e.g., due to the inappropriate location of tools and parts) is waste. Rather than the automating wasted motion, the process is improved itself. Causes of motion waste include:

   - Poor people/machine capability.
   - Irregular work methods.
   - Adverse facility or cell design.
   - Poor co-operation and housekeeping.
   - Unnecessary "busy" activity while resting.

7. **Making defective products**

   This is pure waste. Avoid the situation of faults rather than searching and curing faults. Agents of processing waste include:

   - Delicate mechanism control.
   - Low quality.
   - Unstable inventory level.
   - Low planned maintenance.
   - Weak education/preparation/work instructions.
   - Product layout.
   - Consumer demands not understood.

8. **Underutilizing people**

   Not taking advantage of people's abilities. Causes of people waste include:

   - Old defender thinking, politics, the business culture
   - Cheap rent practices
   - Least or no investment in training
   - Least pay, higher turnover strategy

Nearly every waste in the manufacturing process can fit into at least one of these categories. Those that understand the abstraction keen view waste as the only opponent which highly limits business performance and threatens prosperity unless it is relentlessly reduced over time. Lean manufacturing is an approach that reduces waste by reducing costs in the overall production process, in operations within that process, and in the utilization of production labour. The focus is on making the entire process flow, not the improvement of one or more individual operations.

Types of Lean Manufacturing Process:

- TPS (Toyota Production System). The other survey is the content of what a Lean Manufacturing system really is, and so we shall have a keen glance at the

TPS. Not because the TPS is necessarily perfect. Ohio states reduction of waste in methods to which nobody thinks about them. Seven types of waste:

1. Transportation
2. Waiting
3. Overproduction
4. Defective parts
5. Inventory
6. Movement
7. Excess processing

5-S (five S) When workstations or worker tools are unsystematic, workers can waste time by waiting for goods which are needed for production or provide better service to consumers. At starting stage, 5-S methodology was used to develop an integrated management system which had been developed in Total Production Maintenance (TPM). In other respects, in the West, 5-S has a minimal use and is associated with an activity of maintenance. Often used in conjunction with Kaizen and lean thinking, the 5-S system was developed after World War II as part of a country-wide push to improve quality and efficiency.

Many of the practices in Japan are characterized the techniques which have a part of philosophy and other parts like Japanese fencing (that has its origin in kenjutsu) or judo (jujutsu), the Japanese art of gentle, flexible, yielding, which is used to coach the body and mind through the discipline.

5-S is a workspace management technique which emerged in Japan as a result of the application of the Kaizen culture (continuous improvement in the personal, social, family and professional life). The real concept of the 5-S has philosophical and socio-historical roots. 5-S approach also applies in Japanese administration, which includes both the management philosophy and management techniques.

5-S is a technique which is used to establish a quality environment in an organization and also to maintain that quality environment.

The application of the 5-S methodology in a business as a Kaizen practice was first implemented in 1980 by Takashi Osada. He contributed that need for the continuous improvement philosophy of professional behaviour is enhanced through the combination of *seiri* (to sort), *seiton* (to set in order), *seiso* (to shine or clean), *seiketsu* (to standardize) and *shitsuke* (to sustain) in the workplace. Toyota production system (TPS) is an example of the application of the 5-S practice.

At this time, requirement of improvement in different organizations may be affected by different complexity of systems. Again, it is very important to know which method can help us to initialize the process of continuous improvement in order to achieve safety and increased productivity of the workplace through knowledge and participation of staff. That is why such university methodologies focuses on tools required for the development of future professionals, especially on engineers, and there is no chance that it was one of the best ways to understand fully a methodology is routine use of 5-S.

5-S methodology is based on five Japanese terms that gives principles of industrial housekeeping. These Japanese terms with the English translations are: *seiri* (sort), *seiton* (set in order or systematize), *seiso* (shine), *seikestu* (standardize), and *shitsue* (sustain).

1. Seiri (sorting). It is selecting the items into main categories as necessary and unnecessary items. Remove all unnecessary items which are not needed. Check all tools, materials, and other items in the factory and workspace. Keep only necessary items.
2. Seiton (setting an order of flow). It is straightening all the items that are labelled as necessary to the room. Use the tools where these are kept and return to the proper place after task is completed.
3. Seiso (shining, cleaning). This gives the optimum conditions to the working environment. Regularly clean the workspace and all equipment, and remove all the dirt present in workplace. It is to be kept in mind that cleaning should not be done at the end of day, but it should be at regular intervals.
4. Seiketsu (standardize, visual control). It means that all the above three 'S' should be as followed such that they should be fit in mind as daily work. By visual sign the operator can differentiate the normal and abnormal situations, correct and incorrect behaviour. It means that everything should be clearly identified and labelled. Normal and abnormal situations are distinguished by visible and simple rules.
5. Shitsuke (sustain, discipline and habit). Make it habitual permanently. It means discipline. The effective implementation required commitment of each worker to ensure the 5-S principles.

Six Sigma is a quality improvement approach that seeks to reduce reasons of imperfections in production and service processes. The term "Six Sigma" appears from the statistical measure that permits at most 3.4 defects per million opportunities. In other words, basically no imperfections are permitted in goods under this principle. A fault in Six Sigma is clear as any error that is conceded on to the purchaser in a way that the consumer views the fault as product nonconformance.

Six Sigma is a set of techniques and tools for improvement of process. it had been introduced in 1986 by engineer Bill Smith whereas engaging at Motorola. Jack Welch created it central to his business scheme at General Electric in 1995. Today, it is employed in several sectors of trade.

Six Sigma seeks to enhance the standard of the output of a process by which we identify defects and eliminating the causes of defects and minimizing changeability in producing and trade processes. It uses a group of quality management strategies, chiefly empirical, applied math ways, and it creates a special type of infrastructure of persons within the industry, who are specialists in these methods. The main objective of any business is to create profit. For increasing the profit, the selling price ought to increase and/or the producing value ought to come down. Since the value is decided by the competition within the market, therefore the only way to increase the profit is to cut down the producing price which might be achieved only through continuous improvement within the company's operation. Six Sigma quality programmes offer an overall framework for continuous improvement within the process of a company. Six Sigma uses facts, information and root cause to resolve issues.

Apart from previous quality improvement initiatives, there are a number of additional features set out by Six Sigma:

- A clear focus on achieving measurable and quantifiable money returns from any Six Sigma project.
- An increased stress on robust and perfervid management leadership and support.
- A clear commitment to creating decisions on the idea of verifiable information and applied math strategies, rather than assumptions and guesswork.

Methodologies: DMAIC vs. DMADV

Six Sigma uses two completely different sets of methodologies, DMAIC and DMADV, as lenses to examine and improve business processes of any firm or industry. The DMAIC and the DMADV are two different processes geared towards viewing completely different sectors of a business at the same time however addressing them individually. Despite unique distinctions and differences the methodologies overlap during the examination method and share the result (i.e., same finish goal, improvement of business processes). The goal of both methodologies is the same.

Each methodology has its own set of pointers and goals targeted at rising business processes through the use of knowledge assortment and applied mathematics tools. While the methodologies are designed to succeed constant issue, there are noteworthy variations between the two that ought to be thought about by professionals in leadership roles or in business environments with a good vary of structure settings.

DMAIC

Define   Measure   Analyze   Improve   Control

The set of Six Sigma methodologies that is most applicable to the producing or production aspect of a product or service, DMAIC includes the following project stages through which every product passes:

- Define: address the recognition of specific processes to be examined.
- Measure: record knowledge and use metrics to track effectiveness and judge efficiencies.
- Analyze: utilize critical thinking skills to review knowledge and clarify goals.
- Improve: create changes in business processes intermeshed towards improvement and higher alignment with company goals.
- Control: build a system of checks and changes for in progress improvement in production processes of firm or company.

DMADV

The complementary set of Six Sigma processes that is most applicable to examining and rising the client relations facet of an organization, DMADV includes these project stages:

- Define: address client desires in relation to a product or service.
- Measure: involve the use of electronic knowledge assortment to measure client desires, response to product, or review of services.
- Analyze: utilize metrics to evaluate areas wherever product or service may be higher aligned to client goals and wishes.
- Design: overlap the improvement of business processes that contour company goals to best meet consumer and client desires.
- Verify: In this build a system of models and tests which helps to check the customer specifications and company want to fulfil that needs.

For professionals interested in sorting out more concerning however these powerful methodologies play call at a range of business settings or however they may create an effect for your business, consider following further education in the field of Six Sigma. While each set of Six Sigma methodologies will work hand-in-hand, to Achieve a specific set of structure and monetary goals which provide good services, professionals interested in one set of methodologies from these two, over the opposite can augment skills through an honourable on-line certificate programme.

As Six Sigma continues to evolve and address twenty-first-century business problems and goals, professionals that demonstrate a vast field of these practices could realize several applicable opportunities in a very kind of trade settings. Through online courses instructed by trade leaders, professionals and businesses can attain sensible business solutions and certification as a green belt, black belt and master black belt in Six Sigma.

Applications of Six Sigma

Six Sigma largely finds application in giant organizations. A necessary factor in the spread of Six Sigma was GE's 1998 announcement that with the implementation of Six Sigma process their company saves $350 million, and in next years this figure increase to more than $1 billion.

According to industry consultants of these techniques like Thomas Pyzdek and John Kullmann, consulted that companies having a workforce below five hundred workers are less suited to Six Sigma implementation, or they need to adapt the quality approach to create it work for them. Six Sigma contains a giant range of tools and techniques that employment well in tiny to mid-size organizations.

The infrastructure described as necessary to support Six Sigma is a result of the dimensions of the organization instead of a demand of Six Sigma itself. With the invention of fastest means of communication, better-quality quality computers and swift transportation systems, manufacturing is no longer forced at local level, but it has turned universal in character. Since manufacturing company needs to become competitive for its existence, it has to supply products of reliable high quality at decreased distribution time. Market also stresses on more product alternatives that means decreased lot size and great tractability in operations. Manpower cost has also climbed. All these aspects lead to elevate the product price.

- Theory of Constraints (TOC)
  The Theory of Constraints (TOC) is an idea given by Eliyahu Goldratt while he was trying to build an arrangement course to create chicken coops for a friend. The TOC addresses three major concepts. First, it covers method bottlenecks, the judgement of trouble solving, and contains a tap of business theory that nicely simplifies the subject matter of funds in industrialized business. His arrangement is tough on catalogue elimination, compact direct time, and reduced batch sizes, all desired to go faster cash flow – much as Ohno discusses. There the similarities end, however. His hypothesis is very pathetic on feature and many other aspects of desecrate. I have found that culture and applying the TOC is often a firm place to start for many businesses before they board on a passage into Lean Manufacturing. On the other hand, if you have a pure make-to-order system, with numerous routings and extremely alternate machine cycle times, many tools in the Lean toolkit, turn into less valuable. Some of the tools and techniques of the TOC become more valuable. Since approximately no business is a pure make-to-stock system, it is a superior thought to have an appreciative of the TOC as you go aboard on your Lean journey.
- Just In time
  The company has to sustain the cost at a judicious level. Opposing these challenges, industries worldwide are enforced to discover ways to lessen costs, increase quality, and meet the changing requirements of their consumers. One positive resolution has been the implementation of just-in-time (JIT) manufacturing approach in which many major areas of a company such as engineering, marketing, manufacturing and purchasing are engaged.

Having dependable suppliers allows for a decrease in the number of suppliers and the linked costs. It allows for less possibility catalogue and frees up centre avoiding exhausted interest cost. Main aim in JIT is no catalogue to totally remove safeguard and work-in-all inventory costs.

The main aim is synchronizing claim and manufacture to no units of merchandise until an order is given, which reduces extra manufacture unwanted inventory, and all the waste associated with them.

JIT can be termed as the extension of the novel concept of handling the material flow in a factory in order to minimize the inventory levels. Actually, there is a considerable involvement in the industrial organization than dropping inventories to control costs. Manufacturing needs to cope up with several other issues, such as level of automation, process control, flexible manufacturing, machine set up times, direct employment productivity, Overhead, supplier management, engineering maintenance, and the superiority of product supplied to customers. The present industrial Organization needs to work proficiently on these issues to function in even, prolific, and superiority inclined manner [3]. Also, JIT production system can be described as a combination of a set of principles which are reinforced by three basic elements of JIT which is further well furnished with a set of tools and techniques which are the weapons for reducing the waste. The three basic elements of JIT are removal of waste, total quality and people preparation.

There are two fundamental beliefs of JIT. The first core belief is concerned with the accomplishment of "the excellent company". It assumes that "the rate at which excellence is achieved depends on the rate at which a company can improve relative to its competitors, and continue to improve faster than they can". It does not matter how rapidly a company can progress, it will not become an outstanding company unless it improves faster than its competitors do. The other core belief is that a company "cannot attain such superiority through good management only", rather, an excellent company needs to develop its members to full capabilities which will empower them to handle the perplexing tasks which result from improvements and to contribute their inspiration towards further improvements. In supporting these core beliefs, JIT techniques and tools are necessary for the elimination of waste, total quality is mandatory to develop the organization, and people preparation is desirable to hold the new challenges and chances generated from improvement. The purpose of waste removal over time is to lessen gradually the non-value-added activities and to improve the value-added.

JIT is actually a management philosophy originated in Japan which has come to practice since 1970 in several manufacturing organizations of Japan. The technology was first established in the Toyota manufacturing plants by Taiichi Ohno as a way to fulfil consumer demands with the least delays. For this motivation, Taiichi Ohno is often referred to as the father of JIT manufacturing. The Toyota production plants were the first to introduce JIT. It also provided comprehensive assistance during the 1973 oil prohibition and was later implemented by numerous other organizations. The oil prohibition and the increasing scarcity of other natural assets were observed as a main thrust for the extensive acceptance of JIT. Toyota was capable to cope up with the growing challenges for existence through the methodology. This strategy targeted people, plants and system. Toyota apprehended that JIT can only be efficacious if each individual within the organization was engaged and committed to it, if the manufacturing plant and developments were organized for high output and productivity, and if quality and manufacturing plans were programmed to fulfil demands correctly.

Today, JIT has developed into a management system as a figure of knowledge and surrounding the inclusive set of engineering ideologies and methods. JIT manufacturing has the capability to fortify the industry's competitiveness in the market by dropping wastes and refining quality of product and production efficiency. JIT also appeared as a method of achieving the high usage level from available inadequate resources. The Japanese kept on working towards achieving the optimum rate in their industrial processes despite of constraints. It involved dropping waste and using the existing resources in the judicious manner. The key factor is the constant effort over a longer period of time within the outline of incessant development which is realized by a continuous stream of minor progresses known as "kaizen" in Japan and is known as the most substantial feature of the JIT philosophy [4].

JIT management has wide cultural characteristics rooted in its growth which can be associated as follows:

1. JIT management permits an organization to fulfil customer request irrespective of the level of demand. It can be made promising through the pull system of manufacturing.
2. The time interval between material advents, handling and assemblage of the final product for customers is diminished by the JIT production system.
3. JIT permits decrease in raw material, work in progress and completed goods inventories. This releases a good extent of space and time between processes within manufacturing plants. The equivalent cultural distinctive is apprehension for space due to high population.
4. The JIT production technique has containers for holding fragments. This lets easy identification and checking of inventories. Using selected containers within the production course may be due to the importance of type of packaging preferred by consumers on purchasing goods.
5. JIT production needs plant to be clean, which means that there must be no wastes which hamper production. Japanese are anxious about cleanliness of environment which gives them the impression of larger area.
6. JIT production includes 'visible signals' to present the current position of machinery [4].

Quality management based on JIT is the blend of quality control, inventory control and production management functions which works for improving the quality in two ways. First, it stresses on philosophical trait of quality improvement by making it everyone's concern, and then aims at implementing quality control systems. It considered that its workers are the most respected possessions of an organization, and they give their best output when inspired, cherished, cheered to contribute, and permitted to make decisions. By this approach, Labours examine the quality of product after every consecutive process. Workers are skilled along with supervisors in training and understanding of procedure control charts [4].

JIT manufacturing comprises of numerous components which should be combined together to operate in synchronization to realize the JIT objectives. These components basically include the human assets and the manufacturing, procuring, production, planning and unifying role of an organizational body. These fundamentals can be congregated together into the Toyota production system including people, plants and system [4].

1. **People involvement**

   The ultimate rule for JIT success is gaining support and approval from all individuals engaged in the attainment of managerial objectives. It entails including and notifying all groups who are interested in the industry which significantly decrease the time and struggle required in employing JIT and can diminish implementation complications. Support and contract can be acquired from the groups mentioned below.

   - *Shareholders and the company owners:* long-term realization of turnover should be emphasized, and it must be clear that reimbursements related to JIT can be recognized over the long period.
   - *Workers organization:* All workers should be learned about the objectives of JIT and be informed about how the novel system will affect them. The main shortcoming in JIT is that it usually upsurges the pressure on workers.
   - *Support to management:* It includes assistance to management from all stages. It also entails that management should set instances for the employees. Employees should have continuous improvement not only on the shop floor but should inherent the same in management's attitudes.
   - *Support from Government:* Government can provide sustenance to the companies desiring to implement JIT by encompassing tax and other financial enticements. This inspire companies to be inventive as it tolerates part of the financial burden connected with the implementation cost of JIT [4].

2. **Plants**

   Frequent changes which may arise about the plant include plant layout, workers, demand appeal, kanbans, self-inspection, material requirements planning, manufacturing resource planning and continuous improvement. These are explained below:

   - *Plant layout:* The plant layout is decided in such a way to ensure maximum flexibility to workers and is set in accordance with product. This layout uses "multi-function workers".
   - *Demand appeal production:* The idea of demand pull includes the demand for a product to point when production should take place. It allows a company to yield only what is necessary in the exact amount and at the exact time.
   - *Kanban* It is a Japanese word which means signal and is typically a card convoying products through the plant. The use of kanbans supports in connecting the diverse production procedures.
   - *Self-inspection:* This is done by every worker to assure that their input to production augments worth to the product and is of superior quality. It permits errors and inferiority work to be locked in and amended proficiently.
   - *Continuous improvement:* The continuous improvement includes a variation in attitudes towards the total efficiency of an association. This is a fundamental portion of the JIT and should be embraced by every associate of the company. It demands that with each objective and standard positively seen, these objectives should be increased in a sensible and attainable manner. It allows a firm to continuously develop its actions, goods and its customer contentment.

3. Systems

Systems in an association state to the knowledge and progression to connect, plot and co-ordinate the accomplishments and resources used in manufacturing. For instance MPR and MRP II. MRP is a computer-based method for handling the materials obligatory for carrying a schedule". MRP Planning can be split into two parts including a production plan, indicating the existing size and a master production plan that is an exhaustive plan of what goods to yield in specific time. MRP II is a computer-based plan which provides statistics on monetary resources accessible for carrying the plans of MRP. For instance, information related to inventory investment is provided by MRP II [4].

Many authors have suggested a diverse set of tools and techniques on the basis of their interests and point of views. Moreover, Harrison classified JIT core techniques into two categories:

- JIT1: includes techniques and tools requisite to organize the facility for materializing excellent manufacturing capabilities such as reaction speed, short lead time, low cost and high-quality production.
- JIT2: comprises of techniques and tools needed for the company for constant efforts of removing wastes.

JIT1 Techniques

Harrison references six techniques in this group which are as mentioned below Design.

Design is the soul of value-adding activities. Actually design is the goal of engineering which aids the foundation of new products, software, processes, systems and organizations by means of which engineering contributes to community by satisfying its needs. In a JIT atmosphere of manufacturing instantly with seamless quality and no waste, thus design is reflected to be an obligatory activity directing at total cost saving.

Focus

'Focused factory' or product-oriented manufacturing mean learning to direct each plant on restricted, controllable sets of products, capacities, technologies and markets, and learning to structure basic manufacturing strategies and support services so that they can focus on one unambiguous manufacturing task rather than many unpredictable, contradictory implicit tasks. The JIT system necessitates a focused factory since it is founded on the concept that competence can be refined through simplicity, experience, replication and uniformity of tasks. Such resemblance of tasks can produce a structure that does the significant but limited things efficiently.

Layout and Flow

This technique realized by moving machineries and processes closer whenever is the opportunity, can be measured as an attempt to eradicate or lessen waste as a result of needless movements. This work, which follows rationally from the idea of the focused factory, targets at streamlining and simplifying production flow in such a way that makes it conceivable to transform lot into repetitive production and henceforth, gain the reimbursements of implementing JIT production techniques.

Small machines
This technique emphasize that it is good to install numerous small machines rather than one large machine. The explanations for this option are that small machineries are quite easy to maintain and can produce improved quality over time. Moreover, it is easy to move and to accommodate flexible layout as requisite by JIT manufacturing and have less possibility of making mistakes in investment decisions.

Total Productive Maintenance (TPM)
TPM can be comprehended as the analytical extension of TQC/TQM. JIT system motivates everybody to take accountability for maintenance in the accomplishment of zero breakdown. In augmentation to working of the machine, workers perform dusting and housekeeping, suitable to machine operation, evolving improved consciousness of possible problems, as well as doing routine maintenance tasks. The purpose of TPM is to escalate the equipment up time towards the best of zero breakdown.

Set up Reduction (SUR)
Plummeting set up time is vital to improve the flexibility without dropping capacity, and later sinking inventories and lead periods. SUR is critical in the JIT system, as it will improve the ability of replying to instant demands and the manufacturing of a huge variety of products in small capacities. This movement is an outstanding occasion for endeavouring for the intellect of possession of the ventures amongst shop floor teams and placing upgrading responsibility upon them.

JIT2 Techniques
Harrison proposes eight techniques in this group which are useful to keep up continuous efforts of waste elimination:

Total People Involvement (TPI)
TPI means the condition where company members devote all their abilities to the benefit of the company as a whole. In order to achieve this, workers must be trained, capable and motivated to take full responsibility for all aspects of the job under their authority.

Flow Scheduling
The objective of this method is to develop the situations whereby parts are flowing in an arranged and constant manner and will not stop at all during the course of manufacturing. Positive scheduling can be measured from the proportion of value-added time to total time, or the total flow length of parts or subassemblies. In a JIT environment, material movements and productions are controlled by Kanban.

Inventory Reduction
The JIT system endeavours to eliminate the buffer inventory with the purpose of making problems, concealed by the inventory, more visible. The reduced batch sizes can bring several advantages including decreased production lead times, earlier recognition of defects and less rework, less WIP, and improved flexibility. Therefore, the JIT system strives for achieving less and fewer batch sizes until approaching the size of one.

Process Improvement

Process improvement is the most significant one in recognizing total quality. Also, quality losses are not only produced by defects but also as a result of variability. As an effort to reduce fatalities to society or to upsurge the quality of the product, therefore, producers have to carry on incessant upgrading programme in terms of continuous reduction in the variation of product performance characteristics about their target values.

Visibility

Visibility of processes, problems, and improvement ventures are the main features of JIT systems. In this situation, firm members are stimulated to contribute all their abilities to the profit of the firm as a total, and total people involvement will be easy to be appreciated.

JIT/MRP/OPT

JIT is an outstanding method of shop floor control. Material Requirements Planning (MRP) is a computerized materials management system intended at reducing inventories by working out time-phased material requirements from the Master Production Schedule (MPS). Optimized Production Technology (OPT) is a thinking combined with a computerized system of shop scheduling and capacity planning.

Push vs. Pull production systems

The push system depends on the production of a sales forecast, and is followed by making size planning and scheduling, materials purchase, work orders, etc., with materials being "pushed" at the workshop floor and finished goods out from it. This technique often results in

Inventory whereas the pull production system is introduced by the customers' orders, which gradually "pulls" finished foods out of the plant, with every stage of the manufacturing process gradually "pulling" work pieces from the previous process/stage.

TAKT time

TAKT time is defined as the time requisite to make one finished product from start to finish. With typically U-shaped layout, one operator completes the whole job him/herself. TAKT time is determined by sales records (customers). Hence, the waste rising from overproduction can be removed through the use of TAKT time.

One-piece-flow production

This technique means that one portion is made at a time; i.e., the operator travels from station to station within the cell, usually in a U-shaped layout, within the constraints of TAKT and cycle times. This is valuable in improving a sense of possession of the job.

After discussing JIT philosophy in some detail, the next important stage is to discover the differences between JIT and traditional systems. These differences can be categorized on the basis of three important aspects that includes people preparation, quality consideration and supplier relationship.

In the traditional system, a company employs only specific part of the worker's capability for doing correctly the allotted tasks within the given time period. A worker has diminutive accountability for reassuring the quality of the product, inclines to have specialized skills, and is extra concerned with individual work rather than a team performance. Whereas JIT system employs workers as complete individuals with full acknowledgement of their strengths and limitations. As a result, each worker is responsible for controlling and maintaining the entire job, and henceforth, has accountability for promising quality. To achieve numerous jobs efficiently, every worker is provided with multi-skill teaching and exhilarated to achieve the job as a team.

In systematizing the success of quality, the old-style system splits the planning and execution of tasks. It leads to huge barriers between management and workers, as well as among departments. Consequently, the introduction of curriculums for quality upgrading will always come across confrontation from trade unions. In this system, superiority is a substance of technical practice and training for quality is for quality experts only, hence it is almost difficult to get input from employees who are truly doing the work. In contrast, JIT companies have not experienced any trouble in presenting alterations for improvement because workers believe that it will leads to prosperity for the company and, henceforth, all workers as well. Since everyone is accountable for quality and training for quality will be provided to each worker. Therefore, each worker can contribute his thoughts for development in his own workplace or throughout the organization.

- Kaizen

In today's competitive environment the productivity is key concern of organizations. In most countries the capitalist economy tells to boost the productivity by eliminating various costs and by reducing scraps. To overcome the cost factors, lean manufacturing techniques were initialized. These lean manufacturing techniques are 5-S, Kaizen, Six Sigma, SCM, Just-in-Time etc. The most effective approach is Kaizen approach that was emerged in Japan. Kaizen is the Japanese term (the meaning of "Kai" is "to change" and the meaning of "Zen" is as "good") which is in Indian context or English meaning is to define continuous improvement.

According to Terziovski, "Kaizen means an improvement that is by participating of everyone, including both workers and managers" by using the principle of serving customer needs. The improvements in quality of product, cost, and delivery are main results of Kaizen implementation.

Palmer defines Kaizen implementation as a way to maintain low cost and less inventory, as well as a practice to reduce waste in processes and get continuous change in systems when compared to lean implementation. Unlike other traditional techniques, Kaizen is a philosophical determined technique to achieve quality, functionality, and prices to sustain product competitiveness in the market environment.

Kaizen also differentiate itself from other continuous improvement practices by permitting for team members to change and implement these changes and see the results come from their efforts, as well as encouraging active participation of company workers in industrial engineering and job design. The implementation of Kaizen methods and activities is sometimes called as a "Kaizen event".

In the1980s, management techniques were focusing on involvement of employees through teamwork approaches and interactive communications from top to lower management, and on improving job design, but Japanese companies seemed to be implementing such techniques more effectively than others. The business lesson of the 1980's was that Japanese firms had a greater commitment to the philosophy of continuous improvement than Western companies did. Japanese used these continuous programmes and called them as "Kaizen". Kaizen means continuous improvement by involving everyone in the organization from top management to managers then to supervisors, and last to workers. In Japan, the concept of kaizen is so deeply settled in minds of both managers and workers that they often do not even realize that kaizen was a customer-driven strategy for improvement. According to Imai this philosophy assumes that our way of life, our working life, our home life or our social life deserves to be constantly improved. There is a lot of controversies in the literature as well as the industry as to what kaizen signifies. Kaizen is a Japanese philosophy for process improvement that can be understood in terms of the Japanese words Kai and Zen, which translate roughly into to break apart and investigate and to improve upon the existing situation.

The Kaizen Institute defines kaizen as the Japanese term for continuous improvement. It is a common sense and is both a rigorous, scientific method using statistical quality control and an adaptive framework of organizational values and beliefs that keeps workers and management focused on zero defects. It is a philosophy of never being satisfied with what was achieved last week or last year. Improvement starts with the admission that every organization has problems, which provide opportunities for change. It takes the problems by solving with continuous improvement and largely depends on teams that work cross functionally and can be empowered to challenge the status quo. The need of kaizen is that the people that perform a certain task, have most knowledge about that task; as a result by involving them and showing confidence in their capabilities, ownership of the process is raised to its highest level. Moreover, the team effort encourages innovation and change and, by involving all levels of employees, the imaginary organizational walls disappear to make room for productive improvements. From such a view, kaizen is not only an approach to manufacturing competitiveness but also everybody's business, because its principle depends upon the workshop is to make people's jobs easier by taking them apart, studying them, and making improvements.

2 Green Engineering

2.1 GREEN ENGINEERING

Green Engineering can be defined as environmentally conscious attitudes, values, and principles, combined with science, technology, and engineering practice, all directed towards improving local and global environmental quality. Green engineering encompasses all of the engineering disciplines and is consistent and compatible with sound engineering design principles. Green stands for biological manageability and includes a significant number of separate worries including, but not limited to air, soil pollution, energy utilization furthermore efficiency and waste. Green activities point should minimize those sway for human. The society's rising concern for Green can be grouped into three broad categories:

a. Rising emissions and associated climate change
Greenhouse gas (GHG) emissions have expanded rapidly in the recent past and their gain is further hastening. Global temperatures have risen by 0.74°C over the last century — the quickest warming observed in history. At the current rate, emissions will double by 2050, compared to 2000 levels. This could mean a comparable temperature gain of 4–6°C, over pre–industrial levels by the end of this century. This uncommon change is conventional to have a grave brunt on the global ecosystem, hydrological system, sea level and grains production and related actions.

b. Fast depletion of scarce natural resources
With the increase in population and industrialization, the utilization from claiming regular assets (wood, coal, oil, food, water, and so on) is quickly on the rise, same time their accessibility is contracting. This need prompted occasional mismatches in demand and supply. Furthermore, profoundly fluctuating prices have impacted both corporate edges and purchaser spend. There may be important requirements for using these assets, and finding and establishing the alternatives which are less deficient.

c. Growing waste generation and pollution
Expanded industrialization and urbanization prompted noteworthy growth previously, waste generation and natural contamination. Modern waste for concoction arrangements might conceivably be hazardous to health. Also, its transfer without medication will be prompting area and water contamination. The discharge for mechanical effluents clinched alongside streams and different water forms will be destroying neighbourhood natural surroundings. As the interest and utilization of electronic items rise, e–waste will be additionally turning into major hotspot of natural contamination.

DOI: 10.1201/9781003189510-2

Green engineering is the design, commercialization and use of process and products that are feasible and economical while minimizing risk to human health and environment and generation of pollution at source. Principles of green engineering are:

1. Engineer processes and products holistically, use system analysis and integrate environmental impact assessment tools.
2. Conserve and improve natural ecosystems while protecting human health and wellbeing.
3. Use lifecycle thinking in all engineering activities.
4. Ensure that all material and energy inputs and outputs are as inherently safe and benign as possible.
5. Minimize depletion of natural resources.
6. Strive to prevent waste.
7. Develop and apply engineering solutions, while being cognizant of local geography, aspirations and cultures.
8. Create engineering solutions beyond current or dominant technologies; improve, innovate and invent (technologies) to achieve sustainability.
9. Actively engage communities and stakeholders in development of engineering solutions.

Green companies and green consumers examine corporate social responsibility in terms of the ethical criterion of "greenness" through an assessment of one company's response to green consumers during recent years. There is a need for all companies to shift to Kantian responsibility with the appointment of a chief ethical officer and creation of an ethics department in an attempt to balance the short-term profit-oriented pursuit and the long-term pursuit of fulfilling one's duty (Feng, 2010). The antecedents of Indian firms practicing green manufacturing practices have an impact on extended supply chain performance. The data were collected in two phases and wave analysis was also performed to check non-response bias to avoid any significant impact of non-response bias on statistical analysis. The data has been used to conduct exploratory factor analysis using varimax rotation which reduces variables into five parsimonious and orthogonal factors. The factor analysis output was further used as an input of regression analysis. The results found that the factor analysis output has further validated the findings from literature review. The factor analysis output suggests that total quality management (TQM), supplier relationship management (SRM), research and development, technology and lean manufacturing practices are important determinants of Indian firms practising green manufacturing, which impact extended supply chain performance. The regression analysis output has further established that TQM, research and development, and technology, are strong determinants of extended supply chain performance. However, present study does not support SRM and lean manufacturing practices from respondent's perspective. It needs to be explored further. This study is limited to medium-sized manufacturing firms (Dubey and Ali, 2015).

2.2   GREEN MANUFACTURING

Green manufacturing, also known as environmentally conscious manufacturing, is a modern manufacturing mode. It gives a comprehensive consideration of the environment influence and resource efficiency. In green manufacturing, the hope is that the impact on the environment is minimal, and the resource utilization is maximal. Through this effort, the company can benefit economically and socially. Green manufacturing reflects sustain-able development strategy in the history of modern manufacturing industry. Modern green manufacturing industry mainly deals with green design, process planning, material selection, product packaging, recycling, green management, and equipment utilization. Green manufacturing fully considers the product's entire lifecycle. As in any of the previous manufacturing paradigms, this new green manufacturing paradigm is an outcome of market and technological drivers. Higher global awareness of environmental risks as a result of the new green movement is shaping new customer requirements in many places. In addition, the evolving green technology together with more eco-friendly product designs is helping in realizing the green manufacturing objectives in real practice.

Although interest in green manufacturing is increasing more and more within the research and industrial communities, a clear description of what is meant by this term is becoming more essential. Much confusion arises from failing to describe the meaning, impact and implementation of green manufacturing at various level of manufacturing. In other words, more work is required to differentiate between green manufacturing on the operational level, process level and system level. Furthermore, the relation between sustainability and green manufacturing needs to be better explained to avoid mixing the two terms and at the same time drawing a clear relation between them. The main impartial of green product development is to reduce the crash of industrial extension on the environment over the universe. They perceive out hugely disconnected utilization of elements for executing green product development.

Manufacturing firms are awaited to implement green manufacturing and increase product complication at a competitive price. Nevertheless, a crucial problem for engineering managers is to discover the costs of undertaking on green manufacturing. Thus, a planning and control methodology for costing of green manufacturing at the early plan stage is important for engineering managers. The paper aims to debate these issues. They establish that equipment costs and carbon emission costs are major components of costs in manufacturing. The total lifecycle cost of product in green manufacturing is lower than that of same product in conventional manufacturing. The particular results of this study are limited to the case company but can hopefully accord to further research on discovering cost of implementing "green issues" in manufacturing. The proposed cost calculation model can be logically applied in any manufacturing firm on the basis of attainability of real cost data. The cost model furnishes cost rationale of executing green manufacturing. The reality is that green manufacturing will see its development apex with cost justifications. The consequences of the application show that the advanced detailed cost model can be effective in reducing costs of implementing green manufacturing. Manufacturing firms are approved to adopt energy-saving activities based on the proposed detailed cost calculation model (Orji and Wei, 2016).

The author worked on a topic of green manufacturing and similar frameworks in order to trace the origin, definitions, scope, similarities, differences, and publications of these manufacturing frameworks. He found that that all these eight frameworks have been used interchangeably by researchers, but it requires some standardization. It has been observed during literature review that to standardize the terminology researchers have to clear emphatically in their research the use of various lifecycle engineering approach; clarity on the end-of-life strategies used; clarity in use of various components of triple bottom line perspectives; inclusion of the whole supply chain and integration of environmental improvement strategies with the business strategy. They investigate the applicability of lean and green practices to foundry industry in India for improving productivity and eliminating waste, incorporating the sustainability into business performance measures. The study used survey questionnaire method to collect data. From analysis the found all four constructs are adequate and reliable to illustrate lean and green practices. Descriptive statistics indicates that lean and green practices are applicable for implementation to a certain extent in the foundry industry. Correlation analysis shows that lean practices are positively and moderately interrelated with green practices. Thus, the results present a strong evidence that lean and green practices are moderately applicable for implementation in the foundry industry. The paper provides insights into the applicability of lean and green practices implementation in the context of a developing country and presents evidence that lean and green practices are moderately applicable in the foundry industry.

A continuous process industry, the cement manufacturing industry with the aim of identifying greening opportunities in its production operations. The study analyses areas pertaining to the cement industry that impact the environment with specific focus on the industry within a developing, lower income country. A cleaner production approach was used in a case study approach, focusing on issues such as gaseous emissions and particulate emissions. Both capital intensive and fewer intensive options are proposed. The paper provides insights about how change is brought about within a continuous process industry. It suggests that successful leaders act as "integrating forces" on two levels: integrating the elements of corporate identity structures and mediating between the corporate branding structures and the individual. Capital interventions included redesigning the clinker conveyor, as well as restructuring the dust transportation system. There is a need for the developing countries to track and identify modern interventions that are available within industry and adopt them. The limitation of this study is that the paper focuses on a single cement factory in a low-income country, as the case study approach was used. As such, findings and options generated may not be generalized, as the processes from one industry to another tend to differ in different economies.

The study investigates the relationship between green management and environmental performance. This was accomplished by considering each operational element, including the supply and acquisition of upstream materials, research and development, manufacturing and packaging, marketing, promotion and education, and recycling activities. They made a survey and collect the data from 118 Taiwanese manufacturers. The results indicate a positive relationship between green-value chain management and environmental performance. The results suggest that when firms only implement green management in particular areas the effect is insignificant; however, a comprehensive implementation can result in an overall improvement in environmental performance (Kung, 2012). The electronic industry's reaction to environmental regulations specifically in terms of lead-free solders and halogen free flame retardants. This paper includes examples of how the industry is successful in implementing environmentally the US. While the regulations themselves vary in scope, industry actions to find alternatives do have common purposes. Electronics manufacturers recognize that environmentally motivated changes are beneficial in terms of waste minimization. Regardless of the regulatory motivation, minimization does lead to energy and economic efficiency.

The green manufacturing strategy in large developing countries needs to be enacted for a long-term and with a continuous improvement paradigm. Planning and implementing the strategy requires an integrated model at the whole system level. A theoretical model of a five-layer structure for planning and implementing the green manufacturing strategy under the developing context is proposed. The planning and implementing of the green manufacturing strategy may vary among different sectors, therefore more empirical research is needed to enhance the robustness of the findings.

Green manufacturing has an impact on critical success factors and performance measures in context to Indian cement industry. The authors followed survey method for data collection. For framework development, it uses factor analysis on the identified critical success factors and regression along with the appropriate measures for checking statistical consistency and validity. This was the first research towards green manufacturing framework for Indian cement industry no framework is available which could guide researchers and practitioners of this environment unfriendly industry. Study exposes lack of connectivity between critical success factors and performance measures for a green manufacturing framework and highlights weaknesses of cement industry in this regard. It offers a generalized green manufacturing framework linking performance measures with top management, human resource management, organizational culture, green practices, process management and supply chain management (Seth et al., 2016).

Paul et al. (2014) reviewed a literature on impact of green manufacturing in different firms. The paper discussed the use of green manufacturing, its impacts and the methods to adopt green engineering for decreasing the waste and pollution. The paper also highlighted the use of green manufacturing to obtain a sustainable product and to reuse the product. The authors also discussed about the green accounting and green supply chain management in this article. Green manufacturing and eco-innovation collectively have an impact on sustainability performance of industry. They collected the data from 53 automobile, chemistry and electronics companies through questionnaire base survey and use the methodology to test empirical model by using regression analysis, to verify the hypothetical relationships of the study. The results of this study indicate that the green manufacturing applications have a significant positive impact on environmental performance and social performance. Additionally, eco-process innovation has a significant positive impact on corporate sustainability. However, eco-product innovation was not found to have a significant effect on any of the three types of performance (Sezen and Sibel, 2013).

Despite their widespread use and applications, there are several scientific and economic factors that call for an investigation of current practices and development of new approaches. There are numerous methods that diverge from traditional "wet" machining, which move towards an environmentally friendly and cost-effective machining process. This includes looking at both minimum quantity lubrication and dry machining as methods to reduce recurring costs, lower healthcare premiums associated to metalworking fluid exposure, and to minimize the environmental footprint attributed to machining. Traditional machine lubrication techniques are in use today despite a lack of scientific or economic evidence that they function efficiently. Depending on the machine type and material used, there are several possible methods that can minimize or eliminate metalworking fluids from the machining process.

Wantao Yu et al. worked on the topic integrated green provide chain management and operational performance. The main purpose of this paper is to increase previous green provide chain management analysis by trial and error testing a conceptual framework. This framework investigates the relations between the multiple dimensions of operational performance and three dimensions of integrated green provide chain management. For getting results they done survey and collected knowledge from completely different industries. The study generates important findings of the operational performance in terms of delivery, quality, flexibility and cost. It is important for manager of the industries that they consider the presence of customers and suppliers when implementing environmental sustainability within the provide chains.

The prioritizing barriers to green manufacturing are environmental, social and economic perspectives. Manufacturing firms consume energy and natural resources in highly unsustainable manner and release large amounts of greenhouse gases leading to many economic, environmental and social problems, ranging from climate change to local waste disposal. They concluded that the government should also include the awareness/information campaigns as an obligatory activity for NGOs funded by government. Also, the government should invest more in science and technology to promote the development of indigenous green technologies in association with technical institutions of the country and should build and upgrade necessary infrastructure to enforce the environmental legislation effectively. The government should also ensure the uniform environmental legislation in all states/regions of the country to stop companies from shifting the dirty manufacturing to places with lax environmental legislation.

Green manufacturing factors and its sub factors have a relationship with the organizational performance which include environmental performance, competitive advantage, and economic performance. They found that the industry with large manufacturing capacity can heavily invest on the green supply chain management than the industry with small manufacturing capacity. This is due to the larger firm has more investment capacity on green concept than the smaller firm. Thus, it is concluded that to protect the environment and the earth appropriate methodology should be adopted by the industries to minimize the detrimental effect on the earth. Green manufacturing is core to their competitive strategies. The transformation journey to green manufacturing has just started. While there are a few early adopters, the industry at large needs to develop comprehensive plans to address all three areas that is green energy, green products and green processes. The government has to play an effective facilitator role in this transformation with both stronger incentives on one hand and regulatory mechanisms on the other. The industry associations can bring the different stakeholders together and support the roll-out of a communication strategy.

A system model for the new green manufacturing paradigms has been presented. This model captures various planning activities to migrate from a less green into a greener and more eco-efficient manufacturing environment. The various planning stages are accompanied by the required control metrics as well as various green tools in an open mixed architecture. The system model is demonstrated by an industrial case study. The proposed model is a comprehensive qualitative answer to the questions as how to design and improve green manufacturing systems as well as a roadmap for future quantitative research to better evaluate this new paradigm (Ahmed, 2011). The performance measures for the green manufacturing practices in the Indian manufacturing industries have been explored. The study obtained 108 valid responses from the Indian manufacturing industries. Future research needs to be performed using a larger sample and studying more countries. A total of 12 performance measures of green manufacturing with their 66 items have been developed: top management commitment, knowledge management, employee training, green product and process design, employee empowerment, environmental health and safety, suppliers and materials management, production planning and control, quality, cost, customer environment performance requirement, customer responsiveness and company growth. The performance measures developed in this study enables decision makers to assess the perception of green manufacturing in their organization and in prioritizing GM efforts (Digalwar et al., 2016).

Hong et al. (2009) implemented strategic green orientation in supply chain. The purpose of this paper is to present a research model that defines the inter-relationships between strategic green orientation, integrated product development, supply chain coordination, green performance outcomes and business unit performance. This paper aims to address innovation issues by integrating strategic orientation, internal business practices, supply chain coordination, and performance outcomes measures. This strategic green orientation is supported by a set of inter-organizational innovation practices such as integrated product development practices, effective coordination of supply chain network and relevant and measurable performance outcomes.

Wang et al. worked on planning and implementing the green manufacturing based on a case study of a machine tool manufacturer in China. This work tries to investigate the planning and implementing of a green manufacturing strategy from the perspective of the product lifecycle. The authors explored the model for planning and implementing the green manufacturing (GM) strategy for Chinese enterprises under the background of "Energy Conservation and Pollution Emissions Reduction". The important aspects of green manufacturing where Lean Manufacturing yields sufficient environmental benefits though it does not mainly focus on the environmental results. The elimination of waste represents the ultimate solution to pollution problems that threaten ecosystems at global level. It is also observed that energy saving plays a prominent role in controlling the pollution there by reduction in generation of greenhouse gases to atmosphere is controlled. One of the benefits of green manufacturing would be reducing cost because in the end the company may not have to shell out money to remove the waste when waste has already been eliminated on the first step (Maruthi and Rashmi, 2015).

Orji and Wei (2016) provided detailed calculation model for costing of green manufacturing. The paper integrates "green manufacturing" concepts of industrial dynamics, and product lifecycle aiming at developing a methodology for cost calculation. The methodology comprises of a process-based cost model and a system dynamics (SD) model. The process-based cost model focuses mainly on carbon emission costs and energy-saving activities. The results obtained shows that the equipment costs and carbon emission costs are major components of costs in manufacturing. The total lifecycle cost of product in green manufacturing is lower than that of same product in conventional manufacturing. The green manufacturing and similar frameworks enable tracing the origin, definitions, scope, similarities, differences, and publications of these manufacturing frameworks. A review of 113 research articles was conducted for various terms like green manufacturing (GM). It was observed with reasonable confidence that all these frameworks have been used interchangeably by researchers, but it requires some standardization.

A number of studies have been conducted over the period of time to provide an overview of various aspects and issues related to this research work. The review of literature can lead to draw some significant conclusions and serve as a guide mark for this study. It also gives a fair chance to identify one gap that exists in the area of research. Some of the important studies have been reviewed under different performance measures such as a survey about environmentally conscious design and manufacturing (ECD and M) framework designed in the field of green product development and total lifecycle cost of product in green manufacturing. In the past few years, green manufacturing has attracted the attention of many researchers. This research field is very broad. Zhang et al. as well as Dheeraj and Vishal have given surveys about environmentally conscious design and manufacturing (ECD and M). They considered the social and technological aspects of the design, synthesis, processing and the use of products in continuous or discrete manufacturing industries. Green product development has appeared as a global occurrence. The study recognized 80 unique elements and 11 pillars to suggest a comprehensive conceptual framework in the field of green product development with the help of relative survey. Equipment costs and carbon emission costs are major components of costs in manufacturing. The total lifecycle cost of product in green manufacturing is lower than that of same product in conventional manufacturing (Orji and Wei, 2016). Green manufacturing and similar frameworks like definitions, scope, similarities, differences, and publications have been used interchangeably by researchers but it requires some standardization. The relationship between green management and environmental performance was investigated. The results suggested that when firms only implement green management in particular areas the effect is insignificant; however, a comprehensive implementation can result in an overall improvement in environmental performance.

Lean and green practices improved productivity and eliminated waste in foundry industry. From the analysis it was found that all four constructs are adequate and reliable to illustrate lean and green practices. Thus, the results present a strong evidence that lean and green practices are moderately applicable for implementation in the foundry industry.

Fore and Mbohwa identified greening opportunities in the production operations of a cement manufacturing industry. Study has been carried out by analyzing the areas pertaining to the cement industry that impact the environment with specific focus on the industry pertaining to a developing, lower income of country. A cleaner production approach was used in a case study approach, focusing on issues such as gaseous emissions and particulate emissions. This was the first research towards green manufacturing framework in the context of Indian cement industry no framework is available which could guide researchers and practitioners of this environment unfriendly industry. Seth et al. (2016) exposed lack of connectivity between critical success factors and performance measures for a green manufacturing framework and highlights weaknesses of cement industry in this regard.

Li et al. emphasized that green manufacturing strategy in large developing countries needs to be enacted for a long term and with a continuous improvement paradigm. Planning and implementing the strategy requires an integrated model at the whole system level. The planning and implementing of the green manufacturing strategy may vary among different sectors, therefore more empirical research is needed to enhance the robustness of the findings. Small- and medium-sized enterprises can make themselves greener by making strategic and organizational changes. For greener management, the factors of organizational structure, innovation capability, human resources, cost savings and competitive advantage can influence organizational change. Feng (2010) studied green company and green consumers, objective of which to re-examine corporate social responsibility in terms of the ethical criterion of "greenness" through an assessment of one company's response to green consumers during the past number of years.

Dubey and Ali (2015) investigated green manufacturing practices and their impact on extended supply chain performance studied in Indian firms. The factor analysis output suggests that total quality management (TQM), supplier relationship management (SRM), R and D and technology and lean manufacturing practices are important determinants of Indian firms practicing green manufacturing practices which impact extended supply chain performance. Green manufacturing applications have a significant positive impact on environmental performance and social performance. Additionally, eco-process innovation has a significant positive impact on corporate sustainability. Green technologies can increase the economic gains of manufacturers by reducing costs on energy consumption and shift away from selling low-margin products. However, the local authorities often encounter obstacles when implementing policies for promoting these technologies among manufacturing firms. Based on the econometric analysis of the survey for China's electric motors upgrading project in Guangdong Province, this study shows that three key factors are helpful in the local government's effort to implement the national project: manufacturers' awareness, the understanding of the energy-efficiency technology, and the long-term macroeconomic benefits (Kong et al., 2016).

Small- and medium-sized enterprises (SMEs) are significant to China's emission reduction programme. The research was carried to improve the understanding of the challenge of diffusing green-manufacturing technologies among SMEs in China. Specifically, this study examines the Chinese Government's effort to facilitate reduction of energy consumption among SMEs through Energy Performance Contracts (EPCs) to incentivize domestic manufacturers to adopt energy efficient measures (EEMs) in order to reduce demand for energy and corresponding drop in emissions (Liu et al., 2017).

Rehman et al. designed a diagnostic research survey instrument for data collection from the Indian manufacturing companies that have experienced green manufacturing. The study offered useful insights and guides about how industries should link both aspects critical green manufacturing factors and performance measures to channelize their green manufacturing initiatives, in order to improve environmental, operational and financial performance. Bai et al. proposed a theoretical framework for corporate sustainability development in China to clarify the relationships between the drivers and corporation performance. Woo et al. on the same lines, empirically examined the communication capabilities for green supply chain management and relationship among green integration, green cost reduction, and corporate competitiveness from the suppliers' perspective in Korean context.

Environmental issues would be critical for manufacturing firms in Asia over the next few decades (Diabat and Govindan, 2011; Zhu et al. 2005). Teles et al. (2015) identified reduced consumption of natural resources and waste treatment as the environmental practices are popular, among the best performing green manufacturing practicing Brazilian companies. In China too, the environmental issues have become more prominent (Zhu et al., 2005). Growth of manufacturing industries and dynamic competitive environment encouraged small and medium size enterprises (SMEs) to deliver stand-out performance. SMEs accounted for 99% of total enterprises and furnishing about 60% of employment, that can be considered as a core of economies worldwide. In Indian industrial scenario, SMEs contribute about 45% of the total manufacturing output and 40% of total exports. Moreover, contribution of total manufacturing sector in Indian GDP accounted for 16%, out of which contribution of manufacturing micro, small and medium size enterprises (MSMEs) accounted for 7%. This indicates the significant contribution of manufacturing SMEs in Indian economic growth.

Despite of enormous opportunities to explore RandD activities, the progress of SMEs is hindered by limited resources, either human or financial ones. Implementation of Lean Manufacturing (LM) results in less human effort, less manufacturing space, less lead time and less waste, with fewer defects. SMEs account for at least 13% of global final energy consumption annually. The usage of natural resources rises to 123.5 million tonnes in 2012 which was 83.5 million tonnes in 2002 in India. Also, the Government of India announced the "National Action Plan on Climate Change" (NAPCC), in June 2008 with a goal to reduce India's carbon intensity by 20–25% by 2020, compared to 2005 levels. Hence, there is a need for Indian SMEs to support strategies like green manufacturing (GM) to tackle environmental challenges like depletion of natural resources, pollution, global warming. GM is a collection of harmless activities that helps in minimizing waste and provide a sustainable environment to the society (Singh et al., 2012). These create an essential condition in which SMEs are compelled to redefine the operational strategies by integrating environmental aspects by being lean and green simultaneously.

Factory size is one of the key factors for implementation of LM because operational strategies differ for large scale industries compared to small scale industries. Moreover, this fact stands true in sustainability context, too. Moreover, managerial decisions of SMEs are greatly influenced by the strategies adopted by large scale industries to whom they act as tier I/II suppliers, SMEs need to break the conventional mould and admire the efforts of larger industries by implementing if not all, but few select LM and GM practices.

In recent years, many researchers have explored the possibilities to integrate LM and GM strategically to make the organizations sustainable through improvement in economic, environmental and social performance. Wu et al. investigated relation between lean-green-social (LGS) practices and triple bottom-line (3BL) performance and concluded that optimal 3BL can be achieved by integrated LGS strategies. Also, some studies support the integration of sustainability and supply chain management to improve organizations' sustainable performance. Further, Wu et al. developed a supply chain agility tool and identified key drivers to achieve competitive advantage under uncertainty. In existing literature, a segment of studies concluded with synergic benefits of lean and green integration, while some other studies have investigated positive linkages between LM and GM implementation. Some scholarly studies have highlighted that lean practices are partially green without the explicit intention to being green and hence it is obvious that harmonious integration of lean and green manufacturing can be seen as a positive step towards sustainability. However, Garza-Reyes indicated the limited research on integration of LM and GM. Moreover, Verrier et al. urges for detailed investigation on integrated LM and GM implementation with prime focus on SMEs to provide them convenient path for successful adoption.

2.2.1 Transformation to green manufacturing

Green transformation refers to processes within industries and/or companies that lead to reduced environmental change impact. Since the 1990s, industrial transformation has been one of the core science projects of the International Human Dimensions Programme (IHDP) which has been integrated into the new initiative Future Earth. Manufacturing companies can address these concerns by focusing on three areas:

2.2.1.1 Green Energy

Green energy involves production and use of cleaner energy. This is the first and most obvious step given the dependence of industry on energy. Green energy includes both deploying renewable energy sources like CNG, wind, solar and biomass, and achieving higher energy efficiency in operations.

2.2.1.2 Green Products

Developing greener products is the second step in this transformation. "Recycled", "Low carbon footprint", "Organic" and "Natural" are becoming popular buzzwords which are associated with green products. Developing Green products can often mean higher costs. However, by developing green products that are sought by consumers, and effectively marketing them, companies can derive additional volumes and price premiums, which can offset their cost of development.

2.2.1.3 Green Processes in Business Operations

The third area is implementing green processes in operations. This entails efficient use of key resources, reducing waste generation through lean operations, bringing down the carbon footprint and conserving water. Employing Green processes improves operational efficiency and lowers costs.

Green has moved from being perceived as a "necessary evil" to being seen as "good business". Companies that undertake green initiatives stand to be advantaged on brand enhancement, political traction and regulatory compliance, greater ability to attract and retain talent, enhanced customer retention and potential cost savings. However, these benefits require a long-term commitment and making trade-offs against short term objectives, as the economics of green manufacturing are not well understood yet.

2.2.2 FORCES DRIVING GREEN MANUFACTURING

A number of organizations need to adopt green activities concerning illustration of essential analytics and only operations. These activities are driven by five variables:

1. Increasing energy and input costs.
2. Developing customer draw for green products.
3. Expand regulatory pressures as policy developers create new and stricter environmental and waste management laws.
4. Innovative developments which open up new business chances.
5. The requirement will improve aggressive differentiation, especially to first movers alternately the individuals who have the ability to break that trade off the middle of transient higher costs and various reductions (example: brand premium, new client segments). Green need moved from being discerned concerning illustration an "necessary evil" will be seen similarly as "good businesses".

Organizations that attempt green activities remained to make advantaged ahead mark enhancement, Political footing also administrative compliance, more terrific capability on draw in hold talent, improved client maintenance and possibility cost reserve funds. However, these reductions oblige a long-term duty and settling on trade off against transient objectives, as the trading and lending for green manufacturing are not great comprehended yet. Green manufacturing eludes will multidisciplinary methodologies. Meant on decreasing the energy and material expectation in manufacturing procedures energy can make diminished dependent upon 60–70% with main utilization of renewable energy sources. Separated from the imaginative taking care of energy demands, the green manufacturing will be connected to many other environmental technologies.

Green manufacturing includes conversion for industrial operation in the three ways: (i) utilizing green energy; (ii) creating and offering green products; and (iii) utilizing green processes within those business operations. Green obtaining organize is spreading very much quickly over India. The sway from claiming green processes likewise varies by those industry divisions. For example, green activities control segments bring the greatest sway ahead, lessening CO_2 discharges.

Successful change under green manufacturing will achieve colossal benefits, both unmistakable and immaterial holding to those country and the business. Green manufacturing includes production methods which are exceptionally efficient, and which Produce minimal alternately no waste alternately contamination. Green manufacturing includes encompasses source decrease or called minimum waste or pollution, or prevention, reusing and green product design. Source decrease will be comprehensively characterized will incorporate. Whatever activity diminishing that waste at first created reusing incorporates utilizing or reusing wastes similarly as parts Previously, A transform or concerning illustration a powerful substitute to business product or giving back. Those waste of the first transform which generated it as a substitute to raw material feedstock.

2.2.3 Technologies for Green Manufacturing

Today, there is a plenty of new and rising innovations that support for both, making those universal organizations greener, and in addition making totally new ones. for example, Innovations to diminishing GHG could be ordered under five diverse classes:

a. Carbon sinks
   This classification comprises of developing advances identified with carbon catch and storage (CCS) being produced for use in power plants that would let go by fossil fills like coal. These innovations empower catching and storing CO_2 for approaches such as it doesn't enter the environment. For example, CO_2 starting with fossil fills may be trapped and saved in underground wells under compelling weight which keeps it done condensed.

b. Efficient fuels
   This class includes population of innovations that utilize cleaner fills for generating energy. Cases hydro power, incorporate biomass, integrated gas combined cycle (IGCC), and so on.

c. Consumer Green
   This includes utilizing and proficient fills. In those client end and results coating request side administration. example, off-grid solar powered force requisitions similar to solar water warming and building encasing need aid included in this class.

d. Green transportation
   Electric vehicles, fuel cells, and biodiesel are examples within this category.

e. Industry efficiency
   This class alludes of the utilization of green processing techniques and innovations over accepted commercial enterprises for example: iron and steel, cement,

refining and chemicals. Various such advances need aid rising clinched alongside each about these commercial enterprises.

Every innovation inside these five Classes can be further described for two extents: maturity (nascent versus established) and accessibility (local versus global). Same time some advances for example, biomass, hydro and off-grid solar score higher as far as their relative innovative unrest and business maturity, there would others such as tidal waves, wind seaward and amassed sun powered force which need aid moderately early. Similarly, same techniques for example, IGCC and CCS need aid comprehensively accessible to use others, for example, such that geo–thermal and waste to energy would accessible just in selected geographies. Arranging advances with respect to these two measurements gives direction in settling on business model decisions. It also strikes a harmony between opportunistically tackling the income pools for today and proactively positioning to catching future income pools. Relying upon their craving to asset commitment, organizations could settle on generally different decisions.

2.3 CHALLENGES IN ADOPTING GREEN

Even in tough market conditions, the business case for green remains compelling. There is greater recognition of the imperatives of becoming green and understanding that green has to address all three areas – green energy, green products and green processes. However, companies face challenges on various fronts, most critically in providing leadership for such an effort. Companies have to transition from

a. Approaching green as limited, often isolated initiatives with narrow focus to a more holistic approach,
b. Meeting regulatory compliance to developing eco–advantage, and
c. Viewing initiatives as cost centres to assessing them as business opportunities.

This calls for a major transformation which to succeed, requires a systematic approach and a framework addressing the three principal impediments to decisive action:

1. Companies don't fully understand drivers and issues relevant to them and their industries, and what sustainability means to them.
2. Companies face difficulties in modelling the business case – or even finding a compelling case – for sustainability. The initiatives are not a priority for most, and often the economics are not well understood as technologies and costs are still evolving.
3. Even the companies that adopt green initiatives perform these activities as peripheral to their core business and not integrated into their corporate strategy. Hence the execution is flawed, and they fail in realizing the full benefits.

2.4   ECONOMIC ASSESSMENT AND MAKING STRATEGIC CHOICES

Like any major transformational exercise, success in adopting green requires companies to understand the full set of facts on costs and benefits, and the entire range of green measures available to them. Once this fact base is developed, companies have to select their green initiatives based on both, economic and strategic assessments of the choices they identify. An economic assessment requires estimating the 'value' generated over the long term through these initiatives. It should cover all drivers of value creation – from quantitative metrics like pricing power and cost savings, to qualitative ones like employee recruitment and engagement – otherwise, some of the long-term benefits of green will not get captured as part of the business case.

Performing an economic assessment is only one part of the story. Having made a viable case, companies need to make a strategic choice on how green they want to be, and why. The choice of initiatives could vary depending not only on the underlying economics of the options, but also on the market context and opportunities for strategic differentiation. Potentially, companies can choose to be:

- Planet indifferent: where the measures adopted are minimal,
- Good citizens: where they carry out a few isolated initiatives which are the bare minimum that customers demand or regulators stipulate, or
- Green innovators: where they try to stay ahead of the curve on sustainability and transform the issue from one of risk management to that of top line growth and a key business opportunity.

While the first two choices do not allow the company to fully leverage the potential of green and are only relevant with a short-term lens, the third commits the company to a comprehensive green strategy and to getting the most from the initiatives.

2.5   IMPLEMENTATION FRAMEWORK

Becoming green is a long journey of transformation. To succeed, adequate attention is required on planning and execution of the initiatives. Early wins and successes are important to build momentum. It calls for a fully committed top management, tight periodic reviews and constant internal and external communication. A simple three–step implementation framework can be followed covering all three areas of action – green energy, green products and green processes.

1. Plan

Green initiatives must be factored into the business strategy, future resource planning and budgeting exercises. For example, companies need to plan comprehensively to increase the use of green energy, shift the product portfolio to green products and overhaul business operations towards green processes. A sustainability charter, based on short term and long-term goals, must be laid out with green targets and metrics. Companies should develop. Green indices or scorecards quantifying the impact of the green initiatives they have undertaken, set specific targets on those indices and track progress against those targets.

2. Execute

With a robust plan in place and targets clearly defined and monitored, green needs to be integrated across the value chain and made a part of the core business.

- Green energy: Manufacturing companies with high energy consumption need to shift towards using cleaner energy and plan for increasing the efficiency of its use. Setting up captive wind or solar power generation units and using energy efficient practices, such as installing LED lighting or better use of daylight in building design, can go a long way towards reducing the energy intensity of operations.

- Green products: To move towards a green product portfolio, companies should conduct an evaluation of their products based on (a) how green are the resources and energy being used, (b) how green is the product during the lifecycle of its use, and (c) how green is the manufacturing process. By quantifying these parameters, companies can assess the green value of their product offering. In the planning stage itself, companies should set out targets for this metric, and then periodically assess progress against those targets.

- Green processes in business operations: Companies need to gradually redesign business processes used in different parts of the value chain. This could include shifting to more sustainable manufacturing options, making changes towards reducing waste, increasing recycling, reusing resources and incentivizing all suppliers, channels, customers and employees to adopt similar measures.

3. Communicate

Along with well thought–through implementation, a well formulated promotion campaign for green initiatives is equally important to fully leverage their potential benefits. Customer education campaigns about green product offerings and the green orientation of the firm in terms of energy and processes, can translate into increasing revenues.

2.6 CONSUMER PERSPECTIVE

a. Green Awareness

Green manufacturing will be imperative, barely because of tightening regulations or expense benefits, but also in light of consumers need aid requesting it. Over a BCG survey 10 of shoppers across developed and creating nations, over two–thirds communicated convictions that nature's domain will be for a poor shape and that ecological issues would an essential risk of the culture. Not main would buyers getting to be progressively mindful and acquainted with green, they need aid additionally adopting green propensities and purchasing green products. Those proceeding development about green cognizance around those reality displays an enormous chance to smart organizations. As stated by the BCG overview findings, same time customers accept that as individuals, they can and should help practicality by adopting green products, they also hold organizations on a higher standard when it goes to being green.

The expression green will be distinguished the reality over shorthand for natural cognizance. However, the point when required on characterize green and their desire starting with green products, purchasers required a range for reactions contingent upon the place they existed and the sort for results they purchased. Therefore, incredulous to organizations with uncover how their target customer segments feel regarding green, what they hope from green results and the thing that costs they are eager to pay for them.

An alternate discovering of the overview might have been that over 50% about these consumers bought green items. The overview shown those consumers incredibly quality those regulate reductions that green Items offer, for example, – unrivalled freshness and taste, the guarantee about security also health and Funds for energy fetches. They are eager to pay high costs for green items that need superior personal satisfaction discernment. Same time shopping to green will be getting to be basic in large number countries, shopping propensities shift significantly eventually by categories. Specific green item Classes such as paper, nourishment products, disposable home products, buyer durables also beauty items better known over others and are bought more often.

b. Barriers to Higher Green Consumption

As specified earlier, many consumers, especially in developed countries, would eagerly pay a premium to go green. Their eagerness to pay additional relies around a product's classification and discerned benefits, also may be most elevated for nourishment and buyer durables. The discoveries of the study create plainly that cost is not a critical impediment to large portions purchasers. Previously, cost ranks much bring down likewise obstruction to green buying over absence of attention to green alternately. Discerned absence of choice quite clearly, mindfulness may be a basic lever for expanding offers of green items. It may be assessed that organizations lose with respect to an average, almost 20% about possibility purchasers. When buyers are not educated enough on the manageability part for their offerings. Organizations compelling reason will precisely arrange and put resources into their client mindfulness programmers and fill in with their retailers will give satisfactory Rack space and deceivability to guarantee their green endeavours need aid completely leveraged.

2.7 GREEN SUPPLY CHAIN MANAGEMENT

Green Supply Chain Management (GSCM) is emerged in the automobile organizations and make it cost effective, more environmentally friendly and competitive. The main objective of this research is to review the GSCM practices and to determine the common GSCM practices among the auto-component organization and automobile organization in the Madhya Pradesh. The common practices in their operations were Investment Recovery Cooperation with the customer for Eco-design reduction of toxic emissions at the plant level. Resource allocation, green manufacturing, monitoring of resource consumption, level of information technology and pollution, employee training programmes on green methods, quality of manpower Involvement and commitment, cross-functional cooperation/ self-regulation or management are few recommendations represented in the study. They concluded that all the organizations should go for the improvement of less common practices to participate in a highly competitive international market. The results of the research show that the management should train their employees to work for the safety of the environment and with less wastage. The government should also develop and implement certain policies to help organizations for showing more environment-friendly operations. For example, allowances, tax rebate, and training to the employees on the environmental safety. For effectively implementing the GSCM practices, it is required that every stakeholder contributes to the organization's operations than only we can guard our environment in a better way. The result also indicated that the some of the GSCM practices are at the best stage and most of them are on the primary stage which concluded that there are many opportunities for the business to adopt such types of operations which are environmentally friendly.

The significance of the GSCM was growing by the mounting deterioration of the environment. The waste and discharge were caused due to the supply chain. It was the foremost source of the environmental problems such as acid rain and global warming. Green supply chains help in improving the environmental and economic performance concurrently throughout the chains through creating the long-term buyer-supplier relationships. The results indicated that the green Supply Chain Management improves many of the operations of an organization by employing the environment solutions such as increased the adaptability that leads to the continuous and innovation process enhancement, improved the agility which helps in mitigating the risks, and in promoting the alignment. GSCM helps the organization by improving their environmental performance. They provide the several benefits to an organization such as improved the profitability, enhance the efficiency and cost savings. In this research, some eco-friendly practices can be achieved by adopting the GSCM practices by Indian small, medium and large organizations. After examining the various organizations, a set of bets eco-friendly practices were captured. The captured set can be used as a benchmark for organizations who want to implement the green Supply Chain Management practices.

The main goal of the research is to develop the green supply chain approach for the sustainability and to integrating it into the existing the supply chain of the organization. Green supply chain management impacted by the organizational culture, organizational structure, leadership and employee behaviour. Based on a literature review the constructs were identified. A six-step approach to developing and implementing a sustainable six-step approach to developing for planning and implementing the green supply chain strategy. The different strategies that can be used for effective implementation of GSCM practices. After reviewing the practices of various organizations, few effective and efficient GSCM strategies have been recommended for the research. These include risk-based strategies, closed loop strategies, efficiency-based strategies and innovation-based strategies. GSCM is the concept which involves all the applications of the environmental issues with corporate social responsibility in the traditional supply chain management. The main objective of the green supply chain practice is to minimize the cost and prevent from the pollution which leads to the positive changes in the organization.

This research described the scope of GSCM in the large corporations in India which encourage the GSCM implementation. GSCM incorporates the effective applications of the technology like maintaining the social integrity and environment in an equitable manner. Some large Indian corporation is implementing the green practices for promoting the eco-literacy among the suppliers, promoting eco-friendly products, adopting reverse logistic practices to minimize the waste, adopting the cleaner technology, and for promoting continuous improvement in the products and their design. The results of this research described that the Indian small and medium enterprises (SMEs) have the many opportunities to position themselves in the better way with the help of the green supply chain practices. The top management should adopt these types of strategies in order to gain the confidence of the public and to sustain in the competitive market Shareholders, employees, customers, and stakeholders are essential for building the brand image of the company.

There is high pressure on the organization for using the green practices in sourcing, usage, production, delivery, and disposal of the products. In future, many of the organization will invest in the cross functional collaboration, network design, packaging changes, sourcing, procurement, and on the innovative methods which help in reducing the carbon footprints from every stage of the supply chain. The susceptibility programmes of the organization may change from industry to industry but their basic needs or the communication, transparency, and collaboration will same. Some critical factors which lead to successful green strategy is holistic, result oriented, programmatic, integrated, measurable, and sustained. GSCM has a lot of significance for the organization which includes the reverse logistics, distribution, production, inbound logistics, and purchasing. Green SCM use to ingrates the Supply Chain Management and Environmental management.

The research indicated that the green SCM provide the long-term benefits. It used to recognize the inconsistent environment impact of the supply chains processes in an organization. This research presented the effort which provides the insight on the concept of the green SCM, importance, need, and also exploring the opportunities and challenges which were involved in the Indian market Therefore, the company needs to an emphasis on reducing the carbon content in all of its practices. Align with core business objectives and strategies and, addressing sustainability from an end-to-end viewpoint and focusing against prioritized opportunities are the few recommendations for the organizations for implementing the GSCM practices effectively. This research dealt with global resource exhaustion and enhanced environmental deteriorations in the organizations. GSCM gained a lot of significance among the organizations, which included inbound logistics, purchasing, distribution, production and reverse logistics. GSCM integrated environmental management and supply chain management SCM. Green capabilities can be enhanced and implemented by continuous effort and time. There was a huge pressure on the organization in order to supply those products which are environmentally friendly in disposal, usage, delivery, production, and sourcing. For reducing the carbon footprints at every stage of the supply chain, the organization will invest immensely on the cross functional collaborations, network design, sourcing, packaging changes, procurement, and innovative methods (Raman, 2014).

This research found the need, importance, challenges, opportunities and some crucial factors for implementing and sustaining GSCM with a focus on the Indian Market. This research presented an effort to give an insight on the concept of the green SCM, its challenges, need, opportunities, and the challenges which involved the crucial factors for the sustaining and implementing the GSCM which focuses on the Indian market The major obstacle to implementing the green SCM is the cost of technology used and the complexity of the processes. The other factor which affects the manufacturing companies is the recycling of the raw materials. Implementation of the green warehouses and the distribution initiatives provide the efficient and more lean-to companies. There is a need for the framework which creates the awareness and spread the knowledge of the GSCM practices which provide the cost and efficiency benefits to the companies. Supply chain helps in the sustainable and successful implementation of the GSCM in which the challenges might change, but the fundamentals remain same of doing the business. The result indicated that the green supply chain management could result in the value creation and cost competitiveness in the longer duration.

Most of the Indian manufacturing organizations either small or large developed some quantitative techniques to measure the performance of the product. GSCM helps in the enhancement of the capabilities of the supply chain management. The objective of this research is to study the several activities of the supply chain processes of the various Indian Manufacturing Industries which includes large scale industries and small manufacturing enterprises. The main activities of the supply chain are green manufacturing, green sourcing and procurement, green packaging, green distribution, green warehousing, and green transportation. These activities help in measuring the performance of the various Indian manufacturing industries using various crucial performance indicators and sub indicators. The result indicated the causes which impact the environment that caused by the manufacturing sectors based on some of the methodologies. This research also compares the various sectors by analyzing the lagging and leading sectors which was based on the existing way of the processes (Bhateja et al., 2011).

MSMEs involved GSCM practices to supply to the extent of their participation as distributors, suppliers and in other capacities as business partners. Among internal pressure, on the job training pushed MSMEs in India to adopt GSCM practices and developed the external pressure and adoption of GSCM. Indian MSMEs has the significant pressure from the external stakeholder in order to adopt the GSCM practices. The MSME population carry out the various phases of the GSCM in the heterogeneous manner and heterogeneity size. This research validates and confirms the Indian MSMEs which significantly pressures from the external stakeholder in order to adopt the GSCM practices. The overall strategy of the GSCM is to enhance the eco-efficiency of the business whether the business is of agriculture, mining, transport, service, and manufacturing, etc. It was an integrated approach, ecological efficiency or may be searched economic. The limitations of the empirical study were a weakness which was associated with the cross-sectional surveys, lack of the correct participant database and the constraints on the depth of the information which was provided in this research. A single cross-sectional survey limits the ability to capture the long-term changes and effects. The result declared that the external pressures and adoption of the GSCM could be fully implemented by the internal pressures. In India, GSCM has been described through six important factors. These factors are technology greening, outbound greening, ecological greening, compliance greening, inbound greening, and reverse logistics greening. GSCM use all the resources more efficiently. The result also shows the improvement in the external reliability and generalizability to measure the attributes of the managers at the global firms.

GSCM system used to manage the database of manufacturing facilities. GSCM have many complementary in respect of another management system because it provides better management of the environmental condition. Chinese enterprises increased the environmental awareness due to the market users, drivers, competitive and regulatory. They highlight the exporting by pursuing the international organizational standards IS14001 certification and ISO9000 serial. Chinese enterprises also implement the variety of the GSCM practice in order to improve their environmental performance so that they can more effectively serve as the supplier for the foreign enterprises in China. Internal environmental management manages and supports the mid-level managers who were necessary for the development of GSCM programmes in China (Li, 2011). The main barrier for the implementations of the GSCM lacks the management skills, tools, knowledge, and economic justification in terms of performance. The Chinese government introduced many new policies in order to promote the GSCM and other environmental practices to attract more products and more foreign investments. For example, some of the local government agencies helped the enterprises to pass the ISO14001 certification by providing the training. This research discussed the adoption level, competitive level, and many factors related to GSCM. This research helps in investigating the GSCM practices in China. It explored the performance measurement for the GSCM which was based on the database of 128 manufacturing facilities in China. The result indicated that GSCM has the strongest complementary to the other advanced management practices and also improves the environmental performance.

Procurement management system, mainly for reducing cost and increasing profitability without compromising the quality of the services and goods which are delivered to the customers. Indian industry is growing the environmental awareness, and due to that, there was a problem in the management system. Procurement management system is used to manage the industrial or environment process for management. This system used to increase the strength of supply chain, customer satisfaction, customer service. The objective of the research is to describe and evaluate the world class procurement practice and impact of the performance of the firm among various Indian manufacturing organizations. Procurement has the main impact on the direct material costs which consists of 40–70% of the total cost of the sold goods (Bag, 2012). This research uses the longitudinal methodology which enabling in-birth insight and possibility to be close to data into the procurement practices. It was conducted at bulk and mining material handling equipment manufacturing company which has the multi-location plants across the globe. The procurement directly impacts on the strategic planning process of the firm in order to align the strategic goals the procurement management the firm strategy. Managers should examine the effects of the procurement on the firm performance to manage the supply. Environmental awareness increased among the Indian firms because of the competitive, regulatory, drivers and marketing pressures. Managers should understand the importance of the procurement management and adopt the world class purchasing practice in order to gain the competitive advantage. For this, managers should use the specific framework for determining the performance of purchasing.

GSCM is used to improve the environmental performance of companies. It was viewed as the cross-organizational and closed loop which minimizes the ecological impact of the industrial activity without affecting reliability, cost, quality, energy utilization efficiency, and performance. This is used to check the challenges faced by the GSCM system. It is implemented to review in the improving economy like India. This study used to find out the limitation of the GSCM system and measuring the strength of GSCM System (Kudroli, 2014). In this research, generic integrate approach was developed for implementing the green supply chain practice which generated the important insight. For the effectiveness of the implementation of the GSCM, a framework was developed. The key themes of the GSCM are material management and greening the product design, reverse logistics, distribution, marketing, manufacturing process, material management. This research synthesizes the current and past research in order to develop the viable green supply chain strategy. It determines the overall increase in the environmental issues. For this, it is essential to understand the green supply chain implementation which helps in improving the emerging economy in terms of organizational performance. This research mainly focuses on the implementation of the green supply chain practices with Indian economy in terms of going green.

GSCM is founded as the best system for management as the requirement of the environment. Many other methods that compared with a GSCM system and factor affecting the GSCM system are also evaluated. GSCM is better than another chain supply system. Rapid worldwide industrialization led to the deterioration of the environment by damaging and polluting the environment which leads to the depletion of the ozone layer. In this research, various issues related to the GSCM were described (Luthra et al., 2010). This research also presented the functional model of an organizational supply chain with the environmental influence, the concept of the GSCM, models for implementation of the GSCM, and the difference between conventional GSCM and SCM. It also presented the implementation of the green supply chain, various methods of GSCM and the factors which affect the GSCM. The trend of making the environment-friendly products is increasing with the change in the manufacturing process. Social and the environmental issues are essential for managing any of the business.

GSCM is known as the improving performance approach of the process and the products according to the requirements of the environmental regulations. GSCM includes green packing, green manufacturing, green purchasing, and green marketing and distribution. GSCM also focuses on the ecological and economic causes. On the other hand, SCM focuses on a single economic objective. This research provides the knowledge of many green supply chain management issues and implementation of the various models of GSCM. It also described the various approaches the GSCM and implementation of the green supply chain and those factors which were responsible for affecting the GSCM. Today, for achieving challenges, organizations tried to green their supply chains such as pollution abatement and energy conservation. Going green is the priority of organization to achieve profits. GSCM showed the direct cost and efficiency benefits in the Automobile industry that still incorporated the idea of GSCM in their manufacturing, designs, marketing, etc. In this modern era, the Automobile industries trying to cope up with the demand from the ever-rising population.

The term SCM was first coined in the early 1980s by British logistician and consultant, Keith Oliver. A supply chain consisted of all stages involved directly or indirectly in fulfilling a customer request. SCM is a network of an organization that involved through upstream and downstream linkages in different activities that generated product services and values. Supply chain management has the significant role in the firm performance. This research reveals the considerable spurt in research theory and practices of the SCM. It is also informing and combining the features of the distribution management and supply management. The result of the integration indicated the concept of supply chain and extended enterprise as the collaborative supply chain across the intercompany borders in order to increase the value across the entire supply chain (Jain et al., 2010). This research reviewed the Supply Chain Management. Total 588 articles from the 15 referred academic journals were classified into the five methodologies articles. These five methodologies are hypothesis testing, literature review, methodology, normative and exploratory. This article is further categorized into the 15 categories which were on the basis of the content analysis. SCM is continuously redefining itself. The objective of this report is to provide an extensive review and up-to-date SCM literature which concentrated on the concept of the SCM. It uses the various gaps which were identified to generate the empirical and conceptual work in the SCM which was more influenced by the analysis of the supply chain on a chain wide or network basis. This research categorized the SCM into SCM Frameworks, SCM strategy, relationships trends and challenges. These are the principal areas of SCM domain. The result indicated that the exploratory reviews used most as compared to methodologies. It was followed by the normative study, methodological reviews, Literature review and Hypothesis testing.

Industrialization now contributes to the growth and economic development of the country. Due to the industries, many of the employment opportunities are available, but industries are responsible for the environmental deterioration. With the increase in the growth of the small-scale industries, there is a lack of the pollution control policies, improper waste disposal techniques, use of the obstacle technologies. It results in the weakening of the natural resources, air, oil, noise pollution, global warming, dangerous diseases, and generation of the hazardous wastes. Green supply chain management helps in reducing the pollution and waste management (Vishal and Avinash, 2016). This research described the implementation of the GSCM technique, methods which are used for the protection of the natural environment. And also explained the role of the suppliers, customers, a lean and green manufacturer in implementing the GSCM with its barriers and advantages. It described tools and practices for GSCM adoption (green Purchasing, green manufacturing, green Marketing, etc.). However, in industries, the implementation of GSCM is an important task, but practicing is not a simple task as it is costly and complex. It relies upon the top management, and several barriers are seen at different levels. Therefore, the top management and government take the initiative to successfully apply the GSCM in the industries to save the environment.

The efficient SCM helps organizations in securing position and improving their performance. This research presented the list of the barriers which were identified. The effective supply chain management helps the organization in order to secure its position in the competitive environment. It also helps in improving the performance of the organizations. The key to any manufacturing organization set up the company's efficiency is to satisfy customer's demand at the right time. To achieve this goal, it is mandatory to recognize SCM barriers and analyses it. In this research, the 23 barriers hindered the SCM performance that needs to concentrate during implementation in any organizations.

Green manufacturing processes help in improving the environmental performance. Also, measuring the green index of the manufacturing processes helps in tracking the level of the greenness in order to promote the improvement of the processes. The framework of the green technology also helps the various organization to take the decision related to adopting the green technologies. The greenness of the logistics is an important area of the research (Kumar et al., 2015). In this research, the relation between the lean tools like 5S and KAIZEN and the green objectives was presented. The structure of the operation into the degree of control OEMs (original equipment manufacturer) helps in selecting and improving the alternate technologies for improving the green performance. This research also focused on the packaging practices of the organization, motivating the industries to adopt the green packaging and alternatives of the green packaging technology. For improving the market perception of the manufacturing products, it is essential to address the nature of apprehension and to rectify them. It is required to investigate the benefits of the remanufacturing on the basis of the quality and cost. It results in accelerating the adoption of the re-manufacturing by OEMs.

The success of any of the business depends on the human resources of the organization because employees are the primary source of the strength of the organization. The top management of the organization sets the goals and provide the essential support like allocating the resources. In this research, the behavioural factors affect the willingness and effectiveness of the human resources. Green supply chain management (GSCM) integrates all the ecological concepts related to the supply chain management to reduce the energy and the material usage. It results in decreasing the impacts of the supply chain activities on the environment. In the mining industries, GSCM implementations depend on the various factors which influenced the behaviour of the human being. Basically, the behaviour of the human is dynamic in nature, and the relation which exists between them changes continuously. So, the behavioural factors are essential for identifying and ranking the effects of the implementation of GSCM. It can be taken as the reference while making the decision on the hierarchy of the actions which are essential for the implementation of the green practices in the mining supply chain. This research explores the many behavioural factors that affect the GSCM practices and their interactions. It helps in achieving the green-enabled needs. Interpretive structural modelling (ISM) helps in extracting the inter-relationships between the identified behavioural factors (Muduli et al., 2013).

In this research, 12 behavioural factors were identified. Such a large number of the interrelated elements makes the structure of the system complicated and unclear. ISM tool is used for this type of situation because it was capable of the providing the well-defined and visible structure for such problem. The proposed ISM model is a supportive tool which is used in such type of situation where the management wants to visualize the problem and identify the reason for the problem. In this research, ISM based hierarchical model was used to assist the decision model in order to understand the behavioural factors and for the diagnosis of the crucial behavioural factors for the effectiveness of the implementation of the GSCM system. The initiative of the top management results in the success of the SCM and improvement in the working environment which was related to the educational and training programmes. The result indicated that the improved work culture would help in building and strengthen the employer-employee relationship, motivate the employees to work in the teams initiate the mutual trust and respect among the employees in order to meet the organizational goals. The result also concluded that the effectiveness of GSCM could be improved by the employee teamwork, dedication, and motivation.

The government, stakeholder and the non-government agencies forces on the factor of implementing the GSCM. Implementation of the GSCM is important because of the increase in the economic-environmental performances and to ensure the sustainability of the business. There are many factors presented which were associated with the incorporation of the green initiatives in the supply chain management (Gandhi et al., 2015). For increasing the economic-environmental performance, it is essential for the industries to know the factors. Sixteen factors are essential in implementation and initiation of the successful GSCM which were further evaluated with the help of DEMATEL. This research presented the real-life applicability of the proposed model which helps in determining the interdependence between the factors and divide these factors into effect and cause group. The prime objective of this research is to determine the important factors which were associated with the successful implementation of the GSCM. Decision-making trials and the evaluation laboratory (DEMATEL) are proposed for the development of the structural model for determining the influential factors among the recognized factors.

The proposed method helps in understanding the interrelationship between the evaluated factors using a causal diagram. An empirical case study was conducted in this research of an Indian manufacturing company in order to show the real-life applicability of the DEMATEL. The result indicated that Financial Factors, Human Technical Expertise, and Top Management Commitment has the greatest influential power in the successful adoption of GSCM. Due to the different activities of the supply chain, many of the social and environmental related problems were increasing. This pushes the industries to move towards the green supply chain management (GSCM) practices. To overcome this problem, an attempt has been in order to analyse, identify and model the critical success factors. This helps in the implementation of the GSCM towards the sustainability in the industries in Indian perception. In this research, 26 critical success factors are used for the implement of the GSCM towards the sustainability (Luthra et al., 2015).

In this research, interpretive structural modelling technique was used to propose the structural model. This model helps in understanding the contextual relationship among the critical success factor and their interdependence in order to implement the GSCM towards the sustainability. The importance of the critical success factors (CFCs) can be determined with the help of the analysis which was based on the dependence and driving power. The most important critical success factor which was identified in the research is a scarcity of the natural resources which help in the implementation of GSCM practices. It also ensures the sustainability of the business. In this research, an example of Indian mining industry was presented to show the real-world applicability of the proposed model which helps in regulators, academicians, and practitioners to focus their efforts on the implementation of the sustainable GSCM on various levels of the business. This research recognizes the major critical success factors in facilitating the successful implementation of the GSCM practices in the industry for the sustainable development in India. Consumption and production in the industrial systems initiate with the mining, extractive, industries which started in the emerging economies like Ghana. Supply chain activities have many social and environmental problems in the mining operations which has the serious economic consequences. Greening the supply chain of the mining operations are the essential avenue which provides the beneficial consequences. The important practice of the GSCM is evaluating, developing, selecting and assessing which helps in the successful implementation of the GSCM. These types of the practices have the complex and interrelated relationships. For successful achieving the goals of the implementation of the GSCM in the mining industry, it is essential to properly understand them (Kusi-sarpong et al., 2016).

This research proposed the integrative and comprehensive GSCM practices and the sub practices which helps in determining the relation, relationship and influences within the framework of GSCM. It helps in identifying the perceived impact of the GSCM framework on the sustainable performance of the organization which pertinent to the mining industry. The integrated methodology described in the research limited and determined the interdependencies within the GSCM factors. For the evaluation, Analytical network process (ANP) was used, and fuzzy-DEMATEL was used for the methodology. For determining the applicability of the proposed methodology, multiple field studies are used within Ghana mining industry. The result of the research provides the essential clues and the guidelines needed for making the decision and performing the analysis inside and outside the mining industry. It helps in improving the consumption and corporate sustainable production and making the sustainability decisions like SCM implementation decisions. The application of lean and green thinking in the supply change management. According to the study proposed by Li, the concept of green supply has come up with two major advantages of addressing most important issues in the organization's framework using it which is prevalent (Li et al., 2016).

Those origin of green supply chain management (GSCM), conceptually taken its bases throughout the mechanical upset. Nonetheless morals recently it went of the bleeding edge with expanded sensitivities of the countries and culture towards relief of the mechanical alternately different waste's malefic impacts once surroundings. As the idea of supply chain management (SCM) picked up consideration making manufacturing organizations incorporated with suppliers and clients through Different supply and conveyance logistics networks in place on ship items will clients with aggressive advantage, those natural worries headed the organizations to fuse components with regards to disposal, recovery, reusing and reuse about material/energy waste created inside the ambit about supply chain foundation. Significant manufacturing commercial enterprises over India need aid centring for decreasing energy consumption, water consumption, perilous Substances and waste emanation.

The green scheme research proposed the three main concepts related to the green scheme which is PSS (product services system), lean supply chain management which focused on removal of non-value adding activities associated with the supply chain management across the supply chain process. The third main inclusion is GSCM which is the green supply chain management process the chief component of organizations going green. It focuses on the product lifecycle between the manufacturer to the customer and recycling of the product. The study uses the combination of lean and green supply chain management and the lean supply chain management model with the PSS. The whole paper suggested by Li gives the entire idea of the thing that how can PSS be modified and used for better working with the green scheme. The research tends to follow the next step of a case study of the product-oriented PSS in the organizations using the green supply chain management methodologies. As the meta-analysis is never used much in the study of relationships like the GSCM and the performance of the firm it provides a window to the maturing of the green supply chain management scheme in the industry and the growth of the performance of the firms which are using the GSCM scheme in their practices. A conceptual framework was designed using the meta-analysis of the 130 effects from a large database of 25,680 effects sizes. The study suggested that the use of the green scheme in the manufacturing process helps the company in four major aspects which are economic performance, environmentally friendly approach, better operational performance and better social performance across the market and the customers.

The study also suggested that the firm type, the size of the organization, its ISO registration and the export process orientation. Also, affects the green supply chain management relationships with the performance of the manufacturing unit of the company and consequently affecting all the further processes associated with the organization practices. The study will now be more focused on the performance evaluation of the firms by understanding the relationship between the use of GSCM and production process of the firms (Geng et al., 2017). The green product types related to the development-intensive product or marginal-cost intensive product manufacturing, and the categories of competition related to the price competition and greenness competition. With a game-theoretic method, the research model starts with a humble supply chain with one producer and one vendor. Further, this model is prolonged to take in a straight retailer competition situation and six cases of contending supply chains.

Use of internet GIS as a decision support arrangement in examining and analyzing Geospatial information for wood leftover collection and conveyance in the furniture industry. The study depicted an application which is intended at inspiring the execution of green supply chain management (GSCM) technique in the furniture manufacturing through the creation of the procedure of accumulating and carrying the wood waste for recycling course easier. The proposed study has used SDLC (Software Development Lifecycle) method as an implement for designing the projected application of using internet GIS. There are also many Small and Medium Enterprises (SMEs) in the furniture business and accumulation of wood left-over in Surakarta and Jepara district involved in the proposed request as an introductory of the object for the application. The study gives rise to it, as a decision support system, the application of internet GIS by the Small and Medium Enterprises in the furniture trade and collector of wood waste permitting them to pronounce the geographical position of each party and founded on the convinced criteria. The arrangement will rank the suggested SMEs as the manufacturer of wood waste created at the smallest cost of gathering and transferring the wood waste from each and every one of SMEs

In order to reduce both greenhouse gas (GHG) and expected logistics cost emission in the context of the business environment uncertainty of the Supply chain network (Ameknassi et al., 2016). The result which is a set of the optimal non-dominant green supply chain configuration provided the decision makers with the optimal levels of the logistics outsourcing integration within the decarbonized supply chain. The effective integration helps in the determination of the optimum level of the logistics outsourcing decision which provided the high performances. Uygun and Dede proposed for estimating GSCM model performance of firms in relations of green designing, green purchasing of products, green transformation of the material, green logistics and transport delivery services and reverse transport or logistics. The interrelationship between the cause and effect amongst GSCM scopes is worked out by means of fuzzy DEMATEL technique. After that, based on that cause-and-effect interrelationship, the fuzzy ANP technique is executed for scheming the weightiness of the associated standards. At last, the fuzzy TOPSIS technique is applied by means of the result weights attained from the fuzzy ANP system, for assessing and positioning the GSCM performance of alternate companies. The study comes out with effective results in the study of the relationship between the cause and effect using the GSCM in the firms. In future, it can be the base of effective implementation of GSCM strategies and motivating other companies for adopting the GSCM technique in the production process.

Geng et al. proposed a study to recognize the connection between green supply chain management (GSCM) techniques and a firm presence in the industrial sector in Asian emerging economies which are called AEE. Govindan et al. (2014) evaluated the barriers analysis for the green supply chain management which is implemented in Indian industries with the help of the analytical hierarchy process. Many of the manufacturing industries started to be adopting the green concept in the supply chain management in order to focus the environmental issues. But still, there are many of the industries which struggling in identifying the barriers hindering in the implementation of the green supply chain management. Dube and Gawande discussed the key drivers for the green initiatives for improving the customer and public relations and government compliance. Green supply chain management is the process of using the environmentally friendly inputs and transforming these inputs into the outputs which can be reused at the end of their lifecycle in order to create the sustainable supply chain. The major activities of this research are waste management, reverse logistics, green manufacturing, green design and green operations. GSCM helps in minimizing the ecological impact of the industrial activities without affecting the energy utilization efficiency, performance, cost, reliability, and quality. The key themes related to the GSCM are green manufacturing, waste management, reverse logistics, green operations, green operations, and green design. This result concluded that GSCM helped in minimizing the ecological impacts of the industrial activity.

Puviyarasu reviewed the GSCM and also determined the environmental concern of GSCM. This research mainly presented the development of GSCM which focused on the environmental and the social sustainability towards the operational management and the supply chain management. The important keys of this research are reverse logistics, green management material, green design, and green marketing and distribution. This research presented argues in order to minimize the ecological impacts of the industrial activities. It also presented the diverse methods of the different authors towards the green supply chain management. The result indicated that the implementation of the green supply chain management is necessary for every industry.

Srinivasan and Shrehari reviewed the green supply chain management (GSCM) and evaluated the direct area of the emerging field. This research focused on the development of the green supply chain management in the developing and developed countries which was relevant to the social and environmental sustainability towards the supply chain and operational management. This research also presented the lack of the researchers in order to examine the implementation and adoption of the green supply chain management in the developing countries such as India. It also demonstrated the environmental problems which caused by the business operation for the organizational awareness level.

GSCM helps in minimizing the ecological impacts of the industrial activity without affecting the energy utilization, performance, reliability, cost, quality. It also involves the paradigm shift which was going from the end of the pipe control in order to meet the environmental regulations. It results in reducing the ecological damage and provide the economic profit. The primary areas which emphasize the green supply chain management are product and process technologies, supply-chain management, operations strategy and the quality which helps in the contribution to the more systematic knowledge base. This research involves the state-of-the-art review of GSCM. Also, remanufacturing disassembly has been presented in this. In this research, the green supply chain management was classified on the basis of the problem in the supply chain influential area, methodology, and the adopted approach with the help of the various techniques and mathematical tools. This research also presented the interpretation, findings, issues and the opportunities of GSCM.

The taxonomic approach helps in exploring the GSCM and developed the taxonomic framework which used for formulating the appropriate strategies for green supply chain management on the characteristic dimensions. In this research, the taxonomic framework was developed by three ways. The first method is the development of a taxonomic scheme for selecting or developing the green strategies. The second method is the identification of the key dimensions which influenced the green supply chain management. The last method is the analysis of the green supply chain activities which was found in the existing empirical work. This research yielded the three characteristics dimensions which influence the strategic green chain supply management. The result indicated the development of the specific performance management to the taxonomy of the development of the green strategies. The whole chain from producing a raw material to selling the product to a firm such as a Retail merchant is described as a supply chain. Several companies take part in an organization for creating a product and transmitting it to the end user.

Green supply chain management has become the driver of sustainable strategy. This topic has been gaining increasing attention within both academia and industry for making the industry competitive. With the ever-increasing demand for reducing carbon footprints and greenhouse gas emission, there is a need to study the various parameters and drivers of sustainable development, especially in supply chain management. The need for developing the sustainable model including the drivers of sustainability needs to be designed. The paper aims to discuss these issues. After providing a background discussion on GSCM, the authors categorize and review recent GSCM literature under three broad categories, with a special emphasis on investigation of adoption, diffusion, and outcomes of GSCM practices. Within this review framework, the authors also identified GSCM research questions that are worthy of investigation. The study suggests that the main drivers of GSCM include the environmental policy and the green human resource management by providing them training for adopting sustainability practices. Besides this, another key driver is the sustainability criteria in supplier selection which was found to be enhancing the outcomes of sustainability.

The need for developing the sustainable model including the drivers of sustainability needs to be designed. After providing a background discussion on GSCM, the authors categorize and review recent GSCM literature under three broad categories, with a special emphasis on investigation of adoption, diffusion, and outcomes of GSCM practices. Within this review framework, the authors also identified GSCM research questions that are worthy of investigation. The study suggests that the main drivers of GSCM include the environmental policy and the green human resource management by providing them training for adopting sustainability practices. Besides this, another key driver is the sustainability criteria in supplier selection which was found to be enhancing the outcomes of sustainability. The Global outsourcing shifts manufacturing jobs to emerging countries, which provides new opportunities for improving their economic development. The authors develop and test a theoretical model to predict first, how sustainable supply chain initiatives might influence reverse logistics outcomes and second, the impact of eco-reputation and eco-innovation orientation strategies on the deployment of sustainable supply chain initiatives. The results show that firms that implement sustainable supply chain initiatives can realize positive reverse logistics outcomes; the study also provides new insights into eco-innovation and eco-reputation strategic orientations as theoretically important antecedents of sustainable supply chain initiatives.

The development of supply chain management (SCM) introduction in the construction industry, investigating the risk factors affecting the implementation of SCM principles. There are various perspectives and practices regarding risks, benefits and challenges in global IT outsourcing. They delve into some important issues IT outsourcing, particularly the challenges along with benefits. Finally, we present case studies of two Global 200 organizations and validate some of the claims made by previous researchers on it outsourcing. This study will help the management to identify the risk factors and take the necessary remedial steps. Risk factors are weighed to reflect financial implications as well. Other than effective project management, and participative association of vendors in formulating design specifications, it is very important to have planned and periodic reviews to improve the communication with the team members. The elements affecting supply chain are classified into drivers, facilitators and inhibitors. Sixteen elements are identified and presented in a framework along with their proposed constituents. The elements capture structures and management principles of supply chains that are important for social responsibility.

Moreover, monitoring itself is not sufficient to improve performance; firms need to adopt collaborative practices with their suppliers. Results show that whereas collaboration has a direct effect on performance, monitoring has only an indirect relationship through collaboration. This study analyses the implications in terms of drivers and performance for each GSCM approach (monitoring and collaboration), using a quantitative approach. The standard constructs can represent pillars of SCM excellence. However, frameworks on SCM excellence unlike its contemporary fields are very few. Thus the purpose of this paper is to develop a path analysis for proposed framework of SCM excellence in Indian manufacturing industry proposed by Soni and Kodali using interpretive structural modelling (ISM) and structural equation modelling (SEM). The major findings revealed that ISM based on focal company having highest SCEI, is statistically fit for SCM excellence framework, and finally the structural models of the constructs for each pillar of SCM excellence are also formed by using path analysis.

Strategies that balance economic and environmental performance are increasingly sought after as enterprises that increasingly focus on the sustainability of their operations. GSCM in particular enables the integration of environmentally friendly suppliers into the supply chain to be systematized to fit with specific environmental regulations and policies. More persuasively, GSCM allows enterprises to improve profits whilst lowering impacts on the global environment. Senior managers were found to rank traditional criteria more highly than environmental alternatives – the implication being that for the company, concerned, it may take some time before environmental awareness is fully assimilated into GSCM practice. The more a factor contributes to trust positively (such as participation and communication) or negatively (such as opportunistic behaviour), the more the factor contributes to knowledge sharing correspondingly. The factors with no significant influence on trust (such as shared values and learning capacity) have no or less influence on knowledge sharing. The new research model developed allows the relationships between trust and other influencing factors on interorganizational knowledge sharing to be explored. The model reflects the coexistence of the cooperation and competition relationships between supply chain members, which is not dealt with in previous studies.

Corporate entrepreneurship, social capital and resources contribute to the implementation of supply chain management (SCM) practices in Association for Southeast Asian Nations (ASEAN) automotive industry. The analysis of survey data suggests that corporate entrepreneurship theory and social capital theory play a key role in motivating and preceding SCM practices. However, traditional resource-based explanations of SCM decisions by western manufacturing firms do not always apply to ASEAN automotive suppliers. The moderation effect of environment uncertainties (supply, competition and demand) in the relationship between a firm's drivers (internal and external) and practices (purchasing, design and manufacturing, logistics and internal management) when going green. The result indicates that both the internal and external drivers have significant influence on the adoption of green-related practices when firms go green. It is further confirmed that the practice of green purchasing is significantly influenced by the moderator of environmental uncertainty. Moreover, supply uncertainty has the most significant influence on numerous green practices, such as green purchasing, internal management and green logistics.

Supply chain operations reference (SCOR) model as an enabler for process-oriented supply chain business intelligence. In order to achieve the full benefits from the SCOR model, effective business process management and the SCOR key performance indicators (KPIs) must be implemented and used. Unless data collection to support KPI construction is automated, it is difficult to institutionalize the SCOR model as a measurement and benchmarking framework. We have demonstrated that automated support for KPIs is feasible and achievable.

A comparative analysis shows that large Japanese manufacturers implement one key GSCM practice, internal environmental management, much more actively and effectively than Chinese manufacturers. The sample of Japanese manufacturers implement four other GSCM practices green purchasing, customer cooperation with environmental considerations, eco-design and investment recovery; at similar levels when compared to Chinese manufacturers.

The term GSCM mainly refers to those concepts which integrate the sustainable environmental processes into the outmoded supply chain. This process can include product design, manufacturing, production, material sourcing, and end of life management.

Those examining and managing modern contamination have been discriminating issues for society since the early days of the mechanical upset. Associations have been paying close attention to ecological protection since the negative effects from claiming industrialization were settled on government funded eventually by reports and books for example, such that "Silent Spring" by Rachel Carson in 1962, republished by Mark Lytle in 2007. Government funded and governmental response on this book incorporated propel from claiming extra regulations and formation of the US Environmental Protection Agency.

That history about natural administration in Canada need generally reflected that of the US. Similarly, the inception of the mainstream just-in-time (JIT) intuition manufacturing and supply chain management (SCM) – formed and popularized by Japanese producers in the 1980s – could be followed again on Henry Ford's deliberations on vertically incorporate those automotive supply chain practices, and the standards about JIT were main actualized for manufacturing effectiveness furthermore to decrease waste. However, waste decrease in the early days of JIT might not have been for ecological security, however, for asset-sparing high profit.

Stakeholder consideration and the risk of negative networking consideration rouse organizations with furnish majority of the data around their polishes. Hence, sustainable supply chain administration (SSCM), otherwise called green supply chain management (GSCM) hones have been progressively received likewise associations battle until make green. Looking at those operational techniques and screening supplier exercises need get vital errands to managers, and a number of organizations may be attempting with suppliers to decrease unnecessary bundling and conceivably. Perilous materials and additionally with move forward their ecological profile, expansion benefit margins, and see all the supplier's suppliers on assess and diminishing natural expenses.

Reaction to ecological issues need continuously been a no-win proposition for managers; thus, managers bring translated ecological issues as absurd logic and bring underestimated their company's abilities to turned green. As stated by late thinking, turning green implies that both those benefits of the business and nature's domain could incidentally prove to be a win, and setting off green may be no more an expenses risk on organizations it may be a facilitator for innovation, new business opportunity, and riches production. Nonetheless, some associations even now think that setting off for green practices might wind up for secondary costs which could forestall their results alternately benefits starting with getting focused preference again those rivals.

Business deeds can position a momentous danger to the environment in relationships of emissions of carbon monoxide, packaging materials waste, toxic resources, traffic jamming and other practices causing industrialized pollution. GSCM is deliberated as an ecological revolution. The conception of GSCM is to incorporate environmental philosophy in the methods of supply chain management (SCM). GSCM targets to decrease or eradicate wastages which include lethal chemical, emissions, solid waste and energy alongside supply chain like designing of the product, resourcing and selection of materials, the process of manufacturing, distribution of final product and its end-of-life management.

GSCM theatres a dynamic role in persuading the total environment effect of any industry involved in supply chain actions and backing to sustainable performance development. GSCM is evolved from SCM. In the 1990s, as competition build up, the enhanced cognizance of green practices has caused firms to act in a morally and generally accountable method in the supply chains. In 1995, GSCM fascinated significant academic interest. In 2010, GSCM received uppermost attention. With GSCM practices in concentration, firms advance in environmental managing policies in reaction to the alterations of ecological necessities and their influences on supply chain processes.

According to this definition, green supply chain management refers to a wide range of products from product design by recycling or destroy. In this process, the products are passed through a lifecycle. For example, much like human beings, they also pass through the cycle of life including such events as birth, maturity and death. The product lifecycle involves a degree of structure to the life of products which provide the directions for the functional efforts to produce and deliver the product.

It is generally used to describe a supply chain for improved performance in the measurability, sustainability, and cost reduction through the measurement of other metrics. The supply chain management helps to tells us that how the environmentally-friendly practices help to create value adding facilities for the company. Firstly, the material is extracted for design and production, after that it is ready for consumption and use. In the last stage end of life, management is enabled for recycling and recovery for further processing. It could also be helpful to reduce the waste from the environment.

2.7.1 SCM TO GSCM

The developing issues in the worldwide market for green concerns and the shortage of natural resources have constrained officials to observe supply chain systems from an environmental point of view. Industries with high environmental risks, including automotive, chemical, plastic, and heavy manufacturing, have continuously considered advancements in environmental performance by way of one of the essential competitive needs, adjoining lower costs, lead time, and quality. Green supply chain management (GSCM) is a developing field inspired by the requirement for environmental awareness.

GSCM is one of the best systems for satisfying the challenge to lessen carbon emission and improve sustainability due to its capability to enhance the environmental performance of any business. Organizations could adopt the suitable eco-friendly methods and can make standard to follow for other non-green organizations. Although sustainable supply chain purposes are becoming more crucial, the emphasis value for money, risk, bottom line, delivery times and adaptability are not decreasing. In reality, environmental duty has progressed from a trend to a business importance because it supports the organization to accomplish their business objectives.

GSCM and traditional SCM techniques are highly different at various levels of working from manufacturing to reverse logistics. Traditional SCM is commonly driven by the lone agenda of the economy as its critical objective while GSCM takes into consideration both the environmental as well as economic intentions. SCM out rightly discards eco-friendly techniques whereas GSCM stresses green, combined and environmentally improved practices. Customary SCM is extra dedicated on controlling the final manufactured goods, with no concern for the resultant harmful properties on the atmosphere during distribution and manufacturing.

Increasing energy costs: Increasing power and fuel costs with the cost of related raw materials necessary for operating have carried into focus the need for a more cost-effective green alternative. Low-power IT solutions, energy source substitutes and re-utilizing can have an optimistic impact on increasing the end line in profitable business.

Global panic over carbon dioxide emission: Business policies are focused more on recognizing and depressing the carbon footsteps initiated by their IT gear, setup, and the general public.

Temperature Change: Global warming is affecting the climate, ice caps, and glaciers equally the southern hemisphere and northern hemisphere in an undesirable way. The increase in the sea level due to the decline in the ice caps and glaciers is turning out to be a chief cause of worry for the ecologists all across the globe.

Management and Ecological Protection Agency guidelines: A business organization needs to track certain provisions to attain Energy Star Rating and other eco-friendly certifications. Discipline by regulating agencies to implement carbon recognition obedience is an additional inspirational factor for Green IT enterprises.

Improved environmental awareness among the community: Vendor selection based on green IT practices, sharing of best practices in companies across the supply chain, an end-to-end obedience besides the supply chain are the contributory factors in areas of a fruitful and prosperous green IT policy.

2.7.2   Advantages and Limitations of GSCM

2.7.2.1   Advantages of GSCM

The most fundamental benefits of green supply chain management are a positive long-term benefits and help to improve the financial performance of the organization. The following are some benefits of GSCM.

1. **Sustainability of resources**

   Green supply chain sponsors the operative utilization of all the available resources of the company. By inducing the green supply chain management in entire business making processes help to purchase the green input resources that will support to flow environmentally friendly manufacturing process to the recommended green outputs. It makes the effective use of available resources which are present in the organization and helps to reduce the waste.

2. **Lowered costs/Increased efficiency**

   As it is discussed above, green supply chain management is the principle of reducing the waste by making the effective use of available resources. Within the operative management of resources and suppliers, it can help to decrease the cost of production, promote the recycling and reuse the raw materials which are also helpful to reduce the waste from the environment. It also helps to reduce the production of chemical substances materials for a better resulting of environmental protocols. With the help of these consequences, we can lower the overall costs of the material by increasing the efficiency of products.

3. **Product differentiation and competitive advantage**

   Green supply chain management helps to position the friendly products in the environment according to the perceptual view of customers. It helps to create the assorted products in the market so that it is not similar to anyone else. With the help of this, we can attract new profitable customers for our organization. It will give the competitive edge to the several types of competitors in the market. Besides all these things it also fortifies the brand image and reputation in the marketplace.

4. **Adapting to regulation and reducing risk**

   The organizations which adopt the green supply chain management in their business practices can reduce the risk of manufacturing of that product which is not environmentally friendly. It strengthens the ethical practices in the business process. Green supply chain management makes efforts to create the sustained dedication of possessions, actions and management protocols so that the organization or business can earn more profits.

5. **Improved quality and products**

   It helps to improve the quality of products by enabling the new advanced techniques because some organizations manufacture products which are technologically advanced and environmentally friendly. If these types of products have been manufactured by the company, then it will automatically enhance the brand image and reputation in the minds of customers. So, the green supply chain management helps to improve the superiority because the customers basically get attracted to the products by their quality and affordable prices.

Besides the above five benefits of green supply chain management, there are some additional advantages also generated such as:

- Effective managements of traders and sellers.
- Creating the transparency in the supply chain of products.
- Better control on product safety and quality.
- Helpful to increase the sales and revenues in the organization.
- Reduces the waste and makes effective use of it by recycling and reuse.
- Distribution of technology, capital, and knowledge among the chain partners.

2.7.2.2 Limitations of GSCM

With many advancements in green supply chain management, there are some limitations also arising because the company and organizations must have to spend a lot of money for implementing Research and Development programmes:

- Sometimes the customers may not believe in the effectiveness of firm's green strategies. So, that they should convince the customers sometimes about their green initiatives. On the other hand, it can be done by implementing the eco-label schemes. These schemes offer its approval to "environmentally less harmless" products in the organization which has been famous in Japan and Europe.
- Profits will be incurred by very low and renewable and recyclable products, and green technologies are expensive. The companies and organizations should implement a large amount of cost, and these systems will be applicable only in long run businesses.
- Sometimes the customers cannot pay the required amount of price for the green products which may, directly and indirectly, affect the profitability of the company.
- The companies sometimes feel that it is hard to convince the shareholders to invest in their products because many of them may not believe in these products and cannot co-operate properly.

2.7.3 Environmental and Economic Benefits of GSCM

Over the years, GSCM has pulled in consideration of practitioners and scholastics, concentrating on decreasing waste and maintaining the quality of natural resources and product-life. Eco-proficiency that tries to limit environmental harm whereas increasing production effectiveness, and remanufacturing, have converted to be key advantages for accomplishing best practices. Consumer demands and governmental laws keep on pushing organizations to be increasingly sustainable. Therefore, governmental enactments and public mandates for environmental responsibility have raised these issues during the planning phase of numerous vital organizers, bringing a few green ideas into place.

Concerning the above matters, it can be understood that GSCM is motivated by the increased environmental damage, for example, exhaustion of raw materials, flooding waste landfills, and contamination on the whole. Along these lines, GSCM basically looks to limit the wastes inside the industrial framework, to prevent the scattering of destructive things into the environment, and to preserve natural resources. The goal, nonetheless, is about environmental consideration, as well as the best sense of business and increased benefits.

Organizations have understood the need to redesign their supply chain management from an absolutely functional part to a strategically part to follow current environmental enactments and keep up a persisting competitive advantage by industrial innovation and enhanced eco-efficiency.

Recompenses of going green nowadays include ecological concerns malformed from a corporate mantra to a commercial imperative. Primary adopters of GSCM initiatives and eco-friendly strategies reveal in the following benefits:

1. GSCM policies can help in mitigating business risks and speed up the innovations.
2. GSCM policies and reforms will help in decreasing functioning expenses.
3. GSCM norms will bring growth in adaptability.
4. Promote configuration with the merchants and regulars thus becoming favoured seller in green supply chain.
5. Increase employee satisfaction and attract the attention of top applicants thereby keeping the commercial continuity unharmed.
6. Differentiating themselves from competitors by creating brand distinction and recognition.
7. Green IT solutions can help industries and people to go green.

Green IT resolutions play a critical role in inspection for possible gaps and satisfying them to guarantee the victory of green supply chain initiatives implemented by organizations. Employing green IT solutions in a supply chain enable:

Transportation route optimization which makes sure energy effectual and rate effective way of carriage of goods. Mechanization of transport development process which organizes in advance for unexpected events in the supply chain.

Active usage of collective planning and predicting which in-turn decreases the overall energy necessities of industries. Going green will offer the largest optimistic impact on the return on investment of commerce. Logistics service suppliers are acting on it now to safeguard long term lucrative growth.

GSCM policies help in a decrease of adverse impacts on the ecologies and in improving the situation of the surroundings. Today's socio-economic aspects and supervisory services are convincing corporations to be green and lean in their merchandise sourcing, functioning activities, delivery, and logistics. It is becoming progressively essential for companies to go for GSCM in order to persist sustainably. Also, it is found that by switching to GSCM practices, corporations can decrease budgets by up to 20%. By presenting new technologies companies can help decrease costs much more significantly, the costs of research and development is usually very high and may not provide adequate returns on investment (ROI). Whereas, in the case of GSCM the results are much extra dependable. In addition to all this, by raising their green credentials among staffs, government experts, customers and other shareholders, firms can project an affirmative brand character by safeguarding itself as an institute which defends the environment and ensures maintainable forthcoming for the entire world.

McDonald's, the world's biggest chain of hamburger fast food restaurants is considered to be one of the forerunners in implementing green practices. It assisted its potato provider in Austria to set up a biogas plant to develop all of their dense and liquid wastes accumulated from potato production. The gas formed by the plant is used to generate warmth which in turn is used to heat up the dryer for the french fries production process. Also, the gas formed is converted into electrical energy to supply to the community grid.

The remainder of the adaptation practice is provided to potato growers for spending it as a fertilizer. Through heat retrieval processes, which is serving the dryer, electrical energy of 4.2 gigawatt-hours a year is created. In total, 40% of the facility's energy supplies are provided by this method. Also, re-utilizing of the frying oil which is left out at the end of frying process for producing biofuel so as to power its logistical processes and serving of salads on boards as a substitute for using plastic bowls, are some of the positive green creativities from the company.

Working green also supports companies to come up with gainful initiatives that can be used to provide to the requirements of the Bottom of the Pyramid (BOP). In India, where at minimum 30% of the people have negligible access to electricity, Coca – Cola came up with solar-energy vending machinery which assisted it to reach out to more than 80,000 untouched villages. These mechanisms use padding materials which help them to run deprived of power for up to 16 hours per day and need power supply only for the period of nights when it is mostly available.

2.7.4 GSCM Throughout Product Life Cycle

Detailed GSCM design network, at the diverse product lifecycle phases, is upgraded by simultaneously considering environmental and economic perspectives. This empowers the choice of various substances; specifically: suppliers, production offices, and distribution centres, and also the planning that distinguish the ideal routing of material between the actors (Figure 2.1).

GSCM has developed in a recent couple of years and includes all stages of product lifecycle starting from the production of raw material by design, production, and distribution stages to utilization of products by the consumers and its transfer or disposal towards the completion of product's lifecycle (Figure 2.2).

Under the GSCM reforms and policies, the industries and corporations are told to maintain a relationship between the raw material and manufacturing of the product. The GSCM follows the strategies under which the five steps of product marketing which are raw material, manufacturing, whole selling, retailing and customers service must work in the form of cycle which ensure the idea of green products. The recyclable products which can again help in the production of raw material and maintain that cycle are the main motive of GSCM.

Now we shall discuss the complete product lifecycle of the GSCM strategies.

1. Design means the designing of the suitable raw material for manufacturing which is completely eco-friendly and can give the maximum suitability to the

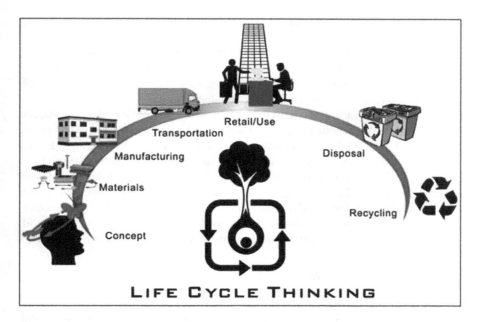

FIGURE 2.1   GSM Lifecycle processes (Raman, 2014).

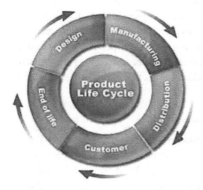

FIGURE 2.2   Product lifecycle.

product manufacturing process to the lower cost and lesser use of energy consumption.

2. Manufacturing part of the product lifecycle involves the use of low or sustainable energy techniques for production. The energy used can be eco-friendly

and the product manufactured must also be completely ecological for its use and disposal in the future.

3. Distribution means the use of conventional resources for the purpose of distributing and selling the products. It mainly includes the idea of ecological transportation with minimum harm to the environment and the minimum cost of operation related to product delivery and distribution.

4. The customer is also considered to be an important part of GSCM as the product is made for the customer with the idea of giving organic and eco-friendly products and in return, it is expected that the customer will help in ensuring safe and eco-friendly use of the product and proper disposal after the use of the product.

5. End of life involves the most important and significant part of the GSCM policy; it involves the recycling of the product for its healthier disposal or the extraction of product which can be reused by the organization. The basic motive is to ensure the use of disposed of material for helping in reducing the overall cost of the complete cycle and the less costly manufacturing of the product.

2.7.5 ACTIVITIES IN GSCM

2.7.5.1 Green Design of Product and Process

Green design includes the designing of products to have a diminished environmental effect for the duration of its life. By a green design of product and process or eco-design, an organization can focus on taking care of ecological issues before they begin. In the green design process, designers may see at the source, composition, and harmfulness of raw materials; the resources and energy required to produce the product; and how the product could be recycled or reused towards the finish of its life.

Adjusted with other product observations, for example, quality, value, producibility, and usefulness, green designed products are economically and environmentally reasonable choices to conventional products. The adequate green design makes products that utilize less energy and resources; products which can be recycled effectively or reused; and products which advance energy and materials effectiveness in customers' lives.

2.7.5.2 Lifecycle Assessment

Lifecycle assessment or analysis (LCA) is a process of evaluating and assessing the environmental, resource, and occupational health related consequences of a product all through the phases of its life. LCA model highlights the immediate linkage between lifecycle examination and GSCM strategies. The focus part of this analysis is an assessment matrix which marks different emission stressors and information certainty values for six steps inside an organization's specific supply chain comprising, material acquisition, production, pre-production, utilization, distribution, and disposal. The instrument can assess different products for analysis.

2.7.5.3 Green Design Methods and Tools

Since different variables must be considered in the development of green design, tools and methods have been created which are expected to encourage the designers and makers throughout the design process. The uniqueness of the Lifecycle Cost management tool lies in the way that it empowers organizations to speak with customers on the lifecycle expenses of various measures. Purchasers regularly concentrate on the price tag alone, which much of the time speaks to just a small amount of a product's lifecycle costs. This tool offers lifecycle costs in a particular and straightforward way.

2.7.5.4   Green Procurement of Product and Process

Green procurement can help company affect its supply chain by asking the trader to follow certain environmental criteria before purchasing, or a contract is signed. Therefore, it promotes closer working relations between trader and customer. Both partners benefit as environmental impact is taken into consideration, mitigating risk and leading to improved green credentials for both parties. For example, green packaging. If the product packaging can be reshaped, this may save the producer money through reduced material use and will reduce the consumption of natural resources. Product's end-users can also save money and achieve environmental aids through reduced volumes of packaging waste. Green procurement can be defined as a combination of supply chain influence tool, a process integral to sustainable development and environmental provenance.

Green manufacturing can be defined as decreasing the environmental pressure by using correct techniques and materials. This is the main concern of manufacturing industries, which included:

- Green energy: includes production and use of clean energy, which is used in deploying renewable source of energy like wind energy, solar energy, CNG, and biomass. These all energy sources achieve higher energy efficiency in operations.
- Green products: the second area for developing green products.
- Green processes: used in business operations, which usually involves reducing waste generation through lean operations.

The key objective of green manufacturing is to reduce the use of the virgin material as it indirectly reduces the amount of waste at the manufacturing stage. Another significant aspect of green manufacturing is 'Emission reduction'.

2.7.6   GREEN OPERATIONS OF PRODUCT AND PROCESSES

Green operations is associated with the factors of SCM operations, that help in reducing the non-ecological raw materials or data, which in turn help in preserving the ecosystem. The following methods can be implemented in the manufacturing industry:

- Green distribution of product and process
- Green packaging
- Green logistics
- Reverse logistics

2.7.6.1 Logistics

As indicated by Prof Bernard La Londe of Ohio State University (1998), co-ordinations are not a centred useful movement but rather one that empowers the integration of exercises crosswise over capacities. A powerful approach to advance this extended part for coordination is to position coordination as a procedure, not as a movement or capacity. These are three important sub-forms as part of the strategic procedure. They are:

- Integrated Production and appropriation methodology improvement
- The renewal procedure
- The order management procedure

An all-round composed gauging framework can contribute essentially to strategic execution. Numerous purchaser items organizations are attempting to work with a 25 to 60 for each penny gauge mistake (on the stockkeeping unit level) in their one month- out estimates. This error range wreaks ruin with stock levels and client benefit execution. "Best Practice" organizations, then again, consistently are ready to accomplish 15 to 20% conjecture error rates. Organizations that perform inadequately in their estimating regularly submit at least two of the "Six of forecasting" given underneath:

- Letting accounts drive estimates
- Having no conjecture "proprietor"
- Having insufficient investigative support
- Using a single gauging approach for everything
- Having no deals and operations planning meeting
- Failing to track gauge mistake

Many organizations are finding that dispersion asset arranging (DRP) frameworks can diminish costs, enhance client administration, and better their stock administration. DRP frameworks give a full view into the distribution centre arrange by first analyzing request towards the finish of the channel and gathering prerequisites back through the distribution centre system. This approach allows for full perceivability of necessities and better administration of inventories. DRP includes both stock administration and dissemination arranging. A module of dissemination prerequisite arranging (DRP) develops the ideas of materials necessities arranging into a multi-echelon-distribution centre stock condition. The outcomes are time-staged renewal plans for moving inventories over the warehousing system. DRP offers a precise re-enactment of conveyance operations with expanded arranging perceivability, permitting coordination's divisions to deal with all resources better.

On the off chance that an organization hopes to accomplish profits by their production network administration handle, they will require some level of interest in innovation. The spine for some huge organizations has been the endlessly costly Enterprise Resource Planning (ERP) suites; for example, SAP and Oracle. These will incorporate an organization's whole store network, from buying of crude materials to guarantee administration of things sold. The many-sided quality of these applications requires a critical cost, a financial cost, as well as the time and assets required to effectively actualize a venture wide arrangement. Purchase in by senior administration and sufficient preparing of staff is vital to the achievement of the usage. There are presently numerous ERP answers for browse and it is vital to choose one which fits the general needs of an organization's inventory network. Since the wide reception of Internet advancements, all organizations can exploit Web-based programming and Internet correspondences. Moment correspondence amongst sellers and clients takes into consideration opportune updates of data, which is enter in administration of the inventory network.

Expanding on globalization and specialization, the expression "SCM" has been authored to portray both changes inside supply chains themselves and in addition the advancement of procedures, strategies, and devices to oversee them in this new "time". The developing ubiquity of community-oriented stages is highlighted by the ascent of a trade card's store network cooperation stage, which associates various purchasers and providers with money related organizations, empowering them to lead mechanized production network fund transactions. Web is a pattern in the utilization of the World Wide Web that is intended to build inventiveness, data sharing, and coordinated effort among clients. At its centre, the basic trait of Web is to help explore the endless data accessible on the Web keeping in mind the end goal to discover what is being purchased. It is the idea of a usable pathway. SCM repeats this idea in inventory network operations. It is the pathway to SCM comes about, a blend of procedures, systems, instruments, and conveyance choices to guide organizations to their outcomes rapidly as the multifaceted nature and speed of the inventory network increment because of worldwide rivalry; quick value variances; changing oil costs; short item lifecycles; extended specialization; close, far-, and off-shoring; and ability shortage.

SCM use arrangements intended to quickly convey comes about with the nimbleness to rapidly oversee future change for nonstop adaptability, esteem, and achievement. This is conveyed through competency systems made out of best-of-breed inventory network mastery to comprehend which components, both operationally and authoritatively, convey comes about, and in addition through personal comprehension of how to deal with these components to accomplish the coveted outcomes. The arrangements are conveyed in an assortment of alternatives, for example, no-touch through business prepare outsourcing, mid-touch by means of oversaw administrations and programming as an administration, or high-touch in the customary programming sending model (Figure 2.3).

A simple supply chain is made up of several elements that are linked by the movement of products along it.

FIGURE 2.3   Structure of SCM.

The supply chain starts and ends with the customer.

- **Customer**: The client begins the chain of occasions when they choose to buy an item that has been offered available to be purchased by an organization. The client contacts the business division of the organization, which enters the business arrange for a particular amount to be conveyed on a particular date. In the event that the item must be fabricated, the business request will incorporate a necessity that should be satisfied by the creation office
- **Planning**: The prerequisite activated by the client's business request will be consolidated with different requests. The arranging division will make a creation plan to deliver the items to satisfy the client's requests. To fabricate the items the organization will then need to buy the crude materials required.
- **Purchasing**: The acquiring office gets a rundown of crude materials and administrations required by the creation division to finish the client's requests. The acquiring office sends buy requests to choose providers to convey the important crude materials to the assembling site on the required date.
- **Inventory**: The crude materials are gotten from the providers, checked for quality and exactness and moved into the stockroom. The provider will then send a receipt to the organization for the things they conveyed. The crude materials are put away until they are required by the creation division.
- **Production**: In view of a creation plan, the crude materials are moved stock to the generation territory. The completed items requested by the client are produced utilizing the crude materials obtained from providers. After the things

have been finished and tried, they are put away back in the stockroom preceding conveyance to the client.

- **Transportation**: At the point when the completed item touches base in the distribution centre, the delivery division decides the most effective technique to send the items with the goal that they are conveyed at the very latest the date indicated by the client. At the point when the merchandise is received by the client, the organization will send a receipt for the conveyed items.

Levels of Supply Chain Management:

- **Strategic**: At this level, organization administration will look to abnormal state key choices concerning the entire association, for example, the size and area of assembling destinations, organizations with providers, items to be made and deals markets.
- **Tactical**: Vital decisions focus on grasping measures that will convey cash sparing preferences, for instance, using industry best chips away at, working up a securing system with favoured suppliers, working with collaborations associations to make cost affect transportation and making circulation focus approaches to reduce the cost of securing stock.
- **Operational**: Choices at this level are made every day in organizations that influence how the items move along the inventory network. Operational choices include rolling out timetable improvements to generation, acquiring concurrences with providers, taking requests from clients and moving items in the stockroom.

Activities of SCM:

SCM (Supply Chain Management) incorporate points from the diverse procedures and assembling operations, buying, transportation, physical appropriation into a solitary programme. After this SCM co-ordinates and incorporates every one of these exercises into a solitary procedure. It connects every one of the accomplices in the chain. Inside any association or industry store network alludes to an extensive variety of practical territories. In this inbound and outbound transportation, warehousing and stock control. Essentially expressed, the store network includes those exercises related with moving merchandise from the crude materials arrange all the way to the finish client. The vital part of the inventory network administration for providing products to their individual spots where they are required. Following activities involved as part of company supply chain management:

1. Inventory management
2. Transportation service procurement
3. Material handling
4. Inbound transportation
5. Warehouse management

There will be a splendid future for the store network administration. Taking after two noteworthy patterns are profiting inventory network administration operations.

1. Customer service focus.
2. Information technology.

Anderson consulted eight principles:

1. Information technology.
2. Segment client in light of administration needs.
3. Customize as indicated by the assets the inventory network administration arrangement.
4. Listen to signs of market requests and plans.
5. Differentiate items nearer to the client.
6. Outsource strategically.
7. Develop a standard network-wide innovation system.
8. Adopt channel-spreading over execution measures.

Implementation procedure:

1. Designing: A first designing the long-term technique structure.
2. Re-engineering: supply chain processes to streamline products, information and the funds flow externally and internally.

Flexible approach. In this approach there are three steps:

1. Strategic analysis
2. Specification
3. Implementation

Strategic analysis: In this, the investigation of present and future needs of business and advancement of those answers for meet these necessities. This procedure includes the models made by total to get the full comprehension of the principal issues and to analyse the viable options.

This approach gives:

1. Confidence in the recommended solution.
2. Identifies a clear way forward.

Specification: This progression gives right intelligent accentuation on every part of the arrangement. It gives details of recommendations limiting the danger of unanticipated cost.

Implementation: This is the last stride. In this progression all exercises and pre-results are actualized to get positive outcome. To achieve superior performance, there are five key dimensions of supply chain management.

Strategy: The alignment of supply chain strategies with the overall business dimensions. Key decision points for managers include:

a. What is needed to align the supply chain with the business strategy.
b. Which type of channels of distribution best meet our goals and needs of the customer.

Infrastructure: infrastructure effects cost service performance of firm or organization and established the boundaries of operation of supply chain for good performance.

Process: the desire to achieve functional excellence and integration across all main processes. Managers must ask themselves the following:

- Which all the main supply chain processes driving the business.
- How can we build linkage with our suppliers and customers?

Organization: giving the counterfeit achievement variables of union, amicability and joining crosswise over association elements. Inquiries to consider incorporates:

a. To oversee COH forms adequately. It chooses what level of cross-utilitarian reconciliation is required to get great outcomes.
b. What execution estimation and detailing structure can help us accomplish our targets.

Technology: technology gives the power to the supply chain to operate on new level of performance and is making new ideas for those companies able to harness it. Companies should address the following important points.

- What data is required to manage the main business processes?
- How can we capitalize on advanced communications of supply chain management?
- How can we leverage enhanced visibility of customer demand and other key operating parameters?

In business, Supply Chain Management (SCM), the administration of the stream of merchandise and enterprises, includes the development and capacity of crude materials, of work-in-process stock, and of completed merchandise from purpose of cause to purpose of utilization. Interconnected or interlinked systems, channels and hub organizations join in the arrangement of items and administrations required by end clients in an inventory network. Store network administration has been characterized as the outline, arranging, execution, control, and observing of production network exercises with the goal of making net esteem, fabricating an aggressive framework, utilizing overall coordination's, synchronizing supply with request and measuring execution all around.

SCM rehearse draws intensely from the territories of mechanical building, frameworks designing, operations administration, coordination's, obtainment, data innovation, and showcasing and makes progress towards an incorporated approach. Showcasing channels assume an imperative part in store network administration if your organization makes an item from parts bought from providers, and those items are sold to clients, then you have an inventory network. Some supply chains are straightforward, while others are fairly confused. The multifaceted nature of the store network will change with the extent of the business and the unpredictability and quantities of things that are produced.

2.7.6.2 Green Distribution of Product and Process

Green Distribution is defined as any mean of transportation between buyer and dealer with lowest possible effect on the ecological and social environment. It includes the entire distribution process from packaging, storage, order processing and picking that improved vehicle loadings, distribution to the purchaser and taking back packaging.

2.7.6.3 Green Packaging

Green packaging refers to any change made by a service provider or product manufacturer to lessen the environment effect of the materials that involved in packaging the product and services while their deployment to the end-user. The material used for packaging is made from plastic and which do not break down easily or disposed of can have a huge effect on the environment. For green packaging, the implementation methods included the use of biodegradable or recycled material, decreasing the amount of material used for packaging a product or reusable packaging containers. Companies must use the environmentally safe product components and finished goods. Usage of biodegradable material for packing can minimize the harmful effect on the environment.

Green purchasing involves the assessing of environmental performance with the help of suppliers that ensure the quality in their operational processing systems. On the other hand, green purchasing involves the environmental plans for firm's long-term material which automatically improves the product quality in the organization. It also helps to evaluate the amount of waste from the processing flow.

2.7.6.4 Green Logistics

The trend of making product environment-friendly in increasing. Due to changing the requirements in the environment affecting manufacturing operations and enhancing the attention to developing a strategy of Environmental Management (EM) for the supply chain. The green logistics are three main approaches:

  a. The top-down approach, where greenness is forced on the logistic industry by government policies through regulations.
  b. The bottom-up approach, where environmental improvement is coming from the industry itself by the best practices adoption.
  c. A compromise between the organizations and government are notable through certification schemes.

2.7.6.5 Reverse Logistics

Several laws and regulation had designed to prevent the companies from disposing of waste arbitrarily, which generally concerned only about the product quality but does not show the similar interest in yoking the product life. Hence, the reverse logistics take it to shape. The company's supply chain start accepting and accommodating the product being returned for recycling and disposal. Thus, there will be closed loop of the supply chain starting from sourcing, making, manufacturing and recycling / disposing of the product.

Reverse logistics (RL) is known as the process of planning, controlling and implementing the cost-effective procedure of finished goods and services, unprocessed material, latest inventory and related information from the point of origin to the consumption point to recapture its value. The product has to be improved followed by segregating. Therefore, for reducing the cost operation, the appropriate network design with redesigning and reuse must be implemented in as many processes as possible.

2.7.7   OPERATIONS OF GSCM

2.7.7.1   Collaboration with Customers

The green supply chain management helps to collaborate with customers to set and achieve the environmental goals. It basically results in the reduction of waste from the environment. On the other hand, in addition to compliance with the customers, they may have to be elaborate their quality of the product which cannot provide the harm to customers and environment. So, If the company or organization should be implemented these things in their business process then it definitely helps to increase the costs and revenues by producing sustainable products with the green packaging.

2.7.7.2   Eco-design and Packaging

Eco-designs basically requires the design products that help to minimize the consumption of materials. It mainly helps to facilitate that material which will be reused or recycle again for further business processes, and it avoids the use of hazardous products in the manufacturing processes of the company.

2.7.7.3   Warehousing and Green Building

The other significant role which the green supply chain management basically involves in their business is that the warehousing and buildings should have safety for storing the products and transportation. The warehousing of products should be done in this way that the manufacturing products cannot get harmful with the other environmental conditions. The investment on warehousing should be made in an elaborative way that the products are getting safe from weather conditions.

2.7.8   NEED OF TOP MANAGEMENT IN GSCM

The efficient management system is the necessity of GSCM system for its effective implementation in the various fields to ensure the sustainable development across the globe which is completely eco-friendly and is also beneficial from the economic point of view. The GSCM is beneficial for all the people who are related to the product usage and manufacturing. The efficient management system ensures the promotion of communication and knowledge sharing between the designer supplier contractor and clients. There is a need for effective understanding between the stake holders to understand the implementation process and benefits of the GSCM.

The positive relationship between the corporations and the GSCM authorities ensure the success rate of GSCM programme implementation. The studies have concluded that without an effective management system it is very difficult for a firm to set up a GSCM model in its whole process of production and distribution. An advanced information and technology system is necessary for the effective working of GSCM model in a company during the various stages of the product lifecycle. It can be very effective and useful in the product development programmes comprising of the programmes of design enhancement related to the environment, the product recovery and the product reuse. Efficient management and information system will help with tracking and trace the product sales and return of products with the previous sales.

The adoption of sustainable culture within an organization helps in the growth of organization with the adoption of GSCM policies. Long term sustainability and vision for future growth and profits with environmentally friendly policies can motivate companies to adopt the green policies in their present agendas. The GSCM adoption involves the implementation and introduction of new technologies. The lack of government support can also be the reason for the unsustainable growth of the industries. There is an urgent need for proper knowledge and information about the effectiveness of the GSCM programmes. There is a need of top-level commitment related to the management of the GSCM projects in the companies. There must be a proper design of the infrastructure and IT management in the process of the GSCM implementation in the organizations.

The GSCM process requires properly skilled workers across the planning and till to the supply chain of the organization for the ecological working of the programme. The skilled professional associated with the programmes can easily adapt to all the changes made in the process related to manufacturing, delivering and reusing the products. The proper management system related to GSCM will help the reduction of the prices which is the major demand of the customers associated with the organization or any kind of particular product.

There must not be any fear related to the initial investment of the plan and the GSCM related authorities can make the organizations informed and understood the future long term benefits of the implementing of the system because the GSCM technology helps in reducing the overall cost of product by minimizing the prices of raw material production, by reducing the energy demand for the manufacturing of the products and the product delivery and transportation charges are also reduced by using GSCM.

The recycling and reusing of the end of the product can also help in creating the raw material at a cheaper cost than the present cost of it. But for that, there is strict need of trust on the suppliers which can only be achieved by effective management system which can ensure and guarantee the effective and workable GSCM plan in a firm or organization or any other industry.

2.7.9 ROLE OF GSCM IN IMPROVING PRODUCTION AND COST

The green supply chain management plays a significant role in increasing the cost and production in the company. It is commonly used for many varieties which are basically performed by the organization to decrease the harmful effects on the natural environment. The green supply chain management helps to increase the efficiency of products by using the waste materials. It generally creates the balance between the economic, environmental and financial resources (Figure 2.4).

Figure 2.4 represents the processing flow of input and output in the green supply chain management which also promotes the environmental behaviour with the help of supplier's management. The mechanism physical and local facilities are coming up within the output by using the waste materials in the manufacturing process.

Mainly the process of green supply chain management is happening between the components of the supply chain which includes the inputs, physical items or services that are necessary to start a business process. It also required the outputs that result from processing an input and bound the green logistics in the manufacturing process of the company. The flow of process basically transforms the input into the output through internal environmental operations. In this process environment basically related to resources such as physical and human which influence the green house practices within the structural and external environment.

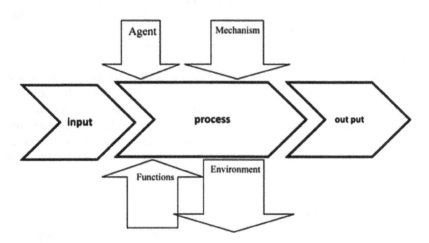

FIGURE 2.4 Components of GSCM process.

2.7.10   ROLE OF EMPLOYEES IN PROMOTING GSCM

The employees also play a significant role in the implementation of green supply chain management in their manufacturing and production process of products. It is the potential concept which helps to formulate the work of entire chain supply according to the environmental priorities. But it is only possible if the employees of the company and customers would endorse the effective implementation of GSCM policies and practices in their production process.

Now, GSCM has become more important to the automobile industries because generally, these industries manufacture those products which create the most pollution in the environment. So, they must be owing those products which are environmentally friendly, cost effective and competitive in the market. But it is only possible with the effective implementation of GSCM in the products by the employees of company and organization.

Employees are basically the main part of the company because they are the ones who implement the new techniques and methods in the manufacturing or production scale of products. It is only possible with the help of employee's engagement with the environment attitude.

2.8   MAINTENANCE REPAIR AND OPERATIONS (MRO)

Maintenance, repair, and operations (MRO) involves fixing any sort of mechanical, plumbing, or electrical device should it become out of order or broken (known as repair, unscheduled, or casualty maintenance). It also includes performing routine actions which keep the device in working order (known as scheduled maintenance) or prevent trouble from arising (preventive maintenance).

MRO can be categorized by whether the product remains the property of the customer (such as when a service is being offered), or whether the product is bought by the reprocessing organization and sold to any customer wishing to make the purchase. In the former case it may be a back shop operation within a larger organization or smaller operation.

The former of these represents a closed loop supply chain and usually has the scope of maintenance, repair, or overhaul of the product. The latter of the categorizations is an open loop supply chain and is typified by refurbishment and remanufacture. The main characteristic of the closed loop system is that the demand for a product is matched with the supply of a used product. Neglecting asset write-offs and exceptional activities the total population of the product between the customer and the service provider remains constant.

2.9   WASTE MANAGEMENT

Waste management (or waste disposal) include the activities and actions required to manage waste from its inception to its final disposal. This includes the collection, transport, treatment and disposal of waste, together with monitoring and regulation of the waste management process. Waste can be solid, liquid, or gas, and each type has different methods of disposal and management. Waste management deals with all types of waste, including industrial, biological and household. In some cases, waste can pose a threat to human health. Waste is produced by human activity, for example, the extraction and processing of raw materials. Waste management is intended to reduce adverse effects of waste on human health, the environment or aesthetics.

Recycling is a resource recovery practice that refers to the collection and reuse of waste materials such as empty beverage containers. The materials from which the items are made can be reprocessed into new products. Material for recycling may be collected separately from general waste using dedicated bins and collection vehicles, a procedure called kerbside collection. In some communities, the owner of the waste is required to separate the materials into different bins (e.g., for paper, plastics, metals) prior to collection. In other communities, all recyclable materials are placed in a single bin for collection, and the sorting is handled later at a central facility. The latter method is known as "single-stream recycling". The most common consumer products recycled include aluminium such as beverage cans, copper such as wire, steel from food and aerosol cans, old steel furnishings or equipment, rubber tyres, polyethylene and PET bottles, glass bottles and jars, paperboard cartons, newspapers, magazines and light paper, and corrugated fibreboard boxes.

PVC, LDPE, PP, and PS (see resin identification code) are also recyclable. These items are usually composed of a single type of material, making them relatively easy to recycle into new products. The recycling of complex products (such as computers and electronic equipment) is more difficult, due to the additional dismantling and separation required.

3 Modern Production Techniques

3.1 ADVANCED MANUFACTURING TECHNIQUES

Advanced Manufacturing Technology (AMT) are resources that can competitively aid modern industry in this volatile and complex environment. Advanced manufacturing uses emerging technologies to critically enhance not only the economic competitiveness of individual manufacturers but also the sustainability of the whole industrial sector. Investment evaluation methods play an important role in today's competitive manufacturing environment. Manufacturing firms have been investing in AMT viz group technology, computer-integrated manufacturing systems, flexible manufacturing systems, etc. to enhance manufacturing firm performance in terms of cost, productivity, flexibility and quality, in order to compete with other industrialized firms.

AMT represents a wide variety of modern technologies devoted to improving the competitiveness of manufacturing firms including design and engineering technologies, fabricating/machining and assembly technologies, automated material handling technologies, automated inspection and testing equipment and information technologies (Small and Chen, 1997). While taking capital investment decisions for enhancing the performance of manufacturing firm, selection of appropriate AMTs should be a vital factor under consideration. Manufacturing companies adopted AMTs over the entire world from past 20 years. In spite of that, the research found that all AMTs did not achieve their performance satisfactorily. A few AMTs perform very poorly, and advances are totally unsuccessful. The performance of many AMTs is good but unable to deliver desired results (Hayes and Jaikumar, 1991; Bessant, 1993; Baldwin and Lin, 2002).

Technology advances more rapidly than people's behaviour. Any organization tries to make changes in the technology usually show up when maximum people of firm are prepared to accept the change. Although, at the same time when the technological change is moving on, a simultaneous practice of preparing people to adopt the change is required (Ghani et al., 2002). Development and advancement are intrinsic parts of technological domains of management. Industry is evolving changes enormously by the introduction of new technologies. Thus, the management accounting reporting systems has to change in order to be effective in meeting the changing needs of organizations, changes in the manufacturing cost structures and the information needs for decision making (Isa and Foong, 2005).

With technology changing at such a fast pace, there is a drastic need to bring changes in the management of the techniques used in the manufacturing process. The pace of development of the technology, bought, sold and traded is remarkable across the globe. The management of resources is essential and crucial for the development of country as well as for the enhancement of technology (Chen and Small, 1996).

DOI: 10.1201/9781003189510-3

"AMT" is a generic term, depicting an assembly of manufacturing technologies, which combines both extent and scale capabilities in a manufacturing environment. AMT is broadly defined by distinguished authors in their terminologies; Chen and Small say, it is

"An automated production system of people, equipment and utensils for the planning and control of the production process, including the procurement of materials, parts and constituents and the shipment and service of completed products".

In meticulous, AMT can be defined as any new manufacturing technique, which is likely to cause constructive changes in a firm's manufacturing practices, management systems and its approach for the designing and production of various engineering products.

In view of the emerging competitive scenario, it is envisioned that AMT would be needed for Indian industries to:

- Respond to business policy or corporate objectives.
- Correct present weaknesses or exploit strengths.
- Cope with the anticipated environmental changes.
- Achieve distinguishing capability which is currently not available.
- Make manufacturing function strong.
- Achieve performance objectives.

Earlier there was a lesser strategic emphasize on manufacturing overpowering focus on structural decisions, such as capacity planning, make v/s buy, and so on. The typical measures of performance were included such as: capacity, planning, utilization of men and machines, labour productivity and manufacturing cost, supply driven environment, manufacturing thrived without much regard to manufacturing excellence, building long term capabilities, benchmarking, global standards improvising on supplier's capabilities and installing quality assurance systems.

The definitions of AMT, which has been adopted by researchers, are often not uniform, and the presence of ambiguity of terms and notations often leads to an unnecessary and unintended controversy in research. Accordingly this section establishes the position and meaning of the fundamental terms as used in this thesis.

The following classifications have been reviewed and used as background for deriving the definition of AMT.

- As defined by Small and Yasin, AMT can be described as a group of computer-based technologies, including computer-aided Design (CAD), robotics, Flexible Manufacturing System (FMS), Automated Material Handling systems (AMHS), and Computer Numerically Control (CNC) or Automated techniques.
- As defined by Y. Park, AMT is "a comprehensive collection of technologies for enhancing the efficiency and flexibility of manufacturing systems".
- As defined by Seetharaman, AMT involves new manufacturing techniques and machines combined with information knowledge, microelectronics and innovative organizational practices in the manufacturing process.

- As defined by Honggeng Zhou, G. Keong Leong, AMTs provide a variety of operational benefits, which includes better coordination between different departments; greater control of the processes; reduced product design time; shorter lead time and stable, high-quality outputs.

The AMTs investigated in this study can be grouped into six domains based on the literature of AMT studies. The five domains are:

- Advanced design and engineering technologies: It concerned with design and engineering technologies such as CAD, CAM, CAE and GT.
- Advanced machining technologies: It concerned with computer numerical control machines (CNC), numerical control/direct numerical control machines (NC/DNC), flexible manufacturing system (FMS), and robotics.
- Advanced planning technologies: It concerned with logistic planning such as MRP, MRPII, ERP and ABC analysis.
- Advanced material handling technologies: It concerned with handling of materials such as AS/RS, AGV and AMHS.
- Advanced management systems: It concerned with production management tools such as TQM, BPR, SPC and JIT.

Advanced process improvement systems: It concerned with advanced process improvement technologies such as Benchmarking, Kaizen, Training and Recycling.

AMT are classified into two classes: hardware and software by Small and Yasin.

I Pure Technical tools (hardware)
II Management tools (manufacturing practice software)

Pure Technical tools or Advanced Technical tools (hardware) can be further classified into the following range of technologies.

A Computer aided design (CAD)
B Computer aided manufacturing (CAM)
C Computer numerical control machines (CNC)
D Direct numerical control machines (DNC)
E Robotics
F Computer aided engineering (CAE)
G Group technology (GT)
H Flexible manufacturing system (FMS)
I Automated material handling systems (AMHS)
J Automated guided vehicles (AGV)
K Bar coding (BC)
L Automated storage and retrieval system (AS/RS)
M Rapid prototyping (RP)

The Manufacturing Practice Software or Production Management tools are additionally classified into the following array of technologies:

A Material requirement planning (MRP)
B Manufacturing resource planning (MRP II)
C Enterprise resource planning (ERP)
D Activity based counting (ABC)
E Office automation (OA)
F Kaizen
G Total quality management (TQM)
H Recycling
I Business process re-engineering (BPR)
J Statistical process control (SPC)
K Just-in-time (JIT)
L Benchmarking (BM)
M Management training (MT)

A manufacturing industry can prefer to compete primarily in one of the two ways: either on cost leadership or on production differentiation, in order to produce similar products at a comparatively lower price; or producing a superior product that differs from its competitors. It is argued that by investing in AMTs, manufacturers would be able to enhance their competitiveness. In other words, AMTs can allow a growth in production of a wide range of varied products, while at the same time, can minimize the overall production cost.

Successful industries have recognized the fact that technology has become a vital competitive tool for success, and the industries are trying to leverage it for their competitive environment. It is a general agreement that the implementation of Advance Manufacturing Technology is a critical component for a firm's success. The most significant competitive weapon, however, does not comprise in the range of technologies, but their effective deployment, implementation and ultimately their management. Many organizational, management procedures and policies have been developed to decrease the overall uncertainty in the traditional manufacturing systems.

These constraints are reduced or have been possibly eradicated with the use of advanced technology. The usage of computer networks and automated machines provides an efficient information and feedback mechanism, not only for the manufacturing system, but also for the tedious and prolonged systems. "Automated processing times" are extremely reliable; the produced data reports from their machines are authentic, unbiased and in the nick of time, thus most of traditional manufacturing management systems, industrial engineering methodology and operational research techniques for increasing the efficiency and effectiveness of manufacturing systems are irrelevant in today's competitive scenario.

The implementation of AMT affects not only the manufacturing division of a plant, but also the Marketing, Person Resource, Research and Development and Engineering Design divisions. These technologies transform the design of a plant as well as the relationship between these various interconnected units. The relationship between the firm and its customers also changes; for example, firms can adjust to frequent changes with respect to the demand, more quickly and would be able to offer superior quality, lesser lead times and enhanced reliability. For organizations that have successfully implemented AMT, the benefits have been outstanding. The liberalization of the economy has opened new windows of opportunities for the manufacturing sector. Overall the growth of manufacturing industry is sustained on modernizations, investigate and expansion.

AMT are resources that can competitively aid modern industry in this volatile and complex environment. Advanced manufacturing uses emerging technologies to critically enhance not only the economic competitiveness of individual manufacturers but also the sustainability of the whole industrial sector. Investment evaluation methods play an important role in today's competitive manufacturing environment. Manufacturing firms have been investing in AMT viz group technology, computer-integrated manufacturing systems, flexible manufacturing systems, etc. to enhance manufacturing firm performance in terms of cost, productivity, flexibility and quality, in order to compete with other industrialized firms.

AMT represents a wide variety of modern technologies devoted to improving the competitiveness of manufacturing firms including design and engineering technologies, fabricating/machining and assembly technologies, automated material handling technologies, automated inspection and testing equipment and information technologies (Small and Chen, 1997).

While taking capital investment decisions for enhancing the performance of manufacturing firm, selection of appropriate AMTs should be a vital factor under consideration. Manufacturing companies adopted AMTs over the entire world from past 20 years. In spite of that, the research found that all AMTs did not achieve their performance satisfactorily. A few AMTs perform very poorly, and advances are unsuccessful. The performance of many AMTs is good but unable to deliver desired results get (Hayes and Jaikumar, 1991; Bessant, 1993; Baldwin and Lin, 2002).

Technology advances more rapidly than people's behaviour. Any organization that tries to make changes in the technology usually shows up when maximum people of the firm are prepared to accept the change. Although, at the same time when the technological change is moving on, a simultaneous practice of preparing people to adopt the change is required (Ghani et al., 2002).

Development and advancement are intrinsic parts of technological domains of management. Industry is evolving changes enormously by the introduction of new technologies. Thus, the management accounting reporting systems has to change in order to be effective in meeting the changing needs of organizations, changes in the manufacturing cost structures and the information needs for decision making (Isa and Foong, 2005).

With the changing technology at such a fast pace that there is a drastic need to bring changes in the management of the techniques used in the manufacturing process. The pace of development of the technology, bought, sold and traded is remarkable across the globe. The management of resources is essential and crucial for the development of country as well as for the enhancement of technology (Chen and Small, 1996).

In the past few years, AMT has attracted the attention of many researchers. This research field is broad. Ghani and Jayabalan (2000) conducted a study about AMT and how it improves the efficiency of performance of manufacturing undertakings in India. They explored the related issues that help to improve the productivity of manufacturing industries. They considered some of the important factors which influence the AMT implementation such as organizational structure, employee's psychology and environment. They found that the performance of AMT implementation depends on the positive feature of organizational structure, employee psychology and environment.

The transfer and implementation process of AMT, a case study of Cypriot manufacturing industry in developing countries. It has been found that management techniques adopted during the transfer of technology plays a vital role into the manufacturing domain (Efstathiades et al., 2000). A cross-sectional survey of 27 AMT firms and data collected from 927 employees revealed significant information to change existing organizational structure and make it appropriate with change in technology to achieve higher productivity (Ghani et al., 2002).

A survey data obtained from 149 companies in the Thai automotive industry identify five quality management practices: employee involvement, leadership, customer focus, continual improvement and vendor relationship. The results revealed that the leadership, employee involvement, and mutually beneficial system vendor relationship are three significant quality management practices while studying the relationship between AMT and performance (Laosirihongthong and Paul, 2004). AMT in manufacturing organizations performs a leading role for improving the quality and flexibility. There are three main AMT implementation steps (AIS) i.e., cost benefit analysis, technology assessment and development and implementation has attracted practitioner's attention, because appropriateness of AMT should be based on their ability to meet the manufacturing strategies and organizational objectives to improve technological competitiveness (Dangayach et al., 2006).

Zhang et al. (2006) extended the research on Flexible Manufacturing Competence (FMC) to its antecedent variables by investigating the impacts of AMT and operations improvement practices (OIP) on FMC. As per the survey from 273 manufacturing firms, there are three research variables which are related viz. additive, moderating and mediating models. The moderating model is best supported amongst the three alternative models. When OIP are effectively implemented, AMTs have stronger and positive impact on FMC.

An analysis was drawn out in the Egyptian industrial sector to examine the impact of organizational characteristics. A survey of 200 Egyptian companies was conducted out of which 61 relevant responses were received. The main area of analysis was on the adoption of AMT by the Egyptian manufacturing sector and the impact on firm size, type of production system, type of ownership and organizational design. The results concluded that larger companies tend to implement AMTs more vigorously and their marketing strategies involved combination of make to order and make to stock products (Salaheldin, 2007).

A survey of 303 companies investigated the manufacturing performance with automation and integration levels under environmental uncertainty of the industry. It has been found that the manufacturing system automation had positive impact on the manufacturing performance under the low uncertainty industrial environment, while the impact of manufacturing system integration is not significant. On the other hand, in the high uncertainty industrial environment, the impact of manufacturing system automation is not significant, but the integration had the positive impact on the manufacturing process (Liao and Tu, 2008).

A survey of 102 Indian small and medium enterprises (SMEs) used to find out the types of AMT adopt to improve the manufacturing parameters that have significant impact on firm performance. It was found that the local area network, CAD and computer-aided manufacturing technologies are the most commonly used and automated storage, whereas the robotics and wide area network technologies are the least commonly used AMT. The firm performance depends upon the manufacturing parameters. It has been observed that the capacity utilization and the finished product inventory has negative impact on the firm performance whereas, product design performance, fixture utilization, setup and production planning performance have positive impact (Koc and Bozdag, 2009).

Singh and Khamba (2009) understand and explicate the nature of interaction between AMTs utilization initiatives on different manufacturing performance parameters for achieving manufacturing success. Their research reported findings of an exploratory study administered in Northern Indian medium and large manufacturing organizations, who are utilizing the AMTs at all levels of manufacturing industry. The statistical results suggest that an organization should deploy multidimensional concept of AMTs utilization initiatives to enhance manufacturing performance parameters in pursuit of agility-based competitive advantages.

The organizational factors that influence the AMT implementation, considering a manufacturing strategy context and an analysis based on an organizational design framework. The research strategy is based on 'empirical iterations' using survey secondary data, experts' interviews information and multiple case studies. It has been showed that there is a set of recommendations, which strongly influence the AMT implementation for integrating these technologies to the organizational design which are framed by structural, process and contextual aspects (Cardoso et al., 2012).

AMTs investment patterns provide new evidence from the Turkish automotive industry and develops a taxonomy by exploring the relationships between AMT investment patterns, ownership structure, firm size and performance. It has been suggested that AMT investment patterns are not only significantly correlated with firm performance or ownership, but also reveals significant differences in manufacturing performance across investment patterns.

The manufacturing industry is the fifth largest employer in Massachusetts and benefits from the state's diversified economy, according to a recent Jobs for the Future (JFF) report. This paper describes an innovative approach that prepares college graduates to launch a second career in the growing advanced manufacturing sector while bringing together various stakeholders including higher education institutions, workforce investment boards and industry. The paper describes the range of services provided to students in the new manufacturing certificate programmes at a community college in Massachusetts and opportunities that exist for additional collaboration. AMT broadly used in automotive industry have limited application for typical UK aerospace manufacturing.

Also discussed in this paper is a framework of key technologies ranging from digital manufacturing concepts to flexible fixturing that enable re-configurability in aerospace manufacturing systems. The overall architecture of the framework is presented illustrating the key components such as a cloud-based data storage mechanism, an intelligent multi-product assembly station, kitting boxes embedded with sensors, a manufacturing network management portal and a decision support tool that combines data analytics and discrete event simulation. The main functionalities and technologies of the components are described and finally an industrial application scenario for the proposed framework is presented (Jackson et al., 2016).

Chen et al. (2017) identified 10 major technologies for a new manufacturing paradigm which can be characterized by two unique features: integrated manufacturing and intelligent manufacturing (I^2M). The author discussed the key technological enablers, such as the Internet of Things and Services (IoTS), cyber-physical systems (CPSs), and cloud computing with applications that are based on commercially available platforms such as General Electric (GE)'s Predix and PTC's ThingWorx.

Correlation analysis and structural equation modelling was used for identifying the influence of AMTs on the manufacturing competitiveness of Maquiladoras in Central America. The use of AMTs in their manufacturing operations can help to improve their performance and competitiveness. It has been found that this method in Maquiladoras in the apparel industry in Honduras shows a positive effect between AMTs use and manufacturing competitiveness, especially in the delivery time and environmental protection factors (Jared et al., 2017).

With the advent of the Fourth Industrial Revolution, the realization of smart manufacturing and Industry 4.0, rapid advancements in technologies will change manufacturing of goods and services. It has been reviewed and discussed that the methods and material technologies present now, along with challenges to overcome, which will be critical for enabling smart manufacturing in the form of the Internet of Things (IoT), cyber-physical systems (CPS), human-robot interaction, augmented and virtual realities.

3.1.1 IMPLEMENTATION OF AMTs

For analyzing the effective implementation process of AMT in organization, the socio-technical systems model is applied. Through technical and social analysis of AMT, it has been observed that the implementation of joint optimization is influenced by four factors in an organization: flexibility, concurrency, congruency and quality of work life (Zhao et al., 1992). AMTs investments in such as flexible manufacturing systems (FMS), computer aided design (CAD), computer aided manufacturing (CAM) and robotics, are more likely lead to improved performance. For this purpose data is collected from 202 manufacturing plants. The investments in the AMTs and the infrastructure are directly related to the performance of the firms. It has been observed that the companies which invested in one of the either, AMT or the infrastructure tends to perform relatively poor than those who invested in both (Boyer et al., 1997).

The introduction of AMT investigates effectiveness by evaluating its impact on SMEs in the key areas of product/market characteristics, competitive priorities and manufacturing parameters in the Cyprus manufacturing industry. There has been an increase in the competitive analysis of the Cypriot manufacturing industry with the introduction of AMT in the industry. Major improvements are seen as improved product market characteristics, improved plant utilization and flexibility and increased local market share (Efstathiades et al., 1999).

The advanced manufacturing strategies based on organizational size have the significant impact. The results indicated that smaller firms get better performance from technology implementation and the size of the firm does interact favourably with the AMT strategy (Gupta and Whitehouse, 2001). A survey of 122 companies on Indian SMEs to analyse how AMTs related to Indian SMEs, AMT implementation criteria, evaluate the degree of investment, competitive priorities in AMTs. It has been found that the preference given to quality is more as compared to preference given to flexibility in Indian SMEs. The steps for implementing AMTs show minimum attention for post implementation evaluation and requirement analysis in Indian SMEs (Dangayach and Deshmukh, 2005).

In organizations for introduction of Advanced manufacturing technologies AMTs some important factors such as efforts for personnel training to employees in companies are gaining importance for technological modernization. A survey of 90 firms on advanced manufacturing technologies in the manufacturing sector found that existence of specific training budget, implementation of AMTs does not appear to determine a company's decision to allocate specific budget items to personnel training programmes. It has been observed that the factors outside the inner context strongly influenced the training policies. AMT investment opportunities evaluation is a complex process for decision making utilized by the organization. A survey on German manufacturers investing in technology provides considerable operational and competitive benefits to the organizations. It has been determined that middle management is more concerned about computer hardware or software AMT investments and necessary technical training provided to employees during the investment is considered (Hofmann and Orr, 2005).

A survey within international project European Manufacturing Survey (EMS) of Slovenian manufacturing companies with the concept of technical innovation they use and to what extent they use them. The descriptive statistics results showed that the trends in using selected technologies in Slovenian manufacturing companies is positive, although the use of specific advanced technologies is slightly missed (Palcic et al., 2015). The up-to-date literature identified outstanding research issues, future trends and directions in advanced manufacturing systems (AMSs) which were extensively reviewed. It has been analyzed that the complex network provides an alternative approach to describe and solve the complicated manufacturing problems in AMSs. Three critical issues are summarized after this investigation: (a) the focused areas of AMSs that have deployed the theory of complex networks; (b) the addressed issues and the corresponding approaches; and (c) the limitations and directions of the existing works (Yongfeng et al., 2016).

Nath et al. solved the problem for selecting the best AMT by fuzzy TOPSIS method. According to this method of TOPSIS, a closeness co-efficient was determined by calculating the distances to both the fuzzy positive ideal solution (FPIS) and Fuzzy negative ideal solution (FNIS). Then, a suitability Index (SI) was calculated by taking into account the Objective Factor Measurement (OFM) to rank the alternatives. Finally, a numerical example using triangular fuzzy numbers has been shown to highlight the proposed method.

A survey of semi-structured interviews in 58 different companies to implement and combine different management approaches, such as "green" and "lean", to meet the needs of the ever-changing market demand. The findings and recommendations of this study can be used to fully utilize the potential of environmental practices to simultaneously improve manufacturing productivity and environmental performance and to identify trends in organizational development.

3.1.2 AMTs and Strategic Success

A comprehensive, firm-level survey of technology adoption and human resource management strategies. It is observed that the firms have downsized with the adoption of AMT. Also the demand for the labour with higher skills has raised. The workforce has to improve their skills with the implementation of the new technologies. In the overall, employee empowerment emphasis is laid down with the adoption of AMTs and the labour demands varied with the category of the technologies implemented (Siegel et al., 1997).

The competition is becoming more knowledge-based and now the competition amongst the firms has shifted from the physical assets to organizational capabilities. In a manufacturing organization, strategic management is a remedial tool for understanding the role of AMTs and to provide practitioners with the understanding necessary for performing this strategic task (Pandza et al., 2005).

Singh et al. (2007) aims to identify and develop the structural relationship among different factors for successful implementation of AMTs. A questionnaire-based survey and interpretive structural modelling (ISM) approach has been applied and 14 factors have been identified, such as top management commitment, organization culture, sound financial condition, training and integration of departments. It has been found that the top management commitment and sound financial condition are the major drivers for implementing AMTs. Effective implementation of AMTs will improve organization performance in terms of lead time, product cost, fast delivery and product quality. For effective implementation of AMTs, management should not ignore managerial aspects such as organization culture, employee training, integration of departments, vendor development, strategy development and customer involvement.

A case study from a semiconductor company located in Taiwan used an analytic hierarchy prediction model based on the consistent fuzzy preference relations to help the organizations become aware of the essential factors affecting the success of Knowledge Management (KM) implementation, forecasting the possibility of successful KM project, as well as identifying the actions necessary before initiating KM. The empirical results not only demonstrate that organizational culture, application of information technology and leadership of superintendent are the three most important influential factors in the KM initiative process, but also reveal the applicability of consistent fuzzy preference relations for solving complicated hierarchical multicriteria prediction problems (Chang and Wang, 2007).

The study in the USA relating to the implementation practices of the advanced manufacturing technologies investigates the competitive strategies and the operational potential of the AMTs. The study was conducted in the manufacturing units which produced 82 different durable goods and discrete parts. The results suggest that the implementation process involving pre planning and justification stages are very crucial for the effective implementation of the AMT (Small et al., 2009). Small and middle-sized companies lack relevant experience and an unsuccessful attempt to adopt AMT can easily lead to serious problems. The several surveys that were carried out in the Czech Republic and selected results focused especially on the problems related to AMT benefits expectations, management attitudes towards AMT, and methods used during the appropriate decision-making processes.

AMT investment patterns in developing countries provides new evidence from the Turkish automotive industry and develops a taxonomy by exploring the relationships between AMT investment patterns, ownership structure, firm size and performance. The results suggested that AMT investment patterns are not only significantly correlated with firm performance or ownership, but also reveals significant differences in manufacturing performance across investment patterns (Singh et al., 2013).

A differentiated technology justification approach relied on AMTs in order to succeed in an environment of high labour costs, increasing competition and rising customer expectations in European companies. The approach developed based on a literature review and a case study suggested a combination of strategic, financial and risk justification methods depend on the integration level of the technical system under consideration, ranging from standalone machines to large and integrated production systems (Natalia et al., 2016).

Robust supply decision making is critical to the advanced manufacturing of prefabricated products. Previous related research focused on minimizing cost overruns in off-site construction supply networks by optimizing purchasing decisions. The proposed optimization models aim to enhance supply network performance with a smaller overall investment. Towards this aim, three research hypotheses on optimization of supply decisions and configurations are developed and tested. The modelling method and results contribute to optimal decision making in advanced manufacturing of prefabricated products (Arashpour et al., 2017).

Due to the recent drop in oil prices and high environmental dynamism, organizations delivering in affected markets need to identify ways to reduce time to market (TtM) and cost of non-quality (CONQ) of their commercialization processes, in addition to pursuing and developing new markets. It has been discussed that the study of a multinational organization's commercialization process of two large and complex projects and their Rand T/D (research and technology/development) and NPI (new product introduction) processes. The first project relies primarily on new knowledge, capabilities and skills and the second on existing ones. The findings provide a review of the operational challenges and best practices for reducing TtM and CONQ of the commercialization process in the context of advanced manufacturing.

The effective implementation of AMTs in an organization is greatly impacted by the size of organization. The large sized organization has larger budgets and they implemented more vigorously. However the implementation in SMEs has better results in terms of productivity, cost analysis and technology assessment, development and flexibility (Dangayach et al., 2006). The organizational design and structure of the firms have varied impacts on the implementation of AMTs (Cardoso et al.,

2012). The middle management is more concerned over the technological implementation whereas the top management is concerned about the costs involved, productivity, knowledge-based competition, training budgets to skilled labour needs. There is a need for the skilled based labour for the AMTs.

Employees at all levels also need be trained, and therefore there is a considerable need to establish a training budget. The employee psychology, leadership and organizational changes are to be brought up for the successful results. The market is so competitive in terms of the technology used and the end products produced that the key focus is on the knowledge-based competition (Pandza et al., 2005). The studies pertaining to factors such as flexibility, quality and quantitative analysis of the impacts of advanced manufacturing techniques, cost benefit analysis, technology assessment, development and implementation of AMTs in the North Indian manufacturing sector.

Yates examined the assessment of what kind of AMT certain organization or any venture needs, should be ascertained and implemented by giving due importance to the factors that gives the business an edge to its competitors and that enhances qualities of the products/services the business offers. Accordingly, AMTs should be implemented in a way that brings a total change in manufacturing capacity, positively alter manufacturing parameters, and lead the organization to become a successful entity which would potentially entice the customers for further investment.

Kaplan contended that the manufacturing adaptability characteristic took into consideration in CIM (computer integrated manufacturing) offers much more valuable, robust and effective life when compared to existing manufacturing processes. Besides that, different advantages – substantial and impalpable – are provided through more investments in AMT. For example, lower inventory stocks, reducing inventory in shop floor, bring down throughput and enhance learning speed at an accelerated pace.

Bessant defined that AMTs can be termed as a spectrum of technologies, that consists of all the automated processes and techniques. AMT is an umbrella term used to portray an extensive variety of computerization and assorted technologies, which proliferated as a repercussion to the advancements in information technologies over the last two decades.

The connection between technology application and business strategy additionally identifies competitive priorities and positioning of the enterprise. In the global market for making success, companies require employing technology strategically by linking it to a firm's competitive strategy.

According to Noori, AMT are picked predominately as indicated by aiming operational criteria, for example, to take care of issues identified with quality, productivity, safety, profitability and reliability. AMT offers much more competitive advantage to organizations and according to strategic criteria these technologies should be selected.

Jonsson described that consideration of supporting infrastructure is an essential requirement so that the full potential of AMTs can be exploited as insufficient attention to company maintenance, infrastructure and organization results in registering several shortcomings in the new techniques. To ensure smooth work and successful results, the three components mentioned above are integral to the operation of AMT.

Lewis and Boyer propounded that for building long-lasting products or services that might give the organization a competitive edge, and potentially enhance business performance; the role of AMTs has gained significant importance over recent years. AMTs are technologies and processes that control firm production through mechanical and automated computer systems; also incorporates the associated machinery that augments the execution.

Workforce development activities are impacted by work atmosphere and personnel induced perceptions. There is a relationship between AMTs with work force training and found it to be directly related. The conceptual framework of human centred technology philosophy would examine the role of personnel perceptions for the purpose of establishing the convoluted or direct relationship between AMTs and workforce performance.

Hayes and Jayakumar dealt with problems that the US companies faced with the implementation of "programmable automation" technologies that were aimed at exploiting the full potential of the firm, especially when their counterparts in Europe and Japan were much more successful in such implementation. It was found that the main hurdle with the effective implementation was embedded in the attitude towards doings things compatible with the capabilities and requirements of the new hardware. Obstacles faced by companies were examined and their managerial practice implications were discussed in detail.

Siegel et al. (1997) reviewed the issues incorporating exhaustive, organization based survey of technology embrace and personnel management strategies. It was observed that the firms implementing AMTs reduced their manpower and relied more on automated processes. Also the demand for the labour with higher skills has raised. The workforce has to improve their skills with the implementation of the new technologies. In the overall, employee empowerment emphasis is laid down with the adoption of AMTs and the labour demands varied with the category of the technologies implemented.

The change is inevitable, and a positive attitude is required to bring in the change. The psychological barriers hammering the technological change can be overcome by the change in work attitude and organizational structure changes. The change in a firm's structure and behaviour of its employees plays an important role in making the technological change a success (Ghani and Jayabalan, 2000).

Karsak and Tolga (2001) designed an advanced fuzzy decision algorithm that helps select the best possible advanced manufacturing system (AMS) available from among a plethora of options that meets the requirement. The criteria for to choose the best alternative among available options are financial evaluation and other performance parameters primarily non-quantitative ones like robustness, performance improvement etc. Cashflow analysis was also brought in to consider the financial aspects of AMS. The fuzzy preferable indices were reckoned and incorporated depending on firm opinion by financial and strategic experts in AMS investment. The ambiguity built in the financial assessment comprising of systematic cash flows, interest rates and inflation factors were justified with these fuzzy numbers.

The impact of the probability of failure of company's technological advancement, industry turbulence and novelty of its technology. Results showed that when new technologies were implemented to result in higher advances through technology especially during low technological turbulence, the firms faced failure at much higher probability. At the same time, when older technologies were brought in to result in such higher advances during high technological period, firms failed at lower probability.

Singh and Khamba (2013) focused on improving the understanding associated with the deployment of new technologies using flexible systems methodology in Indian manufacturing enterprise. For this purpose, study in two different ways was conducted in a leading tractor manufacturing organization which examined the utilization of machines:

- With respect to time.
- Comparing the processing time of different machines.

Results showed a dismal 37.57% overall technology implementation of AMTs in the organization which falls towards a lower side.

Gupta and Whitehouse (2001) assessed the effect of AMT implementation on firms of varied sizes. It was found that technology adoption and implementation impacts small-sized firms favourably as technology positively enhances organization performance. The results implied positive correlation of firm performance and AMT strategy.

A schematic framework regarding AMT implementation has been presented. The aim was to achieve higher performance within the old framework with new technologies. A cross-sectional survey was conducted with sampling size of 927 employees from 27 AMT firms. The study suggested the substantial changes required in the existing organizational structure with the implementation of AMTs. With a Low PL (proactive) level, mechanistic structural changes are imminent at the macro organizations, but when the AMTs increases, there is not enough evidence of any change in the structure, with PL level remaining low (Ghani et al., 2002).

With the introduction of AMTs in the rapidly growing competitive market, it is evident that the production costs had a major impact. New costing methods are required to be brought in, especially methods based on costing. There's a need to put more emphasis on non-financial parameters. The findings of the study did not have conclusive results.

The AMTs implementation process and number of investments in the new technology. The Indian process sector have expressed greater interest in AMTs, standalone technologies such as CNC and AMHS (Dangayach et al., 2006).

Liao and Tu (2008) examined the parameters affecting the quest for higher performance under different uncertainty levels of environment. The impacts of automation on manufacturing performance and associated integration were addressed by two assessment areas: (1) Manufacturing System Integration Strategy; (2) Manufacturing System Automation Strategy. The data sampled from 303 manufacturing companies revealed that the automation has increased the manufacturing performance under low uncertainty environment while integration excelled under high uncertainty levels.

Malek et al. argued that in a competitive environment "a firm must be able to simultaneously produce multiple and diverse products, upgrade and redesign its products in short lifecycles, and execute efficient production changeovers". He discovered that there is little literature to aid companies on how to develop flexible manufacturing (FM) solutions. The authors' paper addresses this issue through the development of a methodology for the design, development and implementation of an FM solution. Their work indicated that much previous FM research concentrated on FMS, usually involving automated metal working facilities. In their publication, Abdel Malek et al. presented an FM solution design method (FMSD) that extends beyond this class of facilities, e.g., into the areas of plastic production, pharmaceuticals and personal products.

The study indicates that most of the AMT implementations were undertaken as a response to market conditions rather than being driven by technological factors. In addition, Burcher and Lee argue that companies assess AMT proposals carefully through evaluation of both quantitative and qualitative factors and that most companies employed more than one appraisal technique. The results of the survey indicated to the authors that there is no pattern of differentiation between larger or smaller companies in terms of the number or types of appraisal techniques employed by a company.

Investment appraised technique for AMT's has been adopted. This research present guidance for manufacturing companies which are preparing to invest in AMT. The purpose of this research is to explain the research is to explain the reasons why company encourage problems while implementing AMT. From this study it is believed that improved justification methods will encourage more firms to invest in AMT and to realize the benefits these investments can offer.

An exploratory survey on AMT's in Indian SMEs of varies sectors. Objective of survey is to assess status of AMT's, identify priorities, AMT's implementation criteria. Responses from 122 companies are analyzed and presented. It is observed that Indian SMEs are giving higher priority to quality and the least priority to flexibility. "Post implementation evaluation" and "requirement analysis". AMT implementation steps have attracted least attention from Indian SMEs (Dangayach and Deshmukh, 2005).

A start-up methodology, the concept is analyzed by means of qualitative and quantitative inquiry, which shows increased problem-solving capacity are related to rate with which manufacturer performance progress as time passes and production capacity is accumulated.

Lower-order AMT represents those technologies that can be implemented incrementally, and the companies implementing such technologies typically develop less complex innovation strategies. In such cases the benefits of AMT are obtained through immediate improvements in production efficiency. Higher-order AMT requires integration of manufacturing units for the development of competitive advantages based on increased flexibility. Companies implementing this level of AMT were shown to be developing more complex innovation strategies.

Hull et al. developed a further process to supplement the six facets model with a process for the evaluation of competing new technologies. This new process, a Modified Analytic Hierarchic Process (MAHP) supports the six facets model through the consideration of strategic factors in the decision-making process. The identified strategic issues are concerned with business and technical factors. Within each of these factors, suggestions are made for appropriate sub-factors that managers can weight in order to assist in selecting the technology that best meets the requirements of the company.

Kearns et al. developed a six-facet model to assist successful technology implementation based on a survey of the available literature and tested through a case study of a US manufacturing and retail company. The specific focus of the model is on the management of change within technology management, stating that such change is a vital aspect of business success. The six facets presented by Kearns et al. are: technology evaluation; product and process integration; planning; implementation; training; and change.

Raymond (2005) worked on operation management technologies in SMEs. The purpose of study is increased requirement for competitive, innovation, quality, flexibility in SMEs. Using a contingency theory, a survey study of 118 Canadians manufacturers to determine performance between critical success factors (CSFs) of SMEs and their level of proficiency in the use of AMT. It was found that while increased CSF and AMT assimilation levels directly impact operation performance in terms of increased production, cost reduction, flexibility, quality and mismatch between two reduces performance.

Small and Yasin worked on topic AMT adoption and performance: the role of management information systems departments. This study used information obtained from the advanced manufacturing literature to develop a conceptual framework that illustrate impact of MIS on different department of AMT adoption. A detailed survey of manufacturing firms in the USA to collect data required to rest five hypotheses. The results of this study indicate that the proposed framework is particularly useful in explaining the role of MIS department in firms that are attempting to integrate advanced process and information technology.

Fulton and Hon worked on topic Managing AMT implementation in manufacturing SMEs. The purpose of this study is to describe new methodology for implementing leading-edge technology into "design and manufacture" companies to gain a competitive advantage. A seven-stage process is applied to 73 SMEs. It finds that success rate was very high. The methodology was embraced by the companies, resulting in very few dropouts. Limitation is that a long-term study is needed to review company performance over an extended period.

"Do foreign owned firms manage AMT better?" This study used regression analysis of factors obtained from measured variables to find statistical relationships between investment in AMT, the planning effort associated with that operational performance of manufacturing firms in Australia and Canada. Hypotheses derived from it were supposed by statistical analysis, lending some support to the persistent idea that Australian managers are not as effective as their overseas counterparts.

Sherer et al. examined the importance of investment in organizational change management in aiding the successful implementation of a new technology. The paper argued that many companies fail to place enough emphasis on the changes that employees must make to the way that they work in order to successfully utilize a new technology. The study focused on a single multinational company's perspective; however, the particular technological implementation examined was a corporate wide system upgrade. The authors concluded that the investment that the company had made in managing the change had a significant impact in improving client satisfaction and reducing resistance from the workforce. The large company technology investment examined was held as an exemplar of how investment in the management of change can assist successful implementation; however, for smaller companies the barriers to such investment may be different.

Ordoobadi evaluated AMT using Taguchi's loss functions. The purpose of this study is to provide a tool for decision maker to consider both tangible and intangible factors while making decisions regarding investment in AMT. It finds from study that investing in new technologies is the only way for manufactures to survive in today's market, Thus there is need to have access to a decision model that will help manufacturer in their investment decisions.

Ordoobadi worked on application of ANP methodology in evaluation of advanced technologies. The aim of this study is to develop decision tool to help managers to make more informed decisions regarding their investments in AMT's. The analytic network process methodology satisfied the requirement of this study. Findings of this study is that Allowing for interdependencies among selection criteria as well as between alternatives and selection criteria provides a more realistic evaluation process than other selection process that ignore such interdependencies.

3.1.3 APPLICATIONS OF AMTs

In globally competing scenario, the application of AMT is emerging as a strategic weapon (Singh et al., 2007). Firms are seeking ways to respond quickly to changes induced by customers, competitors, and technologists and flexibility has become an important tool in this struggle for success.

Flexibility is the organization's ability to meet an increasing variety of customer expectations without excessive costs, time, organizational disruptions or performance losses. To respond more quickly to changing customer needs, manufacturers are enhancing flexible manufacturing competence (FMC) as a source of competitive advantage (Thomas et al., 2008).

The adequate categorization of AMTs has been extensively acknowledged in past years. The organizational ability is enhanced by building sustainable competitive advantage (Raymond and Croteau, 2006; Koc and Bozdag, 2009).

3.1.4 FUTURE PROSPECTS OF NEW TECHNOLOGIES

Technology word finds its roots in the Greek words *techne* and *logia*, which mean art or skill, and science or study, respectively. The systematic treatment of either art or skill is termed as *tecknologia*, or "technology". There are several viewpoints of technology. Depending on the situation, the word means different things for different people.

Competition poses a major threat to all the organizations irrespective of their size and sector. The successful implementation of AMTs by firms can give them an edge over their competitors. The new challenges to the firms include globalization of markets, the knowledge economy, e-business and introduction of new technologies. Management needs to identify and develop the structural relationship among different factors for successful implementation of AMTs. For effective implementation of AMTs, management should not ignore managerial aspects such as organization culture, employee training and integration of departments, vendor development, strategy development and customer involvement (Singh et al., 2007).

The implementation of AMTs not only impacts the manufacturing processes but also the information technologies. Thus the dramatic developments in AMT at various organizational levels can be attributed to number of benefits that improve the competitive position of the adopting companies. AMT impacts not just manufacturing, but the whole business operations, giving new challenges to a firm's ability to manage both manufacturing and information technologies (Sharma et al., 2008). There is an inadequacy to understand an organized effort that by means of what these activities carried out in the industry. This research will be planned to study and propose the strategic impact of advanced manufacturing initiatives that contribute to the success of the industry.

The eternally growing expectations and ineffective conventional manufacturing techniques expects from manufacturers to deploy fresh and more effective techniques in the manufacturing arena. The upcoming AMTs offer much better quality and lesser fixed references at reasonable price. AMTs include procedures that shows manufacturing processes onscreen real time.

The ever-increasing demand and needs of manufacturing industry led to the evolution in manufacturing sector. Price efficient and user-friendly products and services are the need of the hour.

Lower operating costs needs coupled with improved and efficient manufacturing coerced manufacturing firms to tread a greater path of AMT and consider products related to them. The newly inducted AMTs are considered effective for gaining a competitive advantage in this hyper competitive world (Pagell et al., 2000).

Manufacturing forms the backbone of any industrial and booming nation. Any well do economy roughly constitutes 20–30% of the value of all the goods and services produced. Also, country's manufacturing activity level is directly linked with economic health. New manufacturing techniques revolutionized the manufacturing industry gradually but effectively. The slow advancement and eventual revolution metamorphosed the entire industrial sector.

The technical competence of a firm is measured by the importance it gives to AMTs. AMTs help achieve modern world objectives such as delivery, flexibility, cost and quality. The above-mentioned objectives put stringent requirements on manufacturing firms.

3.2 ADVANCED MAINTENANCE TECHNIQUES

Maintenance is the combination of all technical, administrative and managerial actions during the lifecycle of an item intended to retain it in or restore it to, a state in which it can perform the required function. Maintenance includes all activities related to maintaining a certain level of availability and reliability of the system and its components and its ability to perform a standard level of quality. It also includes engineering decisions and associated actions that are necessary for the optimization of specified equipment capability, where capability is the ability to perform a specified function within a range of performance levels that may relate to capacity, rate, quality, safety and responsiveness.

The function of maintenance is total asset lifecycle optimization which means maximizing the availability and reliability of the assets and equipment to produce the desired quantity of products, with the required quality specifications, in a timely manner and this objective must be attained in a cost-effective way and in accordance with environmental and safety regulation.

Latest research on CMMS has been reviewed and is presented briefly in this section. Researchers in the past have proposed many systems related to different strategies in maintenance systems. Some researchers found limitations in the prognostic models for maintenance decisions. The reason behind this was quality and quantity of historical data, assumptions made, and time required in validating models. Maintenance histories from Computerized Maintenance Management System (CMMS) are analyzed for reducing downtimes and Operating Expenditure. The records used for analyzing CMMS was Preventive Maintenance (PM) Intervals, Failure events, cost and maintenance records. The proposed methodologies proved as a case of improved decision making under limited information for maintenance intervals and replacements of a City Council of Australian Local Government organization.

There are different maintenance techniques for each machine, and the selection of these techniques depend on multiple factors here these factors are limited to operational needs and economic factors only. The proposed method combined quality function deployment (QFD) for planning and operational needs, the analytic hierarchy process (AHP) for prioritizing the criteria for selection and ranking the alternative maintenance techniques and the benefit of doubt (BoD) approach for sensitivity analysis through setting the realistic limits for decision making. This proposed method for the selection of maintenance techniques was used in three productive systems of a gear manufacturing organization in India for evaluating its effectiveness (Baidya et al., 2018).

A thorough review on the latest research and standard developments that have influence upon building information modelling (BIM) and its application in facilities management (FM) during the operations and maintenance (O&M) phase. At the same time opportunities for BIM-FM integration is presented. The findings revealed for FM sector in need for greater consideration of long-term strategic aspirations, improvement of data integration, better KM, enriched performance measurement and improved training and competence development for facilities managers to better deal with the amorphous range of services covered by FM. The scope of FM and the growing use of BIM for asset management in future.

As carrying out the proper maintenance processes of power plants has critical importance. Therefore it is necessary for prolonging the effective operational lifetime and as a result improving the sustainable power generation of the system. So the selection of the most applicable maintenance strategy is the first and unignorably stage of maintenance management in power plants as in other manufacturing facilities. The hydroelectric power plants selected in Turkey for the selection of the maintenance strategy. The Technique for Order of Preference by Similarity to Ideal Solution (TOPSIS) is applied under nine evaluation criteria weighted by the AHP for a big scale hydroelectric power plant. With the proposed goal programming (GP) model 77% improvement observed in downtimes by the combinations of maintenance strategies.

A logarithmic fuzzy preference programming was used for the optimum maintenance strategies selection problem. The qualitative as well as quantitative data is used in the methodology. For maintenance strategies selection in the Multiple Criteria Decision-Making (MCDM) field AHP is broadly used. It was observed that the traditional or hybrid AHP methods either produce multiple, even conflict priority results or have complicated algorithm structures which are unstable to obtain the optimum solution. The feasibility and validity of the proposed methodology demonstrated with an example. This maintenance strategy selection methodology is proved a unique optimum solution and consensus results to achieve saving in cost and improving the system reliability and availability.

For improving maintenance strategies, system reliability and reducing costs a conceptual framework for a customized RCM (Reliability-Centred Maintenance) model is proposed for analyzing and improving decisions regarding the maintenance function. A new knowledge base is generated by the transformation of raw information which recorded in a single database for being available for the RCM deployment phases. The decisions in the stages of RCM implementations were supported by MCDM/A (Multi Criteria Decision Making/Analysis) methods.

A procedure is developed to support the planning of preventive involvements to be integrated in a CMMS so as to remove the difficulties in its implementation and to improve maintenance decisions. A new CMMS function is proposed for getting the optimal periodicity of preventive interventions. For achieving accurate solutions the issues based on equipment Failure Mode Effect Analysis (failure records) and reliability were used as strong input to maintenance models.

The targeting of an ongoing project to develop a spare parts classification for integration in a CMMS of a manufacturing company. For improving the performance of maintenance management, Inventory management of spare parts first classification is prepared on the basis of the necessity and importance of spare parts for maintenance. Then, a multi-criteria classification, including the previous maintenance classification is used for defining the groups for which a stock management policy will be associated.

For the risk assessment a CBN model is developed for the safety at level crossing to avoid accidents in Europe. In this model a general approach of Causal Statistic Risk Assessment based on hierarchical Causal Bayesian Networks (CSRA-CBN) is developed to examine the various impacting factors which may cause accidents and identify the factors which contribute most to the accidents at level crossings. The advantage of the model was risk quantification (quantifying the causal relationships between the risk of accident occurring and the impacting factors considered) which can be estimated more clearly thus eliminating the risk of accidents at level crossings. As a result making the level crossing safer.

The maintenance of a water treatment plant is demonstrated with the improved failure mode and effects analysis (FMEA) method. This failure mode and effect analysis method used with two-dimensional uncertain linguistic variables (2DULVs) and alternative queuing method (AQM). The former is used to derive the weights of risk factors and later is proposed for determining the risk ranking of the identified failure modes. The performance of the improved model of failure mode and effects analysis the (FMEA) in ranking the risk of failure modes was found better than other existing methods.

The significance of Multi-Criteria Decision Analysis (MCDA) is highlighted for structuring problems. A literature review was carried out that covers eight PSMs (Cognitive and Causal Maps, DPSIR, Scenario Planning, SSM, Stakeholder Analysis, Strategic Choice Approach, SODA and SWOT) and seven MCDA methods (AHP, ANP, ELECTRE, MAUT, MAVT, PROMETHEE and TOPSIS). It was observed that by combining methods yields a better-off view of the decision-making situation. AHP was found to be the most commonly applied MCDA method. Few limitations and encounters are also identified in combining PSMs and MCDA related to building a value tree and assigning criteria weights.

The application of CMMS is utilized to support a maintenance in "KGHM Polska Miedi S.A – copper mining industry" in Poland. CMMS is used to calculate the intensity of failures of mining machines, its components and systems. These authors also presented a case study of the intensity of failures level analysis for the hydraulic system of the haul trucks and its selected component: a hydraulic pump.

The prospective of advanced content management systems (CMSs) has been explored and tested for applications in the manufacturing engineering domain. The content management systems (CMSs) were widely used in non-engineering sectors such as finance, business, publishing and government organizations. Information and knowledge from the lifecycle of machine tools should be collected and reused for the effective performance and competent maintenance. CMSs have a number of benefits in managing dynamic and unstructured knowledge as compared with traditional engineering information systems. A prototype maintenance and service planning system has been developed and evaluated using a real CNC machine tool.

The functionalities of IT systems for the maintenance management in the manufacturing companies are explored. The maintenance management system which is supported by the information systems comprises of several activities for example PM planning, task scheduling, spare parts management and data analysis to reduce downtime and increase the maintenance performance. The only disadvantage is a poor adjustment to the requirements of enterprises. It was emphasized that plants' production capacities is adversely affected by the failure or incorrect operations of the machines.

Interpretive Structural Modelling (ISM) is a methodology for identifying and summarizing relationships among specific items, which define an issue or problem. ISM is interpretive because the relation among the elements is given by group of members. It is structural also as based on the relationship; an overall structure is extracted from the complex set of variables. It is a modelling technique also as the specific relationships and overall structure is portrayed in a graphical model. The various benefits of this model are competitive capacities for production, highest standards of productivity, reduces overall equipment emergencies, reduces maintenance purchasing, zero accidents in a healthy and clean work environment. It helps to optimize the maintenance cost and provides better services to operations through Computer Integrated Maintenance Management Systems (CIMMS) ((Mishra et al., 2015).

Ahuja and Khamba (2008) highlighted maintenance techniques, framework of Total Productive Maintenance (TPM), overall equipment effectiveness (OEE), TPM implementation practices, barriers and success factors in TPM implementation. It emphasized TPM proved to be one amongst the best of the proactive strategic initiatives which lead the manufacturing organizations to achieve new elevations in becoming successful organizations. It also highlighted the reasons behind failure of TPM programmes in the organizations.

Maintenance performance factors are analyzed with a benchmarking process. The outcome of questionnaire exposed that companies that do not have well planned and defined maintenance strategies have to look for support from external experts to tackle strategic problems in maintenance. It also emphasized for future research work on statistical analysis on the impact of maintenance strategies on production and financial performance.

Verma and Tewari presented a critical literature review on Computerized Maintenance Management Information System (CMMIS) and found that it provides timely information for rigorous decision making for maintenance problems, maximum availability of production equipment and results in the effective planning, controlling and scheduling the maintenance activities. It also shown the importance of training for the employees.

It is assumed that the respective organizations were ready for the implied change, and if users accept the technology, it may bring many future benefits to the business organization. This study aimed to examine post-implementation perception and acceptance of CMMS by users. It also emphasized on the training for users for implementing CMMS deployed for maintenance management.

An integrated RCM and CMMS system for solving and optimizing maintenance problems in Iranian gas industry under Iranian Ministry of Petroleum. A process and functional model is developed for analyzing the plants with small modifications for saving the time. This system works on units and equipment's reliability analysis, failure mode analysis and maintenance benefit cost analysis. It emphasized on human resource training which is considered a Key Performance Indicators (KPI) for maintenance, safety and environment effects caused by equipment malfunction is more essential.

TPM is the significant technique to improve the maintenance management of production equipment. The existing techniques in maintenance management like breakdown maintenance (BM), preventive maintenance (PM), predictive maintenance (PdM) or condition-based maintenance (CBM), reliability-centred maintenance (RCM), CMMS and TPM are explored. This paper revealed that TPM is the latest and corrective maintenance practice is the oldest one.

The role of maintenance from the viewpoint of enhancing company's profitability and competitiveness. This is concluded that maintenance practices related to CBM approach represent the highest opportunity for enhancement. A conceptual model of maintenance impact on company's profitability is developed for improved overall equipment effectiveness and improved cost effectiveness and hence higher margin of a manufacturing organization.

A model with eight various factors and their pointers for Maintenance System Evaluation (MSE) were proposed in this paper. This model helps in measuring the effectiveness of maintenance activities in order to govern the deviations from the prearranged work. It is concluded that computer-aided evaluation is necessity to maintenance activities.

A case study of a company is proposed in which it has developed its own computerized system for solving maintenance problems. This paper presented an ongoing project aiming to develop a CMMS for a manufacturing company. Also proposed optimization for methodologies for decision-making process will be developed taking into account the needs of the company.

A review of current practices followed by a key informant study is done. Then Experts in several major industrial concerns were interviewed along with an opinion leader from a European maintenance federation were interviewed to analyze to what extent technology take-up is likely to affect both purchasing of spares and information management.

Maintenance management in a large-scale industrial operation is complex and play an important role on the profitability of the business. Without computer-based support it is practically impossible to manage maintenance. It is found that there is a low success rate among even large organizations worldwide in implementing CMMS. CMMS used to support improved reliability and performance and to find out the reasons behind the low success rate achieved and a well-resourced programme that can bring success. It is suggested that to improve overall business performance one tool can deliver this support that is a CMMS or eAM software. Without such a system world-class maintenance is almost impossible to achieve (Wienker et al., 2016).

Information technology (IT) is very important tool for attainment efficiency and effectiveness within maintenance, provided that correct and relevant IT is applied. A conceptual model is developed for identifying maintenance management IT requirements with its practical application in a process for the IT requirements identification for maintenance management. By implementing a structured process the demands of IT support in the maintenance organization are fulfilled. IT systems end up in underutilized without considering the actual conditions and maintenance strategy and IT maturity of the maintenance organization and its individuals. Lack of functionality, lack of user knowledge or bad user interfaces are the factors which are considered for underutilized IT system.

New and rapid development of new techniques in maintenance is due to technical developments in smart tags, sensors, data acquisition, signal analysis equipment and wireless communication. Higher overall efficiency in production, e-maintenance can be achieved when technological developments have been linked with new business development ideas.

Organizations must check the suitability according to their needs and objectives of maintenance. A fuzzy-based methodology is proposed for multi-criteria for decision method which is known as AHP making in the field of CMMS selection and lastly a prototype of software is implemented which leads to freedom of estimation of attributes and real alternatives. The programme is developed in MATLAB and run on a desktop PC which was supported by Microsoft Windows XP.

The digitalization as future of the manufacturing industry which realize the use of engineering tools and techniques/methods like Failure Mode Effects Analysis (FMEA) and Fault Tree Analysis (FTA), Event Tree Analysis (ETA) and Hazard and operability studies (HAZOP). For measuring the equipment performance overall equipment effectiveness widely used. For selection of maintenance policy Decision Tree Analysis (DTA) and Variation Mode Effect Analysis (VMEA). For safety and health European Agency for safety and health at work (EU-OSHA) is considered as the measuring tool.

The potential of TPM implementation to enhance work efficiency and productivity of employee and increase overall equipment effectiveness of a company. Indian industry always faces up to challenges from global competition. The need of TPM implementation which needs significant change in the organizational culture and direct and indirect benefits are explored for micro, small, medium enterprises (MSME) (Jain et al., 2014).

The review to recognize the different maintenance models contained by the literature includes a group of preliminary studies. The first review report on maintenance models dates from 1976 in a study entitled "A survey of maintenance models: the control and surveillance of deteriorating systems" (Pierskalla and Voelker, 1976). The concentration is on labour seeming since the 1965 survey, "Maintenance Policies for Stochastically Failing Equipment: A Survey" by John McCall, and the 1965 book, The Mathematical Theory of Reliability, by Richard Barlow and Frank Proschan (McCall, 1965. The survey includes models, which involve an optimal decision to procure, inspect, and repair and/or replace a unit subject to deterioration in service.

Subsequently, Dekker (1996) and Stoneham publish two reviews on models or strategies for maintenance management. In 1996, Dekker reviews the applications of maintenance optimization models and discusses it future prospects. Two years later Stoneham characterized the most used maintenance models up to that date, among which stand out TPM, RCM and CBM. In a critical analysis at the beginning of the 21st century, Sherwin (2000) reviews the general models for maintenance management from a strategic viewpoint to consider maintenance as a "contributor to benefits" instead of "a necessary evil".

A few years later, in a review to identify different maintenance strategies, Mostafa (2004) and Garg et al. list a group of strategies for maintenance management. Fraser et al. (2015) perform a literature review, first with the aim to identify and categorize, the various maintenance management models, and second, to determine the depth of empirical evidence for the popular models in real-world applications (Fraser, Hvolby, and Tseng, 2015). 27 maintenance management models were identified and were named in different ways with particular characteristics and practical utility. Except the Pierskalla and Voelker review from 1976, with a reactive approach according to the period, it is possible to highlight that five of the identified models were listed in all the reviews, so it can be considered as the most relevant model reported in the literature for maintenance management. These models according to the fulfilled review are corrective maintenance (CM), preventive maintenance (PM), total productive maintenance (TPM), reliability-centred maintenance (RCM), and CBM.

Additionally, authors continue searching for the most suitable model for maintenance management in their business (Pramod et al., 2006; Márquez, León, Fernández, Márquez, and Campos, 2009; Campos, Fernández, Díaz, and Márquez, 2010; Shafiee, 2015; Gupta and Mishra, 2016). However, after reviewing the proposed models, it can be verified that theoretical bases form part of the most relevant models with an emphasis on informatics, so they will not be taken into account as new models, but as a specialization of existing models. Table 3.1 summarizes the models identified in the literature, including its focus, the application environment and some examples of implementation in recent years, according to their historical context.

Computerized Maintenance Management Information System (CMMIS) is simply the application of computers for quickly and efficiently deciding, planning and organizing various jobs for effective plant maintenance. Maintenance is a grouping of mechanical, organizational, and management activities throughout the lifecycle of equipment proposed to keep it or to give back it to a state in which it can perform the vital function (Azadeh et al., 2016). The challenge of maintenance is to ensure that the equipment operates at peak efficiency while serving the load with minimal downtime (Aljumaili et al., 2012; García-Sanz-Calcedo and Gómez Chaparro 2017). In the past, maintenance has been treated as an expenditure explanation in which performance measures are developed to track the cost, such as the headcount of maintenance personnel and the total duration of force outages during a specified period (Travis and Casinger, 1997).

Today, maintenance is acknowledged as a pivotal player in the performance and profitability of business organizations (Mostafa et al., 2015) because BM works are both cost-intensive and time-consuming (Dey et al., 2004). Conducting maintenance for an oil and gas (O&G) engineering facility is crucial to ensure high availability of production equipment at a reasonably low cost (Garg and Deshmukh 2006). According to Dey et al. (2004), the archetypal maintenance problems were due to corrosion, external influence, construction and material defects and human errors. In light of this, a paradigm shift from reactive maintenance to preventive and predictive maintenance is crucial for RCM (Tousley 2010) to optimize operations and sustaining the availability of plants (Madu 2000). O&G engineering plays a critical role in driving the global economy, and petroleum is used for numerous products serving as the world's primary fuel resource (Sivalingam 1997; Berntsen et al., 2018).

The processes and systems involved in producing and distributing O&G are highly complex and capital-intensive requiring state-of-the-art technology (Hamraz and Clarkson 2015). O&G is produced from an upstream facility located offshore built from expensive equipment (Antonakakis et al., 2018). An oil platform, offshore platform, or colloquially, "oil rig", is a large structure with facilities to drill, to extract, and to process oil and natural gas, or to temporarily store product until it can be brought to the shore for refining and marketing. Offshore platforms in remote locations have a set of operating requirements in their harsh environments subject to numerous constraints that limit the execution and progression of maintenance activities planned. Platform equipment and process failures have a significant impact on production output (Berntsen et al., 2018).

TABLE 3.1

Maintenance Management Models

First Generation: Pre-1950 Approach: Execute Corrective Actions
Objective: Repair Unforeseen Failures

Model	Main focus	Application	Evidence
Corrective maintenance (CM)	Failure in correction to return the asset immediately to its functionality condition.	Applicable to any work environment. It must be implemented together with a proactive action.	(Wang, Deng, Wu, Wang, and Xiong, 2014; Ben-Daya, Kumar, and Murthy, 2016)
Breakdown, Reactive maintenance or Failure-Based Maintenance (FBM)	The action is performed after the asset fails. It can be more expensive than PM.	Applicable to any work environment. It must be implemented together with a proactive action.	(Jonge et al., 2017)

Second generation: 1950–1959 approach: apply planned actions
Objective: prevent, predict and repair failures

Proactive maintenance	Philosophy focused on reducing the total maintenance required and optimizing the useful life of the asset	Applicable to environments where can be implement risk control strategies	(Mostafa, 2004; Canito et al., 2017)
PM Or Scheduled maintenance	Maintenance frequency is conditioned by the time, production volume and asset condition. Performed regularly on an asset to decrease the probability of failure	Applicable to assets with preventable failure modes, and assets with a probability of failure that increases with time or use.	(Chang, 2014; Ni, Gu, and Jin, 2015; Sheu, Chang, Chen, and Zhang, 2015; Sarker and Faiz, 2016; Maleki and Yang, 2017)
Predictive maintenance (PdM)	Maintenance is carried out when necessary, instead scheduling intervention frequency.	Applicable to assets with a critical operational function. Assets with preferable failure modes cost- effectively with regular monitoring	(McKone and Weiss, 2002; Carnero, 2006)

Third generation: 1960–1989 approach: establish maintenance tactics
Objective: manage and operate under a structured system

RCM	Corporate level maintenance strategy for optimization purposes. It allows determining the maintenance requirements of the assets according to their operating context.	For facilities with critical assets (those that can fail frequently or have large consequences of failures) such as airlines, power plants, oil industries, etc.	(Guck, Spel, and Stoelinga, 2015; Yssaad and Abene, 2015; Piasson, Biscaro, Leão, and Sanches Mantovani, 2016)
TPM	An asset management philosophy of whole company that integrates all business aspects (operators, materials, quality, energy, security, etc.) with maintenance operations.	Industrial and service environments where it is required to demonstrate operational requirements. Companies that implement quality management systems, risk management system, good practices (GxP).	(Chen and Meng, 2011; Jain, Bhatti, and Singh, 2014; Poduval, abd Pramod, 2015)
Total quality maintenance (TQMain)	Achieve and maintaining high overall asset effectiveness to improve manufacturing processes and produce quality products without interruption.	Similar to TPM	(Yang, Tavner, Crabtree, Feng, and Qiu, 2014; Modgil and Sharma, 2016)
Evidence-based asset management (EBAM)	It is the technique of making the right decisions and optimizing asset management processes with the best information available and with clearly defined decision criteria.	Applicable to companies which has implemented a CMMS	(Campbell and Reyes-Picknell, 2015; Chen et al., 2017)
Time-based maintenance (TBM)	Maintenance activity based on time	Applicable in environments where developed a PM strategies and predictive maintenance.	(Jonge, Dijkstra, and Romeijnders, 2015; Wang, 2012; Kim, Ahn, and Yeo, 2016; Jonge et al., 2017)
CMMS	Designed to store, retrieve and analyze information, through computer applications.	Applicable to any work environment, where you need to handle large volumes of information.	(Carnero, 2015)

Fourth generation: 1981–1995 approach: implement a strategy
Objective: costs measuring, compare each other, predict indexes, etc.

Outsourcing model	The transfer of the maintenance programme of the companies to third parties in order to improve maintenance results.	Applicable to any work environment. It must be implemented together with a proactive and reactive action.	(Manning, Larsen, and Bharati, 2015; Sabri et al., 2015)

(Continued)

TABLE 3.1 (Continued)

First Generation: Pre-1950 Approach: Execute Corrective Actions
Objective: Repair Unforeseen Failures

Model	Main focus	Application	Evidence
CBM	Based on assets monitoring and detection to determine vital alerts of imminent failure and decide the type of action to be carried out at each moment	Applicable in any environment where you can monitor and control analysis tools such as: vibration, infrared, ultrasonic, acoustic test, oil analysis, electrical test among others.	(Do, Voisin, Levrat, and Lung, 2015; Engeler, Treyer, Zogg, Wegener, and Kunz, 2016; Goyal et al., 2017; Keizer, Flapper, and Teunter, 2017)
Condition monitoring	Similar to the CBM where the condition monitoring of the selected equipment is undertaken to detect potential failures	The same applications as CMB, with emphasis on operational performance.	(Caesarendra et al., 2016; Moghaddass and Ertekin, 2018)
Risk-based maintenance (RBM)	Prioritize maintenance resources towards the assets that carry the greatest risk in case of failure. It is a methodology to determine the most economical use of maintenance resources.	Suitable for any work environment (equipment and operating systems).	(Bhandari, Arzaghi, Abbassi, Garaniya, and Khan, 2016; Pui et al., 2017)
Value-driven maintenance planning (VDM)	It is a philosophy to optimize the value derived from maintenance at a given time. The decision to perform maintenance at any time is based on the cost / benefit analysis	Applicable to competitive environments in the market, where operations do not imply a high risk. Service companies, basic products factories, etc.	(Macchi et al., 2009; Rosqvist, Laakso, and Reunanen, 2009; Khorshidi, Gunawan, and Ibrahim, 2016)

Fifth generation: 1996–2003 approach: develop skills and competences
Objective: apply science and technology

Effectiveness-centred maintenance	Built on the philosophy of "doing the things correctly" instead of "doing the things right". It is based on the RCM model	Applicable to the environments where the RCM model can be developed	(Pun, Chin, Chow, and Lau, 2002; Andriulo, Arleo, Carlo, Gnonia, and MarioTucci, 2015)
Age-based maintenance	Apply tasks and maintenance intervals to assets, depending on their operating time. Control of the degradation time of a component	Mechanical and structural systems, hydraulic structures, engine monitoring, etc.	(Huynh, Castro, Barros, and Bérenguer, 2012; Shafiee and Finkelstein, 2015; Shafiee, Patriksson, and Chukova, 2016)
Availability-based maintenance (ABM)	The maintenance method based on availability. It is a version of Reliability-Centred Maintenance	The same applications as RCM	(Qiu, Cui, and Gao, 2017)
Prognosis Help Management (PHM)	Evaluate the system based on data of its current condition or status within its lifecycle, determine the occurrence mode and development of failures and, ultimately, mitigate system risks	Applicable to the environments where the CBM model can be developed	(Lei and Sandborn, 2016)

Sixth generation: Since 2004 – modern approach: tangible and intangible assets
Objective: asset integrity management

Terotechnology model	Focused on the lifecycle of the system	Applicable to industrial maintenance.	(Palencia, 2007)
Strategic maintenance management	A global business perspective based on TPM and RCM.	Applicable to the environments where the TPM and RCM models can be developed	(Murthy et al., 2002; Baidya, Dey, Ghosh, and Petridis, 2018)

According to Kusumawardhani et al. (2016), unproductive asset integrity management (AIM) in OandG facilities is mostly due to issues concerning human resources, KM, and information technology (IT). In a similar Labib (1998) emphasized that asset integrity failures are commonplace in the OandG industry, mainly due to poor maintenance decision-making in overly complex situations. The documentation of equipment breakdowns to expenses used can be an overwhelming task without the use of computer applications. The effective planning of technicians and available spares is a dynamic activity (Labib, 1998). These challenges have engendered maintenance managers to adopt tools, methods, and concepts that would provide accurate and timely information for more productive maintenance function and reduce unscheduled equipment downtime (Dey et al., 2004; Tousley 2010).

According to Madu (2000), maintenance and reliability management should be embedded in an organization's strategic planning, specifically with the advancement of computer-based applications. To provide effective maintenance services, the use of a CMMS can simplify maintenance management, which encompasses asset management, work order (WO) management, PM management, inventory control, and report management (Lopes et al., 2016). Today, a CMMS has increasingly been used to manage plants and equipment maintenance in modern industries due to the complexity in maintenance management now considered as a critical element for the improvement of operation and safety, increase of availability, life span enhancement and cost reduction. A CMMS consists of tools for maintenance administration incorporating an open base of information and allows users to programme and to follow the maintenance activities proceeded from the services and maintenance policies. This is consistent with Bacchetti and Saccani (2012), who claimed the need for an integrated knowledge accumulation process for better demand forecasting and inventory management. As such, CMMS infrastructure supports an e-maintenance function to facilitate informed maintenance decisions.

Notwithstanding the various commercial CMMS packages in the market, most are not a perfect match to the peculiarities of each company, which requires further customization to the specific needs of a company (Lopes et al., 2016). Thus, the issues of functionality and user interfaces significantly affect the setup of a CMMS.

According to Wienker et al. (2016), only 6–15% of users exploit CMMSs to their full capability in general facility maintenance. In light of this, the current CMMS implementation fails to generate the return on investment (ROI), and the maintenance software implementation failure rates are as high as 70%. Thus, it is essential for each maintenance department to carefully manage asset-maintenance-related data embedded into software (Carnero and Noves, 2006). The solution for releasing the constraint is to change the way the firm conducts its business by addressing the issues of business model management and its relationship to the theory of constraints (TOC) (Spector, 2011).

Thus, maintenance managers should focus on the few constraints that prevent the CMMS from attaining its intended purpose. Travis and Casinger (1997) outlined the constraints associated with the modern maintenance management to include little or no support from management to implement world-class maintenance practices, and inventory problems, such as the need to reduce spares and still have parts on hand. Accurate information is crucial for maintenance management when making informed decisions related to equipment performance and costs as well as ensuring the reliable operation of equipment. To exploit the potentials of CMMS, this study aims to develop a constraint-free framework and a causal loop diagram (CLD) for a CMMS to improve the conventional maintenance operation system in O&G engineering and to achieve maintenance management success.

In the past few years, much research has been done so that performance of Indian manufacturing industries can be improved. Endrenyi et al. (2001) described the present status of maintenance strategies and the impact of maintenance on reliability. In this, the distinction is created between the strategies in which maintenance consists of replacement by a new component. The new component had the less cost which helps in improving the condition of the component. Various methods were divided into categories in which maintenance is performed at the fixed interval of time. The authors made the distinction between heuristic methods which were based on mathematical models. Maintenance at the fixed intervals is commonly used approach. According to the research, the probabilistic models were advantageous over deterministic models as they are able of describing the actual processes in a realistic way and facilitate optimization for minimal cost or maximal reliability.

Machines in the industries become more complex with the increasing demand for quality, productivity and availability. Mishra et al. (2015) developed a framework for the implementation of the world-class maintenance systems with the help of the ISM approach. A standard template has been provided for describing the way to implement each and every element of WMS in an organization. This framework combines the uniqueness and knowledge of employees working in an organization in order to reach excellence. The organization can use this framework by applying it to their own situation and methods.

RCM is also used for military applications such as heavy tracked armed vehicles. For a long time, the Czech Republic Armed Forces had used reliability and maintainability (R&M) to collect data and to monitor their combat vehicles, but they do not provide a satisfactory level of cost and availability to vehicle maintenance. Vintr and Valis (2006) presented two methods for maintenance improvement based on RCM procedures. The first method is the new optimized method used for PM periods. The other method used to optimize the maintenance procedures and saves additional cost which spent on extra maintenance. The RCM method is suitable for PM and in the cutting maintenance costs.

Today, every company needs a proper maintenance system which keeps the lifecycle cost down and helps in improving the performance of the company. Waeyenbergh and Pintelon (2002) demonstrated several challenges for management in the manufacturing industry. The major challenge is related to production equipment. The highspeed technological innovation put the equipment in higher stress and reduced the lifecycle of equipment. For this, a company strategic investment in production equipment should consider the flexibility, technology trends, cost, capability, etc. Proper maintenance of equipment is essential in the manufacturing industry to ensure smooth internal logistics, proper operations and to keep the lifecycle cost down. Several manufacturing companies seeking the customized maintenance concept.

There are several applications of maintenance optimization models. Dekker (1996) provides an overview of various applications of maintenance optimization models. Maintenance optimization models are the mathematical models which help in determining the optimum balance between the costs and benefits of maintenance process in maintenance industry. Optimization models have four functions: description of the technical system; function and importance; modelling of deterioration of system in time; description of available information about system and action to management. Optimization technique and objective function helps in determining the best balance.

RCM is used to analyze the functions and failures of a system and also determines the consequences of failure to implement the preventive measures with the help of standardized logical resolution procedure. Li and Gao (2010) presented the applications of RCM considering radical maintenance which determines the causes of failure in order to make maintenance decisions. A Root Cause Analysis creates a maintenance plan with the help of combined methods of Fault Tree Analysis (FTA) and Failure Mode, Effects and Criticality Analysis (FMECA). The authors also applied RM approach to an actual engineering project in the petrochemical industry which shows that traditional RCM help in improving the quality of maintenance strategies and assigning the maintenance resources.

Millar defined the requirements for advanced PHM technologies for optimal RCM. Condition Based Maintenance Plus is used as optimal CBM procedures. It helps in determining the least cost maintenance procedure and policy with acceptable levels of safety and readiness.

RCM is also useful for heavy earth-moving machinery in open cast coal mine. Samanta et al. (2001) described that the performance and availability of heavy earth-moving machinery depend upon maintainability and reliability characteristics of the user equipment. The maintenance decision for HEMM should be taken on the basis of scientific analysis of the failure pattern of the machines. Failures of capital-intensive HEMM have an impact on the production cost. RCM was based on the probabilistic models which help in minimizing the cost and increasing the performance of maintenance programme in the manufacturing industry.

RAM engineering is the process of preserving and creating relatability at a high level. Some of the RAM engineering actions influenced the availability and reliability. The high reliability helps in improving the quality of design. Wikstrom et al. (2000) demonstrated that RCM has the important role in RAM engineering in improving its performance by analyzing the complex system and revising the maintenance and design. It helps in increasing the system availability and reliability. The process owners use the procedure of RCM in planning the maintenance strategy which is well suited for VSDS's.

These issues in RCM occurred due to the cultural differences between maritime and aviation industries. RCM is considered as resource demanding in the maritime industry. With the help of reverse logic, saving in efforts and time can be achieved. Also, the failure modes in ships maintenance can be determined by analyzing the maintenance tasks. A fuel oil purification system is used to demonstrate its use. RCM methodology is used as a guiding principle to help in making a safer plan for maintenance strategy (Mokashi et al., 2002).

RCM methodology provides the best strategy for PM optimization. Preventive optimization provides various opportunities as well as challenges in all the aspects of industrial enterprises. PM optimization incorporates a new understanding of different ways in which a particular equipment fails. Deshpande and Modak (2002) demonstrated the application of RCM to a medium scale industry such as steel melting shop. The cause of failures and effects of RCM methodology were analyzed by applying systematically approach. PM categories for various modes were sued in order to preserve the system function in various components such as condition directed, time directed, failure finding and run-to-failure.

The productivity in the manufacturing industry can be enhanced with the help of RCM. The productivity in manufacturing industry can be increased using one-way ANOVA technique. It also helps in reducing the risks and provide better safety climate (Chopra et al., 2016).

The ship maintenance performance measurement (SMPM) is a framework that is used in influencing the decision-making maintenance schemes such as maintenance strategy, employees' strategy, customer, satisfaction, health, safety, budget and environment. Alhouli et al. (2017) described the four criteria of the SMPM framework to develop the RCM. These criteria are developed under the four hierarchical levels of top management, middle management, ship senior staff and ship crew.

The execution of the RCM in wind turbines is performed with the help of operator or owner. Fischer et al. (2012) described that the maintenance service provider analyzed the processing of wind turbines to prevent any failure or the damage to the turbine. The quantitative models were developed for the selection and optimization of the maintenance strategy. This model is effectively implemented in the failure models or the subsystems in which the main drivers for the wind-turbine were unavailable for example the hydraulic system and electrical system. The failure modes, causes and other underlying modules and the wide-ranging parallels between wind turbines are recognized in the analysis phase. V44-600kW and V90-2MW are two turbines that were used to perform the analysis of RCM. The design of the V90-2MW has more causes of the failure has been found in the V44-600kW.

The RCM and its applications are used in the development of the maintenance plan that is used in the steam process plant. The use of RCM in the steam process plant is due to its cost-effective maintenance feature. Afefy (2010) described the design of the steam process plant. It consists of a steam distribution boiler, dryer, fire-tube boiler, process heater and feed-water pump. The use of RCM in the steam process plant showed the time between the failure of plant equipment and sudden failure in the equipment. The RCM is used to decrease this failure time and influenced the PM tasks. It also affects the generation and implementation of the planning. It preferably recommends performing tasks including CD, TD and FF every year, six months, and even monthly.

Productivity is the main strategy used by manufacturing companies to stay competitive in a global market. Increase in the availability of the production equipment is essential for competitiveness. For this, a good maintenance strategy is essential (Sahoo et al., 2014).

Maintenance function importance is increased as it helps in improving the product quality, availability, operating cost levels and safety requirements of the process plants. The selection of the maintenance strategy is an important decision-making process in the manufacturing industry. Vishnu and Regikumar (2016) presented the reliability-based maintenance strategy selection in a process plant. In this research, AHP based framework was used for reliability maintenance strategy selection. The proposed model also validated maintenance history data of titanium dioxide plant. This methodology determined the optimal maintenance strategies for equipment or machinery based FMEA study. The results indicated that the PM strategy is needed for criticality equipment instead of BM and Scheduled maintenance.

Today, the success of the manufacturing business operation depends upon the availability and reliability of plant machinery. In a large number of organization, reliability engineering and reliability management entered into the decision-making process of asset management. Pyne et al. presented the improvement of reliability of process equipment of rolling mill. The result of this research indicated that reliability management in the steel industry is beneficial if this method is applied with dedication and in quantifiable terms. Jain et al. (2014) reviewed the previous papers on the implementation practice of TPM by several manufacturing organizations. It helps in determining the best strategy for improving the SMEs competitiveness in the globalized market. The results of this research indicated that implementation of TPM improves working efficiency and productivity of employees and also improves the effectiveness of equipment.

There are also several challenges faced by the Indian manufacturing industries in the implementation of the TPM. Pathak (2015) presented the implementation of TPM to fine-tune manufacturing performance. This research also analyzed the various factors at the influence the implementation of TPM in Indian manufacturing organization. This analysis concentrates on systematic identification of barriers faced by Indian manufacturing industries to implement TPM practices. The implementation of TPM in manufacturing industry enhance the organization competitiveness, performance, provide better utilization of resources and improve plant profitability.

Maintenance is a support function for every business. It is not a top priority of all the manufacturing industry to manage the performance of their equipment. Several inadequacies of the maintenance practices adversely affected the competitiveness of the organization. Some of the challenges of manufacturing organization foster high availability, reliability, maintainability and availability of the manufacturing systems. Ahuja and Khamba (2007) provided an assessment of maintenance management initiatives in the Indian manufacturing industry. This research proposed prevalent maintenance practices in the manufacturing industry for the development and sustainable growth of the industrial sector. From the past few years, some leading Indian manufacturing companies are taking the proactive initiative to improve the effectiveness of the manufacturing function.

Today several management practices and innovative techniques like TQM, TPM, materials requirement planning (MRP), business process reengineering (BPR), just in time (JIT), and enterprise resource planning (ERP) are becoming more popular. Sharma et al. (2006) presented an analysis of manufacturing excellence by implementing TPM process. The maintenance practices decrease sporadic failures in semi-automated cells and operational and maintenance costs. The results of this research indicated that implementation of TPM increases effectiveness and efficiency of manufacturing systems by minimizing the wastages.

Maintenance is an important method to increase the dependability of the system. Repairs, timely inspections and renewals of a system increase the availability, reliability and lifetime of a system. The good maintenance strategy makes the balance between the given factors and incurs the costs and planned downtime. This research modelled eI-joint as a fault maintenance tree with maintenance aspects. This research shows the way in which complex CBM concept modelled by FMT. It also analyzed the KPI such as a number of failures, system reliability and costs. The results of this research indicated that current maintenance policy is cost-optimal, minimized the cost of failures and increase joint reliability.

RCM is used to develop various maintenance strategies which provide an acceptable level of reliability in a cost-effective method. The RCM technique is used to analyze the potential failures and functions of a transmission component on preserving reliability. A maintenance strategy is an important part of deregulated power industry for transmission systems of ageing components. This strategy helps in providing significant cost savings by taking optimizing maintenance decisions for the power system operations. Heo et al. (2014) implemented the RCM for the transmission components with the help particle swarm optimization. The proposed model was applicable for the transmission components whose degradation is classified on the basis of the severity of the ageing. The result indicated that the maintenance strategy which was based on RCM model was cost effective as compared to CBM and TBM.

RCM is used to enhance the TPM implementation. Ben-Daya (2000) presented the nature of RCM and TPM. The result indicated that an effective PM programme is necessary for the effectiveness of the equipment management. Maintenance system has a crucial role in attaining the organizational objectives and goals. Zhang and Chu (2010) described that maintenance helps in improving the quality, minimizing equipment downtime and increasing productivity. Selection of appropriate maintenance policy is essential for the maintenance management.

Throughout the years, maintenance function mechanization and automation have increased the capital employed and decreased the number of production personnel in civil structures and production equipment. Garg and Deshmukh (2006) reviewed and analyzed the literature on maintenance management. This research determined the various issues in maintenance management include several maintenance techniques, optimization models, information systems and scheduling. Bertling et al. (2005) proposed the reliability-centred asset maintenance method for assessing the impact of maintenance on the power distribution systems. This research is comparing the effect of various maintenance strategies based on cost and system reliability. The proposed method related the reliability theory with the experience that is gained from practical as well as statistical knowledge of maintenance measures and component failures. The result indicated that systematic quantitative approach is appropriate for investing the effect of various maintenance strategies.

Well-designed equipment and the plant will not remain reliable and safe if they are not maintained properly. The aim of the maintenance process is to sue the knowledge of accidents and failures in order to achieve possible safety at lowest possible cost. Arunraj and Maiti (2007) presented applications and techniques for risk-based maintenance. This research determined and analyzed various factors that affect the quality of risk analysis. The result of this research indicated that there is not any unique method to perform risk-based maintenance and risk analysis.

Carnero (2006) proposed an evaluation system for setting predictive maintenance programmes. Predictive maintenance helps in increasing the quality, safety and availability of industrial plants. The evaluation system helps in taking the decision to the feasibility of setting up predictive maintenance programmes. This research uses the combination of various tools like Bayesian tools, decision rules and Analytic Hierarchy Process. The result indicated that the proposed method helps in avoiding the failure of programmes.

3.2.1 Maintenance Types

Maintenance is classified into two main categories, which are as follows:

Preventive Maintenance (PM) is intended to reduce the probability of failure or degradation of functioning of an item and is carried out at predetermined intervals or according to a prescribed condition.

Corrective maintenance (CM), similar to repair work, is undertaken after a breakdown when obvious failure has been allocated. Figure 3.1 represents an overview of maintenance types and their relations.

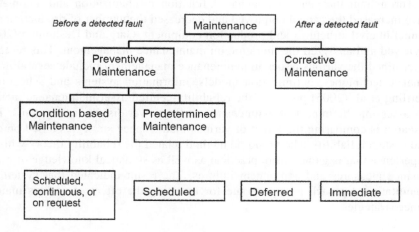

FIGURE 3.1   Maintenance types.

3.2.2 Maintenance Performance and Measurement

Maintenance Performance and Measurement (MPM) is the multidisciplinary process of measuring and justifying the value created by maintenance investment and taking care of the organizations stockholders requirements viewed strategically from the overall business perspective. The prominence of MPM is as follows.

1. Allow companies to understand the value created by maintenance.
2. Re-evaluate and revise maintenance policies and techniques.
3. Justify investment in new trends and techniques.
4. Revise resource allocations and to understand the effects of maintenance on their functions and stakeholders as well as on health and safety.

Different categories of maintenance performance measures/indicators are identified in literature. The commonly used measures of maintenance performance are classified into three categories which are: (1) measures of equipment; (2) measures of cost; and (3) measures of process performance. The commonly-used maintenance performance indicators are maintenance process indicators, which are defined as leading indicators and maintenance results indicators defined as lagging indicators.

Leading indicators measures performance before a possible problem/failure arise, whereas lagging indicators indicates a problem. Reliability is measured by Mean Time Between Failure (MTBF), Maintainability by Mean Time to Repair (MTTR) and Maintenance Supportability by Mean Waiting Time (MWT).

Maintenance management must align with the business activities. Maintenance planning is done at three levels, strategic, tactical and operational levels. An increase in the amount of information available, and an increasing requirement to have this information on hand and real-time decision-making indicates the need to have CMMS to aid maintenance management.

3.2.3 Computerized Maintenance Management System (CMMS)

CMMS are well-adopted in Industries in India. This may render many benefits, including increased productivity, reduced costs and effective utilization of assets in manufacturing and service producers.

A CMMS, also known as Enterprise Asset Management (EAM) software, is designed to help schedule, plan, manage and track maintenance activities associated with equipment, vehicles or facilities. A CMMS solution provides a central storage location for the majority of maintenance data and information for assets, manages and controls your work and materials management/parts usage processes, and tracks maintenance activity over the lifecycle of an asset. All maintenance activities can be monitored and analyzed through robust CMMS reporting and dashboard tools.

In today's fast-paced business environment, an effective CMMS solution is vital for ensuring maintenance management success and driving operational excellence. By implementing a CMMS, organizations are empowered to:

a. Improve work completion rates.
b. Reduce maintenance costs.

c. Increase worker productivity and the life of assets.
d. Create a paperless environment.
e. Make data-driven decisions.
f. Improve customer satisfaction.

CMMS systems can be delivered as a web-based, Software-as-a-Service (SaaS) model, or as an on-premises model. SaaS models have proven to provide a lower Total Cost of Ownership (TCO) and higher ROI. Most modern CMMS solutions are accessible via mobile devices and tablets.

A CMMS is for any organization that is constantly working on reactive maintenance and unable to do PM, frustrated with tracking and managing spare parts inventory, having difficulty with providing documentation for regulatory compliance, or wasting time on costly manual processes for tracking maintenance.

Organizations across all industries can utilize a CMMS system. For manufacturers, a CMMS is used to manage maintenance for equipment and critical assets; for facilities managers, to manage maintenance for buildings and facilities; for service providers, to manage maintenance for clients, staff, tenants and students; and for fleet operators, to management maintenance for vehicles and fleet equipment.

CMMS systems automate most of the logistical functions performed by maintenance staff and management. CMMS systems come with many options and have many advantages over manual maintenance tracking systems. Depending on the complexity of the system chosen, typical CMMS functions may include the following:

a. Work order generation, prioritization, and tracking by equipment/component.
b. Tracking of scheduled and unscheduled maintenance activities.
c. Storing of maintenance procedures as well as all warranty information by component and all technical documentation or procedures.
d. Capital and labour cost tracking by component as well as shortest, median and longest times to close a work order by component.
e. PDA interface to streamline input and work order generation.
f. Outside service call/dispatch capabilities.
g. Real-time reports of ongoing work activity.

Many CMMS programs can now interface with existing Energy Management and Control Systems (EMCS) as well as property management systems. Coupling these capabilities allows for condition-based monitoring and component energy use profiles.

One of the greatest benefits of the CMMS is the elimination of paperwork and manual tracking activities, thus enabling the building staff to become more productive. It should be noted that the functionality of a CMMS lies in its ability to collect and store information in an easily retrievable format. A CMMS does not make decisions, rather it provides the O&M manager with the best information to affect the operational efficiency of a facility.

CMMS can provide the following benefits:

1. Support condition-based monitoring.
2. Track the movements of spare parts.

3. Allow workers to report faults faster.
4. Improve communications between operations and maintenance personnel.
5. Provide maintenance managers with information to have better control of their departments.

They are management information systems that utilize the technologies of computers, telecommunications, etc. to execute the maintenance management processes and provide management with information for decisions making process. Like any other computerized information system, it is made up of the following:

a. Hardware
b. Software
c. Data bases
d. Peripheral equipment
e. Train staff members

We need to acknowledge at the outset that CMMS are not for every organization and that current research shows that as much as 50% of all CMMS start-ups have failed to pay back a meaningful ROI after two years of operations. That is to say, in many cases, the heavy investment in CMMS information technologies have failed to live up to the much-publicized benefits of automation and have delivered some disappointed results. So we do not want to give the impression that CMMS in themselves will cure all the ills of the profession and to advice against walking into the same technology trap that are endemic to the business community at large.

In a rush to automate every job function that affects organizational efficiency and bottom-line profits, many managers are overlooking important caveats inherent in all IT implementations. This highlights the point that an organization needs to know how to find the right CMMS and how to implement and maintain the system. The decreasing costs of computer hardware, and the emerging power of microcomputers and software technologies, have disguised the question of feasibility.

The Systematic Approach to Computerized Maintenance Management is a practical strategy for designing, developing and implementing a complete CMMS. This comprehensive approach is comprised of two proven implementation methodologies:

1. The System Approach to Maintenance Management (SAMM).
2. The CMMS lifecycle.

These concepts have proven through practical applications in various maintenance environment, to be valuable aids to guide companies through the design and implementation of benefits-producing computerized maintenance management systems.

At the core of both the SAMM and CMMS implementation lifecycle is the concept of developing a complete system. The SAMM model is used to establish the relationship between the individual elements that comprises the complete maintenance management system. The CMMS Implementation lifecycle lay out the process or series of activities to design, develop, implement and effectively use the system.

a. The SAMM Model

The SAMM reference model was created for two purposes. Its primary use is to guide the design and implementation of new maintenance management system. Albeit it is equally valuable when used as a diagnostic tool to evaluate ineffective, existing, computer assisted maintenance operations. Its simplicity has made it a valuable educational aid to help facility manager and maintenance industry professional identify and understand the vital elements of a complete information management system.

The SAMM reference model is centred around the holistic concept of the system. It is based on the relationship between people, process and technology. Fundamental to this model is the concept of workflow. By definition, workflow applications automate business process that involve people working together and sharing information to accomplish a predefined set of tasks. A computerized maintenance management software program is a workflow application. Therefore, the application of this technology into a maintenance department must include all elements of the system to become an effective tool for management. The five elements of the SAMM model are the Management Plan, System Resources, IT, Data Medium and Work Methodology.

b. The CMMS Implementation Lifecycle

The CMMS Implementation lifecycle is the related activities required to design, develop, install and improve a complete computerized maintenance system. The CMMS Implementation lifecycle is organized into three sequential phases: Need Analysis, System Design and System Installation.

The CMMS Implementation lifecycle has these characteristics:

1. It is a fully integrated process for implementing new information management technologies into the maintenance operation of business and organizations.
2. It is a sequence of action steps presented in a natural and logical order.
3. It is a process which recycles existing maintenance management practices into new more efficient way of conducting business.
4. The central focus of the lifecycle is the SAMM model – the end product to be achieved from carrying out the implementation process.

Computerized Maintenance Management Information System (CMMIS) is simply the application of computers for quickly and efficiently deciding, planning and organizing various jobs for effective plant maintenance. Maintenance is a grouping of mechanical, organizational, and management activities throughout the lifecycle of equipment proposed to keep it or to give back it to a state in which it can perform the vital function (Azadeh et al., 2016). The challenge of maintenance is to ensure that the equipment operates at peak efficiency while serving the load with minimal downtime (Aljumaili et al., 2012).

In the past, maintenance has been treated as an expenditure explanation in which performance measures are developed to track the cost, such as the headcount of maintenance personnel and the total duration of force outages during a specified period (Travis and Casinger 1997). Today, maintenance is acknowledged as a pivotal player in the performance and profitability of business organizations (Mostafa et al., 2015) because BM works are both cost-intensive and time-consuming (Dey et al., 2004). Conducting maintenance for an oil and gas (OandG) engineering facility is crucial to ensure high availability of production equipment at a reasonably low cost (Garg and Deshmukh, 2006).

According to Dey et al. (2004), the archetypal maintenance problems were due to corrosion, external influence, construction and material defects and human errors. In light of this, a paradigm shift from reactive maintenance to preventive and predictive maintenance is crucial for RCM (Tousley, 2010) to optimize operations and sustaining the availability of plants (Madu, 2000). O&G engineering plays a critical role in driving the global economy, and petroleum is used for numerous products serving as the world's primary fuel resource (Sivalingam 1997; Berntsen et al., 2018). The processes and systems involved in producing and distributing O&G are highly complex and capital-intensive requiring state-of-the-art technology (Hamraz and Clarkson, 2015). O&G is produced from an upstream facility located offshore built from expensive equipment (Antonakakis et al., 2018).

An oil platform, offshore platform or colloquially oil rig is a large structure with facilities to drill, to extract, and to process oil and natural gas, or to temporarily store product until it can be brought to the shore for refining and marketing. Offshore platforms in remote locations have a set of operating requirements in their harsh environments subject to numerous constraints that limit the execution and progression of maintenance activities planned. Platform equipment and process failures have a significant impact on production output (Berntsen et al., 2018).

The documentation of equipment breakdowns to expenses used can be an overwhelming task without the use of computer applications. The effective planning of technicians and available spares is a dynamic activity (Labib, 1998). These challenges have engendered maintenance managers to adopt tools, methods, and concepts that would provide accurate and timely information for more productive maintenance function and reduce unscheduled equipment downtime (Dey et al., 2004; Tousley 2010).

To provide effective maintenance services, the use of a CMMS can simplify maintenance management, which encompasses asset management, WO management, PM management, inventory control, and report management (Lopes et al., 2016). Today, a CMMS has increasingly been used to manage plants and equipment maintenance in modern industries due to the complexity in maintenance management now considered as a critical element for the improvement of operation and safety, increase of availability, life span enhancement and cost reduction. A CMMS consists of tools for maintenance administration incorporating an open base of information and allows users to programme and to follow the maintenance activities proceeded from the services and maintenance policies. This is consistent with Bacchetti and Saccani (2012), who claimed the need for an integrated knowledge accumulation process for better demand forecasting and inventory management. As such, CMMS infrastructure supports an e-maintenance function to facilitate informed maintenance decisions.

Notwithstanding the various commercial CMMS packages in the market, most are not a perfect match to the peculiarities of each company, which requires further customization to the specific needs of a company (Lopes et al., 2016). Thus, the issues of functionality and user interfaces significantly affect the setup of a CMMS. According to Wienker et al. (2016), only 6–15% of users exploit CMMSs to their full capability in general facility maintenance. In light of this, the current CMMS implementation fails to generate the ROI, and the maintenance software implementation failure rates are as high as 70%. Thus, it is essential for each maintenance department to carefully manage asset-maintenance-related data embedded into software (Carnero and Noves, 2006). The solution for releasing the constraint is to change the way the firm conducts its business by addressing the issues of business model management and its relationship to the theory of constraints (TOC) (Spector, 2011).

Given this, maintenance managers should focus on the few constraints that prevent the CMMS from attaining its intended purpose. Travis and Casinger (1997) outlined the constraints associated with the modern maintenance management to include little or no support from management to implement world-class maintenance practices, and inventory problems, such as the need to reduce spares and still have parts on hand. Accurate information is crucial for maintenance management when making informed decisions related to equipment performance and costs as well as ensuring the reliable operation of equipment. To exploit the potentials of CMMS, this study aims to develop a constraint-free framework and a causal loop diagram (CLD) for a CMMS to improve the conventional maintenance operation system in OandG engineering and to achieve maintenance management success.

Maintenance management has flourished as a science along the time but its impact on decision making within organizations is limited so far. Specialized literature on maintenance models was reviewed, considering a large number of papers published in the main databases that publish research related to maintenance function in the period of 2000 to 2017. The information recovered about the of maintenance management models will permit practitioners to reconsider the way to manage the maintenance function, especially in the manufacturing industry.

Finally, improvement of the performance of the maintenance facilities leads to reduced cost and resource efficiency gains by increasing the quality and reliability of services. Therefore, designing a maintenance model that integrates maintenance management, risk management, is the new challenge that mechanical engineers must face nowadays. Maintenance progress allows distinguishing several evolutionary generations, in relation to the different objectives of the productive or service areas over time. Figure 3.2 shows maintenance evolution and the productive or services area, taking into account the approach and its main objective according to its historical context. Let us carry out a brief analysis of each stage.

The priority of the production or service areas in Stage I is the product while the maintenance area focuses on repair of unforeseen events. In this stage, it appears the primary elements required to maintain the assets are elements such as work orders, general tools, spare parts and a maintenance warehouse. It also shows the first information that is later constituted in the databases and then in information systems; then the techniques and technologies of the company in particular are developed; in general, it establishes the requirement for managing the maintenance function.

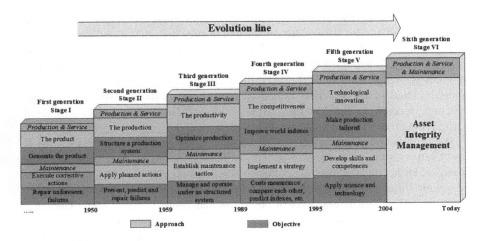

FIGURE 3.2 Approach and objectives of the maintenance and productive areas over the time.

The goal of Stage II is to solve sudden stops, so the maintenance department begins to develop actions of prevention or prediction of failures. In this stage, techniques and technologies specific to prevention and prediction are implemented, such as: maintenance routines, preventive plans, technical measurements, state condition assessment, non-destructive tests, among others; creating in this way the asset's operational control.

Once the companies have reached maturity in the real and conceptual management of maintenance actions, they begin to adopt a structure for a sequential, logical and organized development in order to gestate and operate maintenance under an organized system or maintenance tactic. In Stage III the maintenance tactics are implemented, among them: TPM, RCM, TQM, Evidence-based asset management (EBAM), Time-based maintenance (TBM), CMMS, etc., in sequential and historical order (Modgil and Sharma, 2016; Pramod, Devadasan, Muthu, Jagathyraj, and Dhakshina, 2006; Chen, Maiti, and Agapiou, 2017; Jonge, RuudTeunter, and TiedoTinga, 2017).

Stage IV is reached when companies have adequately developed the previous levels. In this stage, companies are interested in measuring results and knowing how well they do their work, which is why they begin to establish their own maintenance systems such as lifecycle cost analysis (LCC). It is characteristic of this stage that the measurement systems implemented are under international parameters, to compare themselves with similar or different companies to establish the level of success reached, in general, they try to control all the executed actions (Macchi, Márquez, Holgado, Fumagalli, and Martínez, 2009; Sabri, Sulaiman, Ahmad, and Tang, 2015; Goyal, Pabla, Dhami, and Lachhwani, 2017; Pui, Bhandari, Arzaghi, Abbassi, and VikramGaraniya, 2017).

Stage V is characterized by the development of skills and competence in all maintenance staff; it is also dependent on all of the previous stages. At this level the FMECA (Failure Modes, Effects and Criticality Analysis), RCFA (Root Cause Failure Analysis), and RPN (Risk priority number) strategies are consolidated. The company is strengthened and develops skills and competence in whole or some of the topics initiated in the previous stages (Espinosa and Salinas, 2010; Chemweno, Pintelon, Horenbeek, and Muchiri, 2015; Sellappan, Nagarajan, and Palanikumar, 2015; Selim, Yunusoglu, and Balaman, 2016).

The difference between assets and liabilities is that conceptually the first one is associated with the production of wealth, while the second refers to investment or expenses. Under this premise, maintenance is influenced in terms of how to visualize the assets' use. The evolution towards the sixth generation "Assets Integrity Management", has different ways of being reached (Murthy et al., 2002; Dunning, 2006; Palencia, 2007; Kilsby et al., 2017). It focuses on obtaining lower costs, lower labour requirements, reduce the planned repair and maintenance times (increased in operational time), as well as eliminating or reducing the logistics time required for maintenance and/or production.

3.2.4 MAINTENANCE STRATEGIES

Maintenance strategies can be defined as the business approach which is aimed at keeping the business stagnant in the market by maintaining a good position. The maintenance strategies help in securing the brand value and market of the product for the organization. The maintenance strategies are generally applied in markets with the low share which has organizations with limited investments (Waeyenbergh and Pintelon, 2002). The maintenance strategies are applied during the lifetime of a product, from its launch to decline.

3.2.4.1 Applications of Maintenance Strategies

a. The initial phase of a product or early maturity: The organization in the early maturity stage of launching product in marketing applies the maintenance strategies to increase the slowed sales of the product. To bring a stability and avoid declination in the sales, the maintenance strategies such as marketing mix are employed.

b. Habituation of product: When the market which is the target of the product developer, the maintenance strategies are applied to maintain the same position in the market and to continue the current trends to ensure maximum sales. This phase requires the continuous processing of the product along with the analysis of quality, maintain the distribution and positive marketing efforts. Thus, an effective maintenance strategy is adapted to work on all these three processes.

c. The product decline phase: The maintenance strategies are used during this stage to bring the product on lead or make it survive till the decline is assured. The maintenance strategy is adopted by the market-leading brands at the last phase of product lifecycle. This phase requires any changes in the products, the change in prices to ensure the sales and most importantly increased expenses on the advertisement of products. Thus, to retain sales and product position in the market along with customer retention are done using the maintenance strategies.

3.2.4.2 Types of Maintenance Strategies

There are mainly four types of maintenance strategies which are applied in the industry to develop the market situation of the product. Moreover, the maintenance strategies are helpful in working over the product developing operations, establishing the product in the market, distribution of the product in the market, and maintain the position of the product into the market till its decline (Dekker, 1996). The four types of maintenance strategies can be explained as:

Run-to-failure

The run-to-failure strategy is used for the maintenance of the equipment which is not of much use. This equipment may also include those devices which are having low cost and are not essential for product development. This approach works on repair of the equipment by repairing of the parts or by their replacement. The approach works on reducing the cost until the replacement of the entire equipment is much affordable to the repair or the equipment fails completely. This is also known as BM strategy.

Scheduled approach maintenance

The scheduled approach maintenance which is also recognized as PM approach is applied to prevent any failure in equipment. This strategy is implemented from time-to-time inspection and repair of the equipment which are prone to failure on the basis of exposure to operational use. The strategy involves repairs and inspection to be done at fixed intervals. This strategy may prove out to be much costly in the long run as there are chances that money invested on inspection may found to be of no worth. This strategy can be helpful in enhancing the effectiveness of the products and the equipment, but it must only be applied with efficient scheduling.

Predictive approach maintenance

It is a part of asset management process which works on the basis of conditions of use. This approach works by developing the predictions related the equipment failure. The approach does not count the effective lifespan of the equipment rather it works on the assumptions related to the failure of an asset. This approach works by a visual approach for inspection, but it can also be done with the help of meters which can measure the total time period of functioning (Fischer et al., 2012). This approach seems to be much similar to the preventive approach, but it is more stable as it reduces the cost related to inspection and maintenance. Moreover, the time which is required for the system maintenance is decreased with the location of potential issues and predicting failures.

RCM approach

RCM approach is a much broader concept which is not limited to the failure of the equipment. It is a very advanced approach, which takes into consideration of all the possible failure which can occur in a system. The RCM approach has a customized strategy to tackle the failure of every different set of equipment. RCM is a sophisticated approach which works after achieving the expertise in all three above defined approaches.

3.2.5 Reliability-centred Maintenance (RCM)

RCM is based on the concept of developing a customized setting in which all the possible failure modes can be countered. The strategy runs on the approach to find the best solution to the system failure by working on the type of failure in the individual machine. RCM is an overall best maintenance strategy which can be run throughout the product lifecycle in order to ensure product development. It can work very effectively on the product development and establishment in the market (Wikstrom et al., 2000). Any hurdles to the product sales can be managed by using an effective maintenance plan.

3.2.5.1 Principles of RCM

The basic approach of implementing the RCM is to enhance the overall reliability of the system by developing an overall maintenance schedule of the system rather than focusing on an individual function.

Some of the general principles of this approach are:

1. Function orientation: The RCM approach is based on the overall functional maintenance rather than working alone on the operational competence of the system.
2. Focused: The approach is very focused to maintain the function not just a single component which comprises the system.
3. Reliable: The approach holds the account for the age of operation for the equipment and the failures experienced by it. In short, it is concerned with the failures which can occur with age rather than calculating the failure rate for maintenance.
4. Design analysis: The RCM approach works by analyzing the design of the system. It acknowledges the change in reliability to be a matter of design issues instead of any need for the maintenance. The approach goes through the feedback process which is a good tool to make any improved changes in design and maintain the system (Wikstrom et al., 2000).
5. The criteria: The RCM approach has greater priority to the safety criteria for the maintenance of the system. But overall, it is very much concerned with the economics of the system maintenance as well. It works through both the economics and safety of the maintenance of the asset.
6. The unsatisfactory functions: The RCM approach model takes failure as an unsatisfactory function. The loss made to the functioning, or the quality are both considered as inappropriate to the system function. The RCM approach counts for the failure which leads to degradation of quality and reduction in the capability of operating.

7. The effectiveness: The RCM approach tries to reduce the probability or the chances of the failure in equipment by working over the cost related to maintenance at the same time.

8. The acceptance: The RCM approach also has consideration for the approaches related to the maintenance strategies. For example, RCM has special consideration to run-to-failure or the prevention approach as it assesses the requirement for any intervention operation to work on the maintenance.

9. The living system: The RCM approach works on the data which is accumulated over the years. The collected data or the history related to the function and equipment is analyzed in RCM to make any changes in the design that can add to the productiveness of the system. It is a proactive maintenance programme, and the feedback and history of the system form an important part of the RCM approach implementation (Wikstrom et al., 2000).

3.2.5.2 Role of RCM in Improving the Manufacturing Performance

The RCM approach is a powerful technique which can be used in developing the manufacturing performance in the industry. Even though the initial cost related to the implementation of RCM model in the industry is high, but the results are very effective in long run. The approach can be helpful in developing the better system which yields greater productivity with fewer faults (Mkandawire et al., 2015). The overall quality of the system, its functions and the product development are all increased with the reliability enhancement.

The research made on the approach from time to time has given certain results which can be explained as:

a. The efficiency carried by the maintenance programme based on RCM approach is very high, and it is the most effective of all (Vintr and Valis, 2006).

b. The implementation of RCM approach has resulted in decreasing the overall cost of production and maintenance as it works on cutting down the unwanted cost related to inspection, maintenance, repair and overhauls of the system (Vintr and Valis, 2006).

c. The RCM in Indian industry has shown impressive performance as the total number of cases of failures in equipment are decreased with its introduction.

d. The probability of the failure is also reduced with the use of RCM approach as a maintenance strategy in the industry.

e. The RCM approach works on the main or the most significant components of the programme. It identifies the possibility of the faults which can occur in them so that they can be prevented and controlled. It is an approach which works on the critical components of the system (Vintr and Valis, 2006).

f. The introduction of RCM has resulted into an increment in the reliability of every component of the programme which is necessary to continue the production and maintain the market position of shares.

The RCM approach in the industry works on the analysis of root cause or the major reason which is responsible for the failure. This helps in saving the expenses made on the inspection of the entire system as the faulty components are located by RCM with best predictions.

3.2.6 Computer-Aided Facility Management (CAFM)

Computer-aided facilities management (CAFM) refers to the use of IT to effectively manage physical facilities in various ways. This can include long-range facilities management reporting, as well as more direct systems that actively manage aspects of facilities, such as lighting or heating and air conditioning equipment.

Common features of CAFM tools include systems that give information on floor plans and descriptions of the physical space, as well as reporting on energy consumption. These sorts of tools can also provide helpful equipment locations for a facility holding valuable or extensive business assets, such as machinery or hardware. CAFM tools can use extensive databases and visual modelling tools, along with geographic information systems or services, to give leaders and managers a bird's eye view of a particular facility or building.

In addition to providing these sorts of physical tools, computer aided facilities management systems can be part of long-term planning and auditing resources. For example, planners might use these sorts of tools to evaluate the depreciation of a facility or for other tax purposes. A wide range of CAFM solutions has become extremely valuable to those who are tasked with efficiently managing the physical locations of a business or other entity.

3.2.7 New Generation Strategic Asset Management (eXSAM)

Enterprise asset management (EAM) is the optimal lifecycle management of the physical assets of an organization. It covers subjects including the design, construction, commissioning, operations, maintenance and decommissioning or replacement of plant, equipment and facilities. "Enterprise" refers to the scope of the assets across departments, locations, facilities and, potentially, business units.

EAM is a broad term vendors use to describe software that provides managers with a way to view company-owned assets holistically. The goal is to enable managers to control and proactively optimize operations for quality and efficiency. In earlier years, EAM was simply called maintenance scheduling software. EAMs facilitate operations by automating requests for upgrades, regular maintenance and decommissioning or replacement.

eXSAM is a comprehensive strategic asset management solution which gives companies of all natures and size the power to manage, monitor and control all of their assets and their unique attributes with one solution. eXSAM streamlines and optimizes the management of all asset types, from complex mission critical equipment, movable equipment, facilities and plants, to people, livestock, entire mines, vehicles, IT assets, contracts and fixed machinery. With eXSAM, there's no need to deploy and manage different solutions to manage assets with unique attributes. Regardless of what a business's priorities are, or their asset mix, PwC Technology eXSAM keeps it together.

3.3 CONDITION-BASED MAINTENANCE AND RESIDUAL LIFE PREDICTION

Condition based maintenance (CBM) is a maintenance strategy that monitors the actual condition of the asset to decide what maintenance needs to be done. CBM dictates that maintenance should only be performed when certain indicators show signs of decreasing performance or upcoming failure. Checking a machine for these indicators may include non-invasive measurements, visual inspection, performance data and scheduled tests. Condition data can then be gathered at certain intervals, or continuously (as is done when a machine has internal sensors). CBM can be applied to mission critical and non-mission critical assets.

Unlike in planned scheduled maintenance (PM), where maintenance is performed based upon predefined scheduled intervals, CBM is performed only after a decrease in the condition of the equipment has been observed. Compared with PM, this increases the time between maintenance repairs, because maintenance is done on an as-needed basis.

The goal of CBM is to spot upcoming equipment failure so maintenance can be proactively scheduled when it is needed – and not before. Asset conditions need to trigger maintenance within a long enough time period before failure, so work can be finished before the asset fails or performance falls below the optimal level.

3.3.1 ADVANTAGES

- CBM is performed while the asset is working, this lowers disruptions to normal operations.
- Reduces the cost of asset failures.
- Improves equipment reliability.
- Minimizes unscheduled downtime due to catastrophic failure.
- Minimizes time spent on maintenance.
- Minimizes overtime costs by scheduling the activities.
- Minimizes requirement for emergency spare parts.
- Optimized maintenance intervals (more optimal than manufacturer recommendations).
- Improves worker safety.
- Reduces the chances of collateral damage to the system.

3.3.2 DISADVANTAGES

- Condition monitoring test equipment is expensive to install, and databases cost money to analyze.
- Cost to train staff – you need a knowledgeable professional to analyze the data and perform the work.
- Fatigue or uniform wear failures are not easily detected with CBM measurements.
- Condition sensors may not survive in the operating environment.

- May require asset modifications to retrofit the system with sensors.
- Unpredictable maintenance periods.

3.3.3 EXAMPLE OF CONDITION-BASED MAINTENANCE

Motor vehicles come with a manufacturer-recommended interval for oil replacements. These intervals are based on manufacturers' analysis, years of performance data and experience. However, this interval is based on an average or best guess rather than the actual condition of the oil in any specific vehicle. The idea behind CBM is to replace the oil only when a replacement is needed, and not on a predetermined schedule.

In the example of industrial equipment, oil analysis can perform an additional function too. By looking at the type, size and shape of the metal particulates that are suspended in the oil, the health of the equipment it is lubricating can also be determined.

CBM = Cost Savings + Higher system reliability.

CBM allows preventive and corrective actions to be scheduled at the optimal time, thus reducing the TCO. Today, improvements in technology are making it easier to gather, store and analyze data for CBM. In particular, CBM is highly effective where safety and reliability is the paramount concern including the aircraft industry, semiconductor manufacturing, nuclear, and oil and gas.

CBM that arises when needed. This is performed when one of the indicators show deterioration. This is applicable for critical systems that include fault reporting and active redundancy. It is a maintenance strategy that decides the sort of maintenance required. CBM commands that maintenance should be performed when some indicators show signs of upcoming failure or reducing performance. It is the process that predicts the present and future conditions of the machinery when in operation. It gathers information about internal effects of the operating machine. Types of CBM are:

i. Vibration Analysis
    Vibrations are always produced by machines even though they are in good conditions, this is due to periodic events in the machine's operation, such as rotating shafts, meshing gear teeth, rotating electric fields, and so on. The frequency of occurrence of such events often gives a direct indication of the source and thus many powerful diagnostic techniques are based on frequency analysis.
ii. Oil Analysis
    This can be divided in to three categories:
    a. Spectrographic Oil Analysis Procedures (SOAP)
    b. Chip detectors
    c. Ferrography
iii. Performance Analysis
    With different machines, performance analysis is a way of determining the correct functioning of machine. As in gas turbine engines, there are many permanently mounted transducers for various process parameters like flow rates, temperatures and pressures and calculating various efficiencies and comparing

them with normal condition it is called flow path analyses. Modern IC engine control systems, such as for diesel locos, electronic injection control is the fuel supplied to a particular cylinder and when cut off it results in dropped power compared with the theoretical.

iv. Thermography

Thermograph is used in quasi-static situations, such as with electrical switchboards, for detection of local hot spots and faulty refractory linings in hot fluids containers.

v. Infrared – IR cameras can be used to detect high temperature conditions in energized equipment.

vi. Ultrasonic – detection of deep subsurface defects such as boat hull corrosion.

vii. Acoustic – used to detect gas, liquid or vacuum leaks.

viii. Electrical – motor current readings using clamp on ammeters.

ix. Operational performance – sensors throughout a system to measure pressure, temperature, flow etc.

Data can be collected from the system by two different methods:

- Spot readings can be performed at regular intervals using portable instruments.
- Sensors can be retrofitted to equipment or installed during manufacture for continuous data collection.

Critical systems that require considerable upfront capital investment, or that could affect the quality of the product that is produced, need up to the minute data collection. More expensive systems have built in intelligence to self-monitor in real time. For example, sensors throughout an aircraft monitor numerous systems while inflight and on the ground, to help identify issues before they become life threatening. Typically, CBM is not used for non-critical systems and spot readings suffice.

Challenges of CBM

- CBM requires an investment in measuring equipment and staff up-skilling so the initial costs of implementation can be high.
- CBM introduces new techniques to do maintenance, which can be difficult to implement due to resistance within an organization.
- Older equipment can be difficult to retrofit with sensors and monitoring equipment, or can be difficult to access during production to spot measure.

With CBM in place, it still requires competence to turn performance information from a system into actionable proactive maintenance items.

4 Competency and Performance of Manufacturing Industry

4.1 COMPETENCY

Manufacturing competency is a situation for improved competitiveness. More experienced and trained individuals will perform than lesser ones. Also, learning increases reliability and produces fewer surprises. Competencies are broadly classified as organizational level and employee level. Competence is a quality of both people and organizations. Technological competencies are multi-field, highly stable and differentiated. The manufacturing function is a formidable weapon for organizations for achieving competitive superiority.

The constituents of competencies – that is, technological, marketing and integrative competencies – influence company performance. Manufacturing competencies plays an important role in a company's strategic success in order to enable companies improved its competitiveness of manufacturing companies. Competitive strategy affects quality and firm performance.

Quality and business excellence awards are driving forces in improving the competency of Indian firms in the global market. Small and medium enterprises are considered to be an engine for economic growth all over the world.

Hollenbeck et al. argued regarding assumptions for competency models and counters with an investigation of the benefits of leadership competency models for organizations and individuals. Competency model is a more comprehensive model of effectiveness.

In today's competitive world, it is hard for firms to retain sources to respond to new services and new product offerings, such as reducing development time even if, there is rise in development cost. As competition intensifies, it is important that firms reinforce and protect their sources of competitive advantage and try to compensate for organizational weaknesses.

4.1.1 COMPETENCY DEVELOPMENT

Drejer formulated a framework for competency development in accordance with management in firms. The model was followed by some considerations about practicing competency development in management. Understanding of model as a stable entity and using it as basis for dynamic development are the areas to focus on.

In present times, companies are facing rapid evolution in integrating new technologies, competitive environment, and respect for new environmental and safety regulations. Companies must produce distinctive competencies so as to maintain

DOI: 10.1201/9781003189510-4

competitive advantage. Technology acquisition and integration must be strengthened so as to improve the capability of suppliers in order to receive integrated electronic and mechanical components.

To be more competitive, organizations need to develop competencies in a strategic way, and thus develop a strategic architecture for the same. For competence development, a framework, along with competence model, has been presented to form and improve strategies. Traditional ways tend to take a lot of time and are expensive. Competency development in sustainable global manufacturing creates experience by showing how specific competencies are identified and how a scenario has been developed.

Competencies, in a weak manner, capture and portray different emotions and social interactions in everyday job life. Competency frameworks have innovative insight to alternative dimensions to improve firm's performance.

In contemporary environments, organizations measure their performance against a set of predefined performance measures. These measures are governed by the ability of the organization for maintaining necessary sets of 'competencies' that assist in the successful execution of its projects. Competencies being multidimensional and subjective in nature are a lot difficult to be defined and measured. A new modelling approach considering prioritized fuzzy aggregation, factor analysis, and fuzzy neural networks has been applied for identifying the relationship between project competencies and project key performance indicators. The diverse project competencies are analyzed using factor analysis. A standardized framework and methodology for evaluating the impact of project competencies on project key performance indicators has been established.

4.1.2 Competency Management

Competency management concerns with the competency distribution and development. The architecture of the design activities aims to assist competency management through the qualitative feature of the work. For improving business performance, reliable and valid techniques are developed for measuring and managing competency. Apart from development, advancement of these measurement techniques for an end user computing capability is the need of the hour. Knowledge, the major aspect of manpower and assets, is even contained in simplest tool. In market, price is governed highly by quality than by supply and demand. Production factors and industrial processes are combined to minimize the end product cost and thus, managing competency and improving firm's performance.

Competency management, combined with strategic management, represents and evaluates core competencies in relation to the processes and products. Competency management along with the "value creating network concept" and the diffusion of matrix-based tools helps in managing the interdependencies between the project domains: organization, process and product. Competency management experts have underlined the responsibility of design organizations for developing of products in order to satisfy customer requirements.

During recent years, important changes have happened in the automotive industry. With competency management, a new framework has been developed for analyzing the decision of the automakers, whether to develop a new component in-house or outsource it. Competency management has led to pass the decision about the assembler product from supplier to individual's involved.

Hong and Stahle identified various key concepts on competency and competency management. Competency management has led to an integrated and systemic view where managing system towards a self-generative and self-renewable organization is a big challenge.

Competency management and development regarded as vital tools to improve competitiveness of organizations. Competency management helps to identify opportunities and expand organizations in global market. Indian organizations follow various philosophies including 5-S, TPM and TQM, however they have not been able to make any substantial improvement in this regard. Competency management and development contributes to a larger extent for the successful implementation of these philosophies. TQM index, Competency index and 5-S index have been analyzed before and after competency-based training in organizations. Manufacturing industry can improve its competitiveness by focusing on competency management and competency-based training along with training on these philosophies. HRD interventions have an impact on building of employee competencies, thus improving organizational effectiveness. The HRD interventions undertaken in this study are training, performance management and career management. A model has been developed by combining various factors. The validity of the model is tested by applying structural equation modelling (SEM) approach.

4.1.3 CORE COMPETENCY

Prahlad and Hamel described core competencies as collective learning in a firm, especially the integration of multiple streams of technologies and coordinate diverse production skills. "In the short run, an organization's competitiveness derives from the price or performance attributes of products whereas in long run, it derives from the ability to develop, more quickly and at a lower cost than competitors". Prahlad and Hamel, described "competitor differentiation, extendibility and customer value" as conditions for core competency.

With core competency, an organization should be able to provide benefit to customers as well as expand into new markets. Also, competitors should find it hard to replicate. Core competency thinking promotes approach to mobilize and focus on an organization's resources. Technology executives and R and D should describe the core competencies of their companies as core competency thinking enables competitive advantage without disruption to business activities.

Core competency has a dynamic role in improving the potential of project teams. Core competency improves strategies: by balancing itself with the external environment and activities; by reducing path-dependency influences and carefully arranging resources, by guidance rather than control.

Core competencies affect entrepreneurial performance and business success. Core competencies develop strategies in relation to firm's performance. Core competencies enable firms to develop different perspectives in accordance with company values and strategies. Core competencies have an important role in Indian organizations in different conditions. SMEs should be as proactive in making changes such as development of competencies, awareness about market changes, upgrading of technology and human resources.

Core competencies should enhance strategic thinking in order to achieve its goal. Without the core competencies, well-stated and well-conceptualized strategies cannot be successfully realized and implemented. Core competencies are important for organizations in achieving competitive advantage. Core competencies are linked to business profitability as these are cross-culturally valid. Core competency models should focus on selection, feedback, training, and performance management.

Core competency model focuses on competency scoring, competency identification and aligning competency with strategic functions to survive in the competition. Organizations will manage their employee competencies to ensure competitive advantage and better performance. Core competencies help individuals to be able to perform on different positions throughout the organization. Various competency models are used to identify and expand the global competitiveness of organizations (Singh et al., 2013).

4.1.4 RESOURCE-BASED PERSPECTIVE

Resource based perspective is the competitive advantage that is derived from the valuable, sustainable, rare resources and capabilities for a firm. Resource-based perspective uncovers long-term effects of outsourcing. It focuses on organizational resources, for integrating the dispersed knowledge required in developing complex products.

By resource-based analysis, it is argued regarding cooperative competencies that whether they are socially complex and ambiguous or not as they result from historical conditions. Cooperative competencies are competencies relevant to knowledge transfer, communication, information processing, inter- and intra-unit coordination, negotiation and the ability to develop trusting relationships. They can complement technological competencies in dynamic and uncertain industries. Therefore, they can provide organizations with competitive advantage, which cannot be easily competed and imitated with.

Cooperative competency and process-oriented view facilitates the effects of transfer mechanisms, including adaptation and replication of knowledge transfer performance. Cooperative competencies relate to transfer mechanisms in partnering firms, thus knowledge transfer performance improves. A conceptual model shows interrelationships between cooperative competency, knowledge transfer performance and transfer mechanisms. The main focus of companies should be on innovations according to market need, as due to competition, they can be exposed to a tough challenge.

Resource based view, including core competencies, assist organizations in strategic management. Core competencies and the strategies are based on the ideas that are rare and intangible. There is lack of understanding regarding core competencies and their potential value for the company. Higher priority in manufacturing companies is given to delivery, cost and whereas flexibility is given lower priority. For accomplishing these objectives, resource-based view emphasis on shop-floor activities and favours adopting options like periodic reviews, worker training etc. Firms are reluctant in adopting approaches which require either major organizational restructuring or substantial investments.

Individual competencies, composed within self-managed teams, translate into more effectiveness for Multi-Team Systems (MTS). A wide range of self-management competencies by team members combine to influence productivity of a team network. Integration of marketing, R and D, and engineering functions along with strategic thinking and new product development time is vital for developing competitive advantage. Agility of organizations is a prerequisite for export involvement. Resource based view combines with manufacturing excellence to demonstrate best industrial practices and thus achieving competitive advantage. Frameworks have been developed for the assessment and implementation of manufacturing excellence (Sharma et al., 2008).

4.1.5 Economic Effects

The economic, social and environmental pressures contribute towards the phases of automotive lifecycle in global industry. Managing decentralized and dispersed knowledge network is the key challenge confronting Multinational Enterprises (MNEs) today. The design of architectures and economics in MNEs for harnessing individual creativity is a critical component of competitive advantage. A competency typology is a methodology for identifying competencies to aid the transition to competency-based logic from task based for human resource management. Integrating and implementing economics and the competency framework offers guidelines for competitive advantage and managerial insights.

Remanufacturing is a process in which used products are restored to useful form. Reverse logistics is a systematic process for planning, controlling and implementing distribution and manufacturing activities, such as the in-process inventory, packaging of finished goods and backward flow of raw materials to a point of proper disposal or recovery. Remanufacturing and reverse logistics affect company economic and strategic decision making. Competency framework provides the organization with better information regarding selection decisions and understanding of managerial success. Performance ratings, rather than competencies, are influenced by manager's ability to understand the business.

Due to globalization, competitive pressures and strategic responses of organizations have intensified. Financial performances and marketing outcomes are also varied by sectors. The economic realignment focuses on the internal competitive developments, strategic response to these developments, and the financial and marketing outcomes.

4.1.6 Technological Competency

Technology competencies interact with competitive environment to affect firm innovation and competitiveness. Moreover, different types of technological competencies are required during different types of competitive environment for enhancing firm's innovativeness. A technological competency is described as the ability to use technology effectively, through extensive learning and experimentation, development and employment in production. Technological competencies have emerged strongly during the twentieth century in their corresponding fields.

Geels described technological competencies as long term and major technical changes in the way satisfying customers' needs. Technological insights have three levels: socio technical landscape, socio technical regime and technological deliberation.

Technological competency and R and D focus on the creation of competencies and new knowledge and the benefits that firms can reap from collaboration. For acquisition of competencies, a perfect balance between the firm's technological development and the collaboration's strategic orientation is required. Information Technology Competency (ITC) plays a critical role in learning various competencies. In fact, learning competencies mediate the relation between ITC and Commercial Success of Innovation (CSI) as CSI is directly related to competencies.

The technological competencies are to some extent multi-field rather they become more with time and competencies grow beyond their product range. These competencies are highly differentiated and stable, with both the direction of localized search and technology profile strongly influenced by organizations' principal products. Technological competencies have the ability to improve products, and thus customer base, as they create and use technologies effectively. Competency development plays an important role in enhancing the industrial competitiveness. Risk, status, uncertainty, observability, disruptiveness, pervasiveness and centrality are technical characteristics that influence the learning modes selected by an organization. Technological competencies have an impact on organization performance and they possess all the prerequisite competencies required for a given technology-product-market paradigm as the organization enters or remains over time in market. Consequently, high-tech entrepreneurial firms must learn, acquire and develop competencies in response to the changing requirements of industry products.

4.1.7 COMPETITION

Success and survival in today's tough environment depends on competitiveness. Competitiveness is achieved through integration of efforts between various functions of organizations and use of Advanced Manufacturing Technologies (AMT). AMT has a vital role in flexibility and quality improvements in manufacturing organizations. Technology is also a competitive weapon as new products and processes with complexity and higher accuracy are introduced and changes in customer needs and expectations. AMT helps manufacturers in enhancing financial and quality performances and thus, improving competitiveness (Dangayach et al., 2006).

Survival in today's highly fragmented market requires firms to focus on factors such as adherence to standards, quality, rapid response and innovation as the basis for competitive advantage. In order to meet these demands, firms are deploying innovations including reconfiguration of their internal organization, advanced equipment and their external relationships. Competencies in innovations is the need of the hour for organizations, and most importantly, balancing the existing competencies to survive in competitive world. Organizations need to master the competencies in innovation so as to exploit the various phases of an innovation process.

The manufacturing industry plays a key role in a country's economy. Also, it adds high value to exports and generates jobs and contributes to political and social stability to achieve higher profits. Functional competencies are important to an organization's performance as they help the companies in improving their competitiveness.

The strategic Automobile Shredder Residue (ASR) recycling model helps vehicle recyclers in improving their economy as there will be a decrease in disposed ASR quantity with an increase in recycling. Due to factors, such as increases in oil prices, advances in technology and government regulation of emissions, the automobile market has entered into a period of uncertainty. The existing manufacturing industries try to develop and patent Alternative Fuel Vehicle (AFV) technologies.

4.2 STRATEGY

Strategy means deliberately selecting different sets of activities for creating a unique mix of value. Corporate strategy provides an overall plan for the firm since the production of goods is separate, from the purchase and consumption of these goods. Major emphasis in various models, theoretical concepts and frameworks has been given to Manufacturing Strategy (MS). There seems to be a relation between production competency and business competitiveness thus leading to improved strategies.

4.2.1 STRATEGY AGILITY

Strategy agility and learning has three dimensions: process adaptation and experimentation, collaborative technology sourcing and proactive technology posture. These aspects help organizations in gaining competitive advantage. To be more competitive, organizations need to operate in a strategy-driven way and develop a strategic architecture to enable them for developing necessary core competencies. MS contributes to company level competitiveness. Intuitively, it seems obvious that a smoothly running manufacturing system will have significant influence on firm performance.

Alsudiri et al. descried the factors for strategy agility, project management and the business strategy. A framework provides a relation between business strategy and project management. This helped the companies in implementing business strategies by embedding their projects in the overall strategy.

Strategy agility and development is considered as an engine for the economic growth and improving competitiveness of SMEs in the global market. Strategic agility gives a new dimension to thinking about strategic entry barriers whereby competitor's decisions are altered by government rules. Companies attack competitors by modelling government rules so as to create a misalignment of competitor's transactions and governance structures. A firm's governance structure will be established by the guidance from the attributes of the transaction.

Regional strategies are alternative, potentially superior solutions for globally integrated and locally responsive approaches. Companies follow a diverse path for regionalization and globalization. Such an approach involves a cluster of nations that reveal similar market conditions and homogenized regional consumer needs, while minimizing adaptation costs. Regional strategies are associated in evolving a firm's global strategy.

Financial performance is often used to measure firm performance. There is need for an integrated framework to assess manufacturing flexibility and firm performance. Moreover, strategic agility and thinking is reckoned to be an integral parameter towards manufacturing flexibility and competitiveness.

Corporate Social Responsibility (CSR) is more important to managers, still CSR is considered as an informal structure of corporations. According to economic conditions, CSR has an impact on corporate reputation and customer satisfaction in the automotive industry. Although, there does not exist a correlation between corporate reputation, economic responsibility and customer satisfaction. Thus, to increase efficiency in production, the industries need to be strategically agile, so that managers are open to new perspective with most basic and important responsibilities.

A CSR competency framework supply CSR skills and competencies for managers and practitioners. Large companies use these attributes with regard to attitudes, knowledge and practical skills. Organizational competency framework of strategy for integrating CSR and its associated skills into mainstream business has been provided.

4.2.2 Strategy and Business Performance

Strategic thinking has a significant impact on strategy formulation and strategic actions thus affecting business performance. Strategic thinking models consist of conceptual ability, visionary thinking, analytical ability, synthesizing ability, objectivity, creativity and learning ability. This set of abilities and skills are termed "strategic thinking competency". The strategic thinking competency model offers a framework for developing strategic thinking which contributes to better strategy and better business performance. This model is applied for designing training programmes to develop better strategic thinkers.

The major challenges of upgrading technology, reducing costs and building product quality are common to SMEs globally. Indian SMEs lack capacity in product design and development capabilities, but government policies have a prominent impact on development of strategy for competitive nature of SMEs globally. A framework shows the relationship between the process of manufacturing and the strategic thinking. Various forms of MS process and their impact on business performance have been provided. Strategy thinking competencies facilitate process innovation, as organizations can enhance their performance by their innovative efforts for developing and strengthening relevant strategies.

Panda gave the brief overview of the Indian small car industry. The mid-segment cars their concept, evolution, physical aspects and contribution to the growing need of the segment has been highlighted.

Outsourcing along with strategic thinking influences sustainable growth in the organizations. At technological level, machining and composite technologies; at product group level, structural parts and brake system parts are core competence logistics for an organization. Various criteria, such as operation effectiveness, safety, technological feature, cost effectiveness, usage quantity, procuring sufficiency and work force, are affected by core competencies, thus core competencies in an organization effects strategic outsourcing.

4.2.3 MANAGEMENT

Management coordinates the efforts of people to accomplish various objectives by utilizing available resources effectively and efficiently. Competitive advantage is a management concept that describes attributes which allow an organization to outperform its competitors. Basically, it means being self-evident. There may be different competitive advantages including customer support, distribution network, company's product offerings and cost structure. For competitive advantage, customers should be able to distinguish differences between one company's products and services and their competitors. This difference exists because of a capability gap between a company and its competitors. Competitive advantage leads to technological innovation and thus, leading to better strategy formulation and management.

Technological innovation at products or processes level affects environmental and economic condition of the automobile industry. For achieving sustainability, change in processes must be undertaken at the system and functional level. A product service system (PSS), system of products and services, is designed for competitiveness with lower environmental impact and satisfying customer demands. PSS involves developing, maintaining, obtaining and improving products and services in response to market opportunities. PSS is assessed against expanded set of key evaluative criteria: changes in institutional and infrastructural practices, changes in vehicle ownership structure, evidence of "higher-order" learning amongst stakeholders, changes in vehicle design, manufacture and end-of-life management and changes in modes of producer user interactions. Information and Communication Technologies (ICTs) is used by most organizations to offer more sophisticated innovation options.

Firm competencies, such as, New Product Development (NPD), marketing management and business network has an effect on strategic management of an organization. Business network is a kind of competency that covers inter-organizational network, government relationship and R and D partnership. NPD consists of product process innovation and R and D capability, while marketing management includes branding, information management, promotion and distribution channel. Loan amounts play an important role on the forecasting of automobile sales. There exists a relation between automobile production and automobile loan amounts as automobile production through sales varies according to different loan conditions and amounts. Thus, loan amounts from banks have an impact on strategic management of an organization.

Preventive maintenance is carried out on equipment to avoid its breakdown or malfunction. It is a routine and regular action taken on equipment. Preventive maintenance can be extended effectively only if maintenance engineering instruments are adopted to assure that preventive maintenance programmes harmonize well with production schedules and with the actual state of manufacturing equipment. Maintenance performance of an organization leads to growth in firm's performance. Thus it can be said that preventive management affects organization's competencies and strategies in present tough environment.

4.2.3.1 Strategy Management

Strategic management is the formulation and implementation of the initiatives and major goals taken by company's top management based on consideration of resources and environments in which the organization competes. In today's world, the main feature of economy has changed from an individual's effort to teamwork. In inter-organizational network, competencies are built by each firm and are influenced by strategy formulation. Intense competitiveness and rapid developments in manufacturing technology and information technology has led to turbulent and uncertain marketplaces throughout the world. Advances in biological and physical sciences and shortening of product lifecycles to some extent lead to uncertainty. There has been rapid transition in production systems to new organizational forms due to radical changes in technologies, competition and marketplaces. The manufacturing function and strategic management is a formidable weapon to achieve competitive superiority. A model links the action plan of firms and the manufacturing competitive priorities.

A company's internal and external variables are linked regarding strategic management which leads to an improved marketing performance. Strategic management includes human resource management, marketing strategy and strategic thinking. Marketing competency substitute strategic management but formalized organizational structure hampers it. Along with this, the attitude of organizations' management towards risk taking and emphasis of CEOs on strategic thinking also get slow down due formal structure of organization. Strategic thinking is positively related to centralization in the organizational structure. Market performance improves with enhancements strategic management and technological turbulence.

Strategic management elements in the operations unit and business strategies are co related. A model has been presented that associates organizations performance with the challenges in the strategic management field. Managerial cognition along with corporate and individual values have an impact on strategic management. Strategic management and competencies are important to a firm's performance. Along with management, psychological elements provide an understanding of the strategic thinking and decision-making process. Strategic management along with quality management affects the quality as a source of consistent competitive advantage. Quality competency plays an important role in sustaining advantage in today's highly competitive world.

4.2.4 Knowledge Transfer Management

Knowledge, technological skills and capability constitute a major part of firm's competitiveness. For creation of knowledge that will be transformed into new products and services firms have started to form knowledge-based strategic alliances, thus a new form of competition has been created. Nevertheless, this creation and transfer of knowledge through inter-firm cooperation has proven to be quite difficult. The issue of knowledge transfer management is more important for firms lacking in technological capabilities. Strategic variables related to knowledge and flexibility effect an organization's performance. A framework has been presented for capturing knowledge and information from external sources and the process that organizations use to assimilate transform and use this knowledge.

Knowledge management helps in dealing with the complexities of social behaviour in organizations. Knowledge plays an important role in firm's performance as strategic actions are planned according to knowledge and knowledge management involves both workers as well as managers. Along with knowledge management, habitual expressions also form a part in production process. Individuals use various habitual expressions for conveying their desires for product forms. Even oral styling procedure is described to a designer, who progressively sketches the product as it is described. MTS are greatly affected by individual capabilities in self-managed teams. Self-management competencies influence the productivity of a team network. MTS comprise of teams which widely practice self-management and knowledge management strategies to attain higher productivity. MTS having consistent self-managers are the most productive ones.

Knowledge transfer and management has led industries switch to re-insourcing. Besides outsourcing, re-insourcing helps organizations in decision making in MS and in achieving various underlying motives. Re-insourcing implementation gained momentum especially, during situations of financial crisis. In modular assembly, automobile manufacturers can either outsource the units for assembling or assemble them internally. Module assembly units' performance is affected by ownership and location. Even the internal and customer side conditions of different organizations greatly affect module assembly units' performances.

A Fit Manufacturing Framework helps manufacturing companies to operate effectively and become economically sustainable in global competitive market. A Fit manufacturing paradigm, through effective marketing and product innovation strategies, integrates the manufacturing efficiencies, agility and new markets, to achieve long term economic sustainability.

4.2.5 STRATEGY MANAGEMENT AND TECHNOLOGY

There is a strong linkage between technology strategy and business management but organizations can have different approach for technology acquisition and development. Strategic management and technology methods are practiced in various organizations in the auto component industries. Effective strategic management and technology or strategy technology management contributes to faster technology absorption and improved firm performance.

Certain business adaptations are required while entering a new market to have an improved strategic technology and management. MATCH is a new conceptual framework that assesses the strategic management and potential value creation in relation to the business model. Strategy management and technology is affected by the techniques for organizational learning process. Cognitive maps of Indian automobile industry are used for understanding organizational learning process. A simulation experiment, in the light of organizational learning, was performed on uncertainty based cognitive map for generating future scenarios.

Maintenance Quality Function Deployment (MQFD) is a feasible model for nourishing the synergic benefits of TPM and Quality Function Deployment (QFD). Successful implementation of MQFD leads to an enhanced firm performance as by this model strategic thinking, which involves strategic management and technology, gets improved (Pramod et al., 2006). TPM implementation leads to the enhancement of employee competency. It also shows how competency has been improving by implementing TPM. The study uses Analytical Heirarchical Process (AHP) for analysis. This study integrates TPM implementation with employee training, empowerment, teamwork, compensation and management leadership in a theoretical model for studying employee competency within the framework of management system.

Strategic technology management involves concurrent engineering and lean manufacturing towards NPD. Moreover, high degree of similarities exists between concurrent engineering and lean manufacturing. With lean manufacturing, organizations are able to develop new products faster and better with less cost than conventional companies. The benefits of lean manufacturing principles go much beyond frequent deliveries and inventory reduction.

Entrepreneur training and education ensures the improvement in the performance of micro firms. An investment in entrepreneur training and education is especially relevant to firms which are highly competitive. This implication leads to improved competencies and strategic management. A positive association between business training programmes and company performance exists based on four performance variables: organizational improvements, better job satisfaction within a company, increased exports and increased number of employees.

Performance Management and Measurement (PMM) techniques and tools, in recent years, have gained interest as by implementation of PMM yields many advantages. There are number of benefits experienced by organizations, in practice, after introducing PMM. It leads to better strategic formation as with PMM, even strategic technology and management improves, thus, improving the competencies. Management should make PMM advantages explicit before starting its implementation and stress these advantages during and after implementation. With this, the commitment of organizational members' will boost up for PMM and its successful use.

Firms with strategy technology management use open innovation practices and core competencies whereas firms with strategy of diversification use managerial practices. The framework gives useful indications about dependency of firm performance on competitive strategy and open innovation. Firms, with an innovative strategy, invest more on technical skills and core competencies. The integrated model developed, links open innovation, innovation performance and company's strategy in SMEs.

4.3   COMPETENCY AND PERFORMANCE

The literature highlights that the organizations offering flexible production routines, exhibiting product innovations and timely responsiveness have reaped tremendous business success through effective coordination and redeployment of internal and external competences. The organization's short-term competitiveness can be realized through strategic success attributes of different products, while the long-term competitiveness can be attained through the competency of an organization to deliver cost effective innovative products with high degree of flexibility.

MS is influenced by competitive strategy and both affect firm performance in manufacturing industry. There exists a significant relationship between manufacturing and competitive strategies of quality, flexibility, cost and delivery. Firm performance, to a great extent, is affected by quality. An emphasis on quality provides a means by which organizations can mitigate the effects of competitive manufacturing environment.

4.3.1 MANUFACTURING COMPETENCY

Manufacturing competency along with competence management comprises of management, leveraging, building and deployment of operational competencies and strategies. The causal relationships between them and the way competencies are embedded in individual and organizational resources. Competence management and agile management are to some extent inter-dependent. Manufacturing competencies in the form of global and strategic play an important role in organizations' performance and technology development. Manufacturing competencies support strategies to enhance the competitiveness of an organization in global market.

Three concepts of manufacturing competency, that is, organizational capability, administrative heritage and core competency are inter-related with economic condition and strategy formulation. Resource-based view complements economic analysis and both are vital for complete understanding of global strategy. Manufacturing competencies framework consists of competencies such as, research and development, production, information system, human resources and marketing competencies. This model also assesses the level of impact that functional competencies have on organization performance. Also, marketing competencies, research and development competencies and production competencies are key determinants of customer satisfaction and efficiency.

Manufacturing competency and competence-based management has led to major changes in the field of strategic management. As there is an interlinking between design management field and value creating network so changes in one leads to change in other. Therefore, design managers need to use these fields together in order to improve company's competitiveness. Design organizations contribute strongly to the organization's core competence. In-house development and external acquisition, along with organizations' strategic orientations are interrelated. Low and high performing firms differ regarding their strategies and methods for competency development and acquisition. 'The difference', is related to the combination of various integrated and discrete factors.

Technology adoption affects the operational competitiveness in international manufacturing organizations. The mechanism developed provides a deep understanding of trust building for improving operational competitiveness. The managers should focus on their actions, which in turn will help to improve their firm's competitiveness.

Knowledge and manufacturing competency variables affect international performance. Small firms expand into international market by examining the effects of absorptive capacity on the relationship between organizations' networks and knowledge competencies. Drivers of knowledge competency help in performance and early expansion of the firm in global market. Drastic changes in customer expectations, technology and competition have created an uncertain environment. In order to control this situation, manufacturers are seeking to enhance competencies especially, manufacturing competency and flexibility across the value chain. Manufacturing flexibility is the ability of an organization to produce a variety of products according to customer demand and expectation while maintaining high performance. Moreover, it is a critical dimension of value chain flexibility. It is strategically important for enhancing competitiveness and winning customer trust. The existing literature describes a framework for exploring the relationship among flexible capability, flexible competencies and customer satisfaction.

4.3.1.1 Competency-based Business Performance

Technical activities are vital factors in the globalization of multinational firms. The intangible nature of technological assets suggests that R, D and E (Research, Development and Engineering) activities should be managed strategically, sometimes favouring centralization and at times, decentralization. Strategic management of R, D and E activities leads to improved competencies and hence enhanced business performance.

Companies should maintain a higher degree of rationality among order-winning criteria, competitive priorities and improvement activities due to the customer pressures and competitive market. The competitive priorities of Indian companies are improving process and product quality as well as on-time delivery. Companies try to enhance competitive priorities by implementing manufacturing strategies from, TQM, Material Requirements Planning (MRP), Just-In-Time (JIT) and Statistical Process Control (SPC). Manufacturing efficiency and quality are significant criteria in today's industry towards competency and business performance.

These challenges provide the basis for new and advanced MS which aims to create economically sustainable manufacturing organizations. Along with these challenges and their corresponding technologies, strategies and competencies are improved, thus achieving better firm performance.

Competencies influence the performance of different types of services of industries. Services have often been classified as predictability of supply and demand, maintenance level, degree of labour intensity, method of delivery and level of customization and. These dimensions propose different types of services as service factories, service stores, service shops, service complexes. Along with competencies, services often improve by having proper strategic management thus, leading to improved competitiveness and firm performance.

Cloud manufacturing is a manufacturing model which is service oriented, customer centric and demand driven. It presents a strategic vision for the field which is influenced by competencies. Key commercial implementations are critical to enablement of cloud manufacturing, including industrial control systems, automation, service composition, flexibility, business models and architectures. Further improvements in business performance can be made by having higher competition and improvements in the areas of industrial control systems, business models, flexibility enablement and cloud computing applications in manufacturing.

There is a relation between export performance, competencies and MS of manufacturing SMEs. By adopting the MS, SMEs would gain competitive advantage over their rivals and reap higher exports. They could also seek out opportunities and anticipate future threats for further expansions in the global markets.

4.3.2 Performance

Strategy is the direction of the organization. It ideally synchronizes with its resources and changing competencies. It signifies deliberately evolving distinct initiatives to accrue a unique mix of value. Strategic success embodies formulation and execution of key organizational objectives, taking into account available resources and by making holistic consideration of internal and external organizational competitive environments.

Strategic planning must yield the necessary data and facilitate the organization to execute management efficiently to realize the business potential. Strategic planning assists executives to take key business decisions in light of consistent presumptions and a clearer perspective. Strategic thinking involves effective creation and execution of distinct business understanding and opportunities aimed at realizing sustainable competitive advantage. Strategic planning initiatives can be carried out by individual alone or cooperatively for providing favourable organizational benefits. Strategic thinking calls for acquiring and evolving strategic innovative ability, by examining available organizational resources, and confronting contemporary intuition to foster decision making today. Recent strategic thought perpetually focuses obviously on the conclusion that the critical strategic question is not the conventional 'What?', but 'Why?' or 'How?'.

Interdependencies between process, organization and product have been managed by using the diffusion of matrix-based tools. Design management along with strategic management represents and evaluates design core competencies in relation to the organizational, product and process architectures. Small business owners should understand strategies required for growth as they may lead to unintended consequences, like the demise of their firms. Strategic formulation that enables larger organizations to survive and grow, do not necessarily have the same effects for smaller ones. Certain boundary conditions exist for the effectiveness of strategies on firm performance in terms of size.

4.3.2.1 Competitiveness

Competitiveness is the ability and performance of a firm. Competitiveness may be short-term and long-term. The short-term are the ones that last through a business cycle whereas long-term advantages are those that last over more than one business cycle. The "unthreatened competitive advantage" is the noticeable advantage which had the potential of lasting over the entire length of the predictable future. Manufacturing capabilities affect the competencies and strategy formulation and thus competitiveness. The concept of absorptive capacity has been provided that will be applied to clear the view that the manufacturing capabilities are associated with operational performance, and for firms whose main competitive priority is operational performance, the association is the strongest. Manufacturing capabilities have a significant impact on integration of the customers. Manufacturing capabilities have direct contribution to firm performance.

Maintenance is becoming more challenging in the present dynamic business environment as it leads to competitiveness in market. Maintenance management system focuses on improving productivity, equipment effectiveness, environmental issues and workplace safety. Maintenance practices in manufacturing companies have good prospects as all practices are at high level and affect business performance to a larger extent.

Functional strategies of manufacturing, market orientation and human resource management have impact on competitive strategy. They, even, affect performance as it differs among family and non-family firms. There exist significant relationships between the functional strategies and competitive strategy. An HR participation strategy, flexibility and a delivery strategy have a significant impact on profitability for family firms but not for non-family firms; but Cost MS and market orientation is related to cost leadership strategy for both family and non-family firms.

Performance measurement systems has an impact on business performance thus competitiveness. It includes the use of integrated measures related to the perspectives of the balanced scorecard and the stage of development. With performance measurement systems, the organizational performance was higher than that of their competitors. Flexible integrated performance measurement system for greater administrative intensity and higher level of formalizations, leads to an increase the organizational efficiency. Certain quality management practices have a significant effect on customer satisfaction and productivity improvement. Hence, these practices increase competition in the market and lead to an improved firm performance.

Almost all countries try to bridge the gap in competitiveness between their own and foreign firms. The fundamental characteristic of product development strategy is based on variety, and it leads to introduction of the new perspective of product platforms. Furthermore, relating to suppliers, the black box method has improved. Two approaches possible towards product line management are: static and dynamic. The isomorphism between design and production activities enables the lean production system analysis to be applied to design. The evolution of the product development model adopted by organizations has relation with the strategy of product variety. The strategy and organization at the multi-project are considered the most promising.

Industrial competitiveness is vital for nations having export-oriented industrialization policies. Competitiveness of an industry, being a complex process, can be analyzed from various perspectives. The aggregate performance of many organizations can reflect their competitiveness. Based on theories from operations and strategic management, AHP-based model has been presented to explore the varying degrees of significance of the drivers and indicators of industrial competitiveness. The model identifies the degree of importance of organizational performance indicators when assessing industrial competitiveness. Further, it helps to evaluate the factors that are important for companies to perform better.

4.3.2.2 Company Enactment

The automotive sector is flexible in strategies development. These strategies, related to competency development, investment, quality and cost are significantly correlated with competitiveness. Growth-supportive environment, shortage of technical manpower and raising funds from the market are major constraining factors whereas delivery time, quality and cost are the main pressures on the automotive sector. Strategies along with the different dimensions of competitiveness have a relationship with these major factors. Organizations should make investments for developing new competencies and address quality improvement and cost reduction (Singh et al., 2007).

Corporate Financial Performance (CFP) is affected by Corporate Social Performance (CSP). By increasing productivity and lowering costs, CFP might also be affected by the impact of perceived CSP on customer satisfaction. CSP in terms of environmental performance, labour practices and community development contribute to consumer satisfaction. However, determinants outside the empire of CSP, such as product quality, perceived service and understanding with the brand, were much important for customers. The overall importance of CSP for customer satisfaction suggests that in the automobile industry, CSP may contribute indirectly by increasing consumer satisfaction as well as to better financial performance directly by increasing productivity and reducing costs.

According to Kassahun and Molla the Business Process Reengineering Complementary Competences (BPRCC) is composed of the Business Process Reengineering Complementary Transformational Competences (BPRCTC) and Business Process Reengineering Managerial Competences (BPRCMC). The BPRCC has an impact on company performance as it leads to improved strategies, thus, improved business competencies. The BPRCC with measurement instrument for public sector of a developing economy has been modelled.

The impact of an advanced, even authoritative structure on an organization's execution and development encourages the accomplishment of higher worth included and in addition has an immediate effect of administrative abilities on an organization's execution.

Agile manufacturing, a manufacturing paradigm, is the winning strategy to be adopted by manufacturers for drastic performance improvements to become leaders in highly competitive market and changing customer needs. Agility, basically, refers to the efficiency with which an organization accommodates changes in product and process. The drivers of agility and competitive advantages have emerged because of changing manufacturing requirements. The need for achieving competitive advantages of manufacturing and without trade-offs is essential for agile paradigm.

With an increase in turbulent and dynamic nature of competitiveness, there is a tendency to understand organizations in terms of the effective and efficient use of capabilities that creates consistent industrial performance. The main concern of contemporary strategic management is the development of more effective methods for management of knowledge and intangible resources. The relative influences of three constituents of core competencies, that is, technological, marketing and integrative competencies have an impact on strategic competency. Market turbulence and technological turbulence are moderately significant but amongst all the relationships between major constituents of organization performance and core competencies, market turbulence regulates the relationship between integrative competencies and organization performance.

4.4 NEED

Taking into account the literature survey, the need of the present study arose because impact of sustainable green development through advanced manufacturing and maintenance techniques in manufacturing performance of the manufacturing industry has not been yet addressed. For this purpose, the present study has been designed to investigate and suggest the parameters that contribute to the success of manufacturing industry. Moreover, this topic is need of the hour as it involves environment. For this purpose, the present study is so designed to investigate the sustainable green development initiatives that contribute to the performance of the industry. Based on the risks involved in the industry suitable model will be developed based on sustainable green development which will go a long way in serving industries as well as academicians.

4.5 AIM

Objectives of the present study:

1. Synthesize various advanced manufacturing and maintenance techniques in Indian Manufacturing Industries.
2. Explore sustainability and green engineering initiatives in Indian Manufacturing Industries.
3. Analyse the impact of sustainable green initiatives on performance parameters in Indian Manufacturing Industries.
4. Propose future developments of sustainable green initiatives and advanced manufacturing and maintenance techniques in Indian Manufacturing Industries considering the resources and market opportunities.

4.6 ISSUES EXPLORED

The following issues shall be taken up during the research work:

1. Defining advanced manufacturing and maintenance techniques in Indian Manufacturing Industries.
2. Elaborating sustainability and green engineering initiatives in Indian Manufacturing Industries.
3. Relating the various aspects of performance to advanced manufacturing and maintenance techniques in Indian Manufacturing Industries.
4. Analyzing the impact of sustainable green initiatives on performance parameters in Indian Manufacturing Industries.
5. Modelling the results using suitable qualitative and quantitative techniques.

4.7 METHODOLOGY ADOPTED

For accomplishing the objectives of the proposed study, the following methodology has been proposed:

1. A detailed literature review shall be carried out to ascertain the significance of advanced manufacturing and maintenance techniques, sustainability and green engineering.
2. Survey of various Indian Manufacturing Industries shall be carried out through a specially designed questionnaire for understanding and assessing the present situation.
3. Suitable qualitative and quantitative techniques shall be employed to correlate sustainable green initiatives and advanced manufacturing and maintenance techniques with performance of Indian Manufacturing Industries.
4. The results shall be synthesized to come out with a suitable qualitative model.

4.8 SCOPE

The scope of the work shall be limited to Indian Manufacturing Industries of North India. The study investigates the effect of sustainable green development on manufacturing performance through advanced manufacturing and maintenance techniques in manufacturing units. The key factors for realizing overall organizational objectives through various sustainable green development and advanced manufacturing and maintenance attributes have been examined in the study. The research focused on suggesting a model for North Indian manufacturing industry.

The status of manufacturing industry, with regards to various advancement and sustainable green development and performance issues has been elaborated in the study. The study involves investigation of sustainable green development and advanced manufacturing and maintenance techniques. initiatives towards realization of organization performance enhancements and accruing of core competencies in Indian enterprises. Also, a comparative analysis of business performance enhancements will be done by studying sustainable green development and advanced manufacturing and maintenance techniques.

For the purpose, key parameters and organization performance attributes have been evolved in the study. The relationships of various parameters have been analyzed and these were validated by using different statistical tools. Moreover, the study focused upon the impact of sustainable green development on manufacturing performance through advanced manufacturing and maintenance techniques in Indian industry. Finally, a model has been synthesized based upon extensive literature review, learnings from detailed qualitative and quantitative analysis.

4.9 PHASES

The study has been carried out with the objective of developing effective factors for sustainable green development and advanced manufacturing and maintenance techniques in North Indian manufacturing industry. Considering the complexity of theme and taking into view the fact that such studies can be carried out primarily by closely treading and analyzing the approaches adopted by various organizations and results thereof, it was considered appropriate to carry out the study under "Flexible Systems Methodology (FSM)" framework.

The three basic components of FSM are actor, situation and process. The "situation" is to be managed by an "actor" through an appropriately evolved management "process", which recreates the situation. The "actor" forms a part of the "process" as well as the "situation". The research work involves following phases:

a. Clarifying the Context

   The detailed literature review has been conducted regarding sustainable green development and advanced manufacturing and maintenance factors adopted by manufacturing organizations world-wide, from time to time in the past and issues involved with the same. The evolution of processes has been studied through various stages of manufacturing and performance practices along with their relevance and shortcomings. The literature review illustrates tools, techniques employed in implementation processes of these factors and the potential benefits accrued by Western world through effective implementation programmes.

b. Understanding and Assessing the Situation

   A survey of large number of manufacturing organizations (118 manufacturing units) has been completed through a specially-prepared questionnaire for understanding and assessing the present situation regarding manufacturing competencies of Indian entrepreneurs. The survey design and analysis involve following steps:

   i. Design of a questionnaire on various aspects of manufacturing as well as maintenance strategies including organization policies, traditional quality and maintenance attributes, measures and components of manufacturing performance.

   ii. Pre-testing and validation of questionnaire on the representative sample of industries.

   iii. Data collection using detailed questionnaire through google form, postal mail, E-mail, personal visits, interviews and other communication means.

   iv. Summarizing and analyzing the data to investigate status of various traditional maintenance strategies, besides evaluating exploits of Indian entrepreneurs with proactive sustainable green development through advanced manufacturing and maintenance initiatives and strategy initiatives. Thus evaluating the benefits accrued in terms of manufacturing performance achievements.

   v. Statistical analysis pertaining to status of various performance indicators as a result of implementations. Suitable qualitative and quantitative techniques have been employed to analyze the contributions of various manufacturing, maintenance and strategy implementation dimensions towards realization of performance achievements in North Indian manufacturing organizations.

   vi. Identification of stumbling blocks for successful implementation in North Indian manufacturing Enterprises.

   vii. Identification of key success factors for in North Indian manufacturing units.

c. Assessing the Actor's Capability

It emphasizes step-by-step implementation procedure adopted by the organizations towards achieving strategic success through manufacturing competencies.

It has been developed to determine the tools and techniques adopted by manufacturing organizations towards ensuring effectiveness of sustainable green development and results accrued through successful strategies. The data thus obtained regarding key performance indicators has been analyzed for arriving at their role in improving effectiveness of quality and maintenance function in the organizations.

d. Evolving the Management Process

Finally, the inferences drawn from the literature review and survey (analysis of questionnaire) have been effectively deployed to design the model for Indian Manufacturing Organizations. Moreover, the guidelines for strategic measures for overcoming the barriers in implementation programmes have also been evolved in the research.

4.10 RESEARCH FRAMEWORK

Figure 4.1 shows a block diagram for the methodology used for this research. This research has been conducted in and manufacturing units in Northern part of the country for studying the impact of these sustainable green factors on business performance. The aim is to describe the effect of sustainable green factors on performance parameters of manufacturing units. During this research, a large number of units have been surveyed for establishing effects of sustainable green development drivers in the strategy making. Survey of various organizations has been conducted through a specially prepared questionnaire.

The approach has been directed towards analyzing the effect of sustainable green development through advanced manufacturing and maintenance on

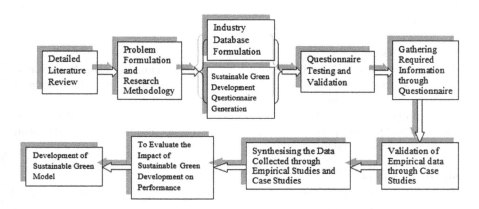

FIGURE 4.1 Block diagram of methodology.

manufacturing performance and thus, in improving the firm's performance. For completion of the survey effectively, the questionnaire was prepared through extensive literature review. This was validated through vast peer review from consultants in the industry and academicians. The questionnaire is based on four-point Likert scale. Each performance parameter and dimension is taken as a group of several related items.

Research is basically to determine new facts, through the process of dynamic changes in the society. Methodology is described as a system of methods and rules to aid in collection and analysis of data. It provides a starting point for making a choice and approach made of concept, data, theories and definition of the topic.

Research Method

There are two basic research methods: qualitative research and quantitative research. Qualitative research is a process of inquiry with a goal of understanding a social or human problem. Quantitative research is an inquiry about an identified problem, based on testing a theory to determine whether the productive generation of theory holds true, using statistical techniques.

Research Design

Claire Selltiz stated that research design should be such that it leads into logical conclusions. In this study both exploratory and descriptive research design have been used. Descriptive studies involve the collection of data in order to reply question regarding to the current status of subject of study (Sellitz, 1965).

The study involves large samples which have been used to give description and define attitude, opinion or behaviour that are measured and observed on a particular environment. The data has been collected in order to reply to questions regarding current status of subject of study.

The study also involves exploratory research design to give answer to the questions "why" and "how". It is process of finding out what other feel and thinks about their words. It is concerned with gathering relevant facts and opinions. So, the study basically involves exploratory research design which takes into consideration descriptive as well as exploratory data.

Sampling Design

Population is a key building block for a solid attributes sampling plan. According to Martin, auditors need to decide what to include in and exclude from the population and the time period examined; is an important consideration.

The purpose of my research is to examine how sustainability green development affects manufacturing performance when industries adopt advanced manufacturing and maintenance techniques.

Size of the Sample

Sampling is described as the selection of a fraction of the total amount of units of interest to decision makers, for the ultimate purpose of being able to draw general conclusions about the entire body of units.

An industrial database among the manufacturing organizations across the Northern region of the country was created for the purpose of conducting survey of 'Sustainable Green Development Questionnaire'. The questionnaires were forwarded to the organizations and they were subsequently contacted through various communication means like: postal mail, email, telephonic interviews, besides personal interviews through visits to various manufacturing units to describe the purpose of the research work, its relevance and to clarify any doubts or queries to facilitate responses to the 'Sustainable Green Development Questionnaire'.

Finalized Sustainable Green Development Questionnaire was forwarded to around 350 industries which are manufacturing s and their parts. Around 150 calls were made to interact with the persons in industry and about 250 mails containing questionnaire were forwarded to various units across the Northern region of the country. Along with this, interviews with the resource persons were made and clarifications were sort.

Furthermore, in case of organizations having multiple products, response for individual product has been received. The responses have been compiled and analyzed to determine the performance of the North Indian manufacturing industry. Most respondents to 'Sustainable Green Development Questionnaire' were from top level of management that included Vice Presidents, General Managers (GM), Head of Operations, Head of Maintenance, Head of Process Engineering, Head of quality Assurance, Quality Managers, etc.

Data Collection
Data is an important tool for the success of the study. In order to make meaningful research a suitable methodology has to be adopted. Data collection is of two types: primary and secondary. A major part of the data is primary, collected through the use of questionnaire or scale. Secondary sources gather information from various national and international journals, books, earlier related studies, reports and survey of government and non-government agencies, including press releases, newspapers, periodicals and use of internet explore various useful sites in relation to study. The questionnaire was pre-tested to judge reliability and validity.

Processing and Analysis of Data
The data has been analyzed by applying appropriate statistical techniques. The statistical tools include chi-square, ANOVA, factor analysis, t-test etc. for analyzing data to meet the objectives. Results and conclusions have been drawn on the basis of analysis of data.

In response to all these efforts, 200 filled questionnaires have been received. The simple, comprehensive and relevant questionnaire, covering different aspects of sustainable green development through advanced manufacturing and maintenance and manufacturing parameters factors gathering data required for attaining objectives of the research. Detailed description of 'Sustainable Green Development Questionnaire' has been presented in Appendix A.

For establishing the benefits realized by an effective sustainable green development approach, it becomes important that the effect of sustainable green development through advanced manufacturing and maintenance on organization performance be analyzed carefully.

The various statistical tools like response analysis, Cronbach's Alpha, percent point score, Multiple Regression Analysis, ANOVA, t-test and Pearson Correlation Coefficient have been employed to evaluate and validate contributions of sustainability initiatives by keeping in mind environmental issues towards building firm performance and realization of core competencies in the manufacturing organizations.

The above work has been extended by applying various qualitative techniques like MDEMATEL, WSM, WPM, WASPAS, GRA, SMART, CRITIC, ENTROPY, EDAS, MOORA, AHP, TOPSIS, VIKOR and Fuzzy Logic. This further has been validated by applying Interpretive Structural Modelling and SEM to the above study. This study uses the confirmatory factor analysis (CFA) approach using Structural Equation Modelling (SEM) in Analysis of Moment Structures (AMOS) 21.0 software to deploy the interrelation between sustainable green development and performance variables involved in the study. The data for the study have been collected through 'Sustainability Green Development Questionnaire' from various North Indian manufacturing industries.

While selecting the organizations, the following factors have been considered:

i.   The selected set of organizations should represent the manufacturing sector in terms of competition, complexity and other aspects need to be included in the study.

ii. The selected set should include organizations, which have different manufacturing sectors.

iii. The organizations participating in the survey through 'Sustainable Green Development Questionnaire' responses have been given preference.

iv. There is the feasibility of getting authentic information and data related to sustainability and performance from the units through personal interactions, observations and published data. Here it is pertinent to mention that although reasonably high numbers of questionnaire responses have been obtained from leading Indian entrepreneurs, very few organizations have come out openly and share their exploits and performance achievements.

v.   The industrial support was sought from various manufacturing organizations regarding the proposed research work and an encouraging response has been received from the industry.

vi. The study has elaborated organizational information, need for implementation, strategies adopted, their time frame, sequence and impact of implementation strategies towards realization of improvements in firm's performance.

Considering the extensive literature review, questionnaire survey, quantitative and qualitative analysis, a model for North Indian manufacturing industry is developed. A summary of the research accomplishments has also been highlighted. Finally, limitations of the research have been presented and recommendations for future research directions have also been suggested.

4.11   RELIABILITY AND VALIDITY

Reliability is defined as accuracy that a measure has in producing stable, consistent measurements. Since in social sciences scale are reliable measurement, social scientist must make sure that these scales are reliable measurements of the constructs they claim to measure.

4.11.1   VALIDITY

Validity is the degree to which the instrument measures what it is intended to measure. As important as reliability is to measure, validity is even more important. There are three principal approaches to validity: face or content validity, predictive or concurrent validity, and construct or factorial validity. In the first instance, efforts were made to improve and ensure the face validity of the scale by carrying out interviews and discussions with some experts in the target field (university researchers and professors in developmental psychology and education) and editing it repeatedly. Initially, 50 items were chosen for development scale measuring industrialists' perception towards sustainability green development.

As, in most of the prior studies a four-point Likert scale (1=not at all to 4=to a great extent) was used as a response option from manufacturing industries. All items underwent the judgement of experts who were given the definition of the proposed construct and were asked to identify: (1) any ambiguity in the wordings; (2) any incompatibility between an item and dimension it is supposed to measure. Construct validity was ensured by factorial validity. Factorial validity is based on the statistical technique known as "factor analysis". Factor analysis is a highly sophisticated statistical technique for examining a series of items to see which items correlate well with one another but are not highly correlated with other items or groups of items. McCroskey used this approach to measure the attitude towards communication sources.

4.12   PILOT STUDY

After the selection of the data collection method, the particular methodology and scale to be used in the survey have been formulated. In the initial phase of the study, several test surveys have been carried out so as to list various significant factors playing central role in the study in hand. In these types of complex studies, it is better to examine various aspects with the help of pilot surveys. The initial scale includes various statements recorded during the direct communication with the respondents, which later on helped to draft a final scale. The questionnaire was tested in two pilot studies.

It was decided to conduct a pilot study for the following reasons:

i.   To identify the problem and revising the items to ensure that all questions were understandable to the respondents.

ii.   To test the method of measuring attitude (impact of sustainability green development on manufacturing performance) which was later used in the main empirical research.

iii. To finalize the scale to be used in the research.

iv.   To gain familiarity with the fieldwork and the problems that can occur at different stages of the research.

4.13   STATISTICAL FRAMEWORK

The data were analyzed by applying both simple as well as advance statistical techniques. The simple tools include frequencies, percentages and averages. Advance statistical techniques include chi-square test, ANOVA, regression and factor analysis. Results and conclusions were drawn on the basis of analysis of data.

4.13.1   CHI-SQUARE TEST

In order to see the association between two-way distribution of respondents, Chi-square test was applied by using the following formula:

$$\chi^2 = \Sigma \frac{(O - E)^2}{E}$$

Where

χ^2 = Chi-square value
O = Observed Frequency
E = Expected Frequency
Σ = Summation

4.13.2   ANALYSIS OF VARIANCE (ANOVA)

To compare more than two means at a time, ANOVA was carried out. This was done to compare a parameter between industries from different regions of North India.

Source of Variation	d.f.	T.S.S.	M.S.S.	F-ratio
Regions	n − 1 = a	S_1	S1/a = x	x ∣ y
Error	b − a = c	S_2	S2/b = y	
Total	N − 1 = b			

where
n = no. regions to be compared (e.g., 3)
N = total no. respondents (e.g., 800)
T.S.S. = Total Sum of Squares
d.f. = Degree of Freedom
M.S.S. = Mean Sum of Squares (TSS/d.f.)

4.13.3 FACTOR ANALYSIS

Factor analysis is an interdependence technique in which all variables are simultaneously considered each related to others. Since the objective of this research was to summarize the variables factor analysis was applied. It studies the structure of interrelationships among a large number of variables by defining a set of common underlying latent dimensions known as factors. As a result, variables within each factor are more highly correlated with variables in that factor than with variables in other factors. This makes it possible to interpret the data from a much smaller number of factors than the original individual variables.

Factor analysis is a statistical method used to describe variability among observed variables in terms of a potentially lower number of unobserved variables called factors. In other words, it is possible, for example, that variations in three or four observed variables mainly reflect the variations in a single unobserved variable, or in a reduced number of unobserved variables. Factor analysis searches for such joint variations in response to unobserved latent variables. The observed variables are modelled as linear combinations of the potential factors, plus "error" terms. The information gained about the interdependencies between observed variables can be used later to reduce the set of variables in a dataset. Factor analysis originated in psychometrics, and is used in behavioural sciences, social sciences, marketing, product management, operations research and other applied sciences that deal with large quantities of data.

Factor analysis is related to principal component analysis (PCA), but the two are not identical. Because PCA performs a variance-maximizing rotation of the variable space, it takes into account all variability in the variables. In contrast, factor analysis estimates how much of the variability is due to common factors ("communality"). The two methods become essentially equivalent if the error terms in the factor analysis model (the variability not explained by common factors, see below) can be assumed to all have the same variance.

Mathematical model

$$\text{for } i = 1,\ldots, 600 \text{ the ith respondent's scores are}$$
$$X_{1,i} = \mu_1 * 1_{1\times600} + L_{1,1}\, F_i + L_{1,2}\, F_2 + \varepsilon_{1,i}$$
$$\vdots$$
$$X_{n,i} = \mu_n * 1_{1\times600} + l_{n,1}F_i + l_{n,2}F_2 + \varepsilon_{n,i}$$

where
  $x_{k,i}$ is the ith respondent's score for the kth statement
  μ_k is the mean of the respondents scores for the kth statement
  n is the number of statements
  F_i is the ith respondent's "first factor"
  F_2 is the ith respondent's "second factor"
  $\varepsilon_{k,i}$ is the difference between the ith respondent's score in the kth statement and the average score in the kth statement of all the respondents,

In matrix notation, we have

$$X = \mu * 1_{1 \times N} + LF + \varepsilon$$

where
N is No. of respondents;
X is a statement × no. respondents matrix of observable random variables;
μ is a number of statements × 1 column vector of unobservable constants;
L is a statements × 2 matrix of factor loadings;
F is a 2 × consumers matrix of unobservable random variables; and
ε is a statement × respondents matrix of unobservable random variables.

4.13.4 TYPE OF FACTORING

4.13.4.1 Principal Component Analysis (PCA)

The most common form of factor analysis, PCA seeks a linear combination of variables such that the maximum variance is extracted from the variables. It then removes this variance and seeks a second linear combination which explains the maximum proportion of the remaining variance, and so on. This is called the principal axis method and results in orthogonal (uncorrelated) factors.

4.13.4.2 Factor Loadings

The factor loadings, also called component loadings in PCA, are the correlation coefficients between the variables (rows) and factors (columns). Analogous to Pearson's r, the squared factor loading is the percent of variance in that indicator variable explained by the factor. To get the percent of variance in all the variables accounted for by each factor, add the sum of the squared factor loadings for that factor (column) and divide by the number of variables. (Note the number of variables equals the sum of their variances as the variance of a standardized variable is 1.) This is the same as dividing the factor's Eigen value by the number of variables.

4.13.4.3 Communality

The sum of the squared factor loadings for all factors for a given variable (row) is the variance in that variable accounted for by all the factors, and this is called the communality. The communality measures the percent of variance in a given variable explained by all the factors jointly and may be interpreted as the reliability of the indicator.

4.13.4.4 Eigen Values

The Eigen value for a given factor measures the variance in all the variables which is accounted for by that factor. The ratio of Eigen values is the ratio of explanatory importance of the factors with respect to the variables. If a factor has a low Eigen value, then it is contributing little to the explanation of variances in the variables and may be ignored as redundant with more important factors. Eigen values measure the amount of variation in the total sample accounted for by each factor.

4.13.4.5 Factor Scores

Factor scores (also called component scores in PCA): are the scores of each case (row) on each factor (column). To compute the factor score for a given case for a given factor, one takes the case's standardized score on each variable, multiplies by the corresponding factor loading of the variable for the given factor, and sums these products. Computing factor scores allows one to look for factor outliers. Also, factor scores may be used as variables in subsequent modelling.

4.13.4.6 Criteria for Determining the Number of Factors

Varimax rotation is an orthogonal rotation of the factor axes to maximize the variance of the squared loadings of a factor (column) on all the variables (rows) in a factor matrix, which has the effect of differentiating the original variables by extracted factor. Each factor tends to have either large or small loadings of any particular variable. A varimax solution yields results which make it as easy as possible to identify each variable with a single factor. This is the most common rotation option.

4.13.4.7 Reliable Measurements

Firstly, the variables should be measured on interval level. Secondly, the variables should be normally distributed, which makes it possible to generalize the results of analysis beyond the sample collected. Thirdly, the sample size should be taken into consideration, as correlations are not resistant and can hence seriously influence the reliability of the factor analysis. The most important factors in determining reliable factor solutions were the absolute sample size and the absolute magnitude of factor loadings. Field states that a researcher should have at least 10–15 subjects per variable. Habing stated that a researcher should have at least 50 observations and at least 5 times as many observations as variables. In the study, these considerations were observed. The scales were framed keeping the above considerations.

4.14 SCORING OF THE VARIABLES

Before data analysis, different variables were developed by assigning scores to the attributes; see Table 4.1.

TABLE 4.1
Scales Used for Variables

Scales Used	Score
To a great extent	4
Reasonably well	3
To some extent	2
Not at all	1

5 Reliability and Factor Analysis of Preliminary Data

5.1 CRONBACH ALPHA

Cronbach alpha is used to estimate the proportion of variance. Higher the coefficient, more is reliability of the generated questionnaire. Nunnaly (1978) has specified 0.7 as an acceptable reliability coefficient but sometimes, lower coefficients are also used. It can range from 0.00 (if no variance is consistent) to 1.00 (if all variance is consistent) For example, if the Cronbach alpha for a set of scores turns out to be.90, it means that the test is 90% reliable, and by extension that it is 10% unreliable. The value of alpha greater the equal to 0.9 means internal consistency is excellent, between 0.7 and 0.9 means good, between 0.6 and 0.7 means acceptable, between 0.5 and 0.6 means poor and less than 0.5 is unacceptable.

According to the response from the respondents, the value of Cronbach alpha came to be 0.975 for overall questionnaire as shown in Table 5.1, means internal consistency between the factors is excellent.

5.2 DEMOGRAPHIC PROFILE

The analysis of demographic profile has been carried out to know the significance of the respondents that is, if the data is significant then there is not much difference in the views from different industries and they can analyzed as such. In other words, when we collect data from around 200 industries, then the manufacturing industries are of different background, they have different turnover, different scales (large, medium and small), etc. So, to know whether the data can be compiled and analyzed, the demographic profile provides with the required results. In the following sections, the demographic profile parameters analyzed are Turnover, No. employees and Market Share.

TABLE 5.1
Cronbach Alpha Reliability Index of Questionnaire

Cronbach Alpha Value for Overall Questionnaire	0.975

5.2.1 Turnover (Table 5.2)

TABLE 5.2
Chi-Square Analysis for Turnover

	<10 crores	10–50 crores	50–100 crores	>100 crores
Punjab	43	24	14	5
Chandigarh-HP	5	3	3	12
Delhi-NCR	14	7	17	24
Haryana-UP	7	7	5	10
Chi-square		1.1944		

Further Table 5.3 shows ANOVA results. Similar results have been given by ANOVA (f-test) as f-value comes out to be 0.83001 and corresponding p-value of 0.516534.

In a nutshell, the mean data was statistically on a par with indicated by chi-square value of 1.19 also indicated the same. Also, the data being not significant at $p < 0.05$ that is, there is not much difference in the views of different respondents belonging to different regions with different turnover

TABLE 5.3
ANOVA Table for Turnover

	Result Details			
Source	SS	Df	MS	
Between treatments	833.3333	2	416.6667	F = 0.83001
Within treatments	1,506	3	502	
Total	2,339.3333	5		

5.2.2 Number of Employees (Table 5.4)

TABLE 5.4
Chi-Square for No. of Employees

	<200	201–500	501–1,000	>1,000
Punjab	41	26	17	2
Chandigarh-HP	5	6	2	10
Delhi-NCR	14	5	19	24
Haryana-UP	12	7	5	5
Chi-square		1.2739		

Further Table 5.5 shows ANOVA results. Similar results have been given by ANOVA (f-test) as f-value comes out to be 1.3855 and corresponding p-value of 0.172857.

It is concluded that the mean data was statistically at par as indicated by chi-square value of 1.2739. Also, the data being not significant at $p < 0.05$ that is, there is not much difference in the views of different respondents belonging to different regions and father's qualification (Table 5.6).

TABLE 5.5
ANOVA Table for No. of Employees

Result Details				
Source	SS	Df	MS	
Between treatments	555.5556	2	277.7778	F = 1.3855
Within treatments	698.6667	6	116.4444	
Total	1,254.2222	8		

5.2.3 MARKET SHARE (TABLE 5.6)

TABLE 5.6
Chi-square Analysis for Market Share

	<200	201–500	501–1,000	>1,000
Punjab	41	24	19	2
Chandigarh-HP	7	3	3	10
Delhi-NCR	17	5	19	21
Haryana-UP	14	10	3	2
Chi-square		1.8761		

TABLE 5.7
ANOVA Table for Market Share

Result Details				
Source	SS	Df	MS	
Between treatments	555.5556	2	277.7778	F = 0.65963
Within treatments	2,526.6667	6	421.1111	
Total	3,082.2222	8		

Further Table 5.7 shows ANOVA results. Similar results have been given by ANOVA (f-test) as f-value comes out to be 0.65963 and corresponding p-value of 0.550874.

It is concluded that the mean data was statistically at par as indicated by chi-square value of 1.8761 also indicated the same. Also, the data being not significant at $p < 0.05$ that is, there is not much difference in the views of different respondents belonging to different regions and mother's qualification.

5.3 RESPONSE ANALYSIS

The data was collected from the respondents on a four-point scale: Not at All (1), To Some Extent (2), Reasonably Well (3) and To a Great Extent (4) Table 5.8.

TABLE 5.8
Response Analysis

S. No	QUESTIONS	No. of Respondents Scoring Points A (1)	B (2)	C (3)	D (4)	Total No. of Responses (N)	Total Points Scored (TPS) **	Percent Points Score (PPS) $\frac{TPS}{5*N}$ 100	Central Tendency TPS/N
A	**Concurrent Engineering**								
1	Employees feel that CE is long and arduous process	8	64	68	60	200	580	59.6	2.98
2	Inadequate internal expertise that required to implement change	24	80	64	32	200	504	52.4	2.62
3	No top management willing to accept responsible as champion of CE	32	56	80	32	200	512	52.8	2.64
B	**Just In Time**								
4	Implementation requires formal approval	36	68	48	48	200	508	53.2	2.66
5	JIT does not fit well with the organization	28	84	32	56	200	516	54.4	2.72
6	Eliminated the waste by producing ZERO defects	20	88	40	52	200	524	54.8	2.74
C	**Predictive Maintenance**								
	Does your organization perform the following activities concerned with Predictive maintenance								
7	Failure pattern Recognition	40	32	56	72	200	560	57.6	2.88
8	Systematic Maintenance	16	92	36	56	200	532	56.4	2.82
9	Improving Unplanned Services	36	88	36	40	200	480	50.4	2.52
D	**Computerized Report Management**								
	How does your organization deal with the following activities concerned with report management								
10	supports real time report generation of ongoing work activity	40	56	72	32	200	496	51.2	2.56
11	report generation of completed maintenance work	32	84	48	36	200	488	50.8	2.54
12	Facilitates the flow of maintenance information	12	72	80	36	200	540	55.6	2.78
E	**Computer-aided Design**								
13	Whether your organization has an effective Design Technology Program (e.g., CAD?)	48	36	48	68	200	536	57.2	2.86
14	Whether the design program includes Aesthetics and Ergonomics of the product?	20	72	44	64	200	552	56.8	2.84
15	Does your organization track Design & Development program costs?	44	72	40	44	200	484	50.4	2.52

F	**Rapid Prototyping**								
16	Does RPT leads to cost and time cutting	8	100	36	56	200	540	56.4	2.82
17	RPT is too expensive	32	72	56	40	200	504	52	2.6
18	RPT is too complex	16	44	80	60	200	584	62.8	3.14
G	**CNC**								
19	Whether your organization use CNC machines?	36	60	52	52	200	520	56	2.8
20	Does your organization prefer using robots?	8	64	72	56	200	576	60	3
21	Does your organization regularly track Production costs?	52	68	36	44	200	472	50	2.5
H	**Residual Life Prediction**								
22	Whether your organization prefer product testing under actual conditions?	28	48	56	68	200	564	58	2.9
23	Does your organization carry out Lifecycle Analysis of the Product?	52	44	48	56	200	508	54	2.7
I	**Automated Storage and Retrieval System**								
24	Does your organization use computer for analysis and record keeping?	40	72	48	40	200	488	50.4	2.52
25	Whether your organization has enough warehouses for Inventory storage?	28	76	64	32	200	500	51.2	2.56
26	Does your organization have sufficient automated equipment to meet market demands?	20	80	68	32	200	512	52.8	2.64
J	**Computerized Material Management and Inventory**								
	Does your organization perform the following computerized maintenance activities concerned with material management / inventory control								
27	track the movement of spare parts affecting costs and ensure its availability when required	28	64	56	52	200	532	55.2	2.76
28	tracking lifecycle of an asset from the original purchase date up until it gets decommissioned	12	56	76	56	200	576	60.8	3.04
29	possess a mechanism for material and machine selection	48	68	32	52	200	488	52	2.6
K	**Reliability-centred Maintenance**								
	To what extent your organization performs following reliability centred maintenance planning and scheduling functions								
30	supporting unscheduled maintenance activities	20	80	64	36	200	516	53.2	2.66
31	prioritizing work and resources for the maintenance activities	24	40	60	76	200	588	62	3.1
32	tracking and managing backlog of the maintenance activities	24	44	68	64	200	572	59.6	2.98
L	**Automated Guided Vehicle**								
33	Are hydraulic and pneumatic systems are employed in your organization?	36	80	24	60	200	508	54	2.7
34	Are robots deployed by your organization	12	32	80	76	200	620	64.8	3.24

(Continued)

TABLE 5.8 (Continued)
Response Analysis

S. No	QUESTIONS	No. of Respondents Scoring Points				Total No. of Responses	Total Points Scored	Percent Points Score (PPS)	Central Tendency
		A	B	C	D	(N)	(TPS)	$\frac{TPS}{5*N} 100$	TPS/N
		1	2	3	4	(N)	**		TPS/N
M	**Finite Element Analysis**								
35	Whether the organization extensively uses Finite Element Method for Analysis purposes?	44	76	28	52	200	488	50.8	2.54
36	Does your organization use simulation and modelling for analyzing designs?	48	56	60	36	200	484	50	2.5
N	**Resource & Asset Management**								
	To what extent your organization supports following Resource management activities								
37	Allocates Tools, equipment and materials (spare parts component assembly) at proper time	40	76	36	48	200	492	50.8	2.54
38	Performs real time machine monitoring and alerts	32	64	52	52	200	524	54.4	2.72
39	Keeping the record of every asset's assemblies in computer like storing manufacturer and model	52	32	36	80	200	544	58.4	2.92
O	**Manufacturing Resource Planning**								
40	Improved order cycle	16	52	96	36	200	552	56.4	2.82
41	Improved decision-making capability	12	72	80	36	200	540	56.8	2.84
42	Organizational resistance to change	20	72	64	44	200	532	54.4	2.72
P	**Product Lifecycle**								
43	Does your organization invest on Quality Control & Inspection	12	52	76	60	200	584	59.2	2.96
44	Does your organization use computer to analyze quality?	24	76	44	56	200	532	54.8	2.74
Q	**Preventive Maintenance**								
	To what extent your organization following Preventive maintenance activities								
45	Failure Mode Effect Analysis	8	64	72	56	200	576	58.8	2.94

46	Root Cause Identification	4	56	80	60	200	596	61.6	3.08
47	Acceptance Testing	56	40	64	40	200	488	50.4	2.52
R	**Reverse Engineering**								
48	Do you use dynamic analysis?	48	52	32	68	200	520	55.2	2.76
49	Do you use static analysis?	44	64	48	44	200	492	51.2	2.56
50	Do you use software metrics?	40	56	52	52	200	516	55.2	2.76
S									
51	Whether the **Kaizen** principles and standards are employed in organization?	12	56	76	56	200	576	59.6	2.98
52	Whether your organization provides training regarding Kaizen?	12	72	60	56	200	560	57.6	2.88
53	Has inter relationship between management & employee improved due to Kaizen?	40	72	36	52	200	500	51.6	2.58
T	**Green Supply Chain Management**								
54	Do you associate with "green" suppliers, or use suppliers that share sustainability commitment?	20	44	80	56	200	572	58.8	2.94
55	Do you have an organizational commitment to implementing green logistics?	56	56	40	48	200	480	50	2.5
56	Do you make "green" strategies to meet customer requirements?	48	64	44	44	200	484	50	2.5
U	**Economic**								
57	New market opportunities	20	68	72	40	200	532	54.8	2.74
58	Commitment from various business stakeholders	48	68	40	44	200	480	50	2.5
59	Industrial sectors initiatives	12	56	52	80	200	600	64	3.2
V	**Greenhouse Gas Reduction**								
60	Do you train your employees for environmental consciousness?	8	40	84	68	200	612	64.4	3.22
61	Do you use fuel efficient tools and machines to make environment friendly?	12	56	72	60	200	580	60.4	3.02
62	Whether your environmental policy specifies your organization's Sustainability Initiative?	12	84	48	56	200	548	57.6	2.88
W	**Material Requirement Planning**								
63	Improved lead time	28	68	64	40	200	516	53.2	2.66
64	Improved interaction with supplier	8	48	116	28	200	564	56.8	2.84
65	Improved information accuracy	44	52	40	64	200	524	55.2	2.76

(Continued)

TABLE 5.8 (Continued)
Response Analysis

S. No	QUESTIONS	No. of Respondents Scoring Points				Total No. of Responses	Total Points Scored	Percent Points Score (PPS)	Central Tendency
		A	B	C	D				
		1	2	3	4	(N)	(TPS)	$\frac{TPS}{5*N}100$	TPS/N
							**		
X	**Computer-aided Inspection & Reporting**								
66	Does Inspection process in your organization improve the quality?	48	76	24	52	200	480	51.2	2.56
67	Does your organization use computer programs for inspection and reporting?	44	56	64	36	200	492	50	2.5
Y	**Social**								
68	Public awareness	24	72	52	52	200	532	56	2.8
69	Customer demand	36	68	60	36	200	496	51.2	2.56
70	Socio-cultural responsibility	48	48	64	40	200	496	50.4	2.52
Z	**Enterprise Resource Planning**								
71	Better resource utilization	4	52	64	80	200	620	64.4	3.22
72	Reduction of redundancy in database	8	48	72	72	200	608	62.4	3.12
73	Top management authority can find easily which department require attention or focus	28	72	36	64	200	536	56.4	2.82
AA	**Automated Material Handling Systems**								
74	Do you think AMHS improves yield?	8	24	96	72	200	632	64	3.2
75	Do you think AMHS reduces damage to product?	12	44	60	84	200	616	63.6	3.18
76	Do you think AMHS reduces dependence on human labour?	12	68	56	64	200	572	58.4	2.92
AB	**Computer-aided Process Planning**								
77	Whether your organization has an effective Process Planning program?	36	60	80	24	200	492	50.4	2.52
78	Does your organization apply Group Technology while planning?	24	40	104	32	200	544	56.4	2.82
79	Does your organization possess a mechanism for material and machine selection?	8	96	40	56	200	544	56	2.8

Code	No.	Item	A	B	C	D	Total	TPS	%	Mean
AC		**Environment**								
	80	How much priority is given to reuse, recycle or recovery of the products, parts or materials?	24	84	32	60	200	528	54.8	2.74
	81	Initiatives taken to avoid the use of hazards materials or manufacturing processes, which affects the environment	12	92	72	24	200	508	52.4	2.62
	82	Promotion about environmental-friendly packaging in organization	12	88	60	40	200	528	54.4	2.72
AD		**Flexible Manufacturing Systems**								
		Kindly indicate the level of following for adopting FMS								
	83	Increased flexibility	8	64	68	60	200	580	59.6	2.98
	84	Capacity increases	24	80	64	32	200	504	52.4	2.62
	85	Reduced floor space requirement	32	56	80	32	200	512	52.8	2.64
AE		**Eco-Friendly**								
	86	Strategy planned for environmental awareness of consumers	36	68	48	48	200	508	53.2	2.66
	87	Promotion of environmental-friendly products by suppliers	28	84	32	56	200	516	54.4	2.72
	88	Role to establish a green corporate image	20	88	40	52	200	524	54.8	2.74
AF		**5-S**								
	89	Whether tools, equipment and materials are managed for smooth flow?	40	32	56	72	200	560	57.6	2.88
	90	Has 5-S made a noticeable contribution to a safe and healthy environment?	16	92	36	56	200	532	56.4	2.82
	91	Do employees feel the 5-S adds the value for customers?	36	88	36	40	200	480	50.4	2.52
AG		**Robotics**								
	92	Do you think robots leads to cleaner operations?	40	56	72	32	200	496	51.2	2.56
	93	Is your management open to the idea of deploying robots?	32	84	48	36	200	488	50.8	2.54
	94	Does the use of robots lead to increased safety and reduced injuries?	12	72	80	36	200	540	55.6	2.78
AH		**Renewable Energy**								
	95	Do you utilize more alternate energy sources?	48	36	48	68	200	536	57.2	2.86
	96	Whether your quality human resources provide green ideas?	20	72	44	64	200	552	56.8	2.84
	97	Whether you consult with environmental specialists while using new technology?	44	72	40	44	200	484	50.4	2.52

** (Total Points Scored (TPS) = A x 1 + B x 2 + C x 3 + D x 4)

It has been observed that the average percent point score of the whole questionnaire is 55.33 and average central tendency of whole questionnaire is 2.77 as shown in the response analysis table.

5.4　FACTOR ANALYSIS

Factor analysis (FA) and Principal Components Analysis (PCA) techniques are used when the researcher is interested in identifying a smaller number of factors underlying a large number of observed variables. Variables that have a high correlation between them and are largely independent of other subsets of variables, are combined into factors. A common usage of PCA and FA is in developing objective instruments for measuring constructs which are not directly observable in real life.

Factor and Component

Factors are produced by FA, while components are produced by PCA. Both FA and PCA essentially are data reduction techniques. Mathematically, the difference is in the variance of the observed variables that is analyzed. In PCA, all the variance in the observed variables is analyzed, whereas in FA, only shared variance is analyzed. Even though PCA is different from other techniques of FA, at many places it is treated as one of the FA techniques.

Exploratory and Confirmatory Factor Analysis

As the name suggests, in exploratory FA (EFA) we are interested in exploring the underlying dimensions that could have caused correlations among the observed variables. In case of confirmatory FA (CFA), the researcher is interested in testing whether the correlations among the observed variables are consistent with the hypothesized factor structure. Thus, while EFA deals with theory building, CFA deals with theory testing.

Factor Extraction

Extraction refers to the process of obtaining underlying factors or components. Besides PCA, SPSS offers several other extraction methods such as principal axis factoring (PAF) and alpha factoring. The differences are primarily mathematical in nature and generate similar results in most of the cases. The two most commonly used extraction methods are PCA and PAF. If the researcher has designed the study based on a theoretical consideration, PFA should be the preferred choice. However, if the main aim of the researcher is simply to reduce the number of variables, PCA is a better choice.

The eigenvalues associated with each component represents variance explained by that particular linear component and displays the eigenvalue in terms of the percentage of variance. It is clear that the large amount of variance is explained by first few components whereas rest of components explain only small amount of variance.

Only five components are extracted as shown. In the next column, extractions sum of squared loadings, the values are the same as the values before extraction, except values for the discarded components are ignored. In the last column rotation sums of squared loadings, the eigenvalues of the components after rotation are displayed.

Communality gives the variance accounted for a particular variable by all the factors. Mathematically, it is the sum of squared loadings for a variable across all the factors. The higher the value of communality for a particular variable after extraction, higher is its amount of variance explained by the extracted factors.

Factor Loadings

FA produces factor loadings for each combination of extracted factors and the observed variables. Factor loadings are similar to correlation coefficients between the factors and the variables. Thus higher the factor loading, the more likely it is that the factor underlies that variable. Factor loadings help in identifying which variables are associated with the particular factors.

Rotation

Factor loadings obtained from extraction may not present a clear picture of the factor structure of the data set. After extraction, while we may be able to identify the number of factors, we may not know the exact way in which the observed variables load on different factors. Unrotated factor loadings are extremely hard to interpret, regardless of the extraction methods. Rotation helps in arriving at a simple pattern of factor loadings by maximizing high correlations and minimizing low ones. For a good factor solution, a particular variable should load high on one factor and low on all other factors in the rotated factor matrix. Researchers commonly use a cut-off of 0.40 to identify high loadings.

Rotation could be orthogonal or oblique. Orthogonal rotation should be used under the assumption that the underlying factors are uncorrelated with each other. However, if the researcher has theoretical reasons to believe that the factors may be correlated, oblique rotation is a better choice. The rotation is used to reduce the number of factors on which the variables under investigation have high loadings. Rotation makes the interpretation of the analysis easier and does not change anything. Values less than 0.55 are concealed. The variables are listed in the order of size of their factor loadings. After rotation factor structure has clarified as most of the variables loaded highly onto the component before rotation.

5.4.1 RESULTS OF FACTOR ANALYSIS (TABLE 5.9)

Descriptive statistics of all the dimensions such as mean standard deviation is shown in Table 5.10.

Following Table 5.11 gives the correlation of each variable with one another.

TABLE 5.9
Dimensions Surveyed from the Respondents

Concurrent Engineering	V1
JIT	V2
Predictive Maintenance	V3
Computerized Report Management	V4
Computer-aided Design	V5
Rapid Prototyping	V6
CNC	V7
Residual Life Prediction	V8
Automated Storage and Retrieval System	V9
Computerized Material Management and Inventory	V10
Reliability-centred Maintenance	V11
Automated Guided Vehicle	V12
Finite Element Analysis	V13
Resource & Asset Management	V14
Manufacturing Resource Planning	V15
Product Lifecycle	V16
Preventive Maintenance	V17
Reverse Engineering	V18
Kaizen	V19
Green Supply Chain Management	V20
Economic	V21
Greenhouse Gas Reduction	V22
Material Requirement Planning	V23
Computer-aided Inspection & Reporting	V24
Social	V25
Enterprise Resource Planning	V26
Automated Material Handling Systems	V27
Computer-aided Process Planning	V28
Environment	V29
Flexible Manufacturing Systems	V30
Eco-Friendly	V31
5-S	V32
Robotics	V33
Renewable Energy	V34

The eigenvalues with each linear component before extraction, after extraction and after rotation is listed in Tables 5.12 and 5.13.

The communalities before and after extraction are listed in Table 5.14.

Communalities show the extent of the variance in the variables has been accounted for by the extracted factors. The component matrix contains the loading of each variable onto each factor. Table 5.15 shows the component matrix before rotation. In the given table, loadings less than 0.55 are suppressed and as a result almost 50% factors are suppressed.

Rotated component matrix is the matrix of the factor loadings for each variable onto each factor and is listed in Table 5.16. In the given table, loadings less than 0.55 are suppressed and as a result almost 50% factors are suppressed.

TABLE 5.10
Descriptive Statistics

	Mean	Std. Deviation	Analysis N
V1	3.240	0.9511	400
V2	2.680	1.0100	400
V3	2.780	0.9869	400
V4	2.560	1.0436	400
V5	2.600	1.3131	400
V6	2.780	1.2552	400
V7	3.240	1.1070	400
V8	2.640	1.2785	400
V9	2.660	1.1781	400
V10	2.360	1.0739	400
V11	2.720	1.0413	400
V12	2.480	1.0060	400
V13	3.140	1.0786	400
V14	3.300	1.0643	400
V15	2.560	1.1874	400
V16	2.720	1.3289	400
V17	2.540	1.0823	400
V18	2.460	0.9647	400
V19	2.844	0.5211	400
V20	2.792	0.6948	400
V21	2.572	0.6773	400
V22	2.852	0.6189	400
V23	2.800	0.4905	400
V24	2.680	0.6126	400
V25	2.724	0.7274	400
V26	2.790000000	0.6106909773	400
V27	2.6900	0.50452	400
V28	2.772	0.5477	400
V29	2.736	0.7656	400
V30	2.840	0.6100	400
V31	2.656	0.5763	400
V32	2.8600	0.54419	400
V33	2.718	0.5990	400
V34	2.73500	0.502899	400

Only five components are extracted as a result of the FA, which have been classified into dimensions. Each dimension is further divided into factors. The association of each factor with its dimension and component is listed in Table 5.17.

5.5 CORRELATION ANALYSIS

The purpose of correlation analysis is to identify the relationship within various parameters. Moreover, perception was measured by correlation by evaluating statements as all were measured on the same scale. The correlation process used is Karl Pearson Correlation with significance level 0.05. Table 5.18 shows the same.

TABLE 5.11
Correlation Matrix

		V1	V2	V3	V4	V5	V6	V7
Correlation	V1	1.000	.310	.291	−.075	.045	−.124	.307
	V2	.310	1.000	.030	−.058	−.142	.118	.176
	V3	.291	.030	1.000	.100	.334	.333	.397
	V4	−.075	−.058	.100	1.000	.018	.263	.022
	V5	.045	−.142	.334	.018	1.000	.153	.135
	V6	−.124	.118	.333	.263	.153	1.000	.370
	V7	.307	.176	.397	.022	.135	.370	1.000
	V8	.220	−.043	.446	.061	.272	.150	.571
	V9	.162	.094	.470	.041	.080	.275	.432
	V10	.033	.402	.245	.195	−.068	.327	.130
	V11	.291	.124	.291	−.261	.035	.183	.441
	V12	.194	.191	.329	−.199	−.067	.211	.436
	V13	.163	.115	.349	−.088	.365	.378	.375
	V14	.424	.090	.025	−.007	−.115	−.116	.160
	V15	.129	−.134	.054	.086	−.319	−.173	.065
	V16	.244	.097	.350	.027	.005	.420	.441
	V17	.030	.030	.018	−.162	.054	−.119	−.159
	V18	−.099	.069	.212	.321	−.044	.051	−.066
	V19	.731	.530	.339	−.119	.161	.076	.343
	V20	.130	.036	.687	.438	.577	.711	.623
	V21	.297	.239	.597	−.040	.100	.375	.672
	V22	.367	.072	.308	−.045	−.014	.164	.345
	V23	.610	.178	.431	.024	.212	.052	.266
	V24	.139	.307	.646	.469	.558	.711	.403
	V25	.316	.223	.585	.025	.153	.403	.810
	V26	.363	.113	.350	−.093	−.030	.197	.411
	V27	.270	.070	.386	.064	.236	.122	.178
	V28	.559	.397	.671	.378	.570	.294	.388
	V29	.181	.217	.586	.180	.186	.661	.770
	V30	.419	.125	.361	−.155	−.045	.158	.508
	V31	.341	.079	.466	.061	.167	.172	.243
	V32	.675	.648	.558	−.100	.132	.234	.430
	V33	.225	.172	.634	.199	.402	.637	.743
	V34	.374	.060	.337	.021	.010	.086	.254

		V8	V9	V10	V11	V12	V13	V14
Correlation	V1	.220	.162	.033	.291	.194	.163	.424
	V2	−.043	.094	.402	.124	.191	.115	.090
	V3	.446	.470	.245	.291	.329	.349	.025
	V4	.061	.041	.195	−.261	−.199	−.088	−.007
	V5	.272	.080	−.068	.035	−.067	.365	−.115
	V6	.150	.275	.327	.183	.211	.378	−.116
	V7	.571	.432	.130	.441	.436	.375	.160
	V8	1.000	.305	.007	.165	.104	.197	.330
	V9	.305	1.000	.192	.184	.459	.353	.209
	V10	.007	.192	1.000	.162	.285	.233	.028
	V11	.165	.184	.162	1.000	.263	.338	.040
	V12	.104	.459	.285	.263	1.000	.271	.221
	V13	.197	.353	.233	.338	.271	1.000	−.002

	V8	V9	V10	V11	V12	V13	V14
V14	.330	.209	.028	.040	.221	−.002	1.000
V15	.239	.165	.014	.095	.228	−.234	.343
V16	.200	.259	.099	.262	.461	.489	.102
V17	.054	.034	.126	.117	.001	−.099	.155
V18	.021	.173	.266	.069	−.021	−.024	−.252
V19	.144	.266	.287	.437	.266	.310	.323
V20	.484	.413	.262	.224	.224	.467	−.029
V21	.567	.717	.521	.563	.667	.455	.284
V22	.378	.382	.183	.321	.456	.434	.573
V23	.179	.312	.244	.440	.195	.273	.207
V24	.329	.343	.383	.136	.159	.432	−.061
V25	.673	.672	.446	.586	.477	.463	.252
V26	.348	.449	.233	.343	.659	.440	.544
V27	.114	.303	.281	.397	.146	.255	.052
V28	.375	.315	.290	.169	.148	.366	.131
V29	.644	.678	.487	.345	.451	.472	.191
V30	.368	.477	.247	.598	.681	.467	.568
V31	.261	.365	.298	.347	.251	.355	.228
V32	.187	.301	.301	.444	.407	.298	.125
V33	.564	.631	.448	.461	.501	.651	.139
V34	.296	.351	.219	.356	.351	.193	.467

		V15	V16	V17	V18	V19	V20	V21
Correlation	V1	.129	.244	.030	−.099	.731	.130	.297
	V2	−.134	.097	.030	.069	.530	.036	.239
	V3	.054	.350	.018	.212	.339	.687	.597
	V4	.086	.027	−.162	.321	−.119	.438	−.040
	V5	−.319	.005	.054	−.044	.161	.577	.100
	V6	−.173	.420	−.119	.051	.076	.711	.375
	V7	.065	.441	−.159	−.066	.343	.623	.672
	V8	.239	.200	.054	.021	.144	.484	.567
	V9	.165	.259	.034	.173	.266	.413	.717
	V10	.014	.099	.126	.266	.287	.262	.521
	V11	.095	.262	.117	.069	.437	.224	.563
	V12	.228	.461	.001	−.021	.266	.224	.667
	V13	−.234	.489	−.099	−.024	.310	.467	.455
	V14	.343	.102	.155	−.252	.323	−.029	.284
	V15	1.000	.201	.201	.265	.122	−.121	.249
	V16	.201	1.000	−.104	.132	.261	.401	.415
	V17	.201	−.104	1.000	−.027	.278	−.117	.108
	V18	.265	.132	−.027	1.000	.039	.137	.167
	V19	.122	.261	.278	.039	1.000	.258	.451
	V20	−.121	.401	−.117	.137	.258	1.000	.545
	V21	.249	.415	.108	.167	.451	.545	1.000
	V22	.577	.676	.401	.054	.475	.238	.568
	V23	.289	.289	.272	.407	.860	.313	.447
	V24	−.205	.328	−.065	.202	.343	.921	.454
	V25	.189	.393	.052	.141	.451	.635	.951
	V26	.550	.697	.339	.040	.474	.262	.663
	V27	.291	.237	.317	.541	.700	.319	.403
	V28	−.105	.259	−.008	.169	.603	.750	.439
	V29	.097	.440	−.021	.132	.335	.775	.873

(Continued)

TABLE 5.11   (Continued)

		V15	V16	V17	V18	V19	V20	V21
	V30	.534	.528	.137	.023	.507	.258	.769
	V31	.399	.544	.479	.430	.643	.354	.501
	V32	−.018	.368	.129	.085	.814	.400	.528
	V33	.020	.498	−.027	.135	.405	.859	.865
	V34	.652	.507	.494	.319	.634	.218	.517

		V22	V23	V24	V25	V26	V27	V28
Correlation	V1	.367	.610	.139	.316	.363	.270	.559
	V2	.072	.178	.307	.223	.113	.070	.397
	V3	.308	.431	.646	.585	.350	.386	.671
	V4	−.045	.024	.469	.025	−.093	.064	.378
	V5	−.014	.212	.558	.153	−.030	.236	.570
	V6	.164	.052	.711	.403	.197	.122	.294
	V7	.345	.266	.403	.810	.411	.178	.388
	V8	.378	.179	.329	.673	.348	.114	.375
	V9	.382	.312	.343	.672	.449	.303	.315
	V10	.183	.244	.383	.446	.233	.281	.290
	V11	.321	.440	.136	.586	.343	.397	.169
	V12	.456	.195	.159	.477	.659	.146	.148
	V13	.434	.273	.432	.463	.440	.255	.366
	V14	.573	.207	−.061	.252	.544	.052	.131
	V15	.577	.289	−.205	.189	.550	.291	−.105
	V16	.676	.289	.328	.393	.697	.237	.259
	V17	.401	.272	−.065	.052	.339	.317	−.008
	V18	.054	.407	.202	.141	.040	.541	.169
	V19	.475	.860	.343	.451	.474	.700	.603
	V20	.238	.313	.921	.635	.262	.319	.750
	V21	.568	.447	.454	.951	.663	.403	.439
	V22	1.000	.497	.169	.508	.970	.431	.241
	V23	.497	1.000	.318	.443	.473	.928	.543
	V24	.169	.318	1.000	.501	.186	.320	.841
	V25	.508	.443	.501	1.000	.560	.389	.486
	V26	.970	.473	.186	.560	1.000	.404	.244
	V27	.431	.928	.320	.389	.404	1.000	.397
	V28	.241	.543	.841	.486	.244	.397	1.000
	V29	.449	.318	.673	.923	.503	.301	.512
	V30	.838	.496	.150	.683	.894	.405	.241
	V31	.756	.820	.339	.471	.708	.836	.419
	V32	.343	.631	.512	.510	.402	.449	.700
	V33	.486	.412	.762	.893	.548	.395	.638
	V34	.869	.774	.175	.461	.830	.764	.286

		V29	V30	V31	V32	V33	V34
Correlation	V1	.181	.419	.341	.675	.225	.374
	V2	.217	.125	.079	.648	.172	.060
	V3	.586	.361	.466	.558	.634	.337
	V4	.180	−.155	.061	−.100	.199	.021
	V5	.186	−.045	.167	.132	.402	.010
	V6	.661	.158	.172	.234	.637	.086

	V29	V30	V31	V32	V33	V34
V7	.770	.508	.243	.430	.743	.254
V8	.644	.368	.261	.187	.564	.296
V9	.678	.477	.365	.301	.631	.351
V10	.487	.247	.298	.301	.448	.219
V11	.345	.598	.347	.444	.461	.356
V12	.451	.681	.251	.407	.501	.351
V13	.472	.467	.355	.298	.651	.193
V14	.191	.568	.228	.125	.139	.467
V15	.097	.534	.399	−.018	.020	.652
V16	.440	.528	.544	.368	.498	.507
V17	−.021	.137	.479	.129	−.027	.494
V18	.132	.023	.430	.085	.135	.319
V19	.335	.507	.643	.814	.405	.634
V20	.775	.258	.354	.400	.859	.218
V21	.873	.769	.501	.528	.865	.517
V22	.449	.838	.756	.343	.486	.869
V23	.318	.496	.820	.631	.412	.774
V24	.673	.150	.339	.512	.762	.175
V25	.923	.683	.471	.510	.893	.461
V26	.503	.894	.708	.402	.548	.830
V27	.301	.405	.836	.449	.395	.764
V28	.512	.241	.419	.700	.638	.286
V29	1.000	.538	.410	.440	.932	.370
V30	.538	1.000	.562	.428	.609	.723
V31	.410	.562	1.000	.418	.476	.906
V32	.440	.428	.418	1.000	.492	.409
V33	.932	.609	.476	.492	1.000	.398
V34	.370	.723	.906	.409	.398	1.000

The purpose of correlation matrix was to establish the relationship and its direction between the parameters of the sustainable green development, modern production techniques and manufacturing performance over the output process followed in the organizations. The hypothesis was also framed for the relationship between the parameters at 0.05 levels of significance.

H_{01}: **There was no relationship between the sustainable development and output process**

The analysis of the correlation matrix showed that the above null hypothesis assumed was not acceptable as the correlations obtained between the sustainable development and all process of output was significant and they were being affected in the organization in a positive manner. It was inference that the correlation of the sustainable development with the parameters; e.g., *reliability* (r = 0.727), *competitiveness* (r = 0.684), *quality* (r = 0.675), *production time* (r = 0.613), *production capacity* (r = 0.606), *growth and expansion* (r = 0.527) and *productivity* (r = 0.500) were significant positive.

H_{02}: **There was no relationship between the natural resources and output process**

The analysis of the correlation matrix showed that the above null hypothesis assumed was not acceptable as the correlations obtained between the natural

TABLE 5.12

Total Variance

Component	Initial Eigenvalues			Extraction Sums of Squared Loadings		
	Total	% Variance	Cumulative %	Total	% Variance	Cumulative %
1	12.860	37.823	37.823	12.860	37.823	37.823
2	4.468	13.140	50.963	4.468	13.140	50.963
3	2.968	8.729	59.692	2.968	8.729	59.692
4	2.355	6.927	66.619	2.355	6.927	66.619
5	1.803	5.303	71.922	1.803	5.303	71.922
6	1.588	4.671	76.593			
7	1.434	4.217	80.810			
8	1.216	3.577	84.386			
9	0.901	2.649	87.035			
10	0.780	2.293	89.328			
11	0.665	1.956	91.284			
12	0.627	1.844	93.127			
13	0.512	1.507	94.634			
14	0.437	1.285	95.919			
15	0.414	1.218	97.138			
16	0.308	0.907	98.045			
17	0.243	0.713	98.758			
18	0.208	0.612	99.370			
19	0.133	0.391	99.760			
20	0.081	0.240	100.000			
21	1.064E-013	1.187E-013	100.000			
22	1.038E-013	1.112E-013	100.000			
23	1.034E-013	1.100E-013	100.000			
24	1.020E-013	1.060E-013	100.000			
25	1.017E-013	1.050E-013	100.000			
26	1.010E-013	1.031E-013	100.000			
27	1.002E-013	1.005E-013	100.000			
28	−1.003E-013	−1.007E-013	100.000			
29	−1.007E-013	−1.020E-013	100.000			
30	−1.015E-013	−1.045E-013	100.000			
31	−1.023E-013	−1.068E-013	100.000			
32	−1.032E-013	−1.094E-013	100.000			
33	−1.038E-013	−1.112E-013	100.000			
34	−1.048E-013	−1.141E-013	100.000			

resources and all process of output was significant and they were being affected in the organization in a positive manner. It was inference that the correlation of the natural resources with the parameters; e.g., *reliability* ($r = 0.758$), *competitiveness* ($r = 0.696$), *quality* ($r = 0.692$), *production time* ($r = 0.635$), *production capacity* ($r = 0.606$), *growth and expansion* ($r = 0.556$), *productivity* ($r = 0.554$), *lead time* ($r = 0.527$) and *profit* ($r = 0.505$) were significant positive.

H_{03}: **There was no relationship between the Green Manufacturing and output process**

The analysis of the correlation matrix showed that the above null hypothesis assumed was not acceptable as the correlations obtained between the Green

TABLE 5.13
Total Variance Rotated

| Component | Rotation Sums of Squared Loadings | | |
	Total	% Variance	Cumulative %
1	8.510	25.028	25.028
2	5.776	16.989	42.017
3	4.113	12.096	54.113
4	3.649	10.733	64.846
5	2.406	7.075	71.922
6			
7			
8			
9			
10			
11			
12			
13			
14			
15			
16			
17			
18			
19			
20			
21			
22			
23			
24			
25			
26			
27			
28			
29			
30			
31			
32			
33			
34			

Manufacturing and all process of output was significant and they were being affected in the organization in a positive manner. It was inference that the correlation of the Green Manufacturing with the parameters; e.g., *reliability* (r = 0.746), *competitiveness* (r = 0.675), *quality* (r = 0.595) and *production capacity* (r = 0.550) were significant positive.

H_{04}: **There was no relationship between the waste management and output process**

The analysis of the correlation matrix showed that the above null hypothesis assumed was not acceptable as the correlations obtained between the waste management and all process of output was significant and they were being affected in the

TABLE 5.14
Communalities

	Initial	Extraction
V1	1.000	.719
V2	1.000	.672
V3	1.000	.580
V4	1.000	.440
V5	1.000	.673
V6	1.000	.600
V7	1.000	.677
V8	1.000	.593
V9	1.000	.465
V10	1.000	.578
V11	1.000	.371
V12	1.000	.602
V13	1.000	.394
V14	1.000	.507
V15	1.000	.670
V16	1.000	.424
V17	1.000	.317
V18	1.000	.675
V19	1.000	.938
V20	1.000	.960
V21	1.000	.892
V22	1.000	.874
V23	1.000	.903
V24	1.000	.905
V25	1.000	.858
V26	1.000	.898
V27	1.000	.837
V28	1.000	.879
V29	1.000	.917
V30	1.000	.904
V31	1.000	.905
V32	1.000	.875
V33	1.000	.974
V34	1.000	.976

organization in a positive manner. It was inference that the correlation of the waste management with parameters; e.g., *reliability* ($r = 0.770$), *competitiveness* ($r = 0.704$), *quality* ($r = 0.690$), *production capacity* ($r = 0.672$), *production time* ($r = 0.631$), *productivity* ($r = 0.553$), *growth and expansion* ($r = 0.552$), *market share* ($r = 0.526$) and *profit* ($r = 0.511$) were significant positive.

H$_{05}$: There was no relationship between the Lifecycle Analysis and output process

The analysis of the correlation matrix showed that the above null hypothesis assumed was not acceptable as the correlations obtained between the Lifecycle Analysis and all process of output was significant, and they were being affected in the organization in a positive manner. It was inference that the correlation of the Lifecycle Analysis with the parameters; e.g., *reliability* ($r = 0.688$), *competitiveness*

TABLE 5.15
Component Matrix

	Component										
	1	2	3	4	5	6	7	8	9	10	11
V33	.885										
V21	.878										
V25	.869										
V29	.829										
V30						.783					
V26						.770					
V31						.748					
V22						.732					
V34						.727					
V23						.702					
V32	.693										
V20	.691	−.640									
V19	.690										
V3	.679										
V7							.672				
V28							.671				
V27									.625		
V9									.619		
V16										.601	
V13											
V12											
V11											
V8											
V24	.634	−.652									
V15		.633									
V6											
V17											
V14											
V2											
V18											
V1											
V4											
V10					.605						
V5											

(r = 0.638), *production capacity* (r = 0.614), *quality* (r = 0.590), *growth and expansion* (r = 0.553), *production time* (r = 0.549) and *market share* (r = 0.508) were significant positive.

H$_{06}$: There was no relationship between the Computer-aided Manufacturing and output process

The analysis of the correlation matrix showed that the above null hypothesis assumed was not acceptable as the correlations obtained between the Computer-aided Manufacturing and all process of output was significant and they were being affected in the organization in a positive manner. It was inference that the correlation of the Computer-aided Manufacturing with the parameters; e.g., *production capacity*

TABLE 5.16
Rotated Component Matrix

	Component										
	1	2	3	4	5	6	7	8	9	10	11
V29	.885										
V21	.876										
V25	.855										
V33						.852					
V7						.753					
V30						.710					
V12							.684				
V9							.642				
V6									.723		
V16					.702						
V13					.662						
V8					.683						
V11										.638	
V34		.924									
V31		.832									
V22		.739									
V27							.721				
V23								.719			
V15								.702			
V26								.662			
V17										.751	
V5			.814								
V28			.756								
V20			.749								
V24			.721								
V3										.803	
V32				.817							
V19				.778							
V2				.773							
V1									.619		
V18									.732		
V10											.756
V14											.749
V4											.721

(r = 0.653), *reliability* (r = 0.652), *production time* (r = 0.628), *quality* (r = 0.586), *productivity* (r = 0.564), *growth and expansion* (r = 0.531) and *competitiveness* (r = 0.525) were significant positive.

H₀₇: There was no relationship between the Automation and output process

The analysis of the correlation matrix showed that the above null hypothesis assumed was not acceptable as the correlations obtained between the Automation and all process of output was significant and they were being affected in the organization in a positive manner. It was inference that the correlation of the Automation with the parameters; e.g., *quality* (r = 0.709), *production capacity* (r = 0.679), *production time* (r = 0.677), *reliability* (r = 0.643), *productivity* (r = 0.612), *growth and*

TABLE 5.17

Associated Factors

Component	Dimensions	Factors
1	Sustainable Development	• Environment • Economic • Social
2	Natural Resources	• Renewable Energy • Eco-Friendly • Greenhouse Gas Reduction
3	Green Manufacturing	• CAD • CAPP • Green SCM • CAIR
4	Waste Management	• 5-S • JIT • Kaizen
5	Lifecycle Analysis	• Product Lifecycle • FEA • RLP
6	CAM	• Robotics • CNC • FMS
7	Automation	• AGV • ASRS • AMHS
8	CIPMS	• MRP • MRP-II • ERP
9	Expert Systems	• RPT • Concurrent Engineering • Reverse Engineering
10	Advanced Maintenance	• RCM • Predictive • Preventive
11	CMMS	• CMM & Inventory • Resource & Asset Management • Computerized Report Management

expansion (r = 0.590), *competitiveness* (r = 0.569), *profit* (r = 0.554), *sales* (r = 0.547) and *lead time* (r = 0.506) were significant positive.

H_{08}: There was no relationship between the CIPMS and output process

The analysis of the correlation matrix showed that the above null hypothesis assumed was not acceptable as the correlations obtained between the CIPMS and all process of output was significant, and they were being affected in the organization in a positive manner. It was inference that the correlation of the CIPMS with the parameters; e.g., *reliability* (r = 0.700), *profit* (r = 0.655), *production time* (r = 0.640), *competitiveness* (r = 0.639), *growth and expansion* (r = 0.606), *lead time* (r = 0.597), *productivity* (r = 0.581), *quality* (r = 0.547), *sales* (r = 0.529), *market share* (r = 0.521), *production capacity* (r = 0.516), and *customer base* (r = 0.515) were significant positive.

TABLE 5.18
Karl Pearson Correlation Matrix

OUTPUTS

		O1	O2	O3	O4	O5	O6	O7	O8	O9	O10	O11	O12
	I1	.606	.613	.450	.675	.727	.500	.527	.684	.404	.453	.448	.348
	I2	.606	.635	.527	.692	.758	.554	.556	.696	.472	.505	.471	.436
	I3	.550	.469	.371	.595	.746	.468	.472	.675	.450	.451	.354	.359
	I4	.672	.631	.451	.690	.770	.553	.552	.704	.478	.511	.526	.412
INPUTS	I5	.614	.549	.384	.590	.688	.496	.553	.638	.443	.422	.508	.481
	I6	.653	.628	.427	.586	.652	.564	.531	.525	.395	.377	.358	.453
	I7	.679	.677	.506	.709	.643	.612	.590	.569	.547	.554	.482	.474
	I8	.516	.640	.597	.547	.700	.581	.606	.639	.529	.655	.521	.515
	I9	.607	.652	.494	.647	.806	.596	.555	.708	.522	.584	.508	.467
	I10	.527	.566	.480	.624	.685	.575	.482	.631	.491	.507	.413	.488
	I11	.528	.554	.450	.553	.738	.470	.449	.610	.400	.432	.475	.498

(O1 – Production Capacity, O2 – Production Time, O3 – Lead Time, O4 – Quality, O5 – Reliability, O6 – Productivity, O7 – Growth and Expansion, O8 – Competitiveness, O9 – Sales, O10 – Profit, O11 – Market Share, O12 – Customer Base, I1 – Sustainable development, I2 – Natural resources, I3 – Green Manufacturing, I4 – Waste management, I5 – Lifecycle Analysis, I6 – Computer-aided Manufacturing, I7 – Automation, I8 – CIPMS, I9 – Expert Systems, I10 – Advanced Maintenance, I11 – CMMS)

H_{09}: **There was no relationship between the Expert Systems and output process**

The analysis of the correlation matrix showed that the above null hypothesis assumed was not acceptable as the correlations obtained between the Expert Systems and all process of output was significant and they were being affected in the organization in a positive manner. It was inference that the correlation of the Expert Systems with the parameters; e.g., *reliability* ($r = 0.806$), *competitiveness* ($r = 0.708$), *production time* ($r = 0.652$), *quality* ($r = 0.647$), *production capacity* ($r = 0.607$), *productivity* ($r = 0.596$), *profit* ($r = 0.584$), *growth and expansion* ($r = 0.555$), *sales* ($r = 0.522$) and *market share* ($r = 0.508$) were significant positive.

H_{10}: **There was no relationship between the Advanced Maintenance and output process**

The analysis of the correlation matrix showed that the above null hypothesis assumed was not acceptable as the correlations obtained between the Advanced Maintenance and all process of output was significant and they were being affected in the organization in a positive manner. It was inference that the correlation of the Advanced Maintenance with the parameters; e.g., *reliability* ($r = 0.685$), *competitiveness* ($r = 0.631$), *quality* ($r = 0.624$), *productivity* ($r = 0.575$), *production time* ($r = 0.566$), *production capacity* ($r = 0.527$) and *profit* ($r = 0.507$) were significant positive.

H_{11}: **There was no relationship between the CMMS and output process**

The analysis of the correlation matrix showed that the above null hypothesis assumed was not acceptable as the correlations obtained between the CMMS and all process of output was significant and they were being affected in the organization in a positive manner. It was inference that the correlation of the CMMS with the parameters; e.g., *reliability* (r = 0.738), *competitiveness* (r = 0.610), *production time* (r = 0.554), *quality* (r = 0.553) and *production capacity* (r = 0.528) were significant positive.

5.6   REGRESSION ANALYSIS

Multiple linear regression analysis has been used for developing regression weights. *Table t-value for 10 degrees of freedom at 5% level is 1.812 and the t-values higher than this in Table 5.19 will give the significant parameters.*

TABLE 5.19
Multiple Linear Regression Analysis of the Production Capacity

(a)

Model Summary				
Model	**R**	**R Square**	**Adjusted R Square**	**Std. Error of the Estimate**
1	.763	.522	.535	.518

ANOVA				
Model	**Sum of Squares**	**Df**	**Mean Square**	**F**
Regression	39.237	11	3.567	14.57
Residual	25.216	105	.269	
Total	67.453	116		

Predictors: (Constant), Sustainable development, Natural resources, Green Manufacturing, Waste management, Lifecycle Analysis, Computer-aided Manufacturing, Automation, CIPMS, Expert Systems, Advanced Maintenance, CMMS.
Dependent Variable: Production Capacity

(b)

	Un Standardized Coefficients		Coefficients	
	B	**Std. Error**	**Beta**	**T**
(Constant)	1.186	.270		4.495
Sustainable Development	.021	.037	.096	1.550
Natural Resources	−.010	.037	−.061	.270
Green Manufacturing	−.005	.027	−.033	1.170
Waste Management	.122	.053	.520	2.279
Lifecycle Analysis	−.043	.044	−.198	.902
Comp Aided Manuf.	.111	.037	.521	3.009
Automation	.095	.031	.405	.081
CIPMS	−.041	.025	−.252	1.629
Expert Systems	−.005	.036	−.033	.133
Advanced Maintenance	−.097	.051	−.307	2.911
CMMS	**.014**	**.028**	**.087**	**.521**

5.6.1 REGRESSION ANALYSIS FOR PRODUCTION CAPACITY

The regression outputs for the dependent variable *Production Capacity* are shown in Table 5.19.

The regression model developed was significant as ANOVA analysis showed F-test = 14.57, p < 05. The predictors identified from the analysis was Sustainable Development, Green Manufacturing, Waste Management, Computer-aided Manufacturing, CIPMS and Advanced Maintenance.

5.6.2 REGRESSION ANALYSIS FOR PRODUCTION TIME

Following are the regression outputs for the dependent variable *Production Time* shown in Table 5.20.

TABLE 5.20
Multiple Linear Regression Analysis of the Production Time

(a)

Model Summary				
Model	R	R Square	Adjusted R Square	Std. Error of the Estimate
1	.7S4	.614	.573	.551

ANOVA				
Model	SUM of Square	Df	Mean Square	F
Regression	51,437	11	4.769	16.23
Residual	32.996	105	.314	
Total	55.453	116		

Predictors: (Constant), Sustainable development, Natural resources, Green Manufacturing, Waste management, Lifecycle Analysis, Computer-aided Manufacturing, Automation, CIPMS, Expert Systems, Advanced Maintenance, CMMS.
Dependent Variable: Production Time

(b)

	Un Standardized Coefficients		Coefficients	
	B	Std. Error	Beta	T
(Constant)	.941	.292		3.088
Sustainable Development	.049	.041	.204	1.220
Natural Resources	.075	.040	.409	1.882
Green Manufacturing	−.099	.029	−.548	3.42
Waste Management	−.013	.058	−.049	.221
Lifecycle Analysis	−.086	.047	−.352	1.818
Comp Aided Manuf.	.130	.040	.541	3.256
Automation	.072	.033	272	2.153
CIPMS	.031	.028	.168	1.129
Expert Systems	.052	.039	317	2.1337
Advanced Maintenance	−.033	.053	−.091	.591
CMMS	−.026	.030	−.141	.875

The regression model developed was significant as ANOVA analysis showed F-test = 16.23, p < 05. The predictors identified from the analysis was Sustainable Development, Natural Resources, Green Engineering, Lifecycle Analysis, Comp. Aided Manufacturing, Automation, CIPMS and Advanced Maintenance.

5.6.3 REGRESSION ANALYSIS FOR LEAD TIME

Table 5.21 shows the Regression outputs for the dependent variable *Lead Time*.

The regression model developed was significant as ANOVA analysis showed F-test = 11.325, p < 05. The predictors identified from the analysis was Sustainable Development, Natural Resources, Green Manufacturing, Waste Management, Lifecycle Analysis, Comp. Aided Manufacturing and Advanced Maintenance.

5.6.4 REGRESSION ANALYSIS FOR QUALITY

Following are the regression outputs for the dependent variable *Quality*. Table 5.22 shows the Regression Analysis of Quality.

The regression model developed was significant as ANOVA analysis showed F-test = 14.9, p < 05. The predictors identified from the analysis was Sustainable Development, Green Manufacturing, Lifecycle Analysis, Comp. Aided Manufacturing and Advanced Maintenance.

5.6.5 REGRESSION ANALYSIS FOR RELIABILITY

Following are the regression outputs for the dependent variable *Reliability* as shown in Table 5.23.

The regression model developed was significant as ANOVA analysis showed F-test = 23.247, p < 05. The predictors identified from the analysis was Sustainable Development, Green Manufacturing, Waste Management, Comp. Aided Manufacturing, CIPMS, Advanced Maintenance and CMMS.

5.6.6 REGRESSION ANALYSIS FOR PRODUCTIVITY

Table 5.24 shows the regression outputs for the dependent variable *Productivity*.

The regression model developed was significant as ANOVA analysis showed F-test = 8.90, p < 05. The predictors identified from the analysis was Sustainable Development, Green Manufacturing, Lifecycle Analysis, Comp. Aided Manufacturing, Advanced Maintenance and CMMS.

5.6.7 REGRESSION ANALYSIS FOR GROWTH AND EXPANSION

Table 5.25 shows the regression outputs for the dependent variable *Growth and Expansion*,

The regression model developed was significant as ANOVA analysis showed f-test = 12.27, p < 05. The predictors identified from the analysis was Sustainable

TABLE 5.21
Multiple Linear Regression Analysis of the Lead Time

(a)

		Model Summary		
Model	R	R Square	Adjusted R Square	Std. Error of the Estimate
1	.616	.457	.400	.614

ANOVA

Model	Sun of Squares	de	Mean Square	F
Regression	33.328	11	3.030	11.325
Residual	39.595	105	.377	
Total	72.923	116		

Predictors: (Constant), Sustainable development, Natural resources, Green Manufacturing, Waste management, Lifecycle Analysis, Computer-aided Manufacturing, Automation, CIPMS, Expert Systems, Advanced Maintenance, CMMS.
Dependent Variable: Lead Time

(b)

Model	Un Standardized Coefficients		Coefficients	T
	B	Std. Error	Beta	
(Constant)	.714	.320		2.234
Sustainable Development	.017	.044	1:177	2.389
Natural Resources	.112	.043	.662	2.568
Green Manufacturing	−.080	.032	−478	1.521
Waste Management	−.074	.063	−.305	1.172
Lifecycle Analysis	−.045	.052	−.200	1.871
Comp Aided Manuf.	.031	.044	.139	1.708
Automation	.028	.037	.114	.760
CIPMS	.108	.030	.632	.575
Expert Systems	−.026	.043	−.169	.601
Advanced Maintenance	.043	.060	.129	2.706
CMMS	−.003	.033	−.019	.097

TABLE 5.22

Multiple Linear Regression Analysis of the Quality

(a)

Model Summary

Model	R	R Square	Adjusted R Square	Std. Error of the Estimate
1	.782	.611	.570	.432

ANOVA

Model	Sum of Squares	Df	Mean Square	F
Regression	38.237	11	3.426	14.393
Residual	24.245	105	232	
Total	62.581	116		

Predictors: (Constant), Sustainable development, Natural resources, Green Manufacturing, Waste management, Lifecycle Analysis, Computer-aided Manufacturing, Automation, CIPMS, Expert Systems, Advanced Maintenance, CMMS.

Dependent Variable: Quality

(b)

	Un Standardized Coefficients		Standardized Coefficients	
	B	Std. Error	Beta	T
(Constant)	1.031	251		4.123
Sustainable Development	.033	.035	.161	1.956
Natural Resources	.049	.034	.313	.933
Green Manufacturing	–.016	.025	–.103	2.640
Waste Management	.027	.050	.120	.544
Lifecycle Analysis	–11,156	.041	–.270	2.388
Comp Aided Manuf.	–1,111	.1:134	–.053	1.819
Automation	.123	.029	.542.	274
CIPMS	–.0131	.024	–.310	.415
Expert Systems	.039	.033	.278	.169
Advanced Maintenance	.057	.047	.187	1.207
CMMS	.013	.026	.095	.587

TABLE 5.23

Multiple Linear Regression Analysis of the Reliability

(a)

		Model Summary		
Model	R	R Square	Adjusted R Square	Std. Error of the Estimate
1	.861	.751	.725	.472

		ANOVA			
Model	Sum of Squares	df	Mean. Square	F	
Regression.	70.624	11	6.420	23.247	
Residual	23.376	105	223		
Total	94.000	116			

Predictors: (Constant), Sustainable development, Natural resources, Green Manufacturing, Waste management, Lifecycle Analysis, Computer-aided Manufacturing, Automation, CIPMS, Expert Systems, Advanced Maintenance, CMMS.

Dependent Variable: Reliability

(b)

	Un Standardized Coefficients		Standardized Coefficients	
	B	Std. Error	Beta	t
(Constant)	.238	.246		0.951
Sustainable Development	.074	.034	.294	2.134
Natural Resources	−.050	.033	−2.61	.997
Green Manufacturing	.081	.024	.426	1.317
Waste Management	.060	.049	.217	1.230
Lifecycle Analysis	−.101	.040	−391	.521
Comp Aided Manuf.	−.031	.034	−.122	1.918
Automation	.003	.028	.010	.095
CIPMS	−.032	.023	−.164	1.373
Expert Systems	.096	.033	.558	.930
Advanced Maintenance	−.091	.046	−.242	2.956
CMMS	.113	.025	.576	2.558

TABLE 5.24

Multiple Linear Regression Analysis of the Productivity

(a)

Model Summary

Model	R	R Square	Adjusted R Square	Std. Error of the Estimate
1	.695	AS3	.429	.708

ANOVA

Model	Sum of Squares	Df	Mean Square	F
Regression	49.149	11	4.468	8.90
Residual	52.663	105	.502	
Total	101.812	1 :...6		

Predictors: (Constant), Sustainable development, Natural resources, Green Manufacturing, Waste management, Lifecycle Analysis, Computer-aided Manufacturing, Automation, CIPMS, Expert Systems, Advanced Maintenance, CMMS.

Dependent Variable: Productivity

(b)

	Un Standardized Coefficients		Standardized Coefficients	
	B	Std. Error	Beta	T
(Constant)	.555	.369		1.506
Sustainable Development	-.016	.051	-.059	2.303
Natural Resources	.045	.050	.242	0.963
Green Manufacturing	-.043	.037	-.220	1.988
Waste Management	-.042	.073	-447	0.580
Lifecycle Analysis	-.114	.060	-.425	1.909
Comp Aided Manuf.	.415	.050	.439	2.282
Automation	.03	.042	.308	0.105
CIPMS	.015	.035	.076	0.442
Expert Systems	.102	.049	.569	0.71
Advanced Maintenance	.117	.070	300	1.681
CMMS	-.093	.035	-.456	2.449

TABLE 5.25

Multiple Linear Regression Analysis of the Growth and Expansion

(a)

Model Summary

Model	R	R Square	Adjusted R Square	Std. Error of the Estimate
1	.763	.522	.535	.518

ANOVA

Model	Sum of Squares	Df	Mean Square	F
Regression	39.237	11	3.567	12.274
Residual	25.216	105	.269	
Total	67.453	116		

Predictors: (Constant), Sustainable development, Natural resources, Green Manufacturing, Waste management, Lifecycle Analysis, Computer-aided Manufacturing, Automation, CIPMS, Expert Systems, Advanced Maintenance, CMMS.

Dependent Variable: Growth and Expansion

(b)

	Un Standardized Coefficients		Coefficients	
	B	Std. Error	Beta	T
(Constant)	1.186	.270		4.495
Sustainable Development	.021	.037	.096	1.550
Natural Resources	-.010	.037	-.061	.270
Green Manufacturing	-.005	.027	-.033	1.170
Waste Management	.122	.053	.520	2.279
Lifecycle Analysis	-.043	.044	-.198	.902
Comp Aided Manuf.	.111	.037	.521	3.009
Automation	.095	.031	.405	.081
CIPMS	-.041	.025	-.252	1.629
Expert Systems	-.005	.036	-.033	.133
Advanced Maintenance	-.097	.051	-.307	2.911
CMMS	.014	.028	.087	.521

Development, Green Manufacturing, Waste Management, Computer-aided Manufacturing, CIPMS and Advanced Maintenance.

5.6.8 REGRESSION ANALYSIS FOR COMPETITIVENESS

Table 5.26 show the regression outputs for the dependent variable *Competitiveness*.

The regression model developed was significant as ANOVA analysis showed F-test = 15.17, $p < 05$. The predictors identified from the analysis was Sustainable Development, Natural Resources, Green Engineering, Lifecycle Analysis, Comp. Aided Manufacturing, Automation, CIPMS and Advanced Maintenance.

5.6.9 REGRESSION ANALYSIS FOR SALES

The regression outputs for the dependent variable *Sales* are depicted in Table 5.27.

The regression model developed was significant as ANOVA analysis showed F-test = 8.035, $p < 05$. The predictors identified from the analysis was Sustainable Development, Natural Resources, Green Manufacturing, Waste Management, Lifecycle Analysis, Comp. Aided Manufacturing and Advanced Maintenance.

5.6.10 REGRESSION ANALYSIS FOR PROFIT

The following regression analysis for the dependent variable *Profit* is given in Table 5.28.

The regression model developed was significant as ANOVA analysis showed F-test = 28.839, $p < 05$. The predictors identified from the analysis was Sustainable Development, Green Manufacturing, Waste Management, Comp. Aided Manufacturing, CIPMS, Advanced Maintenance and CMMS.

5.6.11 REGRESSION ANALYSIS FOR MARKET SHARE

Table 5.29 shows the Regression Analysis of Market Share. The regression model developed was significant as ANOVA analysis showed F-test = 10.32, $p < 05$.

The regression model developed was significant as ANOVA analysis showed F-test = 27.921, $p < 05$. The predictors identified from the analysis was Sustainable Development, Green Manufacturing, Waste Management, Comp. Aided Manufacturing, CIPMS, Advanced Maintenance and CMMS.

5.6.12 REGRESSION ANALYSIS FOR CUSTOMER BASE

Table 5.30 shows the regression outputs for the dependent variable *Customer Base*.

The regression model developed was significant as ANOVA analysis showed F-test = 12.27, $p < 05$. The predictors identified from the analysis was Sustainable Development, Green Manufacturing, Waste Management, Computer-aided Manufacturing, CIPMS and Advanced Maintenance.

TABLE 5.26
Multiple Linear Regression Analysis of the Competitiveness

(a)

Model Summary

Model	R	R Square	Adjusted R Square	Std. Error of the Estimate
1	.7S4	.614	.573	.551

ANOVA

Model	SUM of Square	Df	Mean Square	F
Regression	51.437	11	4.769	15.175
Residual	32.996	105	.314	
Total	55.453	116		

Predictors: (Constant), Sustainable development, Natural resources, Green Manufacturing, Waste management, Lifecycle Analysis, Computer-aided Manufacturing, Automation, CIPMS, Expert Systems, Advanced Maintenance, CMMS.

Dependent Variable: Competitiveness

(b)

	Un Standardized Coefficients		Coefficients	
	B	Std. Error	Beta	t
(Constant)	.941	.292		3.088
Sustainable Development	.049	.041	.204	1.220
Natural Resources	.075	.040	.409	1.882
Green Manufacturing	-.099	.029	-.548	3.42
Waste Management	-.013	.058	-.049	.221
Lifecycle Analysis	-.086	.047	-.352	1.818
Comp Aided Manuf.	.130	.040	.541	3.256
Automation	.072	.033	272	2.153
CIPMS	.031	.028	.168	1.129
Expert Systems	.052	.039	317	2.1337
Advanced Maintenance	-.033	.053	-.091	.591
CMMS	-.026	.030	-.141	.875

TABLE 5.27

Multiple Linear Regression Analysis of the Sales

(a)

		Model Summary		
Model	**R**	**R Square**	**Adjusted R Square**	**Std. Error of the Estimate**
1	.616	.457	.400	.614

ANOVA

Model	**Sun of Squares**	**de**	**Mean Square**	**F**
Regression	33.328	11	3.030	8.035
Residual	39.595	105	.377	
Total	72.923	116		

Predictors: (Constant), Sustainable development, Natural resources, Green Manufacturing, Waste management, Lifecycle Analysis, Computer-aided Manufacturing, Automation, CIPMS, Expert Systems, Advanced Maintenance, CMMS.
Dependent Variable: Sales

(b)

	Un Standardized Coefficients		Coefficients	
	B	**Std. Error**	**Beta**	**T**
(Constant)	.714	.320		2.234
Sustainable Development	.017	.044	1:177	2.389
Natural Resources	.112	.043	.662.	2.568
Green Manufacturing	−.080	.032	−478	1.521
Waste Management	−.074	.063	−.305	1.172
Lifecycle Analysis	−.045	.052	−.200	1.871
Comp Aided Manuf.	.031	.044	.139	1.70S
Automation	.028	.037	.114	.760
CIPMS	.108	.030	.632.	.575
Expert Systems	−.026	.043	−.169	.601
Advanced Maintenance	.043	.060	.129	2.706
CMMS	−.003	.033	−.019	.097

TABLE 5.28
Multiple Linear Regression Analysis of the Profit

(a)

Model Summary

Model	R	R Square	Adjusted R Square	Std. Error of the Estimate
1	.861	.751	.725	.472

ANOVA

Model	Sum of Squares	df	Mean Square	F
Regression.	70.624	11	6.420	28.839
Residual	23,376	105	223	
Total	94.000	116		

Predictors: (Constant), Sustainable development, Natural resources, Green Manufacturing, Waste management, Lifecycle Analysis, Computer-aided Manufacturing, Automation, CIPMS, Expert Systems, Advanced Maintenance, CMMS.

Dependent Variable: Profit

(b)

	Un Standardized Coefficients		Standardized Coefficients	
	B	Std. Error	Beta	t
(Constant)	.238	.246		0.951
Sustainable Development	.074	.034	.294	2.134
Natural Resources	-.050	.033	-2.61	.997
Green Manufacturing	.081	.024	.426	1.317
Waste Management	.060	.049	.217	1.230
Lifecycle Analysis	-.101	.040	-.391	.521
Comp Aided Manuf.	-.031	.034	-.122	1.918
Automation	.003	.028	.010	.095
CIPMS	-.032	.023	-.164	1.373
Expert Systems	.096	.033	.558	.930
Advanced Maintenance	-.091	.046	-.242	2.956
CMMS	.113	.025	.576	2.558

TABLE 5.29

Multiple Linear Regression Analysis of the Market Share

(a)

Model Summary

Model	R	R Square	Adjusted R Square	Std. Error of the Estimate
1	.861	.751	.725	.472

ANOVA

Model	Sum of Squares	df	Mean. Square	F
Regression.	70.624	11	6.420	27.921
Residual	23,376	105	223	
Total	94.000	116		

Predictors: (Constant), Sustainable development, Natural resources, Green Manufacturing, Waste management, Lifecycle Analysis, Computer-aided Manufacturing, Automation, CIPMS, Expert Systems, Advanced Maintenance, CMMS.

Dependent Variable: Market Share

(b)

	Un Standardized Coefficients		Standardized Coefficients	
	B	Std. Error	Beta	t
(Constant)	.238	.246		0.951
Sustainable Development	.074	.034	.294	2.134
Natural Resources	-.050	.033	-2.61	.997
Green Manufacturing	.081	.024	.426	1.317
Waste Management	.060	.049	.217	1.230
Lifecycle Analysis	-.101	.040	-.391	.521
Comp Aided Manuf.	-.031	.034	-.122	1.918
Automation	.003	.028	.010	.095
CIPMS	-.032	.023	-.164	1.373
Expert Systems	.096	.033	.558	.930
Advanced Maintenance	-.091	.046	-.242	2.956
CMMS	.113	.025	.576	2.558

TABLE 5.30

Multiple Linear Regression Analysis of the Customer Base

(a)

Model Summary

Model	R	R Square	Adjusted R Square	Std. Error of the Estimate
1	.763	.522	.535	.518

ANOVA

Model	Sum of Squares	Df	Mean Square	F
Regression	39.237	11	3.567	12.274
Residual	25.216	105	.269	
Total	67.453	116		

Predictors: (Constant), Sustainable development, Natural resources, Green Manufacturing, Waste management, Lifecycle Analysis, Computer-aided Manufacturing, Automation, CIPMS, Expert Systems, Advanced Maintenance, CMMS.

Dependent Variable: Customer Base

(b)

	Un Standardized Coefficients		Coefficients	
	B	Std. Error	Beta	T
(Constant)	1.186	.270		4.495
Sustainable Development	.021	.037	.096	1.550
Natural Resources	-.010	.037	-.061	.270
Green Manufacturing	-.005	.027	-.033	1.170
Waste Management	.122	.053	.520	2.279
Lifecycle Analysis	-.043	.044	-.198	.902
Comp Aided Manuf.	.111	.037	.521	3.009
Automation	.095	.031	.405	.081
CIPMS	-.041	.025	-.252	1.629
Expert Systems	-.005	.036	-.033	.133
Advanced Maintenance	-.097	.051	-.307	2.911
CMMS	.014	.028	.087	.521

6 Qualitative Analysis

6.1 MODIFIED DEMATEL

Modified DEcision-MAking Trial and Evaluation Laboratory (M-DEMATEL) has been developed by modifying DEMATEL method, which is considered as an effective method for the identification of cause-effect chain components of a complex system. It deals with evaluating interdependent relationships among factors and finding the critical ones through a visual structural model. Basically, DEMATEL method involves a matrix where comparison varies qualitatively based on influence from 0 to 4 but pairwise comparison can vary from 0 to 9. Further, DEMATEL method is based on Cause-and-Effect Diagram but sometimes the situation demands analyzing things quantitatively. So, to accommodate these main and some other changes M-DEMATEL has been developed by Dr Chandan Deep Singh in 2020 during the COVID-19 pandemic.

Step 1: Generating Decision Matrix (Table 6.1)
Step 2: Generating Direct Relation Coefficient (Table 6.2)
Step 3: Normalizing the Direct Relation matrix,

$$X = A_{ij}/max. \left(\text{among the SUM}\right)$$

In above matrix the max. among the SUM is 35 (Table 6.3)
Step 5: Identity Matrix (Table 6.4)
Step 6: Calculate (I−X) (Table 6.5)
Step 7: Calculate $(I-X)^{-1}$ (Table 6.6)
Step 8: Calculate Total Relation matrix (Table 6.7)

TABLE 6.1
Decision Matrix

	SD	NR	GM	WM	LCA	CAM	AMT	CIPMS	ES	AMN	CMMS
SD	1	4	0.33	2	6	0.25	3	2	2	3	4
NR	0.25	1	0.33	0.25	2	3	0.5	1	3	2	0.5
GM	3	3	1	4	4	3	0.5	3	4	4	0.5
WM	0.25	0.5	0.5	1	3	0.5	0.33	1	1	0.5	0.25
LCA	0.16	0.17	0.33	0.33	1	0.33	0.25	0.5	0.5	0.25	0.25
CAM	4	4	2	2	3	1	4	4	4	4	3
AMT	0.33	0.33	1	0.33	1	0.25	1	4	3	3	0.5
CIPMS	0.5	0.5	0.33	0.25	1	2	0.25	1	3	2	0.33
ES	0.5	0.5	0.5	0.25	2	4	0.25	0.33	1	0.5	0.25
AMN	0.33	0.33	2	2	4	4	0.33	2	3	1	4
CMMS	0.25	0.25	1	0.33	2	3	0.25	3	2	2	1

DOI: 10.1201/9781003189510-6

TABLE 6.2
Direct Relation Coefficient Matrix

	SD	NR	GM	WM	LCA	CAM	AMT	CIPMS	ES	AMN	CMMS	SUM
SD	1	4	0.33	2	6	0.25	3	2	2	3	4	27.58
NR	0.25	1	0.33	0.25	2	3	0.5	1	3	2	0.5	13.83
GM	3	3	1	4	4	3	0.5	3	4	4	0.5	30
WM	0.25	0.5	0.5	1	3	0.5	0.33	1	1	0.5	0.25	8.83
LCA	0.16	0.17	0.33	0.33	1	0.33	0.25	0.5	0.5	0.25	0.25	4.07
CAM	4	4	2	2	3	1	4	4	4	4	3	35
AMT	0.33	0.33	1	0.33	1	0.25	1	4	3	3	0.5	14.74
CIPMS	0.5	0.5	0.33	0.25	1	2	0.25	1	3	2	0.33	11.16
ES	0.5	0.5	0.5	0.25	2	4	0.25	0.33	1	0.5	0.25	10.08
AMN	0.33	0.33	2	2	4	4	0.33	2	3	1	4	22.99
CMMS	0.25	0.25	1	0.33	2	3	0.25	3	2	2	1	15.08

$$T = X * (I - X)^{-1}$$

Step 9: Calculate C and S as shown in Table 6.8
Step 10: Calculate (C + S) and (C − S) as shown in Table 6.9
Step 11: Calculate Average and Rank alternatives based on the average Table 6.10

$$\text{Average for each parameter is} \left(\frac{(C+S)+(C-S)}{2} \right)$$

6.2 WEIGHTED SUM MODEL

In decision theory, the weighted sum model (WSM), also referred to as weighted linear combination (WLC) or simple additive weighting (SAW), is the best known multi-criteria decision-making method for evaluating a range of alternatives in terms of decision criteria (Table 6.11).

In general, suppose that a given MCDA problem is defined on m alternatives and n decision criteria. Furthermore, let us assume that all the criteria are benefit criteria, that is, the higher the values are, the better it is. Next, suppose that w_j denotes the relative weight of importance of the criterion C_j and a_{ij} is the performance value of alternative Ai when it is evaluated in terms of criterion C_j. Then, the total importance of alternative A_i (i.e., when all the criteria are considered simultaneously), is defined as follows:

$$A_i^{WSM-score} = \sum_{j=1}^{n} w_j a_{ij}, \quad \text{for } i = 1, 2, 3, \ldots, m.$$

In this case, as each criterion has equal importance, so $w_j = 1/11$

TABLE 6.3
Normalized Matrix (X)

	SD	NR	GM	WM	LCA	CAM	AMT	CIPMS	ES	AMN	CMMS
SD	0.02857143	0.114286	0.009429	0.057143	0.171429	0.007143	0.085714	0.057143	0.057143	0.085714	0.114286
NR	0.00714286	0.028571	0.009429	0.007143	0.057143	0.085714	0.014286	0.028571	0.085714	0.057143	0.014286
GM	0.08571429	0.085714	0.028571	0.114286	0.114286	0.085714	0.014286	0.085714	0.114286	0.114286	0.014286
WM	0.00714286	0.014286	0.014286	0.028571	0.085714	0.014286	0.009429	0.028571	0.028571	0.014286	0.007143
LCA	0.00457143	0.004857	0.009429	0.009429	0.028571	0.009429	0.007143	0.014286	0.014286	0.007143	0.007143
CAM	0.11428571	0.114286	0.057143	0.057143	0.085714	0.028571	0.114286	0.114286	0.114286	0.114286	0.085714
AMT	0.00942857	0.009429	0.028571	0.009429	0.028571	0.007143	0.028571	0.114286	0.085714	0.057143	0.014286
CIPMS	0.01428571	0.014286	0.009429	0.007143	0.028571	0.057143	0.007143	0.028571	0.085714	0.014286	0.009429
ES	0.01428571	0.014286	0.014286	0.007143	0.057143	0.114286	0.007143	0.009429	0.028571	0.014286	0.007143
AMN	0.00942857	0.009429	0.057143	0.057143	0.114286	0.114286	0.009429	0.057143	0.085714	0.028571	0.114286
CMMS	0.00714286	0.007143	0.028571	0.009429	0.057143	0.085714	0.007143	0.085714	0.057143	0.057143	0.028571

TABLE 6.4
Identity Matrix (I)

	SD	NR	GM	WM	LCA	CAM	AMT	CIPMS	ES	AMN	CMMS
SD	1	0	0	0	0	0	0	0	0	0	0
NR	0	1	0	0	0	0	0	0	0	0	0
GM	0	0	1	0	0	0	0	0	0	0	0
WM	0	0	0	1	0	0	0	0	0	0	0
LCA	0	0	0	0	1	0	0	0	0	0	0
CAM	0	0	0	0	0	1	0	0	0	0	0
AMT	0	0	0	0	0	0	1	0	0	0	0
CIPMS	0	0	0	0	0	0	0	1	0	0	0
ES	0	0	0	0	0	0	0	0	1	0	0
AMN	0	0	0	0	0	0	0	0	0	1	0
CMMS	0	0	0	0	0	0	0	0	0	0	1

For the maximization case, the best alternative is the one that yields the maximum total performance value (Tables 6.12 and 6.13).

6.3 WEIGHTED PRODUCT MODEL

The weighted product model (WPM) is a popular multi-criteria decision analysis (MCDA)/multi-criteria decision-making (MCDM) method. It is similar to the weighted sum model (WSM). The main difference is that instead of addition in the main mathematical operation now there is multiplication (Table 6.14).

Suppose that a given <u>MCDA</u> problem is defined on m alternatives and n decision criteria. Furthermore, let us assume that all the criteria are benefit criteria; that is, the higher the values are, the better it is. Next, suppose that w_j denotes the relative weight of importance of the criterion C_j and a_{ij} is the performance value of alternative A_i when it is evaluated in terms of criterion C_j. Then, if one wishes to compare the two alternatives A_K and A_L (where $m \geq K, L \geq 1$), then the following product has to be calculated.

$$P\left(A_K/A_L\right) = \prod_{j=1}^{n} \left(a_{Kj}/a_{Lj}\right)^{wj}, \quad \text{for } K, L = 1, 2, 3, \ldots, m.$$

If the ratio $P(A_K/A_L)$ is greater than or equal to the value 1, then it indicates that alternative A_K is more desirable than alternative A_L (in the maximization case). If we are interested in determining the best alternative, then the best alternative is the one that is better than or at least equal to all other alternatives.

The WPM is often called dimensionless analysis because its mathematical structure eliminates any units of measure. Therefore, the WPM can be used in single- and multi-dimensional MCDA/MCDM problems. That is, on decision problems where the alternatives are described in terms that use different units of measurement. An advantage of this method is that instead of the actual values it can use relative ones (Tables 6.15 and 6.16).

TABLE 6.5
(I–X) Matrix

	SD	NR	GM	WM	LCA	CAM	AMT	CIPMS	ES	AMN	CMMS
SD	0.97142857	-0.11429	-0.00943	-0.05714	-0.17143	-0.00714	-0.08571	-0.05714	-0.05714	-0.08571	-0.11429
NR	-0.00714286	0.971429	-0.00943	-0.00714	-0.05714	-0.08571	-0.01429	-0.02857	-0.08571	-0.05714	-0.01429
GM	-0.08571429	-0.08571	0.971429	-0.11429	-0.11429	-0.08571	-0.01429	-0.08571	-0.11429	-0.11429	-0.01429
WM	-0.00714286	-0.01429	-0.01429	0.971429	-0.08571	-0.01429	-0.00943	-0.02857	-0.02857	-0.01429	-0.00714
LCA	-0.00457143	-0.00486	-0.00943	-0.00943	0.971429	-0.00943	-0.00714	-0.01429	-0.11429	-0.00714	-0.00714
CAM	-0.11428571	-0.11429	-0.05714	-0.05714	-0.08571	0.971429	-0.11429	-0.11429	-0.11429	-0.11429	-0.08571
AMT	-0.00942857	-0.00943	-0.02857	-0.00943	-0.02857	-0.00714	0.971429	-0.11429	-0.08571	-0.08571	-0.01429
CIPMS	-0.01428571	-0.01429	-0.00943	-0.00714	-0.02857	-0.05714	-0.00714	0.971429	-0.08571	-0.05714	-0.00943
ES	-0.01428571	-0.01429	-0.01429	-0.00714	-0.05714	-0.11429	-0.00714	-0.00943	0.971429	-0.01429	-0.00714
AMN	-0.00942857	-0.00943	-0.05714	-0.05714	-0.11429	-0.11429	-0.00943	-0.05714	-0.08571	0.971429	-0.11429
CMMS	-0.00714286	-0.00714	-0.02857	-0.00943	-0.05714	-0.08571	-0.00714	-0.08571	-0.05714	-0.05714	0.971429

TABLE 6.6
$(I-X)^{-1}$ Matrix

	SD	NR	GM	WM	LCA	CAM	AMT	CIPMS	ES	AMN	CMMS
SD	1.053331	0.147482	0.040289	0.08847	0.256334	0.083898	0.112843	0.123358	0.139141	0.14796	0.157908
NR	0.031742	1.057369	0.030947	0.030361	0.111498	0.134027	0.038507	0.069721	0.138025	0.097931	0.046387
GM	0.126886	0.14203	1.067151	0.16215	0.23261	0.1771	0.058314	0.161973	0.215569	0.192453	0.077895
WM	0.016632	0.026073	0.023081	1.039445	0.111902	0.035303	0.018433	0.046412	0.052057	0.032228	0.019156
LCA	0.00916	0.011418	0.014168	0.015304	1.042166	0.020608	0.012133	0.024289	0.027003	0.017233	0.013777
CAM	0.157516	0.175634	0.101434	0.11055	0.219571	1.139285	0.161219	0.211525	0.2381	0.212828	0.156772
AMT	0.028017	0.031341	0.0481	0.03179	0.080892	0.059643	1.044617	0.151258	0.138172	0.123682	0.042952
CIPMS	0.03366	0.037561	0.026895	0.026561	0.074544	0.098477	0.026191	1.061149	0.127919	0.089628	0.03651
ES	0.038559	0.043014	0.031987	0.027839	0.101905	0.146464	0.03173	0.046098	1.072209	0.051386	0.03436
AMN	0.048402	0.054455	0.089387	0.095228	0.200113	0.186552	0.044673	0.125308	0.166819	1.095305	0.158401
CMMS	0.034645	0.038736	0.051784	0.036203	0.116248	0.137608	0.032432	0.131553	0.116668	0.103844	1.06291

TABLE 6.7
Total Relation Matrix

	SD	NR	GM	WM	LCA	CAM	AMT	CIPMS	ES	AMN	CMMS	C
SD	0.05333097	0.147482	0.040289	0.08847	0.256334	0.083898	0.112843	0.123358	0.139141	0.14796	0.157908	1.351015
NR	0.03174166	0.057369	0.030947	0.030361	0.111498	0.134027	0.038507	0.069721	0.138025	0.097931	0.046387	0.786515
GM	0.12688567	0.14203	0.067151	0.16215	0.23261	0.1771	0.058314	0.161973	0.215569	0.192453	0.077895	1.614131
WM	0.01663175	0.026073	0.023081	0.039445	0.111902	0.035303	0.018433	0.046412	0.052057	0.032228	0.019156	0.420721
LCA	0.00991605	0.011418	0.014168	0.015304	0.042166	0.020608	0.012133	0.024289	0.027003	0.017233	0.013777	0.208014
CAM	0.15751648	0.175634	0.101434	0.11055	0.219571	0.139285	0.161219	0.211525	0.2381	0.212828	0.156772	1.884434
AMT	0.02801729	0.031341	0.0481	0.03179	0.080892	0.059643	0.044617	0.151258	0.138172	0.123682	0.042952	0.780463
CIPMS	0.03365981	0.037561	0.026895	0.026561	0.074544	0.098477	0.026191	0.061149	0.127919	0.089628	0.03651	0.639095
ES	0.0385591	0.043014	0.031987	0.027839	0.101905	0.146464	0.03173	0.046098	0.072209	0.051386	0.03436	0.625552
AMN	0.04840181	0.054455	0.089387	0.095228	0.200113	0.186552	0.044673	0.125308	0.166819	0.095305	0.158401	1.264641
CMMS	0.03464498	0.038736	0.051784	0.036203	0.116248	0.137608	0.032432	0.131553	0.116668	0.103844	0.06291	0.862631
S	0.57930557	0.765111	0.525223	0.6639	1.547783	1.218966	0.581091	1.152644	1.431682	1.164478	0.807028	

TABLE 6.8
C and S Calculation

	SD	NR	GM	WM	LCA	CAM	AMT	CIPMS	ES	AMN	CMMS	C
SD	0.05333097	0.147482	0.040289	0.08847	0.256334	0.083898	0.112843	0.123358	0.139141	0.14796	0.157908	1.351015
NR	0.03174166	0.057369	0.030947	0.030361	0.111498	0.134027	0.038507	0.069721	0.138025	0.097931	0.046387	0.786515
GM	0.12688567	0.14203	0.067151	0.16215	0.23261	0.1771	0.058314	0.161973	0.215569	0.192453	0.077895	1.614131
WM	0.01663175	0.026073	0.023081	0.039445	0.111902	0.035303	0.018433	0.046412	0.052057	0.032228	0.019156	0.420721
LCA	0.00991605	0.011418	0.014168	0.015304	0.042166	0.020608	0.012133	0.024289	0.027003	0.017233	0.013777	0.208014
CAM	0.15751648	0.175634	0.101434	0.11055	0.219571	0.139285	0.161219	0.211525	0.2381	0.212828	0.156772	1.884434
AMT	0.02801729	0.031341	0.0481	0.03179	0.080892	0.059643	0.044617	0.151258	0.138172	0.123682	0.042952	0.780463
CIPMS	0.03365981	0.037561	0.026895	0.026561	0.074544	0.098477	0.026191	0.061149	0.127919	0.089628	0.03651	0.639095
ES	0.0385591	0.043014	0.031987	0.027839	0.101905	0.146464	0.03173	0.046098	0.072209	0.051386	0.03436	0.625552
AMN	0.04840181	0.054455	0.089387	0.095228	0.200113	0.186552	0.044673	0.125308	0.166819	0.095305	0.158401	1.264641
CMMS	0.03464498	0.038736	0.051784	0.036203	0.116248	0.137608	0.032432	0.131553	0.116668	0.103844	0.06291	0.862631
S	0.57930557	0.765111	0.525223	0.6639	1.547783	1.218966	0.581091	1.152644	1.431682	1.164478	0.807028	

TABLE 6.9
C and S Matrix

	C	S	C + S	C − S
SD	1.351015	0.579306	1.93032	0.771709
NR	0.786515	0.765111	1.551626	0.021404
GM	1.614131	0.525223	2.139354	1.088907
WM	0.420721	0.6639	1.084621	−0.24318
LCA	0.208014	1.547783	1.755797	−1.33977
CAM	1.884434	1.218966	3.1034	0.665468
AMT	0.780463	0.581091	1.361554	0.199372
CIPMS	0.639095	1.152644	1.791739	−0.51355
ES	0.625552	1.431682	2.057234	−0.80613
AMN	1.264641	1.164478	2.429119	0.100163
CMMS	0.862631	0.807028	1.66966	0.055603

TABLE 6.10
Ranking Based on Modified DEMATEL

	C + S	C − S	Average	Rank
SD	1.93032	0.771709	1.351015	3
NR	1.551626	0.021404	0.786515	6
GM	2.139354	1.088907	1.614131	2
WM	1.084621	−0.24318	0.420721	10
LCA	1.755797	−1.33977	0.208014	11
CAM	3.1034	0.665468	1.884434	1
AMT	1.361554	0.199372	0.780463	7
CIPMS	1.791739	−0.51355	0.639095	8
ES	2.057234	−0.80613	0.625552	9
AMN	2.429119	0.100163	1.264641	4
CMMS	1.66966	0.055603	0.862631	5

TABLE 6.11
Decision Matrix

	SD	NR	GM	WM	LCA	CAM	AMT	CIPMS	ES	AMN	CMMS
SD	1	4	0.33	2	6	0.25	3	2	2	3	4
NR	0.25	1	0.33	0.25	2	3	0.5	1	3	2	0.5
GM	3	3	1	4	4	3	0.5	3	4	4	0.5
WM	0.25	0.5	0.5	1	3	0.5	0.33	1	1	0.5	0.25
LCA	0.16	0.17	0.33	0.33	1	0.33	0.25	0.5	0.5	0.25	0.25
CAM	4	4	2	2	3	1	4	4	4	4	3
AMT	0.33	0.33	1	0.33	1	0.25	1	4	3	3	0.5
CIPMS	0.5	0.5	0.33	0.25	1	2	0.25	1	3	2	0.33
ES	0.5	0.5	0.5	0.25	2	4	0.25	0.33	1	0.5	0.25
AMN	0.33	0.33	2	2	4	4	0.33	2	3	1	4
CMMS	0.25	0.25	1	0.33	2	3	0.25	3	2	2	1

TABLE 6.12
Weighted Sum Matrix

	SD	NR	GM	WM	LCA	CAM	AMT	CIPMS	ES	AMN	CMMS	Weighted Sum
SD	0.0909	0.3636	0.0300	0.1818	0.5455	0.0227	0.2727	0.1818	0.1818	0.2727	0.3636	2.5073
NR	0.0227	0.0909	0.0300	0.0227	0.1818	0.2727	0.0455	0.0909	0.2727	0.1818	0.0455	1.2573
GM	0.2727	0.2727	0.0909	0.3636	0.3636	0.2727	0.0455	0.2727	0.3636	0.3636	0.0455	2.7273
WM	0.0227	0.0455	0.0455	0.0909	0.2727	0.0455	0.0300	0.0909	0.0909	0.0455	0.0227	0.8027
LCA	0.0145	0.0155	0.0300	0.0300	0.0909	0.0300	0.0227	0.0455	0.0455	0.0227	0.0227	0.3700
CAM	0.3636	0.3636	0.1818	0.1818	0.2727	0.0909	0.3636	0.3636	0.3636	0.3636	0.2727	3.1818
AMT	0.0300	0.0300	0.0909	0.0300	0.0909	0.0227	0.0909	0.3636	0.2727	0.2727	0.0455	1.2400
CIPMS	0.0455	0.0455	0.0300	0.0227	0.0909	0.1818	0.0227	0.0909	0.2727	0.1818	0.0300	0.9164
ES	0.0455	0.0455	0.0455	0.0227	0.1818	0.3636	0.0227	0.0300	0.0909	0.0455	0.0227	1.0145
AMN	0.0300	0.0300	0.1818	0.1818	0.3636	0.3636	0.0300	0.1818	0.2727	0.0909	0.3636	2.0900
CMMS	0.0227	0.0227	0.0909	0.0300	0.1818	0.2727	0.0227	0.2727	0.1818	0.1818	0.0909	1.3709

TABLE 6.13
Ranking Based on WSM

	Weighted Sum	Rank
SD	2.50727273	3
NR	1.25727273	6
GM	2.72727273	2
WM	0.80272727	10
LCA	0.37	11
CAM	3.18181818	1
AMT	1.24	7
CIPMS	1.01454545	8
ES	0.91636364	9
AMN	2.09	4
CMMS	1.37090909	5

TABLE 6.14
Decision Matrix

	SD	NR	GM	WM	LCA	CAM	AMT	CIPMS	ES	AMN	CMMS
SD	1	4	0.33	2	6	0.25	3	2	2	3	4
NR	0.25	1	0.33	0.25	2	3	0.5	1	3	2	0.5
GM	3	3	1	4	4	3	0.5	3	4	4	0.5
WM	0.25	0.5	0.5	1	3	0.5	0.33	1	1	0.5	0.25
LCA	0.16	0.17	0.33	0.33	1	0.33	0.25	0.5	0.5	0.25	0.25
CAM	4	4	2	2	3	1	4	4	4	4	3
AMT	0.33	0.33	1	0.33	1	0.25	1	4	3	3	0.5
CIPMS	0.5	0.5	0.33	0.25	1	2	0.25	1	3	2	0.33
ES	0.5	0.5	0.5	0.25	2	4	0.25	0.33	1	0.5	0.25
AMN	0.33	0.33	2	2	4	4	0.33	2	3	1	4
CMMS	0.25	0.25	1	0.33	2	3	0.25	3	2	2	1

TABLE 6.15
Weighted Product Matrix

	SD	NR	GM	WM	LCA	CAM	AMT	CIPMS	ES	AMN	CMMS	WPM
SD	1.0000	1.1343	0.9041	1.0650	1.1769	0.8816	1.1050	1.0650	1.0650	1.1050	1.1343	1.7805
NR	0.8816	1.0000	0.9041	0.8816	1.0650	1.1050	0.9389	1.0000	1.1050	1.0650	0.9389	0.8580
GM	1.1050	1.1050	1.0000	1.1343	1.1343	1.1050	0.9389	1.1050	1.1343	1.1343	0.9389	2.1762
WM	0.8816	0.9389	0.9389	1.0000	1.1050	0.9389	0.9041	1.0000	1.0000	0.9389	0.8816	0.6035
LCA	0.8465	0.8512	0.9041	0.9041	1.0000	0.9041	0.8816	0.9389	0.9389	0.8816	0.8816	0.3217
CAM	1.1343	1.1343	1.0650	1.0650	1.1050	1.0000	1.1343	1.1343	1.1343	1.1343	1.1050	2.9504
AMT	0.9041	0.9041	1.0000	0.9041	1.0000	0.8816	1.0000	1.1343	1.1050	1.1050	0.9389	0.8474
CIPMS	0.9389	0.9389	0.9041	0.8816	1.0000	1.0650	0.8816	1.0000	1.1050	1.0650	0.9041	0.5817
ES	0.9389	0.9389	0.9389	0.8816	1.0650	1.1343	0.8816	0.9041	1.0000	0.9389	0.8816	0.7020
AMN	0.9041	0.9041	1.0650	1.0650	1.1343	1.1343	0.9041	1.0650	1.1050	1.0000	1.1343	1.4400
CMMS	0.8816	0.8816	1.0000	0.9041	1.0650	1.1050	0.8816	1.1050	1.0650	1.0650	1.0000	0.8911

TABLE 6.16
Ranking Based on WPM

	Weighted Product	Rank
SD	1.78053574	3
NR	0.85804962	6
GM	2.17619003	2
WM	0.60349308	10
LCA	0.32169388	11
CAM	2.95038303	1
AMT	0.8473612	7
CIPMS	0.70204716	8
ES	0.58165303	9
AMN	1.4399836	4
CMMS	0.89108165	5

6.4 WEIGHTED AGGREGATED SUM PRODUCT ASSESSMENT

The weighted aggregated sum product assessment (WASPAS) method is a unique combination of weighted sum model (WSM) and weighted product model (WPM). Because of its mathematical simplicity and capability to provide more accurate results as compared to WSM and WPM methods, it is now being widely accepted as an efficient decision-making tool.

$$Q_i = (\lambda) \text{WSM} + (1 - \lambda)(\text{WPM})$$

Where $\lambda = 0.5$, equal weightage to WSM and WPM (Table 6.17)

6.5 GREY RELATIONAL ANALYSIS

Grey relational analysis (GRA), also called Deng's Grey Incidence Analysis model, was developed by a Chinese Professor Julong Deng of Huazhong University of Science and Technology. It is one of the most widely used models of Grey system

TABLE 6.17
Ranking Based on WASPAS

	WSM	WPM	Q_i	Rank
SD	2.507273	1.780536	2.143904	3
NR	1.257273	0.85805	1.057661	6
GM	2.727273	2.17619	2.451731	2
WM	0.802727	0.603493	0.70311	10
LCA	0.37	0.321694	0.345847	11
CAM	3.181818	2.950383	3.066101	1
AMT	1.24	0.847361	1.043681	7
CIPMS	1.014545	0.702047	0.858296	8
ES	0.916364	0.581653	0.749008	9
AMN	2.09	1.439984	1.764992	4
CMMS	1.370909	0.891082	1.130995	5

TABLE 6.18
Decision Matrix

	SD	NR	GM	WM	LCA	CAM	AMT	CIPMS	ES	AMN	CMMS
SD	1	4	0.33	2	6	0.25	3	2	2	3	4
NR	0.25	1	0.33	0.25	2	3	0.5	1	3	2	0.5
GM	3	3	1	4	4	3	0.5	3	4	4	0.5
WM	0.25	0.5	0.5	1	3	0.5	0.33	1	1	0.5	0.25
LCA	0.16	0.17	0.33	0.33	1	0.33	0.25	0.5	0.5	0.25	0.25
CAM	4	4	2	2	3	1	4	4	4	4	3
AMT	0.33	0.33	1	0.33	1	0.25	1	4	3	3	0.5
CIPMS	0.5	0.5	0.33	0.25	1	2	0.25	1	3	2	0.33
ES	0.5	0.5	0.5	0.25	2	4	0.25	0.33	1	0.5	0.25
AMN	0.33	0.33	2	2	4	4	0.33	2	3	1	4
CMMS	0.25	0.25	1	0.33	2	3	0.25	3	2	2	1

theory. GRA uses a specific concept of information. It defines situations with no information as black, and those with perfect information as white. However, neither of these idealized situations ever occurs in real world problems. In fact, situations between these extremes, which contain Dispersed knowledge (partial information), are described as being grey, hazy or fuzzy. A variant of GRA model, Taguchi-based GRA model, is very popular in engineering (Tables 6.18 to 6.20).

Step 1: Data is to be normalized and after normalizing the data will range from 0 to 1. In general, it is a method of converting original data into a comparable data. The equation for normalization is (Table 6.21):

$$x_i(k) = \frac{max\ x_i(k) - x_i(k)}{max\ x_i(k) - min\ x_i(k)}$$

TABLE 6.19
Normalized Decision Matrix

	SD	NR	GM	WM	LCA	CAM	AMT	CIPMS	ES	AMN	CMMS
SD	0.094607	0.289226	0.025404	0.222469	0.214286	0.009346	0.434153	0.110132	0.083333	0.116505	0.366636
NR	0.023652	0.072307	0.025404	0.027809	0.071429	0.11215	0.072359	0.055066	0.125	0.07767	0.04583
GM	0.283822	0.21692	0.076982	0.444939	0.142857	0.11215	0.072359	0.165198	0.166667	0.15534	0.04583
WM	0.023652	0.036153	0.038491	0.111235	0.107143	0.018692	0.047757	0.055066	0.041667	0.019417	0.022915
LCA	0.015137	0.012292	0.025404	0.036707	0.035714	0.012336	0.036179	0.027533	0.020833	0.009709	0.022915
CAM	0.37843	0.289226	0.153965	0.222469	0.107143	0.037383	0.578871	0.220264	0.166667	0.15534	0.274977
AMT	0.03122	0.023861	0.076982	0.036707	0.035714	0.009346	0.144718	0.220264	0.125	0.116505	0.04583
CIPMS	0.047304	0.036153	0.025404	0.027809	0.071429	0.074766	0.036179	0.055066	0.125	0.07767	0.030247
ES	0.047304	0.036153	0.038491	0.027809	0.071429	0.149533	0.036179	0.018172	0.041667	0.019417	0.022915
AMN	0.03122	0.023861	0.153965	0.222469	0.142857	0.149533	0.047757	0.110132	0.125	0.038835	0.366636
CMMS	0.023652	0.018077	0.076982	0.036707	0.071429	0.11215	0.036179	0.165198	0.083333	0.07767	0.091659

TABLE 6.20
Max and Min Values from Normalized Matrix

max	0.37843	0.289226	0.153965	0.444939	0.214286	0.149533	0.578871	0.220264	0.166667	0.15534	0.366636
min	0.015137	0.012292	0.025404	0.027809	0.035714	0.009346	0.036179	0.018172	0.020833	0.009709	0.022915

TABLE 6.21
Normalized Data

	SD	NR	GM	WM	LCA	CAM	AMT	CIPMS	ES	AMN	CMMS
SD	0.7813	0.0000	1.0000	0.5333	0.0000	1.0000	0.2667	0.5450	0.5714	0.2667	0.0000
NR	0.9766	0.7833	1.0000	1.0000	0.8000	0.2667	0.9333	0.8174	0.2857	0.5333	0.9333
GM	0.2604	0.2611	0.5988	0.0000	0.4000	0.2667	0.9333	0.2725	0.0000	0.0000	0.9333
WM	0.9766	0.9138	0.8982	0.8000	0.6000	0.9333	0.9787	0.8174	0.8571	0.9333	1.0000
LCA	1.0000	1.0000	1.0000	0.9787	1.0000	0.9787	1.0000	0.9537	1.0000	1.0000	1.0000
CAM	0.0000	0.0000	0.0000	0.5333	0.6000	0.8000	0.0000	0.0000	0.0000	0.0000	0.2667
AMT	0.9557	0.9582	0.5988	0.9787	1.0000	1.0000	0.8000	0.0000	0.2857	0.2667	0.9333
CIPMS	0.9115	0.9138	1.0000	1.0000	1.0000	0.5333	1.0000	0.8174	0.2857	0.5333	0.9787
ES	0.9115	0.9138	0.8982	1.0000	0.8000	0.0000	1.0000	1.0000	0.8571	0.9333	1.0000
AMN	0.9557	0.9582	0.0000	0.5333	0.4000	0.0000	0.9787	0.5450	0.2857	0.8000	0.0000
CMMS	0.9766	0.9791	0.5988	0.9787	0.8000	0.2667	1.0000	0.2725	0.5714	0.5333	0.8000

Step 2: In order to calculate Grey Relational Coefficient, we need to calculate deviation sequence from the normalized matrix as follows (Tables 6.22 and (6.23):

$$\Delta x_i\left(k\right) = \left| x_0\left(k\right) - x_i\left(k\right) \right|$$

TABLE 6.22
Deviation Sequence Matrix

	SD	NR	GM	WM	LCA	CAM	AMT	CIPMS	ES	AMN	CMMS
SD	0.2188	1.0000	0.0000	0.4667	1.0000	0.0000	0.7333	0.4550	0.4286	0.7333	1.0000
NR	0.0234	0.2167	0.0000	0.0000	0.2000	0.7333	0.0667	0.1826	0.7143	0.4667	0.0667
GM	0.7396	0.7389	0.4012	1.0000	0.6000	0.7333	0.0667	0.7275	1.0000	1.0000	0.0667
WM	0.0234	0.0862	0.1018	0.2000	0.4000	0.0667	0.0213	0.1826	0.1429	0.0667	0.0000
LCA	0.0000	0.0000	0.0000	0.0213	0.0000	0.0213	0.0000	0.0463	0.0000	0.0000	0.0000
CAM	1.0000	1.0000	1.0000	0.4667	0.4000	0.2000	1.0000	1.0000	1.0000	1.0000	0.7333
AMT	0.0443	0.0418	0.4012	0.0213	0.0000	0.0000	0.2000	1.0000	0.7143	0.7333	0.0667
CIPMS	0.0885	0.0862	0.0000	0.0000	0.0000	0.4667	0.0000	0.1826	0.7143	0.4667	0.0213
ES	0.0885	0.0862	0.1018	0.0000	0.2000	1.0000	0.0000	0.0000	0.1429	0.0667	0.0000
AMN	0.0443	0.0418	1.0000	0.4667	0.6000	1.0000	0.0213	0.4550	0.7143	0.2000	1.0000
CMMS	0.0234	0.0209	0.4012	0.0213	0.2000	0.7333	0.0000	0.7275	0.4286	0.4667	0.2000

TABLE 6.23
Delta Matrix

Delta min	0	0	0	0	0	0	0	0	0	0	0
Delta max	1	1	1	1	1	1	1	1	1	1	1
0.5*Delta max	0.5	0.5	0.5	0.5	0.5	0.5	0.5	0.5	0.5	0.5	0.5

TABLE 6.24
Grey Relation Coefficient Matrix

	SD	NR	GM	WM	LCA	CAM	AMT	CIPMS	ES	AMN	CMMS	GRA
SD	0.8496	0.8530	1.0000	1.0000	1.0000	0.5172	1.0000	1.0000	0.7778	0.5172	0.9591	0.8613
NR	0.9552	0.9599	0.7325	1.0000	0.7143	0.4054	0.8462	0.7325	0.4118	0.5172	0.8824	0.7416
GM	0.9552	0.8530	0.9152	1.0000	1.0000	0.8824	0.9450	0.7325	0.7778	0.8824	1.0000	0.9040
WM	0.4034	0.4036	0.3333	0.5385	0.4545	0.4054	0.8462	0.4073	0.3333	0.3333	0.8824	0.4856
LCA	0.3333	0.3333	0.5235	0.3333	0.5556	0.3333	0.6471	0.3333	0.3333	0.3333	0.4054	0.4059
CAM	1.0000	1.0000	1.0000	0.9162	0.7143	0.7143	1.0000	0.9152	1.0000	1.0000	1.0000	0.9327
AMT	0.9552	0.9599	0.7325	0.9162	0.7143	0.4054	1.0000	0.4073	0.5385	0.5172	0.9591	0.7369
CIPMS	0.6957	0.3333	1.0000	0.3333	0.3333	1.0000	0.3333	0.5235	0.5385	0.4054	0.3333	0.5831
ES	0.9187	0.9229	0.5235	0.3333	0.4545	0.3333	0.9450	0.5235	0.4118	0.3333	0.7143	0.5300
AMN	0.8496	0.8530	0.9152	1.0000	0.7143	0.3333	1.0000	1.0000	1.0000	0.7143	1.0000	0.8527
CMMS	0.9187	0.9229	0.7325	0.9162	1.0000	0.5172	1.0000	0.7325	0.4118	0.4054	0.8824	0.7672

TABLE 6.25
Ranking Based on GRA

	GRA	Rank
SD	0.861264	3
NR	0.741582	6
GM	0.903953	2
WM	0.485563	10
LCA	0.405899	11
CAM	0.932729	1
AMT	0.736881	7
CIPMS	0.583113	8
ES	0.529975	9
AMN	0.852698	4
CMMS	0.767238	5

Step 3: Grey relational coefficient ξ can be expressed as follows

$$\xi_i(k) = \frac{\Delta\,min + p\Delta\,max}{\Delta\,x_i(k) + p\Delta\,max}$$

and then the relational grade (GRG) follows as:

$$r_i = 1/n\sum\left[\xi(k)\right]$$

ξ is the Grey relational coefficient, $w(k)$ is the proportion of the number k influence factor to the total influence indicators (Tables 6.24 and 6.25).

TABLE 6.26
Decision Matrix

	SD	NR	GM	WM	LCA	CAM	AMT	CIPMS	ES	AMN	CMMS
SD	1	4	0.33	2	6	0.25	3	2	2	3	4
NR	0.25	1	0.33	0.25	2	3	0.5	1	3	2	0.5
GM	3	3	1	4	4	3	0.5	3	4	4	0.5
WM	0.25	0.5	0.5	1	3	0.5	0.33	1	1	0.5	0.25
LCA	0.16	0.17	0.33	0.33	1	0.33	0.25	0.5	0.5	0.25	0.25
CAM	4	4	2	2	3	1	4	4	4	4	3
AMT	0.33	0.33	1	0.33	1	0.25	1	4	3	3	0.5
CIPMS	0.5	0.5	0.33	0.25	1	2	0.25	1	3	2	0.33
ES	0.5	0.5	0.5	0.25	2	4	0.25	0.33	1	0.5	0.25
AMN	0.33	0.33	2	2	4	4	0.33	2	3	1	4
CMMS	0.25	0.25	1	0.33	2	3	0.25	3	2	2	1

6.6 SIMPLE MULTI-ATTRIBUTE RATING TECHNIQUE

SMART (Simple Multi-Attribute Rating Technique) is a compensatory method of multiple-criteria decision-making, developed by Edwards in 1971. In the SMART method, ratings of alternatives are assigned directly, in the natural scales of the criteria (where available). As an example, a natural scale is a range of 100 to 200 miles per hour for evaluating the criterion of the top speed of motor cars. Holding the weighting of criteria and rating of alternatives as separate as possible, the different scales of criteria need to convert to a common internal scale. In SMART, a process is done mathematically by the decision maker using a "Value Function" (Table 6.26).

Step 1: Normalize the decision matrix (Table 6.27)
Step 2: Calculate Utilities by the formula:

$$U_j = \sum k \cdot w_k u_j$$

TABLE 6.27
Normalized Decision Matrix

	SD	NR	GM	WM	LCA	CAM	AMT	CIPMS	ES	AMN	CMMS
SD	0.0946	0.2743	0.0354	0.1570	0.2069	0.0117	0.2814	0.0916	0.0755	0.1348	0.2743
NR	0.0237	0.0686	0.0354	0.0196	0.0690	0.1406	0.0469	0.0458	0.1132	0.0899	0.0343
GM	0.2838	0.2058	0.1073	0.3140	0.1379	0.1406	0.0469	0.1374	0.1509	0.1798	0.0343
WM	0.0237	0.0343	0.0536	0.0785	0.1034	0.0234	0.0310	0.0458	0.0377	0.0225	0.0171
LCA	0.0151	0.0117	0.0354	0.0259	0.0345	0.0155	0.0235	0.0229	0.0189	0.0112	0.0171
CAM	0.3784	0.2743	0.2146	0.1570	0.1034	0.0469	0.3752	0.1832	0.1509	0.1798	0.2058
AMT	0.0312	0.0226	0.1073	0.0259	0.0345	0.0117	0.0938	0.1832	0.1132	0.1348	0.0343
CIPMS	0.0473	0.0343	0.0354	0.0196	0.0345	0.0938	0.0235	0.0458	0.1132	0.0899	0.0226
ES	0.0473	0.0343	0.0536	0.0196	0.0690	0.1875	0.0235	0.0151	0.0377	0.0225	0.0171
AMN	0.0312	0.0226	0.2146	0.1570	0.1379	0.1875	0.0310	0.0916	0.1132	0.0449	0.2743
CMMS	0.0237	0.0171	0.1073	0.0259	0.0690	0.1406	0.0235	0.1374	0.0755	0.0899	0.0686

TABLE 6.28
Utility Calculation

	SD	NR	GM	WM	LCA	CAM	AMT	CIPMS	ES	AMN	CMMS	Utilities
SD	0.8600	2.4938	0.3219	1.4270	1.8807	0.1065	2.5582	0.8328	0.6860	1.2256	2.4938	14.8863
NR	0.2150	0.6235	0.3219	0.1784	0.6269	1.2785	0.4264	0.4164	1.0291	0.8171	0.3117	6.2447
GM	2.5799	1.8704	0.9753	2.8540	1.2538	1.2785	0.4264	1.2492	1.3721	1.6342	0.3117	15.8054
WM	0.2150	0.3117	0.4877	0.7135	0.9403	0.2131	0.2814	0.4164	0.3430	0.2043	0.1559	4.2823
LCA	0.1376	0.1060	0.3219	0.2355	0.3134	0.1406	0.2132	0.2082	0.1715	0.1021	0.1559	2.1059
CAM	3.4399	2.4938	1.9506	1.4270	0.9403	0.4262	3.4109	1.6656	1.3721	1.6342	1.8704	20.6310
AMT	0.2838	0.2057	0.9753	0.2355	0.3134	0.1065	0.8527	1.6656	1.0291	1.2256	0.3117	7.2050
CIPMS	0.4300	0.3117	0.3219	0.1784	0.6269	0.8523	0.2132	0.4164	1.0291	0.8171	0.2057	5.0892
ES	0.4300	0.3117	0.4877	0.1784	0.6269	1.7046	0.2132	0.1374	0.3430	0.2043	0.1559	4.7930
AMN	0.2838	0.2057	1.9506	1.4270	1.2538	1.7046	0.2814	0.8328	1.0291	0.4085	2.4938	11.8712
CMMS	0.2150	0.1559	0.9753	0.2355	0.6269	1.2785	0.2132	1.2492	0.6860	0.8171	0.6235	7.0760

TABLE 6.29
Ranking Based on SMART

	Utilities	Rank
SD	14.88634	3
NR	7.075966	6
GM	15.80543	2
WM	4.28226	10
LCA	2.105866	11
CAM	20.63098	1
AMT	6.244684	7
CIPMS	5.089175	8
ES	4.793038	9
AMN	11.87123	4
CMMS	7.205021	5

Where $U_j = 100/11$ (as each parameter is having equal weightage) (Tables 6.28 and 6.29)

6.7 CRITERIA IMPORTANCE THROUGH INTERCRITERIA CORRELATION

CRITIC (CRiteria Importance Through Intercriteria Correlation) method is one of the weighting methods which determines objective weights for criteria. CRITIC method was proposed by Diakoulaki et al. This method includes the intensity of the contrast and the conflict in the structure of the decision-making problem. It uses correlation analysis to find out the contrasts between criteria. In this method the decision matrix is evaluated and the standard deviation of normalized criterion values by columns and the correlation coefficients of all pairs of columns are used to determine the criteria contrast.

Step 1: The decision matrix X is formed. It shows the performance of different alternatives with respect to various criteria.

$$X = \left[X_{ij}\right]_{mxn} = \begin{bmatrix} X_{11} & X_{12} & \cdots & X_{1n} \\ X_{21} & X_{22} & \cdots & X_{2n} \\ \vdots & \vdots & \ddots & \vdots \\ X_{m1} & X_{m2} & \cdots & X_{mn} \end{bmatrix} \left(i = 1,2,\ldots,m \text{ and } j = 1,2,\ldots,n\right)$$

X_{ij} presents the performance value of ith alternative on jth criterion.

Step 2: Decision matrix is normalized using the following equation:

$$X_{ij} = \frac{X_{ij} - min\left(X_{ij}\right)}{max\left(X_{ij}\right) - min\left(X_{ij}\right)}$$

Step 3: While determining the criteria weights, both standard deviation of the criterion and its correlation between other criteria are included. In this regard, the weight of the jth criterion (w_j) is obtained as:

$$W_j = \frac{C_j}{\sum_{j=1}^{n} C_j}$$

where C_j is the quantity of information contained in jth criterion determined as:

$$C_j = \sigma_j \sum_{j'=1}^{n} \left(1 - r_j'\right)$$

where σ_j is standard deviation of the jth criterion and r_{ij} is the correlation coefficient between the two criteria.

It can be concluded that this method gives the higher weight to the criterion which has high standard deviation and low correlation with other criteria; a higher value of C_j means that a greater amount of information is obtained from the given criterion so the relative significance of the criterion for the decision-making problem is higher (Tables 6.30 to 6.35).

6.8 ENTROPY

Determination of objective criteria weights according to the entropy method is based on the measurement of uncertain information contained in the decision matrix and directly generates a set of weights for a given criteria based on mutual contrast of individual criteria values of variants for each criterion and then for all the criteria at the same time.

TABLE 6.30

Decision Matrix

	SD	NR	GM	WM	LCA	CAM	AMT	CIPMS	ES	AMN	CMMS
SD	1	4	0.33	2	6	0.25	3	2	2	3	4
NR	0.25	1	0.33	0.25	2	3	0.5	1	3	2	0.5
GM	3	3	1	4	4	3	0.5	3	4	4	0.5
WM	0.25	0.5	0.5	1	3	0.5	0.33	1	1	0.5	0.25
LCA	0.16	0.17	0.33	0.33	1	0.33	0.25	0.5	0.5	0.25	0.25
CAM	4	4	2	2	3	1	4	4	4	4	3
AMT	0.33	0.33	1	0.33	1	0.25	1	4	3	3	0.5
CIPMS	0.5	0.5	0.33	0.25	1	2	0.25	1	3	2	0.33
ES	0.5	0.5	0.5	0.25	2	4	0.25	0.33	1	0.5	0.25
AMN	0.33	0.33	2	2	4	4	0.33	2	3	1	4
CMMS	0.25	0.25	1	0.33	2	3	0.25	3	2	2	1

TABLE 6.31

Best and Worst Values

Best	4	4	2	4	6	4	4	4	4	4	4
Worst	0.16	0.17	0.33	0.25	1	0.25	0.25	0.33	0.5	0.25	0.25

TABLE 6.32

Normalized Matrix

	SD	NR	GM	WM	LCA	CAM	AMT	CIPMS	ES	AMN	CMMS
SD	0.2188	1.0000	0.0000	0.4667	1.0000	0.0000	0.7333	0.4550	0.4286	0.7333	1.0000
NR	0.0234	0.2167	0.0000	0.0000	0.2000	0.7333	0.0667	0.1826	0.7143	0.4667	0.0667
GM	0.7396	0.7389	0.4012	1.0000	0.6000	0.7333	0.0667	0.7275	1.0000	1.0000	0.0667
WM	0.0234	0.0862	0.1018	0.2000	0.4000	0.0667	0.0213	0.1826	0.1429	0.0667	0.0000
LCA	0.0000	0.0000	0.0000	0.0213	0.0000	0.0213	0.0000	0.0463	0.0000	0.0000	0.0000
CAM	1.0000	1.0000	1.0000	0.4667	0.4000	0.2000	1.0000	1.0000	1.0000	1.0000	0.7333
AMT	0.0443	0.0418	0.4012	0.0213	0.0000	0.0000	0.2000	1.0000	0.7143	0.7333	0.0667
CIPMS	0.0885	0.0862	0.0000	0.0000	0.0000	0.4667	0.0000	0.1826	0.7143	0.4667	0.0213
ES	0.0885	0.0862	0.1018	0.0000	0.2000	1.0000	0.0000	0.0000	0.1429	0.0667	0.0000
AMN	0.0443	0.0418	1.0000	0.4667	0.6000	1.0000	0.0213	0.4550	0.7143	0.2000	1.0000
CMMS	0.0234	0.0209	0.4012	0.0213	0.2000	0.7333	0.0000	0.7275	0.4286	0.4667	0.2000

Step 1: The decision matrix X which shows the performance of different alternatives with respect to various criteria is formed.

$$X = \left[X_{ij} \right]_{mxn} = \begin{bmatrix} X_{11} & X_{12} & \cdots & X_{1n} \\ X_{21} & X_{22} & \cdots & X_{2n} \\ \vdots & \vdots & \ddots & \vdots \\ X_{m1} & X_{m2} & \cdots & X_{mn} \end{bmatrix} \left(i = 1, 2, \ldots, \text{m}; j = 1, 2, \ldots, \text{n} \right)$$

X_{ij} presents the performance value of ith alternative on jth criterion.

TABLE 6.33
Correlation Matrix

	SD	NR	GM	WM	LCA	CAM	AMT	CIPMS	ES	AMN	CMMS
SD	1	0.811	0.521	0.713	0.355	−0.059	0.674	0.575	0.649	0.757	0.288
NR	0.811	1	0.231	0.696	0.699	−0.248	0.847	0.437	0.483	0.756	0.542
GM	0.521	0.231	1	0.444	0.224	0.235	0.365	0.662	0.571	0.351	0.569
WM	0.713	0.696	0.444	1	0.735	0.094	0.344	0.415	0.54	0.579	0.439
LCA	0.355	0.699	0.224	0.735	1	0.015	0.48	0.171	0.193	0.332	0.741
CAM	−0.059	−0.248	0.235	0.094	0.015	1	−0.451	−0.188	0.193	−0.16	−0.012
AMT	0.674	0.847	0.365	0.344	0.48	−0.451	1	0.522	0.372	0.633	0.641
CIPMS	0.575	0.437	0.662	0.415	0.171	−0.188	0.522	1	0.682	0.8	0.331
ES	0.649	0.483	0.571	0.54	0.193	0.193	0.372	0.682	1	0.827	0.297
AMN	0.757	0.756	0.351	0.579	0.332	−0.16	0.633	0.8	0.827	1	0.285
CMMS	0.288	0.542	0.569	0.439	0.741	−0.012	0.641	0.331	0.297	0.285	1

TABLE 6.34
Criteria Weight Matrix

St. Dev.	0.337	0.402	0.381	0.324	0.313	0.406	0.344	0.366	0.343	0.363	0.411	
	SD	NR	GM	WM	LCA	CAM	AMT	CIPMS	ES	AMN	CMMS	Sum
SD	0	0.189	0.479	0.287	0.645	1.059	0.326	0.425	0.351	0.243	0.712	4.716797
NR	0.189	0	0.769	0.304	0.301	1.248	0.153	0.563	0.517	0.244	0.458	4.745736
GM	0.479	0.769	0	0.556	0.776	0.765	0.635	0.338	0.429	0.649	0.431	5.827966
WM	0.287	0.304	0.556	0	0.265	0.906	0.656	0.585	0.46	0.421	0.561	5.001982
LCA	0.645	0.301	0.776	0.265	0	0.985	0.52	0.829	0.807	0.668	0.259	6.054089
CAM	1.059	1.248	0.765	0.906	0.985	0	1.451	1.188	0.807	1.16	1.012	10.58267
AMT	0.326	0.153	0.635	0.656	0.52	1.451	0	0.478	0.628	0.367	0.359	5.573985
CIPMS	0.425	0.563	0.338	0.585	0.829	1.188	0.478	0	0.318	0.2	0.669	5.592265
ES	0.351	0.517	0.429	0.46	0.807	0.807	0.628	0.318	0	0.173	0.703	5.192133
AMN	0.243	0.244	0.649	0.421	0.668	1.16	0.367	0.2	0.173	0	0.715	4.839036
CMMS	0.712	0.458	0.431	0.561	0.259	1.012	0.359	0.669	0.703	0.715	0	5.87788

TABLE 6.35
Ranking Based on CRITIC Method

	Cj	Wj	%Wj	Rank
SD	2.217882	0.09460841	9.460841	3
NR	1.908934	0.08142959	8.142959	6
GM	2.414118	0.10297925	10.29793	2
WM	1.620462	0.0691242	6.91242	10
LCA	1.590873	0.06786201	6.786201	11
CAM	4.291283	0.18305365	18.30537	1
AMT	1.896987	0.08091995	8.091995	7
CIPMS	1.781	0.076	7.596	8
ES	1.758	0.075	7.498	9
AMN	2.046422	0.0872944	8.72944	4
CMMS	1.917237	0.08178377	8.178377	5
	23.44276			

Step 2: The decision matrix is normalized. Beneficial (maximization) and non-beneficial (minimization) criteria are normalized by Equations (2) and (3) respectively. To have the performance measures comparable and dimensionless, all the entries of the decision matrix are linear normalized using two equations:

$$r_{ij} = \frac{X_{ij} - min(X_{ij})}{max(X_{ij}) - min(X_{ij})} \quad i = 1, 2, \ldots, m \text{ and } j = 1, 2, \ldots, n$$

$$r_{ij} = \frac{max(X_{ij}) - X_{ij}}{max(X_{ij}) - min(X_{ij})} \quad i = 1, 2, \ldots, m \text{ and } j = 1, 2, \ldots, n$$

Step 3: Entropy values (e_j) are determined for each criterion.

$$e_j = -\frac{\sum_{i=1}^{m} f_{ij} \ln f_{ij}}{\ln m} \quad i = 1, 2, \ldots, n \text{ and } j = 1, 2, \ldots, n$$

where $$f_j = \frac{f_{ij}}{\sum_{j=1}^{m} r_{ij}} \text{ and } 0 < e_j < 1.$$

Step 4: Entropy weights (w_j) are calculated.

$$W_j = \frac{1 - e_j}{n - \sum_{i=1}^{m} e_j} \text{ where } \sum_{j=1}^{n} W_j = 1$$

$(1 - e_j)$ represents the inherent contrast intensity of each criterion. In other words it is the degree of divergence of the intrinsic information of each criterion. If $(1 - e_j)$ is normalized, then the final weights of each criterion can be obtained. The entropy weight is a parameter that describes the importance of the criterion. The smaller the value of the entropy, the larger the entropy-based weight, then the specific criterion provides more information, and this criterion becomes more important than the other criteria in the decision-making process (Tables 6.36 to 6.39).

6.9 EVALUATION BASED ON DISTANCE FROM AVERAGE SOLUTION

The evaluation based on distance from average solution (EDAS) method was introduced by Keshavarz Ghorabaee for inventory ABC classification. It was presented that the EDAS method has good efficiency and needs fewer computations in comparison with other ABC classification methods. Moreover, the efficiency of the EDAS method as an MCDM method was demonstrated by comparing it with some commonly used methods. The evaluation of alternatives in this method is based on distances of each alternative from the average solution with respect to each criterion.

TABLE 6.36
Decision Matrix

	SD	NR	GM	WM	LCA	CAM	AMT	CIPMS	ES	AMN	CMMS
SD	1	4	0.33	2	6	0.25	3	2	2	3	4
NR	0.25	1	0.33	0.25	2	3	0.5	1	3	2	0.5
GM	3	3	1	4	4	3	0.5	3	4	4	0.5
WM	0.25	0.5	0.5	1	3	0.5	0.33	1	1	0.5	0.25
LCA	0.16	0.17	0.33	0.33	1	0.33	0.25	0.5	0.5	0.25	0.25
CAM	4	4	2	2	3	1	4	4	4	4	3
AMT	0.33	0.33	1	0.33	1	0.25	1	4	3	3	0.5
CIPMS	0.5	0.5	0.33	0.25	1	2	0.25	1	3	2	0.33
ES	0.5	0.5	0.5	0.25	2	4	0.25	0.33	1	0.5	0.25
AMN	0.33	0.33	2	2	4	4	0.33	2	3	1	4
CMMS	0.25	0.25	1	0.33	2	3	0.25	3	2	2	1

TABLE 6.37
Normalized Matrix

	SD	NR	GM	WM	LCA	CAM	AMT	CIPMS	ES	AMN	CMMS
SD	0.0946	0.2743	0.0354	0.1570	0.2069	0.0117	0.2814	0.0916	0.0755	0.1348	0.2743
NR	0.0237	0.0686	0.0354	0.0196	0.0690	0.1406	0.0469	0.0458	0.1132	0.0899	0.0343
GM	0.2838	0.2058	0.1073	0.3140	0.1379	0.1406	0.0469	0.1374	0.1509	0.1798	0.0343
WM	0.0237	0.0343	0.0536	0.0785	0.1034	0.0234	0.0310	0.0458	0.0377	0.0225	0.0171
LCA	0.0151	0.0117	0.0354	0.0259	0.0345	0.0155	0.0235	0.0229	0.0189	0.0112	0.0171
CAM	0.3784	0.2743	0.2146	0.1570	0.1034	0.0469	0.3752	0.1832	0.1509	0.1798	0.2058
AMT	0.0312	0.0226	0.1073	0.0259	0.0345	0.0117	0.0938	0.1832	0.1132	0.1348	0.0343
CIPMS	0.0473	0.0343	0.0354	0.0196	0.0345	0.0938	0.0235	0.0458	0.1132	0.0899	0.0226
ES	0.0473	0.0343	0.0536	0.0196	0.0690	0.1875	0.0235	0.0151	0.0377	0.0225	0.0171
AMN	0.0312	0.0226	0.2146	0.1570	0.1379	0.1875	0.0310	0.0916	0.1132	0.0449	0.2743
CMMS	0.0237	0.0171	0.1073	0.0259	0.0690	0.1406	0.0235	0.1374	0.0755	0.0899	0.0686

TABLE 6.38
Entropy Matrix

	SD	NR	GM	WM	LCA	CAM	AMT	CIPMS	ES	AMN	CMMS
SD	−0.223	−0.355	−0.118	−0.291	−0.326	−0.052	−0.357	−0.219	−0.195	−0.27	−0.355
NR	−0.089	−0.184	−0.118	−0.077	−0.184	−0.276	−0.144	−0.141	−0.247	−0.217	−0.116
GM	−0.357	−0.325	−0.24	−0.364	−0.273	−0.276	−0.144	−0.273	−0.285	−0.309	−0.116
WM	−0.089	−0.116	−0.157	−0.2	−0.235	−0.088	−0.108	−0.141	−0.124	−0.085	−0.07
LCA	−0.063	−0.052	−0.118	−0.095	−0.116	−0.064	−0.088	−0.086	−0.075	−0.05	−0.07
CAM	−0.368	−0.355	−0.33	−0.291	−0.235	−0.143	−0.368	−0.311	−0.285	−0.309	−0.325
AMT	−0.108	−0.086	−0.24	−0.095	−0.116	−0.052	−0.222	−0.311	−0.247	−0.27	−0.116
CIPMS	−0.144	−0.116	−0.118	−0.077	−0.116	−0.222	−0.088	−0.141	−0.247	−0.217	−0.086
ES	−0.144	−0.116	−0.157	−0.077	−0.184	−0.314	−0.088	−0.063	−0.124	−0.085	−0.07
AMN	−0.108	−0.086	−0.33	−0.291	−0.273	−0.314	−0.108	−0.219	−0.247	−0.139	−0.355
CMMS	−0.089	−0.07	−0.24	−0.095	−0.184	−0.276	−0.088	−0.273	−0.195	−0.217	−0.184

TABLE 6.39
Ranking Based on ENTROPY Method

	Ej (Entropy Values)	dj	Wj (Entropy Weights)	+wj	Rank
SD	−1.42244	0.593204	0.406796	0.242641	0.242641	3
NR	−1.79168	0.747189	0.252811	0.150794	0.150794	6
GM	−1.41108	0.588464	0.411536	0.245469	0.245469	2
WM	−2.76078	1.151333	−0.15133	−0.09027	0.090265	10
LCA	−2.46949	1.029855	−0.02986	−0.01781	0.017808	11
CAM	−0.87844	0.366339	0.633661	0.37796	0.37796	1
AMT	−2.96094	1.234808	−0.23481	−0.14006	0.140056	7
CIPMS	−1.86174	0.776405	0.223595	0.133368	0.133368	8
ES	−1.90884	0.796046	0.203954	0.121652	0.121652	9
AMN	−3.31964	1.384395	−0.38439	−0.22928	0.22928	4
CMMS	−1.57166	0.655432	0.344568	0.205525	0.205525	5
		1.676529			

The mathematical procedure for the EDAS method for a decision-making problem with n criteria and m alternatives can analyzed as per the following procedures:

Step 1: Select the available alternatives and the most important criteria which describes the alternatives to construct a decision-making matrix D as:

$$D = \begin{array}{c} \\ A_1 \\ A_2 \\ A_3 \\ \\ \\ \\ A_m \end{array} \begin{array}{cccccc} C_1 & C_2 & C_3 & \cdots & C_n \\ \left(X_{11} \right. & X_{12} & X_{13} & \cdots & \left. X_{1n} \right) \\ X_{21} & X_{22} & X_{23} & \cdots & X_{2n} \\ X_{31} & X_{32} & X_{33} & \cdots & X_{3n} \\ \cdot & \cdot & \cdot & \cdot & \cdot \\ \cdot & \cdot & \cdot & \cdot & \cdot \\ \cdot & \cdot & \cdot & \cdot & \cdot \\ X_{m1} & X_{m2} & X_{m3} & \cdots & X_{mn} \end{array}$$

Let $A_1, A_2, A_3, \ldots, A_m$ be possible alternatives among which decision makers have to choose C_1, C_2, C_3, C_n are criteria with which alternatives performance are measured, x_{ij} is the performance value of alternatives A_i with respect to criterion C_j, w_j is the weight of criterion C_j and all x_{ij} are positive numbers

Step 2: Determine the average solution (AV_j) according to all the criteria as per the formula:

$$AV_j = \frac{\sum_{i=1}^{n} x_{ij}}{n}$$

Step 3: The Positive Distance from average (PDA) is calculated

$$PDA_j = \frac{max\left(0, \left(X_i - AV_i\right)\right)}{AV_j}$$

Step 4: Calculate the Negative Distance from average (NDA) is calculated

$$NDA_i = \frac{max\left(0, AV_j - X_i\right)}{AV_j}$$

Step 5: The Weighted sum of PDA is obtained from the Average Matrix:

$$SP_i = \sum_{j=1}^{m} w_j PDA_{ij}$$

where w_j denotes the weight of the criteria j

Step 6: The Weighted sum of NDA is obtained from the Average Matrix:

$$SN_i = \sum_{j=1}^{m} w_j NDA_{ij}$$

Step 7: The Normalized values of SP_i and SN_i for all alternatives is calculated as follows:

$$NSP_i = \frac{SP_i}{max_i\left(SP_i\right)}$$

$$NSN_i = 1 - \frac{SN_i}{max_i\left(SN_i\right)}$$

Where NSP_i and NSN_i denote the normalized weighted sum of PDA and NDA respectively

Step 8: The appraisal score AS_i for all alternatives is obtained as:

$$AS_i = \frac{1}{2}\left(NSP_i + NSN_i\right)$$

where $0 < AS_i > 1$

Step 9: The alternatives are ranked according to the decreasing values of appraisal score (AS_i). The alternative with the highest AS_i is the best choice among the alternatives (Tables 6.40 to 6.45).

6.10 MULTI-OBJECTIVE OPTIMIZATION RATIO ANALYSIS MOORA

The MOORA, multi-objective optimization uses ratio analysis method. It considers both benefits and efforts criteria for ranking and selecting best alternative among set of alternatives. Multi-objective problems are found in various field including product design, process design, finance, aircraft design, oil industry, manufacturing sector,

TABLE 6.40
Decision Matrix

	SD	NR	GM	WM	LCA	CAM	AMT	CIPMS	ES	AMN	CMMS
SD	1	4	0.33	2	6	0.25	3	2	2	3	4
NR	0.25	1	0.33	0.25	2	3	0.5	1	3	2	0.5
GM	3	3	1	4	4	3	0.5	3	4	4	0.5
WM	0.25	0.5	0.5	1	3	0.5	0.33	1	1	0.5	0.25
LCA	0.16	0.17	0.33	0.33	1	0.33	0.25	0.5	0.5	0.25	0.25
CAM	4	4	2	2	3	1	4	4	4	4	3
AMT	0.33	0.33	1	0.33	1	0.25	1	4	3	3	0.5
CIPMS	0.5	0.5	0.33	0.25	1	2	0.25	1	3	2	0.33
ES	0.5	0.5	0.5	0.25	2	4	0.25	0.33	1	0.5	0.25
AMN	0.33	0.33	2	2	4	4	0.33	2	3	1	4
CMMS	0.25	0.25	1	0.33	2	3	0.25	3	2	2	1

TABLE 6.41
PDA Matrix

	SD	NR	GM	WM	LCA	CAM	AMT	CIPMS	ES	AMN	CMMS
SD	0.0407	2.0178	0.0000	0.7268	1.2759	0.0000	2.0957	0.0078	0.0000	0.4831	2.0178
NR	0.0000	0.0000	0.0000	0.0000	0.0000	0.5471	0.0000	0.0000	0.2453	0.0000	0.0000
GM	2.1220	1.2634	0.1803	2.4537	0.5172	0.5471	0.0000	0.5117	0.6604	0.9775	0.0000
WM	0.0000	0.0000	0.0000	0.0000	0.1379	0.0000	0.0000	0.0000	0.0000	0.0000	0.0000
LCA	0.0000	0.0000	0.0000	0.0000	0.0000	0.0000	0.0000	0.0000	0.0000	0.0000	0.0000
CAM	3.1627	2.0178	1.3605	0.7268	0.1379	0.0000	3.1276	1.0156	0.6604	0.9775	1.2634
AMT	0.0000	0.0000	0.1803	0.0000	0.0000	0.0000	0.0319	1.0156	0.2453	0.4831	0.0000
CIPMS	0.0000	0.0000	0.0000	0.0000	0.0000	0.0314	0.0000	0.0000	0.2453	0.0000	0.0000
ES	0.0000	0.0000	0.0000	0.0000	0.0000	1.0628	0.0000	0.0000	0.0000	0.0000	0.0000
AMN	0.0000	0.0000	1.3605	0.7268	0.5172	1.0628	0.0000	0.0078	0.2453	0.0000	2.0178
CMMS	0.0000	0.0000	0.1803	0.0000	0.0000	0.5471	0.0000	0.5117	0.0000	0.0000	0.0000

TABLE 6.42
NDA Matrix

	SD	NR	GM	WM	LCA	CAM	AMT	CIPMS	ES	AMN	CMMS
SD	0.0000	0.0000	0.6105	0.0000	0.0000	0.8711	0.0000	0.0000	0.1698	0.0000	0.0000
NR	0.7398	0.2455	0.6105	0.7841	0.2414	0.0000	0.4841	0.4961	0.0000	0.0112	0.6228
GM	0.0000	0.0000	0.0000	0.0000	0.0000	0.0000	0.4841	0.0000	0.0000	0.0000	0.6228
WM	0.7398	0.6228	0.4099	0.1366	0.0000	0.7421	0.6595	0.4961	0.5849	0.7528	0.8114
LCA	0.8335	0.8717	0.6105	0.7151	0.6207	0.8298	0.7420	0.7481	0.7925	0.8764	0.8114
CAM	0.0000	0.0000	0.0000	0.0000	0.0000	0.4843	0.0000	0.0000	0.0000	0.0000	0.0000
AMT	0.6566	0.7510	0.0000	0.7151	0.6207	0.8711	0.0000	0.0000	0.0000	0.0000	0.6228
CIPMS	0.4797	0.6228	0.6105	0.7841	0.6207	0.0000	0.7420	0.4961	0.0000	0.0112	0.7510
ES	0.4797	0.6228	0.4099	0.7841	0.2414	0.0000	0.7420	0.8337	0.5849	0.7528	0.8114
AMN	0.6566	0.7510	0.0000	0.0000	0.0000	0.0000	0.6595	0.0000	0.0000	0.5056	0.0000
CMMS	0.7398	0.8114	0.0000	0.7151	0.2414	0.0000	0.7420	0.0000	0.1698	0.0112	0.2455

TABLE 6.43
SP$_j$ Matrix

	SD	NR	GM	WM	LCA	CAM	AMT	CIPMS	ES	AMN	CMMS
SD	0.004	0.183	0	0.066	0.116	0	0.191	7E-04	0	0.044	0.183
NR	0	0	0	0	0	0.05	0	0	0.022	0	0
GM	0.193	0.115	0.016	0.223	0.047	0.05	0	0.047	0.06	0.089	0
WM	0	0	0	0	0.013	0	0	0	0	0	0
LCA	0	0	0	0	0	0	0	0	0	0	0
CAM	0.288	0.183	0.124	0.066	0.013	0	0.284	0.092	0.06	0.089	0.115
AMT	0	0	0.016	0	0	0	0.003	0.092	0.022	0.044	0
CIPMS	0	0	0	0	0	0.003	0	0	0.022	0	0
ES	0	0	0	0	0	0.097	0	0	0	0	0
AMN	0	0	0.124	0.066	0.047	0.097	0	7E-04	0.022	0	0.183
CMMS	0	0	0.016	0	0	0.05	0	0.047	0	0	0

TABLE 6.44
SN$_j$ Matrix

	SD	NR	GM	WM	LCA	CAM	AMT	CIPMS	ES	AMN	CMMS
SD	0	0	0.056	0	0	0.079	0	0	0.015	0	0
NR	0.067	0.022	0.056	0.071	0.022	0	0.044	0.045	0	0.001	0.056616
GM	0	0	0	0	0	0	0.044	0	0	0	0.056616
WM	0.067	0.057	0.037	0.012	0	0.067	0.06	0.045	0.053	0.068	0.073762
LCA	0.076	0.079	0.056	0.065	0.056	0.075	0.067	0.068	0.072	0.08	0.073762
CAM	0	0	0	0	0	0.044	0	0	0	0	0
AMT	0.06	0.068	0	0.065	0.056	0.079	0	0	0	0	0.056616
CIPMS	0.044	0.057	0.056	0.071	0.056	0	0.067	0.045	0	0.001	0.068275
ES	0.044	0.057	0.037	0.071	0.022	0	0.067	0.076	0.053	0.068	0.073762
AMN	0.06	0.068	0	0	0	0	0.06	0	0	0.046	0
CMMS	0.067	0.074	0	0.065	0.022	0	0.067	0	0.015	0.001	0.022322

TABLE 6.45
Ranking Based on EDAS Method

	SP$_j$	SN$_j$	NSP$_i$	NSN$_i$	A$_{si}$	Rank
SD	0.787788	0.15012728	0.599689	0.804606	0.702147	3
NR	0.177832	0.38520083	0.135372	0.498653	0.317012	6
GM	0.839392	0.10062033	0.638971	0.86904	0.754006	2
WM	0.012539	0.54144348	0.009545	0.2953	0.152422	10
LCA	0	0.76833164	0	0	0	11
CAM	1.313662	0.04402677	1	0.942698	0.971349	1
AMT	0.072036	0.3850524	0.054836	0.498846	0.276841	7
CIPMS	0.025154	0.46528881	0.019148	0.394417	0.206782	8
ES	0.09662	0.56933338	0.07355	0.259	0.166275	9
AMN	0.539848	0.23388152	0.410949	0.695598	0.553273	4
CMMS	0.112641	0.33420735	0.085746	0.565022	0.325384	5
	1.313662	0.76833164				

automobile sector, or fields where decision is taken based on trade-off between conflicting criteria's. Benefit criteria requires maximization and efforts criteria requires minimization. These criteria are conflicting in nature while selecting best alternative. These adds complexity to selection procedure.

MOORA method assists selection process by incorporating ratio analysis in process. The MOORA method consist of two components: i) ratio system; and ii) reference point approach. In ratio system numeric value of criteria corresponding to individual alternative is compared to a denominator which is representation of all alternatives. In reference point ratio calculated in the first component of MOORA is used to determine maximum numeric value of criteria of individual alternative. In MOORA comparison between numerator and denominator is calculated using equation (4) and reference point considering maximization and minimization is calculated.

Step 1: Decision Matrix
Step 2: Calculate sum and square root for each criterion as

$$C_i = \left(C4^\wedge 2 + C5^\wedge 2 + C6^\wedge 2 + C7^\wedge 2 + C8^\wedge 2 + C9^\wedge 2 \right.$$
$$\left. + C10^\wedge 2 + C11^\wedge 2 + C12^\wedge 2 + C13^\wedge 2 + C14^\wedge 2\right)^\wedge 0.5$$

Step 3: X_{ij} as

$$C_{ij} = X_{ij} * C_i$$

Step 4: Calculate weights as (Tables 6.46 to 6.49)

$$Wj = \sum C_{ij} * w_j$$

TABLE 6.46
Decision Matrix

	SD	NR	GM	WM	LCA	CAM	AMT	CIPMS	ES	AMN	CMMS
SD	1	4	0.33	2	6	0.25	3	2	2	3	4
NR	0.25	1	0.33	0.25	2	3	0.5	1	3	2	0.5
GM	3	3	1	4	4	3	0.5	3	4	4	0.5
WM	0.25	0.5	0.5	1	3	0.5	0.33	1	1	0.5	0.25
LCA	0.16	0.17	0.33	0.33	1	0.33	0.25	0.5	0.5	0.25	0.25
CAM	4	4	2	2	3	1	4	4	4	4	3
AMT	0.33	0.33	1	0.33	1	0.25	1	4	3	3	0.5
CIPMS	0.5	0.5	0.33	0.25	1	2	0.25	1	3	2	0.33
ES	0.5	0.5	0.5	0.25	2	4	0.25	0.33	1	0.5	0.25
AMN	0.33	0.33	2	2	4	4	0.33	2	3	1	4
CMMS	0.25	0.25	1	0.33	2	3	0.25	3	2	2	1

TABLE 6.47
Defuzzified Score Based on Sums of Square and Square Root Values

	SD	NR	GM	WM	LCA	CAM	AMT	CIPMS	ES	AMN	CMMS
SD	0.1927	0.6096	0.0955	0.3681	0.5970	0.0311	0.5777	0.2553	0.2261	0.3763	0.6097
NR	0.0482	0.1524	0.0955	0.0460	0.1990	0.3736	0.0963	0.1277	0.3391	0.2509	0.0762
GM	0.5781	0.4572	0.2895	0.7363	0.3980	0.3736	0.0963	0.3830	0.4522	0.5017	0.0762
WM	0.0482	0.0762	0.1447	0.1841	0.2985	0.0623	0.0635	0.1277	0.1130	0.0627	0.0381
LCA	0.0308	0.0259	0.0955	0.0607	0.0995	0.0411	0.0481	0.0638	0.0565	0.0314	0.0381
CAM	0.7708	0.6096	0.5789	0.3681	0.2985	0.1245	0.7703	0.5106	0.4522	0.5017	0.4572
AMT	0.0636	0.0503	0.2895	0.0607	0.0995	0.0311	0.1926	0.5106	0.3391	0.3763	0.0762
CIPMS	0.0963	0.0762	0.0955	0.0460	0.0995	0.2491	0.0481	0.1277	0.3391	0.2509	0.0503
ES	0.0963	0.0762	0.1447	0.0460	0.1990	0.4981	0.0481	0.0421	0.1130	0.0627	0.0381
AMN	0.0636	0.0503	0.5789	0.3681	0.3980	0.4981	0.0635	0.2553	0.3391	0.1254	0.6097
CMMS	0.0482	0.0381	0.2895	0.0607	0.1990	0.3736	0.0481	0.3830	0.2261	0.2509	0.1524

TABLE 6.48
Normalized and Dzefuzzified Rating of Alternatives

	SD	NR	GM	WM	LCA	CAM	AMT	CIPMS	ES	AMN	CMMS
SD	0.0175	0.0554	0.0087	0.0335	0.0543	0.0028	0.0525	0.0232	0.0206	0.0342	0.0554
NR	0.0044	0.0139	0.0087	0.0042	0.0181	0.0340	0.0088	0.0116	0.0308	0.0228	0.0069
GM	0.0526	0.0416	0.0263	0.0669	0.0362	0.0340	0.0088	0.0348	0.0411	0.0456	0.0069
WM	0.0044	0.0069	0.0132	0.0167	0.0271	0.0057	0.0058	0.0116	0.0103	0.0057	0.0035
LCA	0.0028	0.0024	0.0087	0.0055	0.0090	0.0037	0.0044	0.0058	0.0051	0.0029	0.0035
CAM	0.0701	0.0554	0.0526	0.0335	0.0271	0.0113	0.0700	0.0464	0.0411	0.0456	0.0416
AMT	0.0058	0.0046	0.0263	0.0055	0.0090	0.0028	0.0175	0.0464	0.0308	0.0342	0.0069
CIPMS	0.0088	0.0069	0.0087	0.0042	0.0090	0.0226	0.0044	0.0116	0.0308	0.0228	0.0046
ES	0.0088	0.0069	0.0132	0.0042	0.0181	0.0453	0.0044	0.0038	0.0103	0.0057	0.0035
AMN	0.0058	0.0046	0.0526	0.0335	0.0362	0.0453	0.0058	0.0232	0.0308	0.0114	0.0554
CMMS	0.0044	0.0035	0.0263	0.0055	0.0181	0.0340	0.0044	0.0348	0.0206	0.0228	0.0139

TABLE 6.49
Ranking Based MOORA Method

	MOORA Weight	Rank
SD	0.35810481	3
NR	0.188142	6
GM	0.39472663	2
WM	0.11081983	10
LCA	0.05377789	11
CAM	0.49477375	1
AMT	0.16407766	7
CIPMS	0.13443143	8
ES	0.12405021	9
AMN	0.30456066	4
CMMS	0.18996012	5

Where w_j is weightage of each criterion (since equal weightage is given to each criterion so $w_j = 1/11$)

6.11 ANALYTICAL HIERARCHY PROCESS (AHP)

"AHP is a multi-criteria decision-making technique that organizes and analyses multiple criteria by structuring them into hierarchy and thus, assessing their relative importance. It also helps in comparison of alternatives for every criteria and defining ranks to the alternatives", as stated by DSS Resources. AHP is quite helpful in situations where the decision set involves multiple criteria with rating according to multiple value choice. It is based on matrices and their corresponding eigen vector's for generating approximate values.

It is a prescriptive and a descriptive model of decision-making. It is valid for thousands of applications and the results were used by and acceptable to the organizations. Thus, presently, it is the mostly used multiple-criteria decision-making (MCDM) technique. AHP makes comparison of criteria or alternatives in a pairwise mode. For this, AHP uses absolute numbers scale, validated by decision problem and physical experiments.

AHP can be applied to following situations:

- Choice – Choosing one alternative from a given set of alternatives, when there are multiple criteria involved.
- Ranking – Putting alternatives in an order from most to least desirable or vice-versa.
- Prioritization – Determining the relative importance of alternatives, as opposed to selecting only one or simply ranking them.
- Resource allocation – Allocating resources between set of alternatives
- Benchmarking – Comparing the processes in own organization with those of other best organizations
- Quality management – It deals with multidimensional aspects of quality improvement and quality.
- Conflict resolution – Resolving disputes among parties having apparently incompatible goals or positions.

The applications of AHP to complex situations are in the thousands and produces results in problems involving selection, priority setting, resource allocation and planning among choices. Other areas included are total quality management, the Balanced Scorecard, quality function deployment, business process re-engineering and forecasting.

6.11.1 COMPARISON SCALE FOR PAIRWISE COMPARISON

Pairwise comparison is an important stage in AHP for determining priority values of attributes and provides a relative rating for alternatives (Table 6.50).

TABLE 6.50
Comparison Scale Used

Intensity	Definition	Explanation
1	Equal Importance	Two factors contribute equally to the objective
3	Moderately More Important	Experience and judgement favour one factor over another
5	Strongly Morse Important	Experience and judgement strongly favour one factor over another
7	Very Strongly More Important	An factor is strongly favoured and its dominance demonstrated in practice
9	Extremely More Important	The evidence of favouring one factor over another is of the highest possible order of affirmation

2,4,6,8: intermediate values when compromise is needed

A measurement scale provides the relative importance of each factor by providing numerical judgements corresponding to verbal ones. This scale is a discrete one and ranges from 1 to 9, with 9 showing the highest importance of one factor over another, and 1 describing equal importance among two factors, as shown in Tables 6.4–6.27.

6.11.2 PAIRWISE COMPARISON OF ATTRIBUTES

While comparing attributes, the significance of jth sub-objective is calculated from with i^{th} one. For this, according to number of variables, as x in this study, a 7×7 matrix was prepared and used following procedure for filling this:

1. In matrix, the diagonal elements are kept at 1.
2. Values in the upper triangular matrix were filled by using the data compiled through responses from various organizations.
3. For lower triangular matrix, the upper diagonal values are reciprocated as $a_{ji} = 1/a_{ij}$.

6.11.3 ANALYSIS USING AHP

Analysis in AHP is done by squaring the pairwise matrix and then squaring till the eigenvectors calculated are same. When the two successive iterations are almost same, so further squaring and iterations will generate the same solution. Then check for Consistency Ratio (CR). CR is described as the comparison between random index (RI) and consistency index (CI).

$$CR = CI/RI$$

If CR is less than 0.1 that is, 10%, then judgements are considered to be consistent and acceptable. Table 6.4–6.28 gives RI values (Tables 6.51 and 6.52).

TABLE 6.51
Random Index (RI)

N	1	2	3	4	5	6	7	8	9	10	11	12	13	14	15
RI	0	0	0.58	0.89	1.12	1.24	1.32	1.41	1.45	1.49	1.52	1.54	1.56	1.58	1.59

TABLE 6.52
Ranking Based on AHP

Attributes	Priority	Rank
Sustainable Development	14.40%	3
Natural Resources	6.60%	6
Green Manufacturing	16.10%	2
Waste Management	3.70%	10
Lifecycle Analysis	3.00%	11
Comp Aided Manufacturing	22.00%	1
Automation	5.90%	7
Comp Integrated Prod Management System	4.20%	9
Expert System	4.40%	8
Advanced Maintenance	12.90%	4
Computer Maintenance Management System	6.70%	5

Number of comparisons = 55
CR = 7.7%
Principal eigen value = 13.24

6.12 TECHNIQUE FOR ORDER OF PREFERENCE BY SIMILARITY TO IDEAL SOLUTION (TOPSIS)

TOPSIS was developed by Yoon and Hwang and Yoon, for solving MCDM problems. This method is based on the idea that the chosen alternative should be farthest from the Negative Ideal Solution (NIS), and nearest to the Positive Ideal Solution (PIS). This is a more realistic form of modelling as compared to non-compensatory methods, in which alternative solutions are included or excluded according to hard cut-offs. For instance, NIS maximizes the cost and minimizes the benefit whereas PIS maximizes the benefit and minimizes the cost. It assumes that each criterion requires to be maximized or minimized. In this method, options are graded according to ideal solution similarity. Option has a higher grade, if the option is more similar to an ideal solution. Ideal solution is a solution that is the best from any aspect. It assumes that we have m alternatives (options) and n attributes/criteria, and we have the score of each option with respect to each criterion.

It is a technique for ranking different alternatives according to closeness to the ideal solution. The procedure is based on an intuitive and simple idea: optimal ideal solution, having the maximum benefit, is obtained by selecting the best alternative, which is far from the most unsuitable alternative, having minimal benefits. The ideal solution should have a rank of 1 (one), while the worst alternative should have a rank approaching 0 (zero). This method considers three types of attributes or criteria:

1. Qualitative benefit attributes/criteria
2. Quantitative benefit attributes
3. Cost attributes or criteria

In this method, two artificial alternatives are hypothesized:

i. Ideal alternative: the one which has the best level for all attributes considered.
ii. Negative ideal alternative: the one which has the worst attribute values.

Let X_{ij} score of option i with respect to criterion j. We have a matrix $X = (X_{ij})$ $m \times n$ matrix. Let J be the set of benefit attributes or criteria (more is better), and J' be the set of negative attributes or criteria (less is better).

Step 1: Construct normalized decision matrix. Normalize scores or data as follows:

$$r_{ij} = \frac{X_{ij}}{\left(\sum X^2_{ij}\right)} \quad \text{for } i = 1, \ldots, \text{m}; j = 1, \ldots, \text{n}$$

Step 2: Construct the weighted normalized decision matrix. Not all of the selection criteria may be of equal importance and hence weighting was introduced from AHP technique to quantify the relative importance of the different selection criteria. An element of the new matrix is: $v_{ij} = w_j \, r_{ij}$

Step 3: Determine the ideal and NISs.
Ideal solution, $A^* = \{v_1^*, \ldots, v_n^*\}$, where

$$v_j^* = \left\{ max\left(v_{ij}\right) \text{if } j \in J; min\left(v_{ij}\right) \text{if } j \in J' \right\}$$

Negative ideal solution, $A' = \{V_1', \ldots, V_n'\}$, where

$$v_j' = \left\{ min\left(v_{ij}\right) \text{if } j \in J; max\left(v_{ij}\right) \text{if } j \in J' \right\}$$

Step 4: Calculate the separation measures for each alternative.
The separation from the ideal alternative is:

$$S_i^* = \left[\sum \left(v_j^* - v_{ij}\right)^2 \right]^{1/2} \quad i = 1, \ldots, \text{m}$$

$$S_i' = \left[\sum \left(v_j^* - v_{ij}\right)^2 \right]^{1/2} \quad i = 1, \ldots, \text{m}$$

TABLE 6.53
Decision Matrix

	SD	NR	GM	WM	LCA	CAM	AMT	CIPMS	ES	AMN	CMMS
SD	1	4	0.33	2	6	0.25	3	2	2	3	4
NR	0.25	1	0.33	0.25	2	3	0.5	1	3	2	0.5
GM	3	3	1	4	4	3	0.5	3	4	4	0.5
WM	0.25	0.5	0.5	1	3	0.5	0.33	1	1	0.5	0.25
LCA	0.16	0.17	0.33	0.33	1	0.33	0.25	0.5	0.5	0.25	0.25
CAM	4	4	2	2	3	1	4	4	4	4	3
AMT	0.33	0.33	1	0.33	1	0.24	1	1	3	3	0.5
CIPMS	0.5	0.5	0.33	0.25	1	2	0.25	1	3	2	0.33
ES	0.5	0.5	0.5	0.25	2	4	0.25	0.33	1	0.5	0.25
AMN	0.33	0.33	2	2	4	4	0.33	2	3	1	4
CMMS	0.25	0.25	1	0.33	2	3	0.25	3	2	2	1

TABLE 6.54
Ranking Based on TOPSIS

Attributes	S_i^*	S_i'	$S_i^* + S_i'$	$C_i = S_i'/S_i^* + S_i'$	Rank
Sustainable Development	0.0731	0.0523	0.1254	0.4171	3
Natural Resources	0.0739	0.0443	0.1182	0.3752	6
Green Manufacturing	0.0648	0.0545	0.1193	0.4571	2
Waste Management	0.0746	0.0343	0.1089	0.3151	10
Lifecycle Analysis	0.083	0.0345	0.1175	0.2954	11
Comp Aided Manufacturing	0.0724	0.064	0.1364	0.4694	1
Automation	0.0852	0.0502	0.1354	0.3706	7
Comp Integrated Prod Management System	0.083	0.0384	0.1214	0.316	9
Expert System	0.0819	0.0428	0.1247	0.343	8
Advanced Maintenance	0.0729	0.051	0.1239	0.4119	4
Computer Maintenance Management System	0.0763	0.0474	0.1237	0.3832	5

Similarly, the separation from the negative ideal alternative is:

$$S_i' = \left[\sum \left(v_j' - v_{ij} \right)^2 \right]^{\frac{1}{2}} \quad i = 1, \ldots, m$$

Step 5: Calculate the relative closeness to the ideal solution C_i^* (Tables 6.53 and 6.54)

$$C_i^* = \frac{S_i'}{\left(S_i^* + S_i' \right)}, 0 < C_i^* < 1$$

6.13 VIKOR METHOD

The compromise solution is a feasible solution that is the closest to the ideal solution, and a compromise means an agreement established by mutual concession. The compromise solution method, also known as (VIKOR) the *Vlse Kriterijumska*

Optimizacija I KOmpromisno Resenje in Serbian, which means multi-criteria optimization (MCO) and compromise solution, is introduced as one applicable technique to implement within MADM. It focuses on ranking and selecting from a set of alternatives in the presence of conflicting criteria.

The compromise solution, whose foundation was established by Yu and Zeleny is a feasible solution which is the closest to the ideal, and here "compromise" means an agreement established by mutual concessions. The VIKOR method determines the compromise ranking list and the compromise solution by introducing the multi-criteria ranking index based on the particular measure of "closeness" to the "ideal" solution.

The procedure of VIKOR for ranking alternatives is as follows:

Step 1: Determine that best X_J^* and the worst X_j^- values of all criterion functions, where $j = 1, 2, ..., n$.

Step 2: Range Standardized Decision Matrix.

$$X_{ij}' = \left[\frac{\left(X_{ij} - X_j^- \right)}{\left(X_j^* - X_j^- \right)} \right]$$

Step 3: Compute the S_i (the maximum utility) and R_i (the minimum regret) values, $i = 1, 2, ..., m$ by the relations:

$$S_i = \sum W_j * \frac{\left(X_j * - X_{ij} \right)}{\left(X_j - X_j^- \right)}$$

$$R_i = max = \sum W_j * \frac{\left(X_j * - X_{ij} \right)}{\left(X_j - X_j^- \right)}$$

where w_j is the weight of the jth criterion which expresses the relative importance of criteria.

Coefficient of Variation

The weight of the criterion reflects its importance in MCDM. Range standardization was done to transform different scales and units among various criteria into common measurable units in order to compare their weights.

$$X_{ij}' = \left[\frac{\left(X_{ij} - min\ X_{ij} \right)}{\left(max\ X_{ij}^* - min\ X_{ij}^- \right)} \right]$$

$D' = (x')_{mxn}$ is the matrix after range standardization; max x_{ij}, min x_{ij} are the maximum and the minimum values of the criterion (j) respectively, all values in D' are ($0 \leq x_{ij}' \leq 1$). So, according to the normalized matrix. $D' = (x')_{mxn}$.

The standard deviation (σ_j) calculated for every criterion independently as:

$$\sigma_j = \sqrt{1/m}\, \sum \left(X'_{ij} - X'_j\right)^2$$

Where X'_j is the mean of the values of the jth criterion after normalization and $j = 1, 2, \dots\, n$.

After calculating (σ_j) for all criteria, the (CV) of the criterion (j) will be

$$CV_j = \frac{\sigma_j}{X'_j}$$

The weight (W_j) of the criterion (j) can be defined as

$$W_j = \frac{CV_j}{\sum CV_j}$$

Where $j = 1, 2, \dots\, n$.

Step 4: Compute the value Q_i, $i = 1, 2, \dots, m$, by the relation

$$Q_i = \left\{ v \frac{\left(S_i - S^*\right)}{\left(S^- - S^*\right)} \right\} + \left\{ \frac{\left(1-v\right)\left(R_i - R^*\right)}{R^- - R^*} \right\}$$

Where $S^* = \min S_i$, $S^- = \max S_i$, $R^* = \min R_i$, $R^- = \max R_i$ and v is the introduced weight of the strategy of S_i and R_i.

Step 5: Rank the alternatives, sorting by the S, R and Q values in decreasing order (Tables 6.55 and 6.56).

TABLE 6.55

Decision Matrix

	SD	NR	GM	WM	LCA	CAM	AMT	CIPMS	ES	AMN	CMMS
SD	1	4	0.33	2	6	0.25	3	2	2	3	4
NR	0.25	1	0.33	0.25	2	3	0.5	1	3	2	0.5
GM	3	3	1	4	4	3	0.5	3	4	4	0.5
WM	0.25	0.5	0.5	1	3	0.5	0.33	1	1	0.5	0.25
LCA	0.16	0.17	0.33	0.33	1	0.33	0.25	0.5	0.5	0.25	0.25
CAM	4	4	2	2	3	1	4	4	4	4	3
AMT	0.33	0.33	1	0.33	1	0.25	1	4	3	3	0.5
CIPMS	0.5	0.5	0.33	0.25	1	2	1	1	3	2	0.33
ES	0.5	0.5	0.5	0.25	2	4	0.25	0.33	1	0.5	0.25
AMN	0.33	0.33	2	2	4	4	0.33	2	3	1	4
CMMS	0.25	0.25	1	0.33	2	3	0.25	3	2	2	1

TABLE 6.56
Ranking Based on VIKOR

	S_i	R_i	Q_i	Rank
Sustainable Development	0.32011	0.05774	0.23934	3
Natural Resources	0.47443	0.10595	0.72569	6
Green Manufacturing	0.26159	0.05186	0.12943	2
Waste Management	0.58174	0.12571	0.9811	10
Lifecycle Analysis	0.59568	0.1259	1	11
Computer-aided Manufacturing	0.20325	0.04269	0	1
Automation	0.54012	0.09511	0.7442	7
Computer-integrated Product Management System	0.57669	0.11841	0.93082	9
Expert System	0.55216	0.1121	0.86165	8
Advanced Maintenance	0.44091	0.06772	0.45319	4
Computer Maintenance Management System	0.43961	0.09683	0.69018	5

TABLE 5.36
Ranking Based on VIKOR

7 Fuzzy Techniques

7.1 FUZZY MDEMATEL

A new tool has been developed in fuzzy systems which is a combination of fuzzy and MDEMATEL. MDEMATEL has already been developed by Dr Chandan Deep Singh and combination of fuzzy and MDEMATEL results in a new tool named "Fuzzy MDEMATEL".

Fuzzy MDEMATEL was developed by Dr Chandan Deep Singh and Dr Harleen Kaur in September 2020. MDEMATEL method is a well-known and comprehensive method to obtain ranking between complex real-world factors. The MDEMATEL method is superior to other techniques such as AHP, TOPSIS, VIKOR, DEMATEL since it accounts for the interdependence among the factors of a system, which is overlooked in traditional techniques. The concepts of fuzzy is introduced for real-world problems where there is uncertainty, because of goals, constraints and possible actions are ambiguous.

The analysis procedures of Fuzzy DEMATEL method are explained as follows:

Step 1: Define the evaluation criteria.
Step 2: Define the fuzzy linguistic scale: No influence, Very low influence, Low influence, High influence and Very high influence. The fuzzy numbers for these linguistic terms are given in Table 7.1.
Step 3: Obtain an initial decision matrix with pair wise comparison. Develop the initial fuzzy decision matrix.
Step 4: Obtain the normalized fuzzy decision matrix.
Step 5: Compute the total relation matrix T.

$$T = D(I - D)^{-1}$$

Determine row (ri) and column (cj) sums for each row and column from the T matrix, respectively, with following equations.

TABLE 7.1
Fuzzy Numbers for Linguistic Terms

Linguistic Terms	Corresponding Triangular Fuzzy Numbers (TFNs)
No influence (NO)	(1,1,1)
Very Low influence (VLI)	(1,3,5)
Low Influence (LI)	(3,5,7)
High Influence (HI)	(5,7,9)
Very High Influence (VHI)	(9,9,9)

DOI: 10.1201/9781003189510-7

$$ri = \sum_{j=1}^{n} tij \left(i = 1,2,\ldots,n \right)$$

$$cj = \sum_{i=1}^{n} tij \left(j = 1,2,\ldots,n \right)$$

Following tables gives the detailed description of this new tool. Table 7.2 represents the decision matrix for fuzzy MDEMATEL.

As mentioned in Step 4, Table 7.3 represents the fuzzy direct relation matrix.

According to Step 6, Table 7.4 represents total relation matrix (formulae already described in Step 6).

Following the calculations, as initially the data was in fuzzy form, we need to defuzzify it. Table 7.5 represents the defuzzification matrix. Where C_i and S_i are the required defuzzified parameters

Table 7.6 represents the final ranking based on Fuzzy DEMATEL as mentioned in step 8.

As per the results obtained from fuzzy MDEMATEL, the significant parameters for Green Sustainability are CAM, GM, SD, AMN.

7.2 MODIFIED FUZZY TOPSIS

Technique for Order Preference by Similarity to Ideal Solution (TOPSIS) was developed by Yoon and Hwang and Yoon, for solving Multiple-Criteria Decision-Making (MCDM) problems This method is based on the idea that the chosen alternative should be farthest from the Negative Ideal Solution (NIS) and nearest to the Positive Ideal Solution (PIS). This is a more realistic form of modelling as compared to non-compensatory methods, in which alternative solutions are included or excluded according to hard cut-offs. For instance, NIS maximizes the cost and minimizes the benefit whereas PIS maximizes the benefit and minimizes the cost. It assumes that each criterion requires to be maximized or minimized. In the TOPSIS approach an alternative that is nearest to the Fuzzy Positive Ideal Solution (FPIS) and farthest from the Fuzzy Negative Ideal Solution (FNIS) is chosen as optimal. The technique called Modified fuzzy TOPSIS can be used to rank various criteria. As the criteria are often of inconsistent dimensions, which may create problem in evaluation of multi criteria problems. So, to avoid this problem a need of fuzzy system is necessary. Using fuzzy numbers in TOPSIS for criteria analysis make it simple for evaluation. Hence, Modified Fuzzy TOPSIS is simple, realistic form of modelling and Compensatory method for MCDM problems. This method "Modified Fuzzy TOPSIS" has been developed by Dr Chandan Deep Singh and Dr Harleen Kaur in 2020. Existing fuzzy TOPSIS technique has been modified by introducing certain changes so as to make it more convenient to decision-making. The linguistic variables and their corresponding fuzzy numbers are shown in Table 7.7. The steps involved in the implementation are presented as follows:

TABLE 7.2
Decision Matrix for Fuzzy MDEMATEL

	SD	NR	GM	WM	LCA	CAM	AMT	CIPMS	ES	AMN	CMMS
SD	(1,1,1)	(3,4,5)	(1/4,1/3,1/2)	(1,2,3)	(5,6,7)	(1/5,1/4,1/3)	(2,3,4)	(1,2,3)	(1,2,3)	(2,3,4)	(3,4,5)
NR	(1/5,1/4,1/3)	(1,1,1)	(1/4,1/3,1/2)	(1,2,3)	(1,2,3)	(2,3,4)	(1/3,1/2,1)	(1,2,3)	(2,3,4)	(1,2,3)	(1/3,1/2,1)
GM	(2,3,4)	(2,3,4)	(1,1,1)	(3,4,5)	(3,4,5)	(2,3,4)	(1,1,1)	(2,3,4)	(3,4,5)	(3,4,5)	(1,1,1)
WM	(1/3,1/2,1)	(1/3,1/2,1)	(1/5,1/4,1/3)	(1,1,1)	(2,3,4)	(1/3,1/2,1)	(2,3,4)	(3,4,5)	(1,1,1)	(1/3,1/2,1)	(1/5,1/4,1/3)
LCA	(1/7,1/6,1/5)	(1/3,1/2,1)	(1/5,1/4,1/3)	(1/4,1/3,1/2)	(1,1,1)	(1/4,1/3,1/2)	(1/5,1/4,1/3)	(1/3,1/2,1)	(1/3,1/2,1)	(1/5,1/4,1/3)	(1/5,1/4,1/3)
CAM	(3,4,5)	(3,4,5)	(1,2,3)	(1,2,3)	(2,3,4)	(1,1,1)	(3,4,5)	(3,4,5)	(3,4,5)	(3,4,5)	(2,3,4)
AMT	(1/4,1/3,1/2)	(1,2,3)	(1,1,1)	(1/4,1/3,1/2)	(1,1,1)	(1/5,1/4,1/3)	(1,1,1)	(3,4,5)	(2,3,4)	(2,3,4)	(1/3,1/2,1)
CIPMS	(1/3,1/2,1)	(1/3,1/2,1)	(1/4,1/3,1/2)	(1/5,1/4,1/3)	(1,1,1)	(1,2,3)	(1/5,1/4,1/3)	(1,1,1)	(2,3,4)	(1,2,3)	(1/4,1/3,1/2)
ES	(1/3,1/2,1)	(1/4,1/3,1/2)	(1/5,1/4,1/3)	(1,1,1)	(1,2,3)	(1/5,1/4,1/3)	(1/4,1/3,1/2)	(1/4,1/3,1/2)	(1,1,1)	(1/4,1/3,1/2)	(1/3,1/2,1)
AMN	(1/4,1/3,1/2)	(1/3,1/2,1)	(1/5,1/4,1/3)	(1,2,3)	(3,4,5)	(1/5,1/4,1/3)	(1/4,1/3,1/2)	(1/3,1/2,1)	(2,3,4)	(1,1,1)	(3,4,5)
CMMS	(1/5,1/4,1/3)	(1,2,3)	(1,1,1)	(3,4,5)	(3,4,5)	(1/4,1/3,1/2)	(1,2,3)	(2,3,4)	(1,2,3)	(1/5,1/4,1/3)	(1,1,1)

TABLE 7.3
Fuzzy Direct Relation Matrix

	SD	NR	GM	WM	LCA	CAM	AMT	CIPMS	ES	AMN	CMMS
SD	0.040, 0.029, 0.023	0.120, 0.118, 0.114	0.010, 0.010, 0.011	0.040, 0.059, 0.068	0.200, 0.176, 0.159	0.008, 0.007, 0.008	0.080, 0.088, 0.091	0.040, 0.059, 0.068	0.040, 0.059, 0.068	0.080, 0.088, 0.091	0.120, 0.118, 0.114
NR	0.008, 0.007, 0.008	0.040, 0.088, 0.023	0.010, 0.010, 0.011	0.040, 0.059, 0.068	0.040, 0.059, 0.068	0.080, 0.088, 0.091	0.013, 0.015, 0.023	0.040, 0.088, 0.068	0.080, 0.118, 0.091	0.040, 0.118, 0.068	0.013, 0.015, 0.023
GM	0.080, 0.088, 0.091	0.080, 0.088, 0.091	0.040, 0.029, 0.023	0.120, 0.118, 0.114	0.120, 0.118, 0.114	0.080, 0.088, 0.091	0.040, 0.029, 0.023	0.080, 0.088, 0.091	0.120, 0.118, 0.114	0.120, 0.118, 0.114	0.040, 0.029, 0.023
WM	0.013, 0.015, 0.023	0.013, 0.015, 0.023	0.008, 0.007, 0.008	0.040, 0.029, 0.023	0.080, 0.088, 0.091	0.013, 0.015, 0.023	0.080, 0.088, 0.091	0.120, 0.118, 0.114	0.040, 0.029, 0.023	0.013, 0.015, 0.023	0.008, 0.007, 0.008
LCA	0.006, 0.005, 0.005	0.013, 0.015, 0.023	0.008, 0.007, 0.008	0.010, 0.010, 0.011	0.040, 0.029, 0.023	0.010, 0.010, 0.011	0.008, 0.007, 0.008	0.013, 0.015, 0.023	0.013, 0.015, 0.023	0.008, 0.007, 0.008	0.008, 0.007, 0.008
CAM	0.120, 0.118, 0.114	0.120, 0.118, 0.114	0.040, 0.059, 0.068	0.040, 0.059, 0.068	0.080, 0.059, 0.068	0.040, 0.029, 0.023	0.120, 0.118, 0.114	0.120, 0.118, 0.114	0.120, 0.118, 0.114	0.120, 0.118, 0.114	0.080, 0.088, 0.091
AMT	0.010, 0.010, 0.011	0.040, 0.059, 0.068	0.040, 0.029, 0.023	0.010, 0.010, 0.011	0.040, 0.029, 0.023	0.008, 0.007, 0.008	0.040, 0.029, 0.023	0.040, 0.029, 0.023	0.080, 0.088, 0.091	0.080, 0.088, 0.091	0.013, 0.015, 0.023
CIPMS	0.013, 0.015, 0.023	0.013, 0.015, 0.023	0.010, 0.010, 0.011	0.008, 0.007, 0.008	0.040, 0.029, 0.023	0.040, 0.059, 0.068	0.008, 0.007, 0.008	0.010, 0.010, 0.011	0.040, 0.029, 0.023	0.040, 0.059, 0.068	0.010, 0.010, 0.011
ES	0.013, 0.015, 0.023	0.010, 0.010, 0.011	0.008, 0.007, 0.008	0.040, 0.029, 0.023	0.040, 0.059, 0.068	0.008, 0.007, 0.008	0.010, 0.010, 0.011	0.010, 0.010, 0.011	0.080, 0.088, 0.091	0.010, 0.010, 0.011	0.013, 0.015, 0.023
AMN	0.010, 0.010, 0.011	0.013, 0.015, 0.023	0.008, 0.007, 0.008	0.040, 0.059, 0.068	0.120, 0.118, 0.114	0.008, 0.007, 0.008	0.010, 0.010, 0.011	0.013, 0.015, 0.023	0.080, 0.088, 0.091	0.040, 0.029, 0.023	0.120, 0.118, 0.114
CMMS	0.008, 0.007, 0.008	0.040, 0.059, 0.068	0.040, 0.029, 0.023	0.120, 0.118, 0.114	0.120, 0.118, 0.114	0.010, 0.010, 0.011	0.040, 0.059, 0.068	0.080, 0.088, 0.091	0.040, 0.059, 0.068	0.008, 0.007, 0.008	0.040, 0.029, 0.023

TABLE 7.4
Total Relation Matrix

	SD	NR	GM	WM	LCA	CAM	AMT	CIPMS	ES	AMN	CMMS
SD	0.060, 0.051, 0.049	0.161, 0.164, 0.169	0.032, 0.030, 0.032	0.092, 0.117, 0.131	0.292, 0.271, 0.256	0.038, 0.043, 0.049	0.117, 0.130, 0.138	0.105, 0.134, 0.151	0.110, 0.142, 0.159	0.124, 0.141, 0.150	0.162, 0.160, 0.160
NR	0.029, 0.032, 0.037	0.069, 0.064, 0.066	0.023, 0.025, 0.030	0.068, 0.095, 0.111	0.092, 0.120, 0.139	0.099, 0.111, 0.119	0.042, 0.049, 0.063	0.081, 0.109, 0.127	0.128, 0.146, 0.158	0.072, 0.099, 0.116	0.041, 0.049, 0.063
GM	0.118, 0.127, 0.134	0.140, 0.153, 0.163	0.066, 0.055, 0.049	0.184, 0.187, 0.187	0.245, 0.242, 0.237	0.119, 0.132, 0.139	0.098, 0.092, 0.089	0.167, 0.180, 0.188	0.218, 0.223, 0.223	0.187, 0.192, 0.193	0.104, 0.095, 0.092
WM	0.026, 0.028, 0.041	0.034, 0.039, 0.056	0.020, 0.018, 0.020	0.060, 0.051, 0.050	0.123, 0.129, 0.137	0.029, 0.034, 0.047	0.100, 0.108, 0.115	0.158, 0.156, 0.158	0.082, 0.075, 0.077	0.041, 0.048, 0.064	0.026, 0.027, 0.034
LCA	0.011, 0.010, 0.012	0.021, 0.023, 0.034	0.012, 0.011, 0.012	0.019, 0.019, 0.023	0.056, 0.044, 0.041	0.016, 0.016, 0.020	0.015, 0.015, 0.017	0.025, 0.027, 0.038	0.027, 0.029, 0.041	0.017, 0.017, 0.021	0.015, 0.014, 0.017
CAM	0.157, 0.156, 0.158	0.187, 0.193, 0.199	0.071, 0.088, 0.097	0.111, 0.142, 0.157	0.218, 0.200, 0.211	0.084, 0.081, 0.081	0.178, 0.181, 0.182	0.212, 0.222, 0.227	0.229, 0.241, 0.244	0.196, 0.205, 0.208	0.151, 0.159, 0.165
AMT	0.026, 0.026, 0.031	0.064, 0.085, 0.100	0.053, 0.041, 0.035	0.041, 0.044, 0.049	0.096, 0.087, 0.083	0.029, 0.033, 0.037	0.060, 0.050, 0.047	0.157, 0.156, 0.156	0.132, 0.145, 0.151	0.113, 0.125, 0.130	0.042, 0.044, 0.056
CIPMS	0.027, 0.031, 0.044	0.032, 0.039, 0.054	0.018, 0.020, 0.024	0.028, 0.034, 0.041	0.077, 0.074, 0.075	0.052, 0.073, 0.086	0.025, 0.029, 0.034	0.064, 0.060, 0.061	0.112, 0.128, 0.138	0.061, 0.086, 0.101	0.030, 0.036, 0.044
ES	0.020, 0.021, 0.031	0.021, 0.021, 0.028	0.013, 0.012, 0.013	0.053, 0.042, 0.039	0.064, 0.082, 0.095	0.015, 0.015, 0.017	0.022, 0.021, 0.025	0.028, 0.028, 0.033	0.058, 0.047, 0.045	0.022, 0.022, 0.027	0.024, 0.025, 0.036
AMN	0.022, 0.022, 0.027	0.035, 0.040, 0.055	0.021, 0.019, 0.019	0.075, 0.094, 0.105	0.175, 0.173, 0.172	0.021, 0.023, 0.028	0.032, 0.037, 0.042	0.051, 0.057, 0.071	0.116, 0.128, 0.137	0.060, 0.052, 0.050	0.143, 0.138, 0.137
CMMS	0.026, 0.026, 0.030	0.067, 0.090, 0.107	0.055, 0.043, 0.037	0.154, 0.152, 0.150	0.181, 0.179, 0.177	0.033, 0.038, 0.044	0.071, 0.091, 0.103	0.133, 0.145, 0.152	0.091, 0.117, 0.131	0.041, 0.048, 0.055	0.062, 0.052, 0.050

TABLE 7.5
Defuzzification Matrix

	C	C_i	S	S_i
SD	1.294029, 1.383445, 1.444412	1.373962	0.521758, 0.529056, 0.593315	0.548043
NR	0.743321, 0.89893, 1.027672	0.889975	0.831273, 0.910777, 1.029986	0.924012
GM	1.793698, 1.865474, 1.926897	1.862023	0.535418, 0.599027, 0.66618	0.600208
WM	0.338875, 0.33659, 0.388385	0.354617	1.302244, 1.41955, 1.502893	1.408229
LCA	0.233858, 0.224708, 0.274106	0.244224	1.620122, 1.600723, 1.623645	1.61483
CAM	1.64643, 1.676409, 1.69392	1.672253	0.384513, 0.362533, 0.367331	0.371459
AMT	0.699636, 0.714667, 0.798055	0.737453	0.883919, 0.977231, 1.042929	0.968027
CIPMS	0.526871, 0.60943, 0.702354	0.612885	1.181491, 1.273043, 1.362039	1.272191
ES	0.750948, 0.782157, 0.843514	0.792207	0.934307, 1.033589, 1.114587	1.027494
AMN	0.912752, 0.981833, 1.037909	0.977498	0.801422, 0.799381, 0.853416	0.818073
CMMS	0.815775, 0.835341, 0.875004	0.84204	0.759726, 0.804075, 0.855909	0.80657

TABLE 7.6
Ranking Matrix Based on Fuzzy MDEMATEL

	C_i	S_i	$C_i + S_i$	$C_i - S_i$	Rank
SD	1.373962	0.548043	1.922004	0.825919	3
NR	0.889975	0.924012	1.813987	−0.03404	6
GM	1.862023	0.600208	2.462231	1.261815	2
WM	0.354617	1.408229	1.762846	−1.05361	10
LCA	0.244224	1.61483	1.859054	−1.37061	11
CAM	1.672253	0.371459	2.043712	1.300794	1
AMT	0.737453	0.968027	1.705479	−0.23057	7
CIPMS	0.612885	1.272191	1.885076	−0.65931	9
ES	0.792207	1.027494	1.819701	−0.23529	8
AMN	0.977498	0.818073	1.795571	0.159425	4
CMMS	0.84204	0.80657	1.64861	0.03547	5

TABLE 7.7
Fuzzy Numbers for Linguistic Terms

Linguistic Terms	Corresponding Triangular Fuzzy Numbers (TFNs)
No influence (NO)	(1,1,1)
Very Low influence (VLI)	(1,3,5)
Low Influence (LI)	(3,5,7)
High Influence (HI)	(5,7,9)
Very High Influence (VHI)	(9,9,9)

Step 1: Criteria weightage by decision makers and apply fuzzy numbers.
To start with, create a decision matrix by weightage given by decision makers in terms of linguistic terms and then apply fuzzy numbers to it so as to convert linguistic terms into numbers. Fuzzy numbers for linguistic terms are given in Table 7.7.

Step 2: Aggregated alternative and criteria weightage fuzzy decision matrix.
Now, calculate weighted fuzzy decision matrix from above matrix.

Step 3: Normalized weighted matrix.
Calculate normalized weighted decision matrix as shown in appendix from weighted decision matrix.

Step 4: Positive and negative ideal solution for each criterion.
Calculate positive and negative ideal solutions:
Positive Ideal Solution

$$A^* = \left\{ v_1^*, \ldots, v_n^* \right\}, \quad (\mathrm{i})$$

where

$$v_j^* = \left\{ max\left(v_{ij}\right) \text{if } j \in J; \ min\left(v_{ij}\right) \text{if } j \in J' \right\}$$

Negative Ideal Solution

$$A' = \left\{ v_1' \cdots, v_n' \right\}, \quad (\mathrm{ii})$$

where

$$v' = \left\{ min\left(v_{ij}\right) \text{if } j \in J; \ max\left(v_{ij}\right) \text{if } j \in J' \right\}$$

Step 5: Separation from positive ideal solution and negative ideal solution.
Next step is to calculate the distance of each alternative from both the ideal solutions.
The separation from the positive ideal alternative is:

$$S_i^* = \left[\Sigma \left(v_j^* - v_{ij} \right)^2 \right]^{1/2} \quad (\mathrm{iii})$$

where i = 1, ..., m
Similarly, the separation from the negative ideal alternative is:

$$S_i' = \left[\Sigma \left(v_j' - v_{ij} \right)^2 \right]^{1/2} \quad (\mathrm{iv})$$

where i = 1, ..., m
Tables 7.8 and 7.9 show separation from positive and negative ideal solution.

TABLE 7.8
Separation from Negative Ideal Solution

	SD	NR	GM	WM	LCA
SD	4.07405498973471E-05, 4.67323772228285E-05, 8.87092385455731E-05	0.000260944245400749, 0.00056948491750658, 0.00237235404532855	5.81620707700978E-05, 0.00018352729280349,2 0.000911371537583564	1.84356507386981E-06, 1.83885883032676E-05, 0.000175138587966737	2.27649450505213E-07, 0, 0
NR	0, 0, 0	0.0000327753366483, 2.91070004124562E-05, 4.33913924050633E-05	0.000114680886977557, 0.000392453166632295, 0.00175564444556962	6.81215965596022E-06, 6.52198484223551E-05, 0.000431542116455696	2.16746136272007E-06, 6.97587234481336E-06, 1.83464911392405E-05
GM	8.20149631932932E-07, 4.6139512075518E-06, 3.33577279752705E-05	0, 0, 3.18519319938177E-07	2.32155919566394E-05, 2.74510530832414E-05, 3.95294466769706E-05	0.000354034994287874, 0.00083845421601788,8 0.00314838762287481	3.51392951322379E-06, 1.33828809611377E-05, 3.70064914992272E-05
WM	0.000016675376611933, 7.54057817717712E-05, 0.00087965884248058	5.70043888634708E-06, 1.91996433379373E-05, 0.000265043077804661	0, 0, 0	3.28345279853592E-05, 4.01084322604332E-05, 8.43541589201579E-05	1.61285709928321E-05, 4.95998391524031E-05, 0.000169316135234942
LCA	0.000542019846153846, 0.0014781866666667, 0.00862708003635537	0.000243858615384615, 0.000439103739837399, 0.00309688417177914	0.000148659846153846, 0.000292261463414634, 0	0.000073034, 0.0001290731707317,07 0.00128901868666212	0.000135360615384615, 0.000163934959349594, 0.000736850861167916
CAM	0, 0, 0	0.000152879821958457, 0.000404035878759446, 0.00165581096491228	1.17522255192878E-05, 9.14602770448549E-05, 0.000497467105263158	4.23753709198813E-05, 0.000129825448548813, 0.000535149631578948	2.99111275964392E-06, 9.9167414240211E-06, 3.17844912280702E-05
AMT	1.30641357730485E-05, 6.07539880798134E-05, 0.000729800122591944	3.02389290672856E-06, 9.67251619590568E-06, 0.000161085866900175	0, 0, 0	2.95425741343225E-05, 2.74047784400104E-05, 2.59654465849387E-05	1.25300321196925E-05, 3.60917958020213E-05, 8.45185347043848E-05
CIPMS	0.000276596328849419, 0.0013633664505222, 0.00468189511278195	0.000120586236123808, 0.000474768028401833, 0.00142687339849624	7.15355896565235E-05, 0.000954003383458647	9.71537482042576E-05, 0.000343872904801262, 0.000859225278195489	7.96129162857515E-06, 8.58477128259073E-05, 0.00041210864661654
ES	3.23668773249383E-06, 9.89795475513895E-06, 3.53747709661967E-05	0, 0, 0	1.37919236173325E-07, 8.56926043473448E-07, 5.7026236744968E-06	3.51057534646524E-08, 8.9308779569694E-07, 1.30824187322131E-05	0.00014852622569464, 0.000570424770269772, 0.0042785429208502
AMN	8.99454309614688E-06, 1.40440413318025E-05, 2.16092659385319E-05	0.000019628653219012, 3.08794489092997E-05, 0.000140566611633223	2.55695259234889E-05, 7.18714580941447E-05, 0.000719926847853696	9.06623032924819E-06, 0.0000275121010332950, 0.000342062484124968	0.000123338879764718, 0.000280633019517796, 0.00069157260181187
CMMS	0.000112275946028203, 0.000696072328767123, 0.00627840527472527	4.15542254235569E-05, 0.000182522818003914, 0.00187995956043956	0.00042219742315106, 0.000772280313111546, 0.00124586901098901	4.73328598965207E-08, 0, 0	0.000192783022217713, 0.000947431780821918, 0.0033610710989011
Si'	0.0318500166997503, 0.0612296785907365, 0.146204960218047	0.0296808265712324, 0.0464577871685121, 0.105082289702018	0.0295957949605121, 0.0428037609355496, 0.078291215350569	0.0254318620868417, 0.0402585714643184, 0.0830898696117407	0.0254072586260128, 0.046521386183885, 0.0991015553519898

M	AMT	CIPMS	ES	AMN	CMMS
00236145243750252,	1.42280906565758E-06,	6.93309448089853E-08,	6.37077412342498E-05,	6.78235175717563E-05,	0,
0950179613532772,	1.70928933684278E-05,	3.16389548693586E-06,	0.000129593159144893,	0.000118041728188997,	7.48796302240483E-07,
441877607043861	0.000175138587966737	1.12326756888962E-06	0.000605718369476602	0.000184174766019892	4.19455144301321E-05
103211933879E-07,	5.74504502083053E-06,	1.43037293374546E-06,	0.000211087337723424,	1.04523155489853E-05,	7.32385432065582E-07,
0005671272427E-06,	6.21088069705094E-05,	0.000023965808414106,	0.000450972952155083,	0.00003995733656424,	1.39717065374304E-05,
0015060053164557	0.000431542116455696	3.14037569620253E-05	0.00177328900253164	7.53066227848101E-05	0.000152606825316456
589981016844E-06,	6.20632714591261E-05,	2.49084986127694E-06,	7.51575258334121E-05,	6.5432618387033E-07,	1.47223391370824E-06,
422042417555E-05,	0.000247198725021454,	3.74090670589677E-05,	0.00022039286992767,	1.60297364227044E-05,	5.80291773936496E-07,
03525885625966	0.00121848938485317	0.00005689057187017	0.00102775504173107	4.00618238021638E-05	0
111178892786E-06,	2.92578923288089E-05,	6.52222628031111E-06,	7.21891108738753E-05,	6.34680494128412E-06,	0.000156808906512124,
813818906586E-05,	3.83309963809291E-05,	5.14279616937951E-05,	0.000253211916708918,	5.63092819553473E-05,	0.000382869066559435,
0154782407996944	8.43541589201579E-05	0.0000713805793964409	0.0013104065210 7475	0.000177638763529861	0.00191100231885904
0220432153846154,	0.000065,	6.34098461538462E-05,	0,	0.000013754,	4.81984615384616E-06,
07553092682 92683,	0.000122600325203252,	0.00104314829268293,	0,	1.43414634146341E-05,	4.68292682926829E-06,
53476736400818	0.00128901868666212	0.00390822478754829	0.000224638148148148	0.000210192965235174	0.000378881092933424
548961424332E-05,	0.000110253353115727,	0.000548823798219585,	2.35548961424332E-07,	2.59300296735905E-05,	3.78872997032641E-05,
243403693931E-05,	0.000267031675461741,	0.00425543007915567,	8.76286279683377E-06,	5.68024406332454E-05,	7.97715171503958E-05,
0106600438596491	0.000995545421052631	0.0072289368596 4912	6.89875263157895E-05	6.02387543859649E-05	0.000370099105263158
630001865014E-06,	2.58088153014071E-05,	3.69732391155687E-06,	8.38212072859896E-06,	0.000122363594918872,	6.31419275959964E-06,
898419279606E-06,	2.58106659756414E-05,	3.77941461518528E-05,	8.20792536926665E-05,	0.000294911179061933,	6.00034827675564E-05,
163455925277E-06	2.59654465849387E-05	1.85586047869235E-05	0.0005356523117338	0.000492923064798599	0.00046001826619965
	8.68964986287058E-05,	8.48631592007314E-05,	3.63676753297636E-05,	4.85965913543163E-06,	0.000029752551913282,
844165602224E-06,	0.000331638801562852,	0.000420649876775115,	0.000157562071530543,	0.000048097782853708,	0.000124048990157037,
	0.000859225278195489	0.00015523863 1578947	0.000377294451127819	1.51883458646617E-05	0.000320829488721804
021824115839E-05,	9.80020628464326E-07,	1.52317784707999E-05,	2.80536027256684E-05,	0.000108687725542366,	2.25477943444641E-05,
0163863158283205,	8.5825737166476E-06,	0.000110533569214304,	3.11842639406576E-05,	0.000327981990626269,	0.000159927962505074,
16145879593121	0.000165303544130216	0.000140610963191164	6.67169884191643E-05	0.000703283305375274	0.00112888966966911
262665196524E-05,	1.29650233525919E-07,	0.000101015423158746,	0,	5.34504532692517E-05,	7.65845645036157E-05,
618369690011E-05,	5.00114810562573E-08,	0.000589241056257176,	0,	4.33884730195178E-05,	0.000441663182548795,
0189690968588604	0	0.000906995935991872	1.21920243840488E-06	7.92786385572772E-06	0.00246340157480315
929735213554E-05,	5.55503702952217E-06,	4.69660302323222E-05,	5.55544283250482E-07,	0,	6.65618342294816E-05,
0101195225048924,	3.89060665362035E-05,	0.000477758923679061,	6.90481409001958E-06,	7.67201565557731E-07,	9.80165166340509E-05,
0235345201465201	0.000591956043956044	0.000499840146520147	0.00022271098901 0989	1.37195604395604E-05	0.00018642989010989
51697066137274,	0.0198270621326453,	0.0295722866839115,	0.0222651343515746,	0.0203549116133038,	0.0200868516563809,
66786301340339,	0.0340492517051214,	0.0839673905547261,	0.0366150811003784,	0.0318846454317145,	0.0366231134635659,
1924737823236	0.076397242546948	0.114101727002986	0.0788592889462432	0.0445045597224789	0.0861051900079537

TABLE 7.9
Separation from Positive Ideal Solution

	SD	NR	GM	WM	LCA
SD	9.54711968117226E-05, 0.0005754661359699, 0.00325530918636882	0, 4.84569198176798E-05, 0.000315668345018751	7.27159132080029E-05, 0.00029852095782243, 0.00131659718897766	0.000218921299464595, 0.0007042013224626605, 0.00283448497635741	0.000245757120888853, 0.00095019613532772, 0.00441877607043861
NR	0.000211087337723424, 0.000450972952155083, 0.00177328900253164	7.75081306276038E-05, 0.000250938337801608, 0.00126189943291139	1.45918559333423E-05, 2.03260053619302E-06, 4.41113924050573E-08	0.000142058594274963, 0.000173191998350175, 0.000455261012658227	0.000170475194194329, 0.000345771647762425, 0.00143089386329114
GM	0.000320775139796769, 0.000718672233734216, 0.00253360012673879	0.000354034994287874, 0.000838454216010788, 0.00308537140340031	0.000195931729356892, 0.000562481794777492, 0.00248235624111283	0, 0, 0	0.000287006624004673, 0.00063997928650239, 0.00250272060587326
WM	7.12131225323234E-05, 0.000118448179100302, 0.000197570273780721	0.000102713707149272, 0.000230593352798224, 0.000752672028524131	0.00015680890651212, 0.000382869066559435, 0.00191100231885904	4.61339026994052E-05, 0.000175136598073326, 0.0011923596077932	7.23570901326826E-05, 0.000156858716366243, 0.000942665559658729
LCA	0, 0, 0	5.87575384615385E-05, 0.000305983739837398, 0.00138625312428993	0.000122959384615385, 0.000455888130081301, 0.00862708003635537	0.000217129846153846, 0.000733659837398374, 0.00324662576687117	0.000135649384615385, 0.000657588292682927, 0.00432136355373779
CAM	0.000548823798219585, 0.00425543007915567, 0.00722893685964912	0.000122379584569733, 0.00203799526385224, 0.00196528168421053	0.000399995347181089, 0.00309916792875989, 0.00393369607017544	0.000286196795252226, 0.0028986987176781, 0.0038303539649128	0.000470781735905044, 0.00385449405013192, 0.00630203875438596
AMT	5.54633731893819E-05, 8.79561440787769E-05, 0	8.69159707399963E-05, 0.000197765472920446, 0.000205144090073555	0.000122363594918872, 0.000294911179061933, 0.000729800122591944	3.16575004662536E-05, 0.00014251634102099, 0.00048045057793345	5.65809262904863E-05, 0.000124664669603524, 0.000317602895504962
CIPMS	0, 0, 0	3.19226015410735E-05, 0.000229056728529567, 0.000939446857142857	6.68030612511427E-05, 0.0013633664505222, 0.00140905864661654	4.58941935483871E-05, 0.000337823740326095, 0.00152973527819549	0.000190705310173697, 0.000764986448268089, 0.00231591127819549
ES	0.000107911664293032, 0.000430042472598443, 0.00353583678112878	0.000148526225694864, 0.000570424770269772, 0.0042785429208502	0.000139612156508697, 0.000527063517179023, 0.00397184247057829	0.000143994439699106, 0.000526176329482969, 0.003818450149880886	0, 0, 0
AMN	6.57188037604231E-05, 0.000421347462686567, 0.00202356832105664	4.45607019337858E-05, 0.000350339563719862, 0.0014270705486411	3.65924819103554E-05, 0.000249532078071183, 0.000519895351790703	6.55255558939452E-05, 0.000362106268656716, 0.000969558547117094	0, 5.65832376578645E-05, 0.000544517483701634
CMMS	9.90305366744446E-05, 1.93353424657534E-05, 0	0.000198843461499442, 0.000298262544031311, 0.00128722285714286	0, 8.94277886497063E-06, 0.00193068131868132	0.0004133041004697, 0.00094743178082191, 0.0062784052747252	4.43930455513848E-05, 0, 0.000452057472527472
Si*	0.0396925052497459, 0.0841288951879939, 0.14334612150754	0.0350166091520179, 0.0732002111307672, 0.130017588426357	0.0364462968767048, 0.0851162527502008, 0.163804926290791	0.0401349751731566, 0.0836716349090955, 0.156957590311436	0.0409109573556588, 0.0868970998509626, 0.153455360080106

M	AMT	CIPMS	ES	AMN	CMMS
8976691759592E-07,	0.00023830119560404,	0.00025250675294 8754,	6.67824966788777E-05,	6.26989251640434E-05,	0.000260944245400749,
	0.000712389641137574,	0.00084368460165 6288,	0.000377955765551775,	0.0003984128805 28985,	0.00089758083327 9835,
	0.00283448497635741	0.00427899557149845	0.00175247131257133	0.00279870357084624	0.00359968073699657
0019408011356 0005,	0.00014718451820 9918,	0.00017776523652 7348,	0,	0.00012759602204 0048,	0.00018695229135 8688,
00398065481542586,	0.0001783616250 77335,	0.0002670163580 11961,	0,	0.00022245550010 3114,	0.00030618872344 8134,
0146151070632911	0.00045526101265 8227	0.00133272692658228	0	0.00111773201012658	0.00088548051645 5696
02839957395270 53,	0.00011963531725921,	0.0002971339230 3662,	0.00010295092725 4142,	0.0003242489284 39516,	0.00030984664015 324,
00577070511217359,	0.00017512603162 9275,	0.00052165549098 9334,	0.00019910449429 9375,	0.0006226201986 02427,	0.00079491883780 8017,
0139376431530139	0.00044959381761 9784	0.0023588419659 9691	0.00057849273570 3246	0.00247815331066461	0.00314838762287481
5106374866555E-05,	5.05987494280 921E-05,	9.93704193991154E-05,	1.62080219612628E-05,	0.00010006100350 7702,	0,
00210231445705194,	0.00017891301991 3632,	0.00015365365534 9057,	1.33546864346032E-05,	0.00014551812157 9803,	0,
00978053987011334	0.001192359607 7932	0.0012437125990 0675	5.64823634279894E-05	0.00092336328027 5054	0
1384615384616E-05,	0.000231619846 153846,	0.00023465,	0.00054201984615 3846,	0.0003830898461 53846,	0.00044461538461 5385,
0012021593495935,	0.00074937365853 6585,	3.78149593495935E-05,	0.00147818666666667,	0.001201328130 0813,	0.00131364695934 9594,
00390231822313111	0.0032466257668 7117	0.0009221109406 95296	0.00606749744376278	0.00614405816859804	0.00539008640 0818
00234076913946588,	0.00016710290801 1869,	0,	0.0005263195252 22552,	0.00033616617210 6825,	0.00029831240356 0831,
0315522742742 74406,	0.00239048180738786,	0,	0.0038779818601 5831,	0.0033289343667 5462,	0.00316993405013192,
0557985185964912	0.0028591360701 7544	0	0.00588554133333333	0.0059693844912 2807	0.00432769185964912
7341906873614E-05,	3.57791822947966E-05,	0.0000835206863253,	6.66936610232712E-05,	0,	7.30854383819964E-05,
00234657310183985,	0.00014622996631 2516,	0.0001215568826 12076,	6.58243068152371E-05,	0,	8.88643068152371E-05,
00597865732632808	0.00048045057793345	0.0005156007238 7624	1.49819264448336E-05	2.31644133099824E-05	3.09890017513134E-05
00276596328849419,	5.34266893039 049E-05,	5.50425284053807E-05,	0.00011237322188 8468,	0.00020081303069 08711,	0.0001249162857516,
0117565341949057,	0.00035017036892 3285,	0.0002694207648 95935,	0.0005939668009 6176,	0.00089930364114509,	0.0006649211090 23969,
04681895112781 95	0.00152973527817 9549	0.0031320695338 3459	0.0024010300150 3759	0.00416375338345 865	0.0025515298640 601
2726042002473E-05,	0.00012537669887 2212,	6.86303306549928E-05,	4.74799333007194E-05,	3.10391480287825E-06,	5.53339873500765E-05,
00122825405026387,	0.00043906860538 0669,	0.00017785834003764,	0.00033486363804 1112,	3.33309222423146E-05,	0.00012627700483 4483,
00636484084569217	0.0027618734467 3097	0.0028678833838 9578	0.00327670668457485	0.00151251631930421	0.0010119790737 2099
00030643766469635,	0.00011547080169 7697,	1.11336464055237E-06,	0.0001233388797 64718,	0.000014400675 435652,	5.54387339582921E-06,
00264523536165327,	0.0005784340298 50746,	0,	0.0005892410562 57176,	0.00031284041331 8025,	1.49207807118255E-05,
0129307120480908	0.0024634015748 0315	0.0003808856997 71399	0.00235501447802896	0.0021918333756 6675	0
00238978496499949,	0.00033089540428 1221,	0.0001875329369 99087,	0.0003921229583 03743,	0.00042219742315106,	0.00015348483311 3523,
00429351389432485,	0.0006023542537 14285,	7.96142661448141E-05,	0.0007925733072 40704,	0.0008942778864 97064,	0.00043597651663 4051,
0375144322344322	0.0030146953846 51538	0.0032325528937 7289	0.0041173041758 2417	0.0057051428571 4286	0.0043010584615 3846
394769938875814,	0.04001150128 46953,	0.0381741568106513,	0.044679855321516,	0.0445162129758393,	0.0437382599457491,
817791029326399,	0.080628177703975,	0.049731034706839,	0.0912307615969588,	0.0897720561246802,	0.0884084371323428,
44097786412007	0.145902767327264	0.142366008017822	0.162805167205188	0.181735536372557	0.158892676471293

TABLE 7.10
Defuzzification and Closeness

	S_i^*	S_i'	C_i
SD	0.104	0.063	0.379
NR	0.102	0.053	0.342
GM	0.102	0.052	0.340
WM	0.097	0.046	0.321
LCA	0.082	0.064	0.439
CAM	0.095	0.058	0.380
AMT	0.108	0.044	0.287
CIPMS	0.096	0.059	0.381
ES	0.095	0.052	0.353
AMN	0.111	0.038	0.254
CMMS	0.099	0.053	0.350

Step 6: Defuzzification and closeness coefficient of each alternative
Defuzzify the values obtained and based on these de-fuzzified values calculate the closeness coefficient for each alternative.

De-fuzzified values for separation from positive and negative ideal solution and corresponding closeness coefficient are shown in Table 7.10.

Closeness coefficient is calculated as

$$C_i^* = \frac{S_i'}{\left(S_i^* + S_i'\right)}(v)$$

$$0 < C_i^* < 1$$

Step 7: Ranking of each alternative.
Rank the option with closeness coefficient, C_i^* closest to 1 as best alternative, and so on. The ranking is shown in Table 7.11.

TABLE 7.11
Ranking Based on Modified Fuzzy TOPSIS

	C_i	Rank
SD	0.380	3
NR	0.350	6
GM	0.381	2
WM	0.287	10
LCA	0.254	11
CAM	0.439	1
AMT	0.342	7
CIPMS	0.321	9
ES	0.340	8
AMN	0.379	4
CMMS	0.353	5

Above we describe the application of Modified Fuzzy TOPSIS for a scenario where there are 11 evaluation criteria and rating scale is as shown in Table 7.7. Key input from decision makers typically identifies the proper weightage to various criteria. As result of above fuzzy TOPSIS steps, Closeness coefficients is calculated. Hence the ranking order is given in Table 7.11. So, based on above analysis of modified fuzzy TOPSIS, the significant parameters for strategic success and competency are **CAM, SD, GM and AMN**. As a result, application of optimization techniques reduces human efforts. Modified Fuzzy TOPSIS is a method which can use data in any form like linguistic and numerical etc. After collecting data and converting it into fuzzy system, the chances of errors are reduced. As errors may be caused by units of parameters which also creates problem for mathematical calculations, so Modified Fuzzy TOPSIS is an ideal method. Modified fuzzy TOPSIS is a simple, superior and full proof solution to multi criteria decision-making.

7.3   MODIFIED FUZZY VIKOR

As human judgement involves some indecisiveness and ambiguity, fuzzy theory has been introduced for expressing the linguistic terms in decision-making process. This method "**Modified Fuzzy VIKOR**" has been developed by *Dr Chandan Deep Singh, Dr Harleen Kaur* and *Dr Rajdeep Singh* in 2020. Existing fuzzy VIKOR technique has been modified by introducing certain changes so as to make it more convenient to decision-making. The linguistic variables and their corresponding fuzzy numbers are shown in Table 7.12. The steps involved in the implementation are presented as follows:

Step 1: Identification of objectives of the decision-making process.
Step 2: D describing a set of relevant attributes.
Step 3: The fuzzy decision matrix is constructed as shown in Table 7.13.
Step 4: Normalized Decision Matrix if formed as shown in Table 7.14.
Step 5: Determine the best f^*_j and the worst f^-_j values of all criteria.

TABLE 7.12
Fuzzy Numbers for Linguistic Terms

Linguistic Terms	Corresponding Triangular Fuzzy Numbers (TFNs)
No influence (NO)	(1,1,1)
Very Low Influence (VLI)	(1,3,5)
Low Influence (LI)	(3,5,7)
High Influence (HI)	(5,7,9)
Very High Influence (VHI)	(9,9,9)

TABLE 7.13

Modified Fuzzy VIKOR Decision Matrix

	SD	NR	GM	WM	LCA	CAM	AMT	CIPMS	ES	AMN	CMMS
SD	(1,1,1)	(3,4,5)	(1/4,1/3,1/2)	(1,2,3)	(5,6,7)	(1/5,1/4,1/3)	(2,3,4)	(1,2,3)	(1,2,3)	(2,3,4)	(3,4,5)
NR	(1/5,1/4,1/3)	(1,1,1)	(1/4,1/3,1/2)	(1,2,3)	(1,2,3)	(2,3,4)	(1/3,1/2,1)	(1,2,3)	(2,3,4)	(1,2,3)	(1/3,1/2,1)
GM	(2,3,4)	(2,3,4)	(1,1,1)	(3,4,5)	(3,4,5)	(2,3,4)	(1,1,1)	(2,3,4)	(3,4,5)	(3,4,5)	(1,1,1)
WM	(1/3,1/2,1)	(1/3,1/2,1)	(1/5,1/4,1/3)	(1,1,1)	(2,3,4)	(1/3,1/2,1)	(2,3,4)	(3,4,5)	(1,1,1)	(1/3,1/2,1)	(1/5,1/4,1/3)
LCA	(1/7,1/6,1/5)	(1/3,1/2,1)	(1/5,1/4,1/3)	(1/4,1/3,1/2)	(1,1,1)	(1/4,1/3,1/2)	(1/5,1/4,1/3)	(1/3,1/2,1)	(1/3,1/2,1)	(1/5,1/4,1/3)	(1/5,1/4,1/3)
CAM	(3,4,5)	(3,4,5)	(1,2,3)	(1,2,3)	(2,3,4)	(1,1,1)	(3,4,5)	(3,4,5)	(3,4,5)	(3,4,5)	(2,3,4)
AMT	(1/4,1/3,1/2)	(1,2,3)	(1,1,1)	(1/4,1/3,1/2)	(1,1,1)	(1/5,1/4,1/3)	(1,1,1)	(3,4,5)	(2,3,4)	(2,3,4)	(1/3,1/2,1)
CIPMS	(1/3,1/2,1)	(1/3,1/2,1)	(1/4,1/3,1/2)	(1/5,1/4,1/3)	(1,1,1)	(1,2,3)	(1/5,1/4,1/3)	(1,1,1)	(2,3,4)	(1,2,3)	(1/4,1/3,1/2)
ES	(1/4,1/3,1/2)	(1/4,1/3,1/2)	(1/5,1/4,1/3)	(1,1,1)	(1,2,3)	(1/5,1/4,1/3)	(1/4,1/3,1/2)	(1/4,1/3,1/2)	(1,1,1)	(1/4,1/3,1/2)	(1/3,1/2,1)
AMN	(1/4,1/3,1/2)	(1/3,1/2,1)	(1/5,1/4,1/3)	(1,2,3)	(3,4,5)	(1/5,1/4,1/3)	(1/4,1/3,1/2)	(1/3,1/2,1)	(1,1,1)	(1,1,1)	(3,4,5)
CMMS	(1/5,1/4,1/3)	(1,2,3)	(1,1,1)	(3,4,5)	(3,4,5)	(1/4,1/3,1/2)	(1,2,3)	(2,3,4)	(1,2,3)	(1/5,1/4,1/3)	(1,1,1)

TABLE 7.14
Normalized Decision Matrix

	SD	NR	GM	WM	LCA	CAM	AMT	CIPMS	ES	AMN	CMMS
SD	0.0899, 0.1005, 0.107	0.0, 0	0.0242, 0.018, 0	0.041, 0.0328, 0.0275	0.2102, 0.2102, 0.2102	0, 0, 0	0.0364, 0.0271, 0.0218	0.1771, 0.1767, 0.1739	0.0078, 0.0065, 0.0057	0, 0, 0	0.0341, 0.0227, 0.0171
NR	0.1258, 0.1256, 0.1248	0.0568, 0.0635, 0.0676	0.0242, 0.018, 0	0.041, 0.0328, 0.0275	0.2102, 0.2102, 0.2102	0.1251, 0.1248, 0.1229	0.0364, 0.0271, 0.0218	0.1771, 0.1767, 0.1739	0, 0, 0	0.0176, 0.0149, 0.0137	0.0341, 0.0227, 0.0171
GM	0.1236, 0.1228, 0.1204	0.0781, 0.0776, 0.076	0.0484, 0.0541, 0.0541	0, 0, 0	0.2102, 0.2102, 0.2102	0.1192, 0.117, 0.1053	0.0182, 0.0136, 0.0109	0.1771, 0.1767, 0.1739	0.0155, 0.013, 0.0114	0.0235, 0.0199, 0.0183	0.0341, 0.0341, 0.0341
WM	0.1198, 0.1172, 0.107	0.0757, 0.074, 0.0676	0.0676	0.041, 0.0437, 0.0458	0.2102	0.1251, 0.1248, 0.1229	0.0364, 0.0407, 0.0436	0.1822, 0.1822, 0.1822	0.0233, 0.0195, 0.017	0.0235, 0.0199, 0.0183	0, 0, 0
LCA	0.0, 0	0, 0, 0	0.0, 0.0685	0.0137, 0.0109, 0.0092	0, 0, 0	0, 0, 0	0, 0, 0	0.1012, 0.0663, 0.0497	0.0311, 0.026, 0.0227	0.0117, 0.01, 0.0091	0.0171, 0.0114, 0.0085

(Continued)

TABLE 7.14 (Continued)

	SD	NR	GM	WM	LCA	CAM	AMT	CIPMS	ES	AMN	CMMS
CAM	0.1236,	0.0284,	0.0484,	0.0273,	0.1971,	0.0715,	0,	0,	0.0311,	0.0117,	0,
	0.1228,	0.0212,	0.0361,	0.0219,	0.1868,	0.0936,	0,	0,	0.026,	0.01,	0,
	0.1204	0.0169	0.018	0.0183	0.1577	0.1053	0	0	0.0227	0.0091	0
AMT	0.1198,	0.0757,	0.0665,	0.041,	0.2102,	0.1287,	0.0364,	0.1822,	0.0311,	0.0117,	0.0341,
	0.1172,	0.074,	0.0661,	0.0437,	0.2102,	0.1287,	0.0407,	0.1822,	0.026,	0.01,	0.0227,
	0.107	0.0676	0.0631	0.0458	0.2102	0.1287	0.0436	0.1822	0.0227	0.0091	0.0171
CIPMS	0.0449,	0.0284,	0.0242,	0.0137,	0.1752,	0.1251,	0,	0.1012,	0.0155,	0.0176,	0,
	0.0335,	0.0212,	0.0676,	0.0109,	0.1401, 0	0.1248,	0,	0.1325,	0.013,	0.0149,	0,
	0.0268	0.0169	0	0.0092		0.1229	0	0.1491	0.0114	0.0137	0
ES	0.1273,	0.0811,	0.0677,	0.0512,	0.1752,	0.1192,	0.0485,	0.1822,	0.0311,	0.0176,	0.0341,
	0.1273,	0.0811,	0.0676,	0.051,	0.1401, 0	0.117,	0.0475,	0.1822,	0.0326,	0.0149,	0.0227,
	0.1271	0.0811	0.0661	0.0504		0.1053	0.0436	0.1822	0.0341	0.0137	0.0171
AMN	0.1284,	0.0781,	0.0645,	0.0501,	0.2102,	0.1287,	0.0509,	0.1771,	0.0369,	0.0235,	0.0341,
	0.1284,	0.0776,	0.0631,	0.0492,	0.2102,	0.1287,	0.0509,	0.1767,	0.0369,	0.0249,	0.0227,
	0.1284	0.076	0.0541	0.0458	0.2102	0.1287	0.0509	0.1739	0.0369	0.0274	0.0171
CMMS	0.1198,	0.0757,	0.0484,	0.0519,	0.1971,	0.1287,	0.0485,	0.1822,	0.0363,	0.0274,	0.0341,
	0.1172,	0.074,	0.0541,	0.0519,	0.1868,	0.1287,	0.0475,	0.1822,	0.0358,	0.0274,	0.0341,
	0.107	0.0676	0.0541	0.0519	0.1577	0.1287	0.0436	0.1822	0.0341	0.0274	0.0341

TABLE 7.15
S, R and Q Values for Fuzzy Matrix

	S	R	Q
SD	0.6207,0.5945,0.5632	0.2102,0.2102,0.2102	0.7909,0.7781,0.753
NR	0.8483,0.8163,0.7795	0.2102,0.2102,0.2102	0.9282,0.9094,0.8913
GM	0.8479,0.839,0.8146	0.2102,0.2102,0.2102	0.9422,0.9229,0.9138
WM	0.9057,0.9007,0.8822	0.2102,0.2102,0.2102	0.9804,0.9594,0.957
LCA	0.1748,0.1246,0.1677	0.1012,0.0663,0.0685	0,0,0
CAM	0.5391,0.5184,0.4684	0.1971,0.1868,0.1577	0.6837,0.6518,0.5071
AMT	0.9374,0.9215,0.8971	0.2102,0.2102,0.2102	0.9933,0.9717,0.9665
CIPMS	0.5458,0.5585,0.35	0.1752,0.1401,0.1491	0.6081,0.5133,0.401
ES	0.9352,0.884,0.7207	0.1822,0.1822,0.1822	0.8417,0.8522,0.7549
AMN	0.9825,0.9693,0.9494	0.2102,0.2102,0.2102	1.0229,1,1
CMMS	0.9501,0.9397,0.8884	0.1971,0.1868,0.1822	0.9445,0.9012,0.8622

Step 6: Compute the values S_i, R_i and Q_i. The values of S, R and Q are calculated for all concept designs and are presented in Table 7.15

$$S_i = \sum W_j * \frac{\left(X_j * -X_{ij}\right)}{\left(X_j - X_j -\right)}$$

$$R_i = \max\left[\sum W_j * \frac{\left(X_j * -X_{ij}\right)}{\left(X_j - X_j -\right)}\right]$$

where w_j is the weight of the jth criterion which expresses the relative importance of criteria.

$$Q_i = \left\{ v\frac{\left(S_i - S^*\right)}{S^- - S^*}\right\} + \left\{\frac{\left(1-v\right)\left(R_i - R^*\right)}{R^- - R^*}\right\}$$

Where $S^* = \min S_i$, $S^- = \max S_i$, $R^* = \min R_i$, $R^- = \max R_i$ and v is the introduced weight of the strategy of S_i and R_i.

Step 7: The fuzzy decision matrix is defuzzified as shown in Table 7.16. Rank the alternatives, sorting by the S, R and Q values in decreasing order. The results are shown in Table 7.16.

The significant parameters that affect the manufacturing performance of an organization are CAM, GM, SD and AMN.

TABLE 7.16
Defuzzified Values and Ranking
Based on Modified Fuzzy VIKOR

	Q (avg)	Rank
SD	0.6142	3
NR	0.9026	6
GM	0.5075	2
WM	0.9772	10
LCA	1.0076	11
CAM	0	1
AMT	0.9096	7
CIPMS	0.9656	9
ES	0.9263	8
AMN	0.774	4
CMMS	0.8163	5

7.4   FUZZY AHP

Fuzzy AHP method is used to calculate the weight of criteria. Decision Matrix for Fuzzy AHP is collected from the experts. The weightage for calculation is taken from the analytical hierarchy process. The standard procedure is followed for the calculation of Fuzzy Weights and then defuzzfied number is taken for prioritization of CMMS criteria.

The values in the scale of relative importance are crisp numeric values like 1,3,5,7,9 etc. in fuzzy these crisp numeric values are converted into fuzzy number. Triangle membership function is used. The fuzzy values which are assigned to the different numbers are given in Table 7.17:

Step 1: This is the matrix with fuzzy numbers assigned for the crisp values given by the experts. Here fuzzified pairwise matrix was obtained by replacing all the crisp and reciprocal values with fuzzy numbers which are given in the above table.

TABLE 7.17
Fuzzy Values Which are Assigned to the Different
Crisp Variables

Number & Fuzzy value	Reciprocal Number & Fuzzy value
1= 1, 1, 1	1/2 = 1/3, 1/2, 1
2= 1, 2, 3	1/3= 1/4, 1/3, ½
3= 2, 3, 4	1/4= 1/5, 1/4, 1/3
4= 3, 4, 5	1/5= 1/6, 1/5, ¼
5= 4, 5, 6	1/6= 1/7, 1/6, 1/5
6= 5, 6, 7	1/7= 1/8, 1/7, 1/6
7= 6, 7, 8	1/8= 1/9, 1/8, 1/7
8= 7, 8, 9	1/9= 1/9, 1/9, 1/9
9= 9, 9, 9	

Step 2: Fuzzy geometric mean is calculated for measuring the weights by the equation given below. This is achieved by multiplying all the a, b, and c components of the rows and then taking seventh root for getting the desired fuzzy geometric mean.

$$r_i = \left\{ \left(a_1 * a_2 * a_3 * a_4 * a_5 * a_6 * a_7\right)^{1/7}, \left(b_1 * b_2 * b_3 * b_4 * b_5 * b_6 * b_7\right)^{1/7}, \right.$$
$$\left. \left(c_1 * c_2 * c_3 * c_4 * c_5 * c_6 * c_7\right)^{1/7} \right\} = (a,b,c)$$

Step 3: The following formulae are used for calculation of weighted Fuzzified matrix.

$$w_i = r_i * \left(r_1 * r_2 * r_3 * r_4 * r_5 * r_6 * r_7\right)^{-1}$$

$$A^- = (I,m,u)^{-1} = \left(\frac{1}{u}, \frac{1}{m}, \frac{1}{1}\right);$$

where $\frac{1}{u}$ corresponds to the reciprocal of the upper value, $\frac{1}{m}$ corresponds to reciprocal of the middle value, and $\frac{1}{1}$ corresponds to the lower value of the component of matrix.

The fuzzified numbers are calculated by adding all the a, b, c elements of the rows. Then defuzzified number are calculated by simply taking the average of the fuzzified number. subsequently the ranks of the alternatives are determined

Based on above steps and formulae, Tables 7.18 and 7.19 depict the detailed fuzzy AHP analysis for Sustainable Green Development. Table 7.18 represents the decision matrix for Sustainable Green Development.

Table 7.19 represents complete analysis based on fuzzy AHP for manufacturing competency starting from geometric mean value to normalized weight through defuzzification.

As per the results obtained from fuzzy logic, same have been verified by fuzzy AHP that is same parameters have been ranked higher in fuzzy AHP which were under study in fuzzy logic. So, from Sustainable Green Development, significant parameters are SD, GM, CAM and AMN

7.5 FUZZY LOGIC

Fuzzy Logic (FL) is based on the concept of a fuzzy set, which is without a crisp, clearly defined boundary. It contains elements having a partial degree of membership. A membership function (MF) defines mapping of each point in the input space to a membership value, which lies between 0 and 1. MF can have arbitrary curves whose shape can be define as a function that is simple, convenient, fast and efficient. It defines the relationship between input and the output variables, thus, facilitating the optimization of process output. A single fuzzy if–then rule assumes the form "if

TABLE 7.18
Fuzzy AHP Decision Matrix for Sustainable Green Development

	SD	NR	GM	WM	LCA	CAM	AMT	CIPMS	ES	AMN	CMMS
SD	(1,1,1)	(3,4,5)	(1/4,1/3,1/2)	(1,2,3)	(5,6,7)	(1/5,1/4,1/3)	(2,3,4)	(1,2,3)	(1,2,3)	(2,3,4)	(3,4,5)
NR	(1/5,1/4,1/3)	(1,1,1)	(1/4,1/3,1/2)	(1,2,3)	(1,2,3)	(2,3,4)	(1/3,1/2,1)	(1,2,3)	(2,3,4)	(1,2,3)	(1/3,1/2,1)
GM	(2,3,4)	(2,3,4)	(1,1,1)	(3,4,5)	(3,4,5)	(2,3,4)	(1,1,1)	(2,3,4)	(3,4,5)	(3,4,5)	(1,1,1)
WM	(1/3,1/2,1)	(1/3,1/2,1)	(1/5,1/4,1/3)	(1,1,1)	(2,3,4)	(1/3,1/2,1)	(2,3,4)	(3,4,5)	(1,1,1)	(1/3,1/2,1)	(1/5,1/4,1/3)
LCA	(1/7,1/6,1/5)	(1/3,1/2,1)	(1/5,1/4,1/3)	(1/4,1/3,1/2)	(1,1,1)	(1/4,1/3,1/2)	(1/5,1/4,1/3)	(1/3,1/2,1)	(1/3,1/2,1)	(1/5,1/4,1/3)	(1/5,1/4,1/3)
CAM	(3,4,5)	(3,4,5)	(1,2,3)	(1,2,3)	(2,3,4)	(1,1,1)	(3,4,5)	(3,4,5)	(3,4,5)	(3,4,5)	(2,3,4)
AMT	(1/4,1/3,1/2)	(1,2,3)	(1,1,1)	(1,2,3)	(1,1,1)	(1/5,1/4,1/3)	(1,1,1)	(3,4,5)	(2,3,4)	(2,3,4)	(1/3,1/2,1)
CIPMS	(1/3,1/2,1)	(1/3,1/2,1)	(1/4,1/3,1/2)	(1/5,1/4,1/3)	(1,1,1)	(1/5,1/4,1/3)	(1/5,1/4,1/3)	(1,1,1)	(2,3,4)	(1,2,3)	(1/4,1/3,1/2)
ES	(1/3,1/2,1)	(1/4,1/3,1/2)	(1/5,1/4,1/3)	(1,1,1)	(1,1,1)	(1/5,1/4,1/3)	(1/4,1/3,1/2)	(1/4,1/3,1/2)	(1,1,1)	(1/4,1/3,1/2)	(1/3,1/2,1)
AMN	(1/4,1/3,1/2)	(1/3,1/2,1)	(1/5,1/4,1/3)	(1,2,3)	(3,4,5)	(1/5,1/4,1/3)	(1/4,1/3,1/2)	(1/3,1/2,1)	(2,3,4)	(1,1,1)	(3,4,5)
CMMS	(1/5,1/4,1/3)	(1,2,3)	(1,1,1)	(3,4,5)	(3,4,5)	(1/4,1/3,1/2)	(1,2,3)	(2,3,4)	(1,2,3)	(1/5,1/4,1/3)	(1,1,1)

TABLE 7.19

Complete Fuzzy AHP Matrix for Sustainable Green Development

	Fuzzy Geometric Mean value after multiplication	Fuzzy Geometric Mean value by 11th root	Fuzzy weights,	De-Fuzzification	Normalized weight	Rank
SD	(9,576,12600)	(1.22,1.78,2.36)	(0.185,0.173,0.149)	0.169	0.132761438	3
NR	(1/45,3,216)	(0.71,1.10,1.63)	(0.071,0.077,0.081)	0.07633	0.059962607	6
GM	(864,20736,160000)	(1.85,2.47,2.97)	(0.206,0.207,0.189)	0.20066	0.157632604	2
WM	(4/675,9/64,80/9)	(0.63,0.84,1.22)	(0.051,0.049,0.05)	0.05	0.039278532	10
LCA	(1/1890000,1/110592,1/720)	(0.27,0.35,0.55)	(0.027,0.025,0.028)	0.02666	0.020943313	11
CAM	(2916,147456,2250000)	(2.06,2.95,3.78)	(0.037,0.034,0.035)	0.35333	0.277565674	1
AMT	(1/20,1,20)	(0.76,1,1.31)	(0.076,0.07,0.065)	0.07033	0.055249183	7
CIPMS	(1/800,1/48,1)	(0.51,0.70,1)	(0.062,0.059,0.061)	0.06066	0.047652715	9
ES	(1/57600,1/2592,1/48)	(0.37,0.49,0.70)	(0.063,0.059,0.061)	0.061	0.047919809	8
AMN	(1/200,1/6,25/3)	(0.62,0.85,1.21)	(0.122,0.125,0.118)	0.12166	0.095572524	4
CMMS	(9/50,8,150)	(0.86,1.21,1.58)	(0.086,0.085,0.079)	0.08333	0.065461601	5
Sum		(9.86,13.74,18.31)		1.27296		
Reciprocal		(0.10,0.07,0.05)				

x is A then y is B", where A and B are defined by fuzzy sets. The *if* part of the rule is called the premise, while the *then* part of the rule is called the conclusion. For example, "If the product concept is very low" and "quality is considerably high" then the result is "acceptable". The rules are determined through expert knowledge and are further refined following real-life application and appraisal, which either confirm them or require them to be modified.

The function itself can be arbitrary curves whose shape can be define as a function that suits from the point of view of simplicity, convenience, speed and efficiency. A function is a mathematical representation of the relationship between the input and output of a system or a process. It facilitates the optimization of process output by defining the true relationship between input and the output variables. Basically, it has been applied to validate the input factors determined from earlier tools. Therefore, only the identified factors are tested, and results obtained justify the earlier obtained results. The fuzzy logic toolbox graphical user interface (GUI) tool to build a FIS is shown in Figure 7.1.

Fuzzy inference systems
Fuzzy inference is the process of formulating the mapping from a given input to an output using FL. The mapping then provides a basis from which decisions can be made, or patterns discerned. FIS have been successfully applied in fields such as automatic control, data classification, decision analysis, expert systems and computer vision. Because of its multidisciplinary nature, FISs are associated with a number of names, such as fuzzy-rule-based systems, fuzzy expert systems, fuzzy modelling, fuzzy associative memory, FL controllers, and simply (and ambiguously) fuzzy systems. Figure 7.2 shows the procedure of FIS for the present study.

Fuzzification
The first step is to take the inputs and to determine the degree to which they belong to each of the appropriate fuzzy sets via MFs. In fuzzy logic toolbox software, the input is always a numerical value limited to the input variable and the output is a

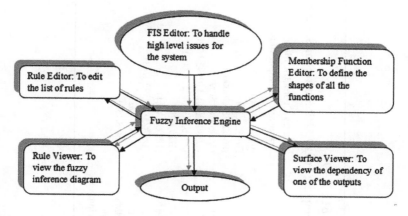

FIGURE 7.1   Tools used in fuzzy logic toolbox.

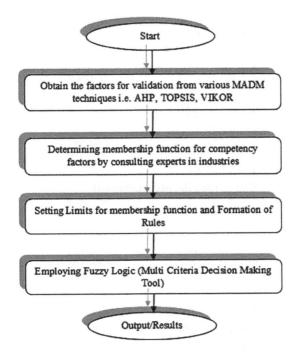

FIGURE 7.2   FIS procedure for present study.

fuzzy degree of membership in the qualifying linguistic set (always the interval between 0 and 1).

Rule evaluation
The FIS develops appropriate rules and on the basis of the rules the decision is made. This is principally established on the concepts of the fuzzy set theory, fuzzy IF-THEN rules and fuzzy reasoning. FIS uses "IF... THEN..." statements, and the connectors existent in the rule statement are "OR" or "AND" to create the essential decision rules. The basic FIS can accept either fuzzy inputs or crisp inputs, but the outputs it provides are virtually all the time fuzzy sets.

Defuzzification
The input for the defuzzification process is a fuzzy set (the aggregate output fuzzy set) and the output is a single number. As much as fuzziness helps the rule evaluation during the intermediate steps, the final desired output for each variable is generally a single number.

RESULT: CHECKING SUITABILITY
By consulting various experts from the industries, the fuzzy set rules defined for SD as: If it is less or greater than 3% of the actual, then it is considered as low or high else it is optimum as shown in Table 7.20.

TABLE 7.20
Range for SD Measurement

Fuzzy	Linguistic Value	Range
1	Low	−5 to −3
2	Optimum	−3 to 3
3	High	3 to 5

TABLE 7.21
Range for GM Measurement

Fuzzy	Linguistic Value	Range
1	Low	−4 to −2
2	Optimum	−2 to 2
3	High	2 to 4

TABLE 7.22
Range for CAM Measurement

Fuzzy	Linguistic Value	Range
1	Low	−6 to −4
2	Optimum	−4 to 4
3	High	4 to 6

TABLE 7.23
Range for AMN Measurement

Fuzzy	Linguistic Value	Range
1	Low	−5 to −3
2	Optimum	−3 to 3
3	High	3 to 5

By consulting various experts from the industries, the fuzzy set rules defined for GM are: If the control is less or greater than 2% of the actual, then it is considered as low or high else it is optimum (as shown in Table 7.21).

By consulting various experts from the industries, the fuzzy set rules defined for CAM as: If the actual quality is less or greater than 4% of the quality, then it is considered as low or high else it is considered optimum as shown in Table 7.22.

By consulting various experts from the industries, the fuzzy set rules defined for AMN as: If the support is less or greater than 3% of the required, then it is considered as low or high else it is optimum as shown in Table 7.23.

7.5.1 Fuzzy Evaluation Rules and Solution

The inputs here are the factors like Product Concept, Production, Planning and Control, Quality Control and Management. Table 7.24 shows the formation of fuzzy rules. There are 81 rules following the format "if (condition a) and (condition b) and (condition c) and (condition d) then (result c)" corresponding to the combination of input conditions

The result value lies between 0 and 3 is considered as rejected by the system, between 3 and 6 is considered poor (under consideration), between 6 and 8 is considered as acceptable, and between 8 and 10 is considered optimum (as shown in Table 7.24). The transfer function in fuzzy is shown in Figure 7.3.

These if–then rule statements are used to formulate the conditional statements that comprise FL. For example, "if SD is high" and "GM required is high" and "CAM is optimum" and "AMN is low" then the result is "acceptable". These rules are formed with the expert knowledge, feedback and guidance given by experts in the

TABLE 7.24

Range for Result Measurement

Fuzzy	Linguistic Value	Range
1	Reject	0–3
2	Under Consideration	3–6
3	Accept	6–8
4	Optimum	8–10

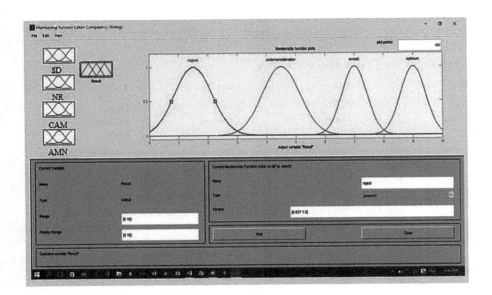

FIGURE 7.3 Transfer function in fuzzy format of RESULT.

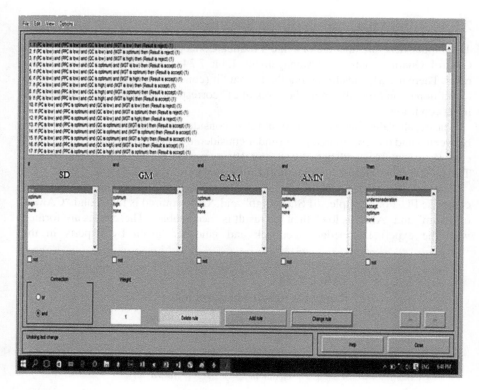

FIGURE 7.4   Fuzzy rules.

TABLE 7.25
Fuzzy Rules for Competency-Strategy

SD	GM	CAM	AMN
Low	Low	Low	Low
Optimum	Optimum	Optimum	Optimum
High	High	High	High

manufacturing industries and are further refined with experienced persons in the field of operation and production management from different manufacturing industries across India. The fuzzy set rules have been formed considering three different cases between of "SD, GM, CAM, AMN", when they are low, optimum and high. Figure 7.4 shows various rules for the fuzzy logic.

A continuum of fuzzy solutions is presented in Figure 7.5 using the rule viewer of fuzzy toolbox of MATLAB. The inputs SD, GM, CAM and AMN can be set within the upper and lower specification limits and the output response is calculated as a score that can be translated into linguistic terms. In this instance, if the value of SD

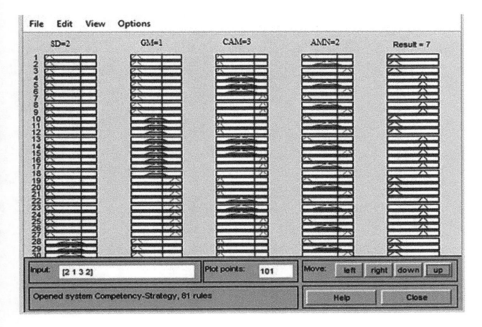

FIGURE 7.5 Rule viewer.

is entered as 2 (optimum), GM 1 (optimum), CAM 3 (optimum) and AMN 2 (optimum), then the order output is 7, which indicates the system is "acceptable" linguistically.

Thus, from analysis of empirical data, various MCDM analysis, factor selected for model development through ISM and SEM and verified by Fuzzy Logic are CAM, GM, SD, AMN.

8 Model Development Techniques

8.1 INTERPRETIVE STRUCTURAL MODELLING

Interpretive Structural Modelling (ISM) is an emerging modelling methodology which is useful as an aid to individuals or small groups in developing and understanding of complex situations. This modelling tool was introduced with the objective of understanding of complex relationships among the research variables related to the subject. In this process, a set of different directly and indirectly related elements are structured into a comprehensive systematic mode. The model formed after the process predicts the structure of a complex issue in a carefully designed pattern implying graphics as well as words.

ISM is an interactive learning process. The method is interpretive in that the group's judgement decides whether and how items are related; it is structural relationships among elements of a system. However, the direct and indirect relationships between the factors describe the situation far more accurately than the individual factor taken in isolation. Therefore, ISM develops insights into collective understandings of these relationships. The various steps involved in the ISM technique are:

Step 1: List all the research variable of system under the study; including factors, criteria and dimensions which can be objective, actions and individuals.

Step 2: Establish a contextual relationship among the variables with respect to which pair of variables is being examined.

Step 3: Develop the Structural Self-Interaction Matrix (SSIM) for the variables which can indicate pairwise relationships among the variable of the system under consideration.

Step 4: Develop the Binary Initial Reachability Matrix (IRM) from SSIM and the matrix is checked for transitivity, leading to development of "final reachability matrix". The transitivity of the contextual relations is basic assumptions made in ISM. It states that if a variable A is related to B and B is related to C, then A is necessarily related to C.

Step 5: The final reachability matrix obtained in Step 4 is partitioned into different levels.

Step 6: Based on the relationship given in the reachability matrix and the determined levels for each variable a directed graph is drawn, and the transitive links are removed.

Step 7: The resultant diagram is converted into ISM by replacing variable nodes with statements.

Step 8: The ISM model developed in Step 7 is reviewed to check for conceptual inconsistency and necessary modifications are made.

DOI: 10.1201/9781003189510-8

8.1.1 STRUCTURAL SELF-INTERACTION MATRIX (SSIM)

For analyzing the criteria a contextual relationship of "leads to" is chosen here. For developing contextual relationships among variables, expert opinions based on management techniques such as brainstorming were considered.

8.1.2 FINAL REACHABILITY MATRIX

The final reachability matrix is obtained by incorporating the transitivity as enumerated in Step 4 of the ISM methodology. In Table 8.1, the driving power and dependence of each variable is also shown. Driving power for each variable is the total number of variables (including itself), which it may help to achieve. On the other hand, dependence is the total number of variables (including itself), which may help in achieving it. These driving powers and dependencies will later be used in the classification of variables into the four groups of autonomous, dependent, linkage and drivers (independent).

8.1.3 LEVEL PARTITION

From the final reachability matrix, the reachability and antecedent set for each factor are found. The reachability set consists of the element itself and other elements to which it may help achieve, whereas the antecedent set consists of the element itself and the other elements which may help achieving it. Then, the intersection of these sets is derived for all elements. The element for which the reachability and intersection sets are same is the top-level element in the ISM hierarchy. The top-level element of the hierarchy would not help in achieving any other element above their own. Once the top-level element is identified, it is separated out from the other elements. Then, by the same process, the next level of elements is found. These identified levels help in building the diagraph and final model.

TABLE 8.1
Final Reachability Matrix of Factors

	SD	NR	GM	WM	LCA	CAM	AMT	CIPMS	ES	AMN	CMMS	Driving Power
SD	1	0	0	1	1	0	1	1	0	0	1	6
NR	0	1	0	1	1	1	1	1	0	0	0	6
GM	1	1	1	1	1	0	1	1	1	1	1	10
WM	0	0	0	1	1	1	0	0	0	0	0	3
LCA	0	0	0	0	1	0	0	0	0	0	0	1
CAM	1	1	1	1	1	1	1	1	1	1	1	11
AMT	0	0	0	1	1	1	1	1	1	1	1	8
CIPMS	0	0	0	1	1	1	1	1	0	0	0	5
ES	0	0	0	1	1	0	0	1	1	0	0	4
AMN	0	0	0	1	1	1	1	1	0	1	1	7
CMMS	0	1	1	1	1	1	1	1	1	0	1	9
Dependence	3	4	3	10	11	7	8	9	5	4	6	

8.1.4 MICMAC ANALYSIS

Matrice d'Impacts croises-multiplication *applique* and *classment* (cross impact matrix multiplication applied to classification) is abbreviated as MICMAC. The purpose of the MICMAC analysis is to assess the driving power and the dependence of the variables. Driving power and dependence of each benefit is shown in the final reachability matrix. In this section, the critical success factors described earlier are classified into four clusters (Figure 8.1). The first cluster consists of the "autonomous factors" that have weak driving power and weak dependence. These factors are relatively disconnected from the system, with which they have only few links, which may not be strong. The "dependent factors" constitute the second cluster which has weak driving power but strong dependence. Third cluster has the "linkage factors" that have strong driving power and strong dependence. These factors are unstable due to the fact that any change occurring to them will have an effect on others and also a feedback on themselves. Fourth cluster includes the "independent factors" having strong driving power but weak dependence. The driving power and dependence of each of these factors are shown in Table 8.1. Subsequently, the driver power dependence diagram is constructed as shown in Figure 8.2.

ISM model of the critical success factors for coordinated and responsive supply chain indicates the relationship between different critical factors and also gives the level of critical factors as determined in different iterations from Table 8.2 to 8.11. Driving power and dependence diagram of the critical factors for responsive supply chain divides the factors in four categories such as: autonomous, dependent, linkages and drivers, due to which analysis of factors becomes easier.

1. Autonomous variables generally appear as weak driver as well as weak dependent and are relatively disconnected from the system. These variables do not have much influence on the other variables of the system. Thus, these have weak drive as well as dependence power and are somewhat disconnected from other factors in the organization. Figure 8.1 shows that there is one autonomous factor which is ES.

DRIVING POWER	11						CAM				
	10		GM								
	9		DRIVERS			CMMS			LINKAGES		
	8						AMT				
	7			AMN							
	6		SD	NR							
	5								CIPMS		
	4		AUTONOMOUS		ES		DEPENDENT				
	3								WM		
	2										
	1										LCA
		1	2	3	4	5	6	7	8	9	10	11
		DEPENDENCE

FIGURE 8.1 MICMAC analysis.

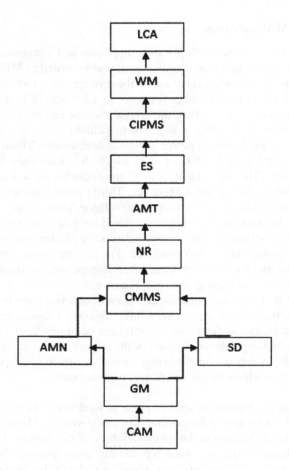

FIGURE 8.2 ISM based model.

2. There are three linkage variables: CMMS, AMT, CAM. These have strong driving power as well as strong dependence. Thus, it can be inferred that of all the 11 variables chosen in this study, 3 are unstable. Therefore, these have compelling drive power but weaker dependence. A factor of using a very strong drive power, referred to as "key factor" is categorized as class of independent or "linkage" factors.

3. The driver power dependence diagram indicates that variables such as SD, NR, GM and AMN. These variables will help organizations to achieve a coordinated and responsive supply chain and are classified as independent variables or drivers. Thus, these factors have strong drive power that is likely to be strong dependence power. These variables are unstable within the indisputable fact that any impact on these variables can have an impact on others as well as are sponsor result on their own.

4. Factors such as WM, LCA, and CIPMS have weak derive power and strong dependence power.

TABLE 8.2
Iteration 1

	Reachability Set	Antecedent Set	Intersection
SD	1,4,5,7,8,11	1,3,6	1
NR	2,4,5,6,7,8	2,3,6,11	2,6
GM	1,2,3,4,5,8,9,10,11	3,6,11	3,11
WM	4,5,6	1,2,3,4,6,7,8,9,10,11	4,6
LCA	5	1,2,3,4,5,6,7,8,9,10,11	5
CAM	1,2,3,4,5,6,7,8,9,10,11	2,4,6,7,8,10,11	2,4,6,7,8,10,11
AMT	4,5,6,7,8,9,10,11	1,2,3,6,7,8,10,11	6,7,8,10,11
CIPMS	4,5,6,7,8	1,2,3,6,7,8,9,10,11	6,7,8
ES	4,5,8,9	3,6,7,9,11	9
AMN	4,5,6,7,8,10,11	3,6,7,10	6,7,10
CMMS	2,3,4,5,6,7,8,9,11	1,3,6,7,10,11	3,6,7,11

TABLE 8.3
Iteration 2

	Reachability Set	Antecedent Set	Intersection
SD	1,4,7,8,11	1, 3, 6	1
NR	2,4,6,7,8	2,3,6,11	2,6
GM	1,2,3,4,8,9,10,11	3,6,11	3,11
WM	4,6	1,2,3,4,6,7,8,9,10,11	4,6
CAM	1,2,3,4,6,7,8,9,10,11	2,4,6,7,8,10,11	2,4,6,7,8,10,11
AMT	4,6,7,8,9,10,11	1,2,3,6,7,8,10,11	6,7,8,10,11
CIPMS	4,6,7,8	1,2,3,6,7,8,9,10,11	6,7,8
ES	4,8,9	3,6,7,9,11	9
AMN	4,6,7,8,10,11	3,6,7,10	6,7,10
CMMS	2,3,4,6,7,8,9,11	1,3,6,7,10,11	3,6,7,11

TABLE 8.4
Iteration 3

	Reachability Set	Antecedent Set	Intersection
SD	1,7,8,11	1,3,6	1
NR	2,6,7,8	2,3,6,11	2,6
GM	1,2,3,8,9,10,11	3,6,11	3,11
CAM	1,2,3,6,7,8,9,10,11	2,6,7,8,10,11	2,6,7,8,10,11
AMT	6,7,8,9,10,11	1,2,3,6,7,8,10,11	6,7,8,10,11
CIPMS	6,7,8	1,2,3,6,7,8,9,10,11	6,7,8
ES	8,9	3,6,7,9,11	9
AMN	6,7,8,10,11	3,6,7,10	6,7,10
CMMS	2,3,6,7,8,9,11	1,3,6,7,10,11	3,6,7,11

TABLE 8.5
Iteration 4

	Reachability Set	Antecedent Set	Intersection
SD	1,7,11	1,3,6	1
NR	2,6,7,	2,3,6,11	2,6
GM	1,2,3,9,10,11	3,6,11	3,11
CAM	1,2,3,6,7,9,10,11	2,6,7,10,11	2,6,7,10,11
AMT	6,7,9,10,11	1,2,3,6,7,10,11	6,7,10,11
ES	9	3,6,7,9,11	9
AMN	6,7,10,11	3,6,7,10	6,7,10
CMMS	2,3,6,7,9,11	1,3,6,7,10,11	3,6,7,11

TABLE 8.6
Iteration 5

	Reachability Set	Antecedent Set	Intersection
SD	1,7,11	1,3,6	1
NR	2,6,7	2,3,6,11	2,6
GM	1,2,3,10,11	3,6,11	3,11
CAM	1,2,3,6,7,10,11	2,6,7,10,11	2,6,7,10,11
AMT	6,7,10,11	1,2,3,6,7,10,11	6,7,10,11
AMN	6,7,10,11	3,6,7,10	6,7,10
CMMS	2,3,6,7,11	1,3,6,7,10,11	3,6,7,11

TABLE 8.7
Iteration 6

	Reachability Set	Antecedent Set	Intersection
SD	1,11	1, 3, 6	1
NR	2,6	2,3,6,11	2,6
GM	1,2,3,10,11	3,6,11	3,11
CAM	1,2,3,6,10,11	2,6,10,11	2,6,10,11
AMN	6,10,11	3,6,10	6,10
CMMS	2,3,6,11	1,3,6,10,11	3,6,11

TABLE 8.8
Iteration 7

	Reachability Set	Antecedent Set	Intersection
SD	1,11	1, 3, 6	1
GM	1,3,10,11	3,6,11	3,11
CAM	1,3,6,10,11	6,10,11	6,10,11
AMN	6,10,11	3,6,10	6,10
CMMS	3,6,11	1,3,6,10,11	3,6,11

TABLE 8.9
Iteration 8

	Reachability Set	Antecedent Set	Intersection
SD	1	1, 3, 6	1
GM	1,3,10	3,6	3
CAM	1,3,6,10	6,10	6,10
AMN	6,10	3,6,10	6,10

TABLE 8.10
Iteration 9

	Reachability Set	Antecedent Set	Intersection
GM	3	3,6	3
CAM	3,6	6	6

TABLE 8.11
Iteration 10

	Reachability Set	Antecedent Set	Intersection
CAM	6	6	6

Apart from this, from Figure 8.2 we can see that LCA is at the top, followed by WM at second stage and CIPMS at third. Then ES comes at fourth stage, followed by AMT at fifth stage, NR at sixth stage and CMMS at seventh stage. Finally, all these factors will lead to responsive supply chain. CAM, GM, SD and AMN are at the bottom level with highest driving power. It means these are the major drivers.

8.2 STRUCTURAL EQUATION MODELLING

In the present study structural equation modelling has been done by using the AMOS (Analysis of Moment Structures) software. Structural equation modelling (SEM) encompasses such diverse statistical techniques such as path analysis, confirmatory factor analysis, causal modelling with latent variables, and even analysis of variance and multiple linear regressions. SEM is a technique that is able to specify, estimate and evaluate models of linear relationships among a set of observed variables in terms of a generally smaller number of unobserved variables.

It examines the structure of interrelationships through a number of equations and these equations depict the relationships among the dependent and independent variables, referred to as the constructs, which are the unobserved or latent variables represented by multiple indicators. Observed variables are also termed measured, indicator, and manifest, and researchers traditionally use a square or rectangle to designate them graphically. The response to a Likert scaled item, ranging from 4 (strongly agree) to 1 (strongly disagree) is an example of an observed variable. Unobserved variables are termed as latent factors or constructs and are depicted graphically with circles or ovals.

Figure 8.3 shows a model of three observed predictors predicting one outcome variable. Amos introduced a way of specifying models in terms of path diagrams. These path diagrams follow a set of standard conventions. It is an important skill to be able to convert theoretical hypotheses and the data into a path diagram in consisting of:

Rectangle: observed variables (Ob1, Ob2, Ob3), such as items from a questionnaire.

Ellipse: latent lariables (LV), that are estimated from observed variables.

Circle: error (e), in predicting a variable.

Single-headed arrow: Relationships those are predictive.

Double-headed arrow: Covariance

The structural equation model consists of two components: the inner model, which shows the linear relationships among the exogenous and endogenous latent variables, and the outer model, which relates each latent variable to its corresponding manifest indicators. SEM has been described as a combination of exploratory factor analysis and multiple regressions. Exploratory factor analysis (EFA) is designed for the situation where links between the observed and latent variables are unknown or uncertain. In contrast to EFA, confirmatory factor analysis (CFA) is appropriately used when the researcher has some knowledge of the underlying latent variable structure.

Based on knowledge of the theory, empirical research or both, the relations are postulated between the observed measures and the underlying factors a priori and then tests this hypothesized structure statistically. It takes a confirmatory rather than an exploratory approach for the data analysis. The present study has been done using the confirmatory factor analysis (CFA) approach using Structural Equation Modelling (SEM).

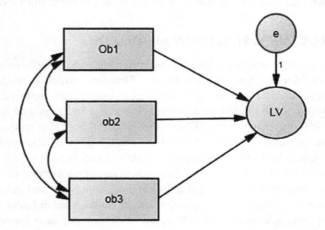

FIGURE 8.3   Basic model of three observed predictors predicting one outcome variable.

The core of the SEM analysis should be an examination of the coefficients of hypothesized relationships and should indicate whether the hypothesized model was a good fit to the observed data. In general, fit means consistency of two or more factors and it is believed that a good fit among relevant factors will lead to better performance.

In reference to model fit, researchers use numerous goodness-of-fit indicators to assess a model. Some common fit indices are the Normed Fit Index (NFI), Non-Normed Fit Index (NNFI, also known as TLI), and Incremental Fit Index (IFI), Comparative Fit Index (CFI), and root-mean-square error of approximation given by Schreiber et al. are shown in Table 8.12.

The questionnaire used was divided into four parts. The first part was dedicated for gathering demographical information about the respondents and their respective organizations such as position, name of the organization, years of experience, job title etc to ensure that the respondents are having suitable back rounds. It is also very useful in identifying discrepancies or errors in responses obtained. The second, third and fourth parts of the questionnaire were dedicated to measuring the effectiveness of sustainable green development through advanced manufacturing and maintenance techniques in the respective organizations. Each statement in the questionnaire was designed to extract the respondent's opinion on the above parts in the context of business performance measurement using a 4-point Likert scale, with point 1 representing "disagree" to point 4 representing "strongly agree".

Screening of the Data with Preliminary Analyses

After the data was been collected through the questionnaires, various data examination techniques were applied to the data such as testing for skewness and kurtosis, a normality test, CFA, test for the reliability of the data, so as to check and increase confidence in the data obtained. And lastly, the data was used to construct SEM_MC model using the Structural Equation Modelling (SEM) using AMOS 21.0 to employ the interrelationship among the variables used in this study. The result of the SEM analysis allows to understand which variables best explained the constructs and to understand the nature of the relationship between constructs. SEM analysis requires that the data sample should be multivariate normally distributed. Screening of the variables for normality is an important early step in almost every multivariate test. As there is no method to test the multivariate normality of the sample data using AMOS or SPSS software. Therefore, in the present study, a univariate normality test has been done. Skewness and kurtosis (as shown in Figure 8.4) are two important components used to measure the univariate normality of the data. As skewness relates to the symmetry of the distribution, a skewed variable is a variable whose mean is not in the centre of the distribution. On the other hand, kurtosis measures the spread of data relative to a normal distribution and relates to the peakedness of a distribution.

According to Currie et al. the values of skewness $<\pm 2$ and kurtosis $<\pm 7$ are considered acceptable.

Confirmatory Factor Analysis

To measure the determination of the data and stablish whether it is suitable for CFA, the strength of the intercorrelations among the items was checked by Bartlett's Test

TABLE 8.12
Cut-off Criteria for Several Fit Indices

Index	Shorthand	General Rule for Acceptable Fit if Data are Continuous	Categorical Data
Absolute/predictive fit Chi-square	x^2	Ratio of x^2 to $df \leq 2$ or 3, useful for nested models/model trimming	
Akaike information criterion	AIC	Smaller the better; good for model comparison (non-nested), not a single model	
Browne-Cudeck criterion	BCC	Smaller the better; good for model comparison, not a single model	
Bayes information criterion	BIC	Smaller the better; good for model comparison (non-nested), not a single model	
Consistent AIC	CAIC	Smaller the better; good for model comparison (non-nested), not a single model	
Expected cross-validation index	ECVI	Smaller the better; good for model comparison (non-nested), not a single model	
Comparative fit		Comparison to a baseline (independence) or other model	
Normed fit index	NFI	≥.95 for acceptance	
Incremental fit index	IFI	≥.95 for acceptance	
Tucker-Lewis index	TLI	≥.95 can be 0 > TLI > 1 for acceptance	0.96
Comparative fit index	CFI	≥.95 for acceptance	0.95
Relative non-centrality fit index	RNI	≥.95, similar to CFI but can be negative, therefore CFI better choice	
Parsimonious fit			
Parsimony –adjusted NFI	PNFI	Very sensitive to model size	
Parsimony –adjusted CFI	PCFI	sensitive to model size	
Parsimony –adjusted GFI	PGFI	Closer to 1 better, though typically lower than other indexes and sensitive to model size	
Other			
Goodness-of-fit index	GFI	≥.95 Not generally recommended	
Adjusted GFI	AGFI	≥.95 Performance poor in simulation studies	
Hoelter.05 index		Critical N largest sample size for accepting that model is correct	
Hoelter.01 index		Hoelter suggestion, =200, better for satisfactory fit	
Root-mean-square residual	RMR	Smaller, the better; 0 indicates perfect fit	
Standardized RMR	SRMR	≤.08	
Weighted root mean residual	WRMR	≤.90	<.90
Root-mean-square error of approximation	RMSEA	<.06 to.08 with confidence interval	<.06

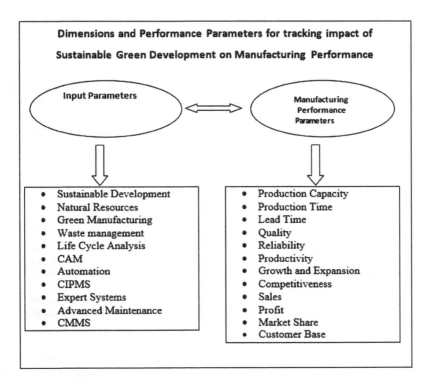

FIGURE 8.4   Parameters of the study.

of Sphericity and using exploratory factor analysis (EFA). The adequacy of the sample size has been checked using the Kaiser-Meyer-Olkin (KMO) test. Bartlett's Test of Sphericity should be significant at $p < 0.05$ for CFA to be considered appropriate, and KMO index should range from 0 to1, with 0.5 as minimum value for CFA.

The KMO and Bartlett's Test for the independent and dependent variable are shown in the Table 8.13 and the values of the test recommended that the data is suitable to continue with a CFA procedure.

TABLE 8.13
KMO and Bartlett's Test for the Independent and Dependent Variable of Model

Variable	KMO Measure	Bartlett's Test of Sphericity	
		Chi-Square Value	P-value
CAM	0.838	306.74	0.000
GM	0.783	418.793	0.000
SD	0.844	464.750	0.000
AMN	0.885	452.097	0.000
OUTP	0.893	918.154	0.000

TABLE 8.14
Model Fit Summary

Model Fit Summary	Before Modification Indices	After Modification Indices	Recommended Value for Model Fit*
CMIN/Df	3.73	2.26	x2/df < 3.0
Degrees of Freedom	514	189	Smaller is better
Probability level	0.00	0.00	
Root-Mean-Square Residual Index (RMR)	0.29	0.13	Smaller is better; 0 indicates perfect fit
Root-Mean-Square Error of Approximation (RMSEA)	0.134	0.071	<0.08
Baseline Comparisons			
Goodness-of-Fit Index (GFI)	0.350	0.984	>0.95
Adjusted Goodness-of-Fit Index (AGFI)	0.631	0.961	>0.95
Comparative Fit Index (CFI)	0.543	0.953	>0.95
Incremental Fit Index (IFI)	0.717	0.971	>0.95
Normed Fit Index (NFI)	0.710	0.963	>0.95
Relative Fit Index (RFI)	0.803	0.986	>0.95
Tucker-Lewis index (TLI)	0.452	0.969	>0.95

It was seen that after doing the required medications in the model, there has been slight improvement in it as the value of RMR after doing the modification indices further decrease to 0.13, which is less as compared to RMR value before doing the modification indices. Similarly, the value of GFI increased to 0.980 which is close to 1.

The other values shown in Table 8.14 which are related to SEM_SGD model as they are required to make model fit like Comparative Fit Index (CFI), Normed Fit Index (NFI), Relative Fit Index (RFI) etc. The values of standardized regression weights for various output factors as obtained from Structural Equation Modelling are Quality (0.92), Productivity (0.90), Competitiveness (0.86), Lead Time (0.82), Reliability (0.80), Production Time (0.80), Production Capacity (0.77), Growth and Expansion (0.72), Sales (0.66), Profit (0.66), Market Share (0.60), Customer Base (0.54).

9 Case Studies in Manufacturing Industries

9.1 CASE STUDY IN A 2-WHEELER MANUFACTURING INDUSTRY

This organization is the globally largest manufacturer of two wheelers. It started its operations in India in 2001 at Manesar (Haryana) and has acquired over 12 million customers in 12 years of operations. Now days, it is recognized as the fastest growing two-wheeler company in India.

Two-wheeler segment is the most important among the automobile sector that has experienced significant changes over the years. The two-wheeler sector consists of three segments: motorcycles, mopeds and scooters. The key manufacturers in this sector are TVS, Yamaha, Hero and Bajaj. Governance structure of this manufacturing unit in shown in Figure 9.1.

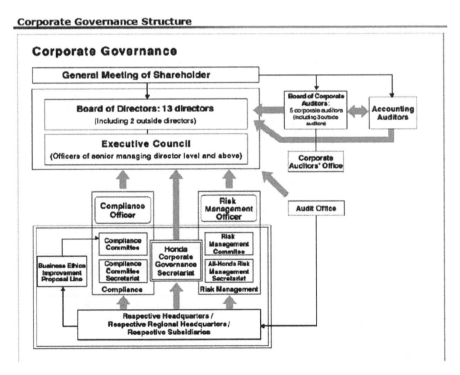

Corporate Governance Structure

FIGURE 9.1   Corporate governance structure.

DOI: 10.1201/9781003189510-9

9.1.1 COMPANY STRATEGY

The principle that it follows, is followed by all its companies worldwide.

Company Principle (Mission Statement)

People here are committed to provide products of best quality and at reasonable prices in order to satisfy customers worldwide.

Fundamental Beliefs

Respect for the Individual

- **Equality:** to respect and recognize differences in one another and fair treatment to everyone. It is dedicated to this principle, thus, creating equal opportunities for everyone. Figure 9.2 depicts its philosophy.
- **Initiative:** implies thinking creatively and acting on one's own judgement without being bound by preconceived notions and one must be responsible for the results from those actions.
- **Trust:** mutual trust is the basis for the relationship between associates here. Trust is created by helping each other, sharing knowledge, recognizing and making efforts for fulfilling one's responsibilities.

Management Policies

- Always have ambition and youthfulness.
- Make effective use of time and developing new ideas.
- Enjoy work and encourage open communication.
- Consistently strive for a harmonious workflow.

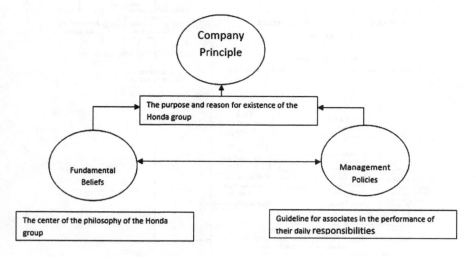

FIGURE 9.2   Its philosophy.

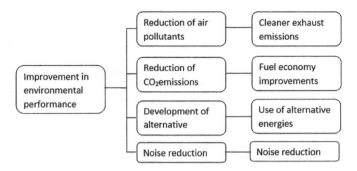

FIGURE 9.3   Principle initiatives in product development.

- Be mindful of the value of endeavour and research. Figure 9.3 depicts principle initiatives in product development. Principle initiatives in product development are shown in Figure 9.3.

Innovation in Manufacturing: Strengthening the Fundamentals

To meet demand, it is pursuing innovations in manufacturing technology. They meet the demands and the expectations of customers and their stakeholders.

Vision of Environmental Technology

Implementing different technologies, it is delivering on the promise of genuine value in environmental responsibility and driving pleasure. Figure 9.4 and 9.5 shows principle initiatives in production and recycling respectively. Table 9.1 gives 3R for recycling.

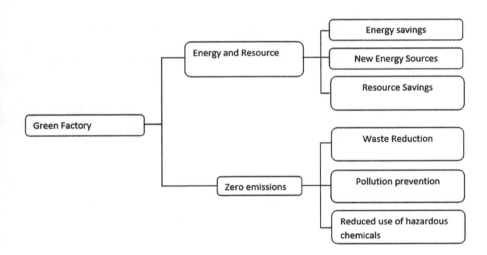

FIGURE 9.4   Principle initiatives in production.

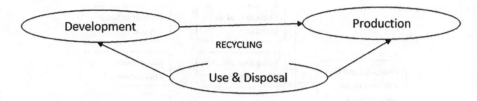

FIGURE 9.5   Principal initiatives in recycling.

TABLE 9.1
Recycling (3R)

	Development	Products	Use	Disposal
Reduce	Design for reduction			
Reuse	Design for reusability & recyclability	Recycled/Reused parts		
	Recycling and recovery of bumpers			Recycling of MIA batteries
		Recycling of by products		Compliance with the end-of-life vehicle
Recycling				recycling law in Japan
	Reduction in hazardous or toxic substances			Voluntary measures for recycling motorcycles

---

9.1.2 INITIATIVES TAKEN TOWARDS TECHNOLOGICAL ADVANCEMENT

Cutting-edge technology
The fundamental design philosophy strives to maximize comfort and space for people, while minimizing the space for mechanical components. With this in mind, its R and D activities include fundamental research and product-specific development.

Combi Brake System
Generally, it is quite difficult to control a two-wheeler while braking during bad road conditions and emergencies. Combi brake system allows easy and simultaneous operation of the rear and front brake, and also providing optimal braking performance.

Matic Transmission
The efficient, compact and oil pressure-controlled transmission is globally the first fully automatic transmission system, delivering a dynamic combination of torque and accelerator response for superior and constant driving experience.

Fuel Injection System
Its fuel injection system is designed to realize ideal combustion, resulting maximum power output, improving fuel efficiency and yet stay environment friendly.

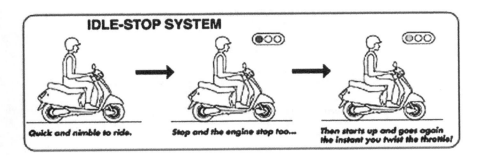

FIGURE 9.6 Idle stop system.

Idle Stop System

It has developed an advanced Idle Stop System, as shown in Figure 9.6, which reduces fuel consumption and totally blocks out toxic exhaust gases and any unwanted noise. As soon as the vehicle stops, the engine is stopped automatically. The engine restarts when the throttle is opened and the vehicle moves off smoothly.

9.1.3 Management Initiatives

1. *Respecting Independence*: Challenge
   Expect associates to express their independence and individuality. Currently, associates are encouraged to think, act and accept responsibility. Anyone with proposals and ideas should express them.
2. *Ensuring Fairness*: Equal Opportunity
   Offer a simple system with fair rewards for anyone having same abilities in handling similar sort of work and producing similar results, having no concern for nationality or race or gender, making no distinctions on educational basis or career history and objectively assessing each individual's strengths and aptitudes.
3. *Fostering Mutual Trust*: Sincerity
   Mutual respect and tolerance lay the foundation for trust that binds the employee and the company (Figure 9.7).

Fun Expansion

It is the first industry to promote green environment and safety in India. For 5 years, it has expanded popular initiatives such as Asia Cup, One Make Race, Gymkhana and Racing Training by Moto GP riders from Japan.

Environment Conservation

On environmental front, it believes that tomorrow should be greener than today. To ensure enjoyment of the environment for the next generation, it has implemented

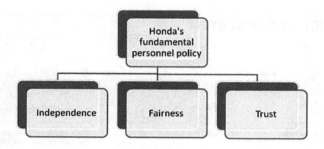

FIGURE 9.7   Principles of personnel management.

environmental management at its premises. Various effort are made, such as reusing and reducing waste to achieving zero emissions, improved efficiency and promotion of Green Factory, Green Supplier, Green Dealer initiatives and resource conservation.

Quality assurance

Quality Innovation centres were established so that quality issues do not arise, and to enhance the capacity to resolve problems whenever they do. Specialized departments at these centres are fully equipped to handle cases globally. They provide the resolution of any quality issues, rapid information and timely diagnosis. They also keep technicians and customers to date by providing the updates on recommended maintenance techniques. Its quality circle is shown in Figure 9.8.

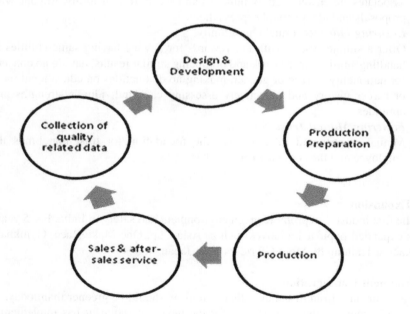

FIGURE 9.8   Quality circle.

9.1.4 SUSTAINABLE DEVELOPMENT GOALS

Being the world's leading manufacturer in the two-wheeler sector, it is working to increase fuel efficiency and lower emissions. People here are working hard to improve environmental performance. For this, Programmed Fuel Injection (PGM-FI) has been implemented. It adapts to changes in engine load caused due to acceleration and deceleration, driving conditions, adjusting the volume and timing of fuel injection as well as the timing of ignition for optimal electronic control. With this, fuel efficiency improves, and emissions are reduced, without compromising performance.

The Sustainable Development Goals (SDGs) or Global Goals are a collection of 17 interlinked global goals designed to be a blueprint to achieve a better and more sustainable future for all. Five critical dimensions: people, prosperity, planet, partnership and peace; also known as the 5Ps. However, it actually refers to four distinct areas: human, social, economic and environmental; known as the four pillars of sustainability. Human sustainability aims to maintain and improve the human capital in society. The SDGs aim to ensure that all human beings can enjoy prosperous and fulfilling lives and that economic, social and technological progress occurs in harmony with nature. Inequality is one of the defining issues of this generation and requires a commensurate focus that, to date, has been lacking. SDGs include:

1. No poverty.
2. Zero hunger.
3. Good health and wellbeing.
4. Quality education.
5. Gender equality.
6. Clean water and sanitization.
7. Affordable, clean energy.
8. Decent work and economic growth.
9. Industry, innovation and infrastructure.
10. Reduced inequalities.
11. Sustainable cities and communities.
12. Responsible production and consumption.
13. Climate action.
14. Life below water.
15. Life on land.
16. Peace, justice and strong institution.
17. Partnerships for the goals.

These 17 objectives are interrelated, and often the key to one's success will involve the issues most frequently linked to others. They can be summarized as follows:

- Eradicate poverty and hunger, guaranteeing a healthy life.
- Universalize access to basic services such as water, sanitation and sustainable energy.
- Support the generation of development opportunities through inclusive education and decent work.

- Foster innovation and resilient infrastructure, creating communities and cities able to produce and consume sustainably.
- Reduce inequality in the world, especially that concerning gender.
- Care for the environment, combating climate change and protecting the oceans and land ecosystems.
- Promote collaboration between different social agents to create an environment of peace and sustainable development.

Develop sustainable, resilient and inclusive infrastructures; promote inclusive and sustainable industrialization; increase access to financial services and markets; upgrade all industries and infrastructures for sustainability; enhance research and upgrade industrial technologies. The remaining three targets are "means of achieving" targets: Facilitate sustainable infrastructure development for developing countries; support domestic technology development and industrial diversification; and universal access to information and communications technology.

Implement the 10-Year Framework of Programmes on Sustainable Consumption and Production Patterns; achieve the sustainable management and efficient use of natural resources; reducing by half the global food waste per capita at the retail and consumer levels; achieving the environmentally sound management of chemicals and all wastes throughout their lifecycle; reducing waste generation through prevention, reduction, recycling and reuse; encourage companies to adopt sustainable practices; promote public procurement practices that are sustainable; and ensure that people everywhere have the relevant information and awareness for sustainable development. The three "means of achieving" targets are: support developing countries to strengthen their scientific and technological capacity; develop and implement tools to monitor sustainable development impacts; and remove market distortions, like fossil-fuel subsidies, that encourage wasteful consumption.

Some of the goals conflict. For example, seeking high levels of quantitative GDP growth can make it difficult to attain ecological, inequality reduction and sustainability objectives. Similarly, increasing employment and wages can work against reducing the cost of living. On the other hand, nearly all stakeholders engaged in negotiations to develop the SDGs agreed that the high number of 17 goals was justified because the agenda they address is all-encompassing. Environmental constraints and planetary boundaries are underrepresented within the SDGs. For instance, the paper "Making the Sustainable Development Goals Consistent with Sustainability" points out that the way the current SDGs are structured leads to a negative correlation between environmental sustainability and SDGs. This means, as the environmental sustainability side of the SDGs is underrepresented, the resource security for all, particularly for lower-income populations, is put at risk. This is not a criticism of the SDGs per se, but a recognition that their environmental conditions are still weak. The SDGs have been criticized for their inability to protect biodiversity. They could unintentionally promote environmental destruction in the name of sustainable development.

Several years after the launch of the SDGs, growing voices called for more emphasis on the need for technology and internet connectivity within the goals. In September

2020, the UN Broadband Commission for Sustainable Development called for digital connectivity to be established as a "foundational pillar" for achieving all the SDGs. In a document titled "Global Goal of Universal Connectivity Manifesto", the Broadband Commission said: "As we define the 'new normal' for our post-COVID world, leaving no one behind means leaving no one offline".

Despite organizations adopting SDGs, organization growth has improved over the years so leading to an improved profit.

Figure 9.9 shows operating revenue for the last 5 years of this 2-wheeler manufacturing unit. The operating revenue has increased consistently, even though the industries are working towards sustainable development along with environmental issues.

The graph in Figure 9.10 shows the total income in the last five financial years. A gradual rise in total income has been witnessed during this phase. Total income is the sum of the money received, including income from services or employment, payments from pension plans, revenue from sales or other sources.

Figure 9.11 shows profit for the last 5 years. Even though there is a dip in the financial year 2018–19, and a rise during 2019–20.

Similar to the empirical data results, it has been analyzed through case studies that sustainable green development and production techniques have an impact on overall performance of the organization. The factors Sustainable Development, Green Manufacturing, Advanced Production Techniques (Computer-aided Manufacturing and Advanced Maintenance) have a considerable impact compared to others.

From the above data, it has been observed that the company has been growing for the last five years. This is due to introduction of new strategies and technologies in their products. It is otherwise very difficult to withstand the competitive world of the market. Every company has to make use of competency in their products in the

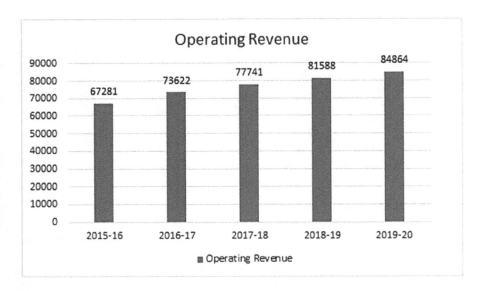

FIGURE 9.9 Operating revenue for the last 5 years.

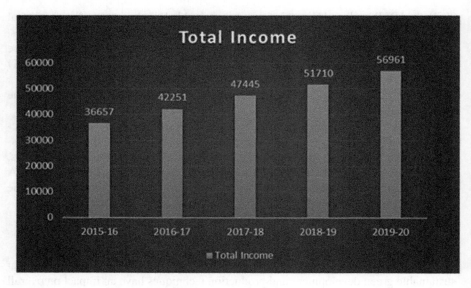

FIGURE 9.10   Total income of IT for the last 5 years.

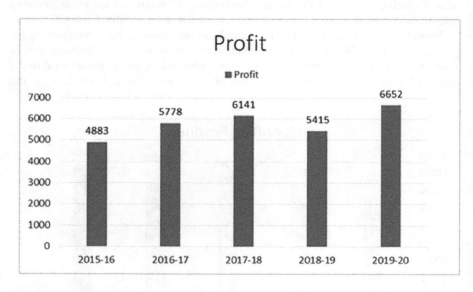

FIGURE 9.11   Profit for the last 5 years.

present times. If no innovation is made in the product, it becomes obsolete. It has legacy of cutting-edge Research and Development resulting in customer-oriented products. Today, due to the new technical centre, India is the centre of attention worldwide. They are devoted for delivering the best quality products at reasonable prices and at faster speed by having Research and Development, engineering, purchasing, quality and designing at same place.

9.1.5 GROWTH FRAMEWORK WITH CUSTOMER NEEDS

1. **Premises/Process**
   - *Voice of the customer at dealerships*: evaluating customer feedback and bring it on operations.
   - *Process efficiency improvement*: Improve work efficiency by elimination of wasteful operations at individual dealerships.
   - *Single repair programmes*: Ensure that customer's most issues are solved in a single repair. Figure 9.12 shows customer satisfaction initiatives.
2. **Product**
   - *Pre-emptive prevention, expansion prevention and mis-delivery prevention*: Boosting product-service quality.
3. **People**
   - *Developing a comprehensive dealership training system*: Strengthening training programmes to improve human resources and skill levels.

9.1.6 VISION FOR THE FUTURE

1. **Future Initiatives**
   Structural changes surface in the economy because of awareness about environmental issues globally and the growth of developing countries have a significant effect on their business activities. With the growth of emerging economies, competition in the market has intensified, and online information is exerting a significant influence on performances. In future, this will require them to provide tailor made products to every region of the world more affordably and speedily.
2. **Triple Zero**
   Zero CO_2 emissions will be guaranteed by using original renewable energy. Also, zero energy risk and zero waste will also be ensured with the

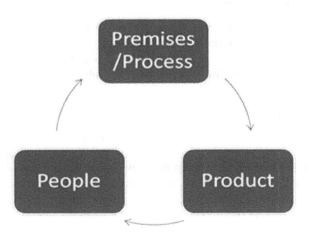

FIGURE 9.12 Customer satisfaction initiatives.

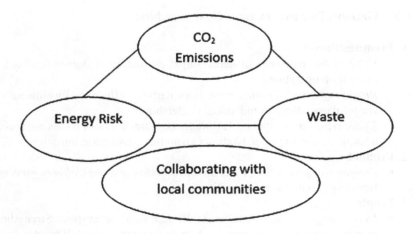

FIGURE 9.13   Triple Zero + coexistence with local communities.

collaboration of local communities. Figure 9.13 depicts Triple Zero and its coexistence with local communities.

9.2   CASE STUDY IN A 4-WHEELER MANUFACTURING UNIT

This unit was established in Feb 1981 with the objectives of modernising the Indian automobile industry, producing fuel efficient vehicles and producing indigenous utility cars for Indian population. It is the leader in the car sector, both in terms of revenue earned and volume of vehicles sold. Production of cars commenced in 1983. By 2004, over 5 million vehicles had been produced. Its two manufacturing facilities are sited at Manesar and Gurgaon.

9.2.1   COMPANY PRINCIPLES

It has adopted uniform fabric and colour working clothes for all employees, thereby giving them an identity. In order to minimise time loss between shifts, employees report early for shifts. It has an open-office system and practices kaizen activities, job-rotation, teamwork, quality circles and on-the-job training.

9.2.2   COMPANY OBJECTIVES

There was a need to provide a reliable, better quality and cost-effective car to the customers. This was established in such a scenario with a resolve to bring about technological modernization and expansion of the automobile sector. This has been entrusted with the task of achieving the following policy objectives:

- Modernization of the Indian automobile industry.
- For economic growth, a large volume of vehicles had to be produced.
- For conservation of scarce resources, fuel-efficient vehicles were required.

9.2.3 Company Strategy and Business Initiatives

For three decades, it has been the world's leader in mini and compact cars. Its technical superiority lies in its capability to pack performance and power into a lightweight and compact engine that is fuel-efficient and clean. This organization is clearly an "employer of choice" for young managers and automotive engineers across the country.

9.2.4 Technology Initiatives

Indian customers have passion for fuel efficiency when they choose automobiles. Achieving more energy per car from a single drop of fuel is a challenge for the designer, but important for the economy, the planet and the customer. At the same time, a speed conscious, young and fast-growing India demands better pick-up and instant response during acceleration. A third requirement is space efficiency, so that the car can cope with car parks and congested roads.

The company's new K-series engines deliver on all these fronts. The organization believes that the technology's purpose is to serve mankind with products that use minimum resources and reach out to maximum customers, good for their long-term safety, happiness, wellbeing, health and meet the needs of society. Better technologies, better thinking, better processes, more ideas and sensitivity that makes a difference in customer's life, help them develop better cars and thus, a better living. Today, the R and D team has many achievements:

- It has launched many new models in India in the last few years.
- In India, some of the most fuel-efficient petrol cars come with its badge.
- Launch of factory-fitted CNG variants. The factory-fitted CNG (Compressed Natural Gas) vehicles use advanced i-GPI (Intelligent Gas Port Injection) technology. State-of-the-art i-GPI technology is used here.
- The new concept Single Minute Exchange of Dies (SMED) is being adopted. This helps in changing of die setup within single digit minute, thus, improving operating efficiency and machine utilization.
- Almost all its cars obey ELV norms, which means they can be fully recycled and are free from any hazardous material.
- Plastic Intake in K-series is an example of technologies adopted for light weight construction. Light Piston, Nut-less ConRod and Optimized Cylinder Block for light weight configuration, High Pressure Semi-return Fuel System, Smart Distributor Less Ignition (SDLI) with committed advanced injectors and plug top coils for better performance.
- Wagon R Green: Wagon R is a balance of performance, space and comfort in a new design. Its new model known as Wagon R Green is available on CNG. It ensures fuel efficiency, safety, reliability and more power. CNG technology is another step for keeping low cost of ownership for customers.
- ESP (Electronic Stability Programme): An onboard microcomputer displays vehicle's stability and behaviour with sensors on a real time basis. During instability due to lane change or high-speed cornering, it automatically applies

differential brakes at the four wheels to keep the vehicle stable and on intended track without any additional driver involvement.

- Sequential injection has been introduced in LPG (liquefied petroleum gas) vehicles to ensure reduced emissions, better fuel economy and improved performance.
- Variable Geometry Turbocharger (VGT) has been introduced in diesel engines for improving performance and fuel efficiency.

9.2.5 MANAGEMENT INITIATIVES

The organization develops a culture in which higher standards of individual's accountability, transparent disclosure and ethical behaviour are ingrained in all business dealings and are shared by management, employees and board of directors. The firm has established procedures and systems to ensure that its board of directors are well-equipped and well-informed to fulfil their overall responsibilities and provides the management with strategic direction needed for creating long term shareholder value.

To meet the organizational responsibilities of safe working environment, the company has established an OHSMS (Occupational Health and Safety Management System) for:

- Managing risks – They identify all hazards by undertaking assessments, external and internal audits as well as all the necessary actions to prevent and control injury, loss, damage or ill health.
- Complying with legal and other obligations – They ensure that business is managed in accordance with occupational health standards and safety legislations.
- Establishing targets and review mechanism – They manage their commitments by using coordinated safety plans and occupational health for each site and area. They tend to measure progress, leadership support and ensure continual improvement. Health and safety performance is always among parameters for evaluation.
- Providing appropriate training and information – They provide all the necessary tools to all its vendors, employees, visitors and contractors to ensure safe performance at work.
- Ensuring meaningful and effective consultation – They involve all interested people and employees in the issues that harm health and safety at workplace.
- Communicating – They believe in the transparent relations of the performance and OHS commitments.
- Promoting a culture of safety – They believe that all incidents and injuries can be prevented, and everyone is responsible for their own and their processes safety. All responsibilities are clearly defined for all personnel, managers and supervisors. Figure 9.14 shows materiality matrix.

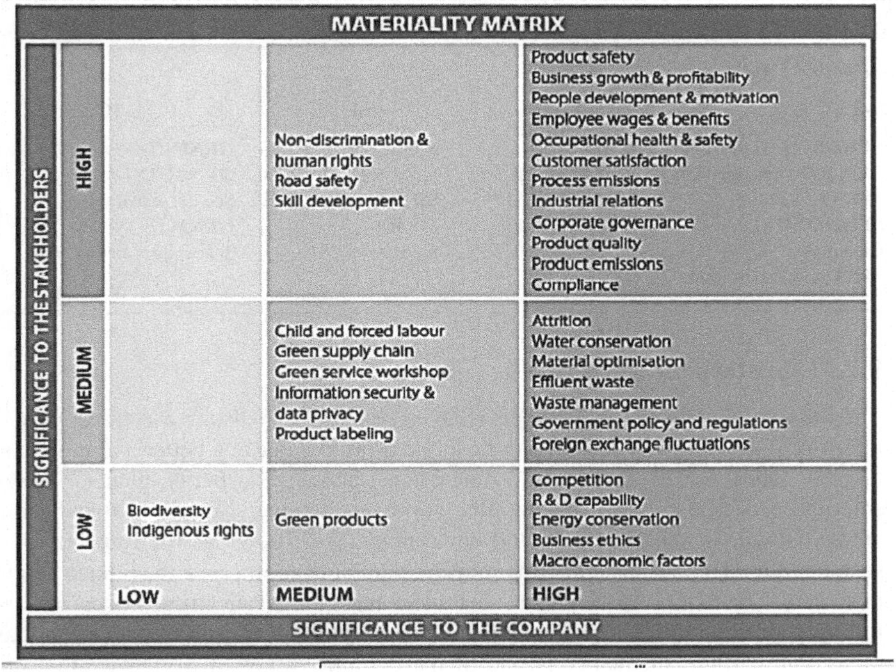

FIGURE 9.14 Materiality matrix.

9.2.6 QUALITY

The company was awarded ISO 27001 certification by Standardization, Testing and Quality Certificate (STQC), Government of India. The quality management is certified against ISO 9001:2008 standard. These systems are re-assessed at regular intervals by a third party. To increase customer satisfaction through improvement of services and products, PDCA functions and levels of organizations are followed. Table 9.2 depicts the quality tools employed for realizing overall organizational objectives.

It recently enhanced its product range with an aim to meet customer needs. A striking new look and a more daring approach to design began with the launch of Swift Dzire and Swift. Another major development is its entry into used car market, where customers are allowed to bring their vehicles to 'True Value' outlet, where it can be exchanged it for a new one, by paying the difference.

TABLE 9.2
Quality Tools

5-S	4M	3M	3G
SERI-Proper Selection	**MAN**	**MURI-**	**GENCHI-**Go to actual place
SEITION-Arrangement	**MACHINE**	Inconvenience	**GENBUTSU**
SEISO-Cleaning	**MATERIAL**	**MUDA-**Wastage	See the actual thing
SEIKETSO-	**METHODS**	**MURA-**	**GENJITS-**
Cleanliness		Inconsistency	Take appropriate action
SHITSUKE-Discipline			

9.2.7 SUSTAINABLE DEVELOPMENT GOALS

The Sustainable Development Goals (SDGs) or Global Goals are a collection of 17 interlinked global goals designed to be a blueprint to achieve a better and more sustainable future for all. Five critical dimensions: people, prosperity, planet, partnership and peace; also known as the 5Ps. However, it actually refers to four distinct areas: human, social, economic and environmental – known as the four pillars of sustainability. Human sustainability aims to maintain and improve the human capital in society. The SDGs aim to ensure that all human beings can enjoy prosperous and fulfilling lives and that economic, social and technological progress occurs in harmony with nature. Inequality is one of the defining issues of this generation and requires a commensurate focus that, to date, has been lacking. SDGs include:

1. No poverty
2. Zero hunger
3. Good health and wellbeing
4. Quality education
5. Gender equality
6. Clean water and sanitization
7. Affordable and clean energy
8. Decent work and economic growth
9. Industry, innovation and infrastructure
10. Reduced inequalities
11. Sustainable cities and communities
12. Responsible production and consumption
13. Climate action
14. Life below water
15. Life on land
16. Peace, justice and strong institution
17. Partnerships for the goals

These 17 objectives are interrelated, and often the key to one's success will involve the issues most frequently linked to another. They can be summarized as follows:

- Eradicate poverty and hunger, guaranteeing a healthy life
- Universalize access to basic services such as water, sanitation and sustainable energy
- Support the generation of development opportunities through inclusive education and decent work
- Foster innovation and resilient infrastructure, creating communities and cities able to produce and consume sustainably
- Reduce inequality in the world, especially that concerning gender
- Care for the environment combating climate change and protecting the oceans and land ecosystems
- Promote collaboration between different social agents to create an environment of peace and sustainable development.

Develop sustainable, resilient and inclusive infrastructures; promote inclusive and sustainable industrialization; increase access to financial services and markets; upgrade all industries and infrastructures for sustainability; enhance research and upgrade industrial technologies. The remaining three targets are "means of achieving" targets: Facilitate sustainable infrastructure development for developing countries; support domestic technology development and industrial diversification; universal access to information and communications technology.

Implement the 10-Year Framework of Programmes on Sustainable Consumption and Production Patterns; achieve the sustainable management and efficient use of natural resources; reducing by half the per capita global food waste at the retail and consumer levels; achieving the environmentally sound management of chemicals and all wastes throughout their lifecycle; reducing waste generation through prevention, reduction, recycling and reuse; encourage companies to adopt sustainable practices; promote public procurement practices that are sustainable; and ensure that people everywhere have the relevant information and awareness for sustainable development. The three "means of achieving" targets are: support developing countries to strengthen their scientific and technological capacity; develop and implement tools to monitor sustainable development impacts; and remove market distortions, like fossil-fuel subsidies, that encourage wasteful consumption.

Some of the goals compete with each other. For example, seeking high levels of quantitative GDP growth can make it difficult to attain ecological, inequality reduction and sustainability objectives. Similarly, increasing employment and wages can work against reducing the cost of living.

On the other hand, nearly all stakeholders engaged in negotiations to develop the SDGs agreed that the high number of 17 goals was justified because the agenda they address is all-encompassing.

Environmental constraints and planetary boundaries are underrepresented within the SDGs. For instance, the paper "Making the Sustainable Development Goals Consistent with Sustainability" points out that the way the current SDGs are structured leads to a negative correlation between environmental sustainability and SDGs. This means, as the environmental sustainability side of the SDGs is underrepresented, the resource security for all, particularly for lower-income populations, is put at risk. This is not a criticism of the SDGs *per se*, but a recognition that their environmental conditions are still weak. The SDGs have been criticized for their inability to protect biodiversity. They could unintentionally promote environmental destruction in the name of sustainable development.

Several years after the launch of the SDGs, growing voices called for more emphasis on the need for technology and internet connectivity within the goals. In September 2020, the UN Broadband Commission for Sustainable Development called for digital connectivity to be established as a "foundational pillar" for achieving all the SDGs. In a document titled "Global Goal of Universal Connectivity Manifesto", the Broadband Commission said: "As we define the 'new normal' for our post-COVID world, leaving no one behind means leaving no one offline".

Despite organizations adopting Sustainable Development Goals, Organization growth has improved over the years so leading to an improved profit.

The graph in Figure 9.15 shows the total income in the last five financial years. A gradual rise in total income has been witnessed during this phase. Total income is the sum of the money received, including income from services or employment, payments from pension plans, revenue from sales or other sources.

The sales and profit of the company have been shown in Figures 9.16 and 9.17 respectively whereas the growth of the company has been represented in Figure 9.18.

Similar to the empirical data results, it has been analyzed through case studies that sustainable green development and production techniques have an impact on overall performance of the organization. The factors Sustainable Development, Green

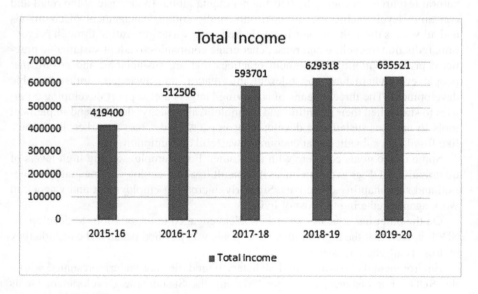

FIGURE 9.15   Total income for the last 5 years.

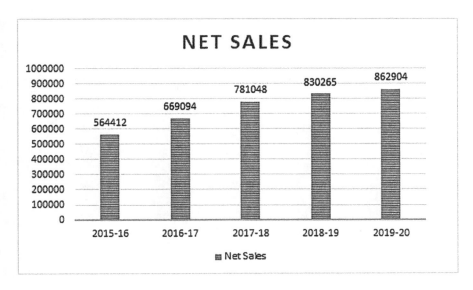

FIGURE 9.16 Sales for the last 5 years

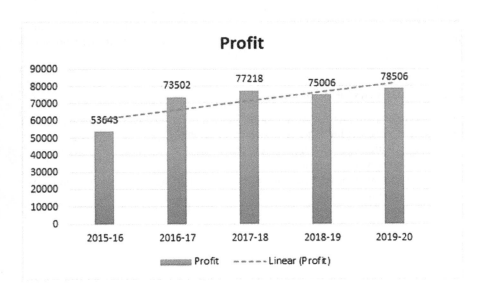

FIGURE 9.17 Profit for the last 5 years.

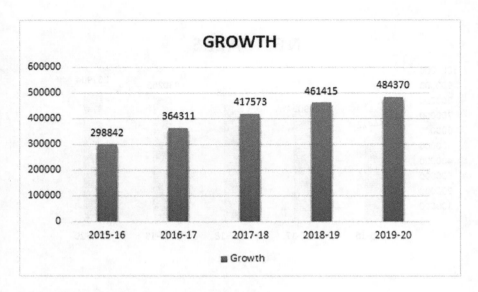

FIGURE 9.18   Growth for the last 5 years.

Manufacturing, Advanced Production Techniques (Computer-aided Manufacturing and Advanced Maintenance) have a considerable impact as compared to others.

From the above data, it has been seen that the company sales have been growing. This is due to the introduction of new strategies and technologies in their products which is a prerequisite for survival in the market.

9.2.8   FUTURE PLAN OF ACTION

- Continuously upgrade existing models.
- Develop products having alternative fuel options.
- Comply with safety and emission regulations.
- Introduce new technologies.
- Develop knowledge of different automotive technologies through standard cost benchmarking and tables.

10 Sustainable Green Development Model

10.1 SUMMARY

The study is aimed at identifying the attributes of sustainable green initiatives and advanced manufacturing and maintenance techniques of the Indian manufacturing organizations in order to enhance performance. The study also critically examines sustainable green initiatives and advanced manufacturing and maintenance factors affecting the performance of these organizations. Moreover, the study illustrates the relationship of sustainable green initiatives and advanced manufacturing and maintenance techniques and performance in Indian manufacturing industries to have overall business performance. The major objective of this research is to examine how sustainable green initiatives and advanced manufacturing and maintenance techniques affect the performance and an organization's success. Lastly, the research culminates with development of a model for Indian manufacturing units for growth and competitiveness. Primarily, the focus of this research was to investigate the impact that sustainable green initiatives and advanced manufacturing and maintenance techniques have on performance when viewed from manufacturing organization's perception.

To provide for the impact that sustainable green initiatives and advanced manufacturing and maintenance techniques have on performance, it was important to include the human and technology interaction while developing a model. This chapter presents the conclusions and recommendations for future from this study.

After reviewing more than 350 papers and books, it was observed that the impact of sustainable green initiatives and advanced manufacturing and maintenance techniques on performance has not been addressed yet. Based on the research gaps, the objectives are framed and issues for the study were listed along with the methodology adopted for the research work. Initially, there were 11 input factors, having 34 sub-variables and 12 output variables.

During this research work, a questionnaire was prepared for the survey to be conducted in the North Indian manufacturing units. A pilot survey was made for finalizing the questionnaire. During pilot survey, academicians, industrialists and existing literature were consulted. Responses to the questionnaire were received from 200 units. Telephone interviews were conducted, emails and letters were sent, and visits to the industries were even made.

After completing the survey, preliminary analysis of the data was carried out. Firstly, Cronbach alpha, a reliability analysis, was performed to analyze the questionnaire prepared. Then, demographic analysis involving chi-square and ANOVA was conducted to justify that the responses from different organizations did not have a significant difference among their views. Factor analysis was then employed to combine factors into one, thus reducing the number of input factors. Next, various

DOI: 10.1201/9781003189510-10

quantitative techniques were employed, including PPS and central tendency. This was followed by correlation and regression analysis of the data. Based on the data analysis, factors were selected for detailed study in various manufacturing units.

Data from each manufacturing unit was collected by visiting the organizations during the research work.

This was followed by qualitative analysis of the data. Firstly, MDEMATEL (a new tool), WSM, WPM, WASPAS, GRA, SMART, CRITIC, ENTROPY, EDAS, MOORA, AHP, TOPSIS, and VIKOR were employed for parameter selection according to importance, and then for development of a model, ISM, followed by SEM. SEM was employed by using AMOS 21.0 in SPSS 21.0 tool. Various important factors required for SEM_SGD model including CAM, Green manufacturing, sustainable development and advanced maintenance were formulated from the questionnaire, and from the extensive literature review. Further various data analysis techniques such as the test for kurtosis and skewness and for checking the normality variables were applied on the model SEM_SGD. Through Confirmatory Factor Analysis (CFA), various items which were affecting for the model to unfit were removed from independent and dependent variables. During this a model was developed to conclude the results of whole research work.

10.2 IMPLICATIONS

The research highlights the attributes of sustainable green initiatives and advanced manufacturing and maintenance techniques and performance of the Indian manufacturing organizations in order to enhance performance. The study also critically examines the sustainable green initiatives and advanced manufacturing and maintenance factors affecting the performance of these organizations. Moreover, the study illustrates the relationship of sustainable green initiatives and advanced manufacturing and maintenance techniques and performance factors in Indian manufacturing industries to have overall business performance.

The research critically examines the impact of sustainable green initiatives and advanced manufacturing and maintenance techniques on strategy formation and thus organization's success. Finally, the research culminates with development of a sustainable green initiatives and advanced manufacturing and maintenance techniques model for Indian manufacturing industry for sustained performance. This study is a legitimate reaction to a developing need of both academicians and professionals for better comprehension of the relationship of various sustainable green initiatives and advanced manufacturing and maintenance techniques and performance attributes.

The empirical analysis has been conducted in this research to evaluate the critical contribution of sustainable green initiatives and advanced manufacturing and maintenance techniques factors in realizing performance in the organizations. The association amongst sustainable green initiatives and advanced manufacturing and maintenance techniques parameters and performance factors have been deployed to critically examine the impact of distinct sustainable green initiatives and advanced manufacturing and maintenance techniques and strategy factors towards fulfilment of organizational sustainability objectives. In this admiration, notwithstanding exhibiting a most recent understanding of the present status of the impact of four capacities on execution of vehicles organizations, it formulates valuable ramifications for managers with respect to the technique development. The conclusions drawn from research work have been highlighted below.

10.2.1 RELIABILITY ANALYSIS

According to the response from the respondents, the value of Cronbach alpha came to be 0.975 for overall questionnaire as shown in Table 6.1.

10.2.2 DEMOGRAPHIC ANALYSIS

The data being not significant at $p < 0.05$; that is, there is not much difference in the views of different respondents belonging to different regions with different turnover, different market share and different numbers of employees. Thus, enabling analysis of the data as a whole.

10.2.3 PPS RESULTS

The research provides an insight into sustainable green development through advanced manufacturing and maintenance techniques. The average percent point score for whole questionnaire is 55.33 and central tendency 2.77.

10.2.4 FACTOR ANALYSIS

The research has highlighted the role of sustainable green development through advanced manufacturing and maintenance techniques. The data analysis has been conducted in this research to evaluate the impact that sustainable green development through advanced manufacturing and maintenance techniques have on performance of Indian manufacturing industries. 11 components were extracted as a result of the factor analysis, which have been classified into dimensions. Each dimension is further divided into factors. These components may be reviewed by the managers as a productive result in increasing their sales, profit and building good relationships with their customers.

The empirical analysis has highlighted different issues from adolescents' and parents' points of view, which are listed in Table 10.1.

10.2.5 CORRELATION RESULTS

The research has highlighted contributions of various sustainable green initiatives and advanced manufacturing and maintenance techniques attributes in Indian manufacturing industry for realizing performance achievements for competing successfully in fiercely competitive marketplace. The data analysis has been conducted in this research to evaluate the impact of sustainable green initiatives and advanced manufacturing and maintenance techniques in realizing performance in the organizations. The association amongst sustainable green initiatives and advanced manufacturing and maintenance techniques and strategy factors towards fulfilment of organizational sustainability objectives. Thus manufacturing managers must develop

TABLE 10.1
Results of Factor Analysis

Component	Dimensions	Factors
1	Sustainable development	• Environment • Economic • Social
2	Natural resources	• Renewable Energy • Eco-Friendly • Greenhouse Gas Reduction
3	Green Manufacturing	• CAD • CAPP • Green SCM • CAIR
4	Waste management	• 5-S • JIT • Kaizen
5	Lifecycle Analysis	• Product Lifecycle • FEA • RLP
6	CAM	• Robotics • CNC • FMS
7	Automation	• AGV • ASRS • AMHS
8	CIPMS	• MRP • MRP-II • ERP
9	Expert Systems	• RPT • Concurrent Engineering • Reverse Engineering
10	Advanced maintenance	• RCM • Predictive • Preventive
11	CMMS	• CMM & Inventory • Resource & Asset Management • Computerized Report Management

competencies for managing manufacturing initiatives efficiently for realizing global performance. Therefore, effective adoption of sustainable green initiatives and advanced manufacturing and maintenance techniques factors contributes towards realization of sustained performance.

a. The analysis of the correlation matrix showed that the above null hypothesis assumed was not acceptable as the correlations obtained between the sustainable development and all processes of output was significant and they were affected in the organization in a positive manner. It was inference that the correlation of the sustainable development with the parameters *reliability* (r = 0.727), *competitiveness* (r = 0.684), *quality* (r = 0.675), *production time* (r = 0.613), *production capacity* (r = 0.606), *growth and expansion* (r = 0.527) and *productivity* (r = 0.500) were significantly positive.

b. The analysis of the correlation matrix showed that the above null hypothesis assumed was not acceptable as the correlations obtained between the natural resources and all process of output was significant and they were being affected in the organization in a positive manner. It was inference that the correlation of the natural resources with the parameters *reliability* (r = 0.758), *competitiveness* (r = 0.696), *quality* (r = 0.692), *production time* (r = 0.635), *production capacity* (r = 0.606), *growth and expansion* (r = 0.556), *productivity* (r = 0.554), *lead time* (r = 0.527) and *profit* (r = 0.505) were significantly positive.

c. The analysis of the correlation matrix showed that the above null hypothesis assumed was not acceptable as the correlations obtained between the green manufacturing and all process of output was significant, and they were being affected in the organization in a positive manner. It was inference that the correlation of the green manufacturing with the parameters *reliability* (r = 0.746), *competitiveness* (r = 0.675), *quality* (r = 0.595) and *production capacity* (r = 0.550) were significantly positive.

d. The analysis of the correlation matrix showed that the above null hypothesis assumed was not acceptable as the correlations obtained between the waste management and all process of output was significant and they were being affected in the organization in a positive manner. It was inference that the correlation of the waste management with parameters *reliability* (r = 0.770), *competitiveness* (r = 0.704), *quality* (r = 0.690), *production capacity* (r = 0.672), *production time* (r = 0.631), *productivity* (r = 0.553), *growth and expansion* (r = 0.552), *market share* (r = 0.526) and *profit* (r = 0.511) were significantly positive.

e. The analysis of the correlation matrix showed that the above null hypothesis assumed was not acceptable as the correlations obtained between the Lifecycle Analysis and all process of output was significant, and they were being affected in the organization in a positive manner. It was inference that the correlation of the Lifecycle Analysis with the parameters *reliability* (r = 0.688), *competitiveness* (r = 0.638), *production capacity* (r = 0.614), *quality* (r = 0.590), *growth and expansion* (r = 0.553), *production time* (r = 0.549) and *market share* (r = 0.508) were significantly positive.

f. The analysis of the correlation matrix showed that the above null hypothesis assumed was not acceptable as the correlations obtained between the computer-aided manufacturing and all process of output was significant, and they were affected in the organization in a positive manner. It was inference that the correlation of the computer-aided manufacturing with the parameters *production capacity* (r = 0.653), *reliability* (r = 0.652), *production time* (r = 0.628), *quality* (r = 0.586), *productivity* (r = 0.564), *growth and expansion* (r = 0.531) and *competitiveness* (r = 0.525) were significantly positive.

g. The analysis of the correlation matrix showed that the above null hypothesis assumed was not acceptable as the correlations obtained between the automation and all processes of output was significant and they were being affected in the organization in a positive manner. It was inference that the correlation of the automation with the parameters *quality* (r = 0.709), *production capacity* (r = 0.679), *production time* (r = 0.677), *reliability* (r = 0.643), *productivity* (r = 0.612), *growth and expansion* (r = 0.590), *competitiveness* (r = 0.569), *profit* (r = 0.554), *sales* (r = 0.547) and *lead time* (r = 0.506) were significantly positive.

h. The analysis of the correlation matrix showed that the above null hypothesis assumed was not acceptable as the correlations obtained between the CIPMS and all process of output was significant, and they were being affected in the organization in a positive manner. It was inference that the correlation of the CIPMS with the parameters *reliability* (r = 0.700), *profit* (r = 0.655), *production time* (r = 0.640), *competitiveness* (r = 0.639), *growth and expansion* (r = 0.606), *lead time* (r = 0.597), *productivity* (r = 0.581), *quality* (r = 0.547), *sales* (r = 0.529), *market share* (r = 0.521), *production capacity* (r = 0.516), and *customer base* (r = 0.515) were significantly positive.

i. The analysis of the correlation matrix showed that the above null hypothesis assumed was not acceptable as the correlations obtained between the expert systems and all processes of output were significant, and they were affected in the organization in a positive manner. It was inference that the correlation of the expert systems with the parameters *reliability* (r = 0.806), *competitiveness* (r = 0.708), *production time* (r = 0.652), *quality* (r = 0.647), *production capacity* (r = 0.607), *productivity* (r = 0.596), *profit* (r = 0.584), *growth and expansion* (r = 0.555), *sales* (r = 0.522) and *market share* (r = 0.508) were significantly positive.

j. The analysis of the correlation matrix showed that the above null hypothesis assumed was not acceptable as the correlations obtained between the advanced maintenance and all processes of output were significant, and they were affected in the organization in a positive manner. It was inference that the correlation of the advanced maintenance with the parameters *reliability* (r = 0.685), *competitiveness* (r = 0.631), *quality* (r = 0.624), *productivity* (r = 0.575), *production time* (r = 0.566), *production capacity* (r = 0.527) and *profit* (r = 0.507) were significantly positive.

k. The analysis of the correlation matrix showed that the above null hypothesis assumed was not acceptable as the correlations obtained between the CMMS and all processes of output was significant, and they were affected in the organization in a positive manner. It was inference that the correlation of the CMMS with the parameters *reliability* (r = 0.738), *competitiveness* (r = 0.610), *production time* (r = 0.554), *quality* (r = 0.553) and *production capacity* (r = 0.528) were significantly positive.

10.2.6 Regression Results

The research has been extended to establish a mathematical model between the dependent and independent variables involving sustainable green initiatives and advanced manufacturing and maintenance techniques and performance attributes. For this purpose, ANOVA analysis and t-test have been performed.

a. The key predictors identified from the regression analysis of production capacity were sustainable development, green manufacturing, waste management, computer-aided manufacturing, CIPMS and advanced maintenance.

b. The predictors identified from the regression analysis of production time were sustainable development, natural resources, green engineering, lifecycle analysis, computer-aided manufacturing, automation, CIPMS and advanced maintenance.

c. The predictors identified from the regression analysis of lead time was sustainable development, natural resources, green manufacturing, waste management, lifecycle analysis, computer-aided manufacturing and advanced maintenance.

d. The predictors identified from the regression analysis of quality were sustainable development, green manufacturing, lifecycle analysis, computer-aided manufacturing and advanced maintenance.

e. The predictors identified from the regression analysis of Reliability were sustainable development, green manufacturing, waste management, computer-aided manufacturing, CIPMS, advanced maintenance and CMMS.

f. The predictors identified from the regression analysis of Productivity included sustainable development, green manufacturing, lifecycle analysis, computer-aided manufacturing, advanced maintenance and CMMS.

g. The predictors identified from the regression analysis of Growth and Expansion were sustainable development, green manufacturing, waste management, computer-aided manufacturing, CIPMS and advanced maintenance.

h. The key predictors identified from the regression analysis of Competitiveness were sustainable development, natural resources, green engineering, lifecycle analysis, computer-aided manufacturing, automation, CIPMS and advanced maintenance.

i. The key predictors identified from the regression analysis of Sales were the predictors identified from the analysis was sustainable development, natural resources, green manufacturing, waste management, lifecycle analysis, computer-aided manufacturing and advanced maintenance.

j. The predictors identified from the regression analysis of Profit were sustainable development, green manufacturing, waste management, computer-aided manufacturing, CIPMS, advanced maintenance and CMMS.

k. The key predictors identified from the regression analysis of market share were sustainable development, green manufacturing, waste management, computer-aided manufacturing, CIPMS, advanced maintenance and CMMS.

l. The predictors identified from the regression analysis of the customer base were sustainable development, green manufacturing, waste management, computer-aided manufacturing, CIPMS and advanced maintenance.

10.2.7 RESULTS OF PRELIMINARY DATA ANALYSIS

The empirical analysis has highlighted that sustainable development, green manufacturing, computer-aided manufacturing, CIPMS and advanced maintenance have emerged as significant contributors for realizing sustained competitiveness in the organization.

10.2.8 Qualitative Analysis Results

For parameter selection from the questionnaire, MCDM techniques have been employed and, in the process, a new tool has been developed and results have been compared with the existing tools and the results have been encouraging (Table 10.2).

10.2.9 Fuzzy Techniques Results

To validate the parameters for model development, fuzzy logic has been employed. Finally, the research culminates with the development of sustainable green development model. The validation of the model justifies that the factors that emerged as significant are rightly so. The work presents the evolution of a sustainable green initiatives and advanced manufacturing and maintenance techniques and performance model in Indian manufacturing industry. The model has been based upon the extensive literature review, learnings from sustainable green initiatives and advanced manufacturing and maintenance techniques Questionnaire analysis and results from surveys conducted in selected manufacturing organizations.

10.2.10 Sustainable Green Development Model

For further validation of results obtained from qualitative techniques, Interpretive Structural Modelling and Structural Equation Modelling analysis have been conducted.

ISM model of the critical success factors for coordinated and responsive supply chain indicates the relationship between different critical factors and also gives the level of critical factors as determined in different iterations from Table 8.2 to 8.11. Driving power and dependence diagram of the critical factors for responsive supply chain divides the factors in four categories such as: autonomous, dependent, linkages and drivers due to which analysis of factors become easier.

1. Autonomous variables generally appear as weak driver as well as weak dependent and are relatively disconnected from the system. These variables do not have much influence on the other variables of the system. Thus, these have weak driving as well as dependence power and is relatively disconnected from other factors in the organization. Figure 8.1 shows that there is one autonomous factor which is ES.
2. There are three linkage variables namely, CMMS, AMT, CAM which have strong driving power as well as strong dependence. Thus, it can be inferred that among all the 11 variables chosen in this study, 3 are unstable. Thus, these have compelling drive power but weaker dependence power. A factor by using a very strong drive power, referred to as 'key factor' is categorized as class of independent or *linkage factors*.
3. The driver power dependence diagram indicates that variables such as SD, NR, GM and AMN. These variables will help organizations to achieve a coordinated and responsive supply chain and are classified as independent variables or drivers. Thus, these factors have strong drive power that is likely to be strong

TABLE 10.2

Comparison of Various MCDM Tools with MDEMATEL

	MDEMATEL	WSM	WPM	WASPAS	GRA	SMART	CRITIC	EBTROPY	EDAS	MOORA	AHP	TOPSIS	VIKOR
SD	3	3	3	3	3	3	3	3	3	3	3	3	3
NR	6	6	6	6	6	6	6	6	6	6	6	6	6
GM	2	2	2	2	2	2	2	2	2	2	2	2	2
WM	10	10	10	10	10	10	10	10	10	10	10	10	10
LCA	11	11	11	11	11	11	11	11	11	11	11	11	11
CAM	1	1	1	1	1	1	1	1	1	1	1	1	1
AMT	7	7	7	7	7	7	7	7	7	7	7	7	7
CIPMS	8	8	8	8	8	8	8	8	8	8	8	8	8
ES	9	9	9	9	9	9	9	9	9	9	9	9	9
AMN	4	4	4	4	4	4	4	4	4	4	4	4	4
CMMS	5	5	5	5	5	5	5	5	5	5	5	5	5

dependence power. These variables are unstable within the indisputable fact that any impact on these variables can have an impact on others as well as are sponsor result on their own.

4. Factors such as WM, LCA, CIPMS have weak derive power and strong dependence power.

Apart from this, from Figure 8.2, it is understood that LCA is at the top, followed by WM at the second stage and CIPMS at the third. Then ES comes at the fourth stage, followed by AMT at the fifth stage, NR at the sixth stage and CMMS at the seventh stage. Finally, all these factors will lead to responsive supply chain. CAM, GM, SD and AMN are at the bottom level with highest driving power. It means these are the major drivers.

This study uses the CFA approach using Structural Equation Modelling in AMOS 21.0 software to employ the relationship between sustainable green initiatives and advanced manufacturing and maintenance techniques and performance in the study.

a. Model Fit summary of SEM_SGD model RMR value was 0.48. Similarly, Goodness-of-Fit Index (GFI) value was 0.530. Normed Fit Index (NFI) value was 0.550

b. Model Fit summary of SEM_SGD model after deploying Modification Indices has indicated that the RMR value was observed.22, and also the GFI for the model was observed.82, This indicated that the model after modifications does provide a better fit with respect to the NFI also which was observed.9110. Thus, the SEM study confirms and validate SEM_SGD model.

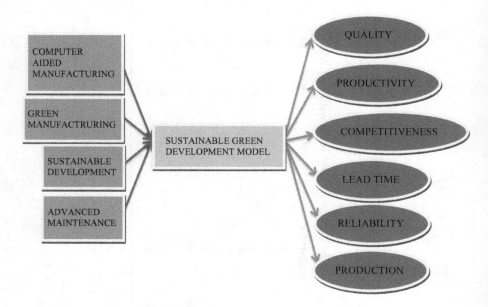

FIGURE 10.1 Final sustainable green development model.

10.2.11 Case Study Results

Further, detailed multiple-descriptive case studies have been conducted in selected manufacturing organizations across northern part of the country that has made serious interventions regarding sustainable green development. The following key issues have been highlighted through the case study:

a. The case studies have depicted organizations have deployed various modern technologies for attaining strategic success, thereby evolving significant production system innovations successfully, attaining cost-effective production capabilities, mitigating production wastages, evolving and aligning personnel competencies with organizational sustainability objectives through empowerment and facilitation.

b. The manufacturing organization has been successful in creating a congenial atmosphere for implementation of modern technologies through establishing improved communication in the organization, ensuring enhanced employee involvement, motivation and empowerment; and by putting in resources for improving the employee competencies through training and multi-skilling.

c. Finally, an evaluation of achievements accrued through sustainable green development and modern production techniques has been highlighted to evolve the consensus on strategic success of organization in highly competitive environment. The study reveals that the companies have kept on growing from the past experiences by introducing innovative strategies and technologies in their products. Thus to be able ensure realization of sustained strategic success, the organizations must consistently continue to foster modern technologies.

10.3 FINDINGS

This research is a legitimate reaction to the developing needs of both academicians and professionals for understanding the relationship of various sustainable green initiatives and advanced manufacturing and maintenance techniques and performance attributes. In this admiration, notwithstanding exhibiting a most recent understanding of the present status of the impact of four capacities on execution of vehicles organizations, it formulates valuable ramifications for managers with respect to the technique development. The conclusions from this study are:

1. Sustainable development, green manufacturing, computer-aided manufacturing and advanced maintenance have emerged as significant contributors to sustained competitiveness in the organization.

2. Sustainable development has a significant impact on an organization's competency as it involves innovation, sustained development, implementation and sustaining the performance.

3. Green manufacturing plays a vital role in enhancing the sustainable green initiatives and advanced manufacturing and maintenance techniques as it directly deals with manufacturing strategy planning, execution and controlling the

operations. Its contribution to performance is higher than that of sustainable development.

4. Computer-aided manufacturing directly affects the market value of a product and contributes significantly to the performance of an organization as it improves the productivity, quality and performance of the product.

5. Advanced maintenance provides the much-needed impetus for motivating employees towards organizational goals by making available the required resources which ultimately lead to the success and growth of any organization.

6. The qualitative sustainable green development model developed for Indian industry has highlighted the significant contributions of sustainable green initiatives and advanced manufacturing and maintenance techniques factors to performance of an organization.

10.4 LIMITATIONS

The research limitations of the present work, presents suggestions for future studies. The samples in this study were collected among organizations. The validity of the findings regarding the relationship between sustainable green initiatives and advanced manufacturing and maintenance techniques and organization performance may be hampered by as data on manufacturing practices and organizational performance were collected around the same point in time. At last, organization performance may be affected by other variables not accounted for in this work. It would be useful to examine the organization performance by taking factors like the legal situation and economic ones into account. Further limitations of the study are:

1. This study has been conducted in manufacturing industry only. Factors may vary according to manufacturing industries of different other products like bicycle, machine and machine tools, material handling equipment, Farm and agricultural machinery.

2. The scope of this research has been limited to North India; significance of issues may differ in other parts such as South, Central or the whole of India.

3. A qualitative sustainable green development model has been developed. Other modelling techniques can be explored

10.5 SUGGESTIONS

The primary aim of this research is to synthesis performance concept and exploring sustainable green initiatives and advanced manufacturing and maintenance techniques for manufacturing organizations, while a similar study can also be conducted in future for other Indian product, process and service industries as well.

The work is aimed at developing sustainable green initiatives and advanced manufacturing and maintenance techniques and performance model for North Indian and autoparts manufacturing organizations and various manufacturers have been treated alike irrespective of the sector of manufacturing organizations. Another direction for future research is developing area-wise, sector-wise and product-wise model for manufacturing industry. Thus, individual case study could be conducted for different areas, products and sectors of manufacturing industry and accordingly the typical methodologies can also be evolved in future.

While this research provided an insight into sustainable green initiatives and advanced manufacturing and maintenance techniques and their relationship with performance, it also discovered areas that could improve from further research. This work focused only on sustainable green initiatives and advanced manufacturing and maintenance techniques of organizations. Future works could focus on other competencies as well.

By doing so, a better and broader understanding of the effects that other competencies have on organization's performance may be accomplished.

1. Sustainable green initiatives and advanced manufacturing and maintenance techniques of manufacturing units have been explored. Future research could focus on the other competencies like innovation, design and development, supply chain, green manufacturing and such others.
2. Future research could also concentrate on sectors like large scale, medium scale and small scale industries for model development in those industries.
3. Such studies can also be conducted in other regions of India to develop a holistic model for manufacturing industry.
4. A mathematical model could be attempted in future, as in the present study only a qualitative model has been developed.

10.6   FINAL MODEL DEVELOPED

Based on the analysis and findings a qualitative model has been developed which is as follows (Table 10.3, Figure 10.1):

TABLE 10.3
Generalized Model

CAM Green Manufacturing Sustainable Development Advanced Maintenance	SUSTAINABLE GREEN DEVELOPMENT MODEL	Quality Productivity Competitiveness Lead Time Reliability Production Time

References

Acharya, S. G., Jeetendra, A. V., and Acharya, G. D. (2014). "A review on evaluating green manufacturing for sustainable development in foundry industries", *International Journal of Emerging Technology and Advanced Engineering*, 4(1), pp. 232–237.

Adebambo, H., Ashari, H., and Nordin, N. (2015). "An empirical study on the influence of sustainable environmental manufacturing practice on firm performance", *Journal of Sustainability Science and Management*, 10(2), December 2015: 42–51.

Adhikary, S., Jana, K., and Chattopadhyay, S., (2015) "Green manufacturing is the focus for the nation", *IOSR Journal of Mechanical and Civil Engineering*, 12(2), 13–17.

Afefy, I. H. (2010). "Reliability-centered maintenance methodology and application: A case study", *Engineering*, 02(11), 863–873.

Ahmad, N., Hossen, J., and Ali, S. M. (2018). "Improvement of overall equipment efficiency of ring frame through total productive maintenance: A textile case", *The International Journal of Advanced Manufacturing Technology*, 94(1–4), 239–256.

Ahmed, M. (2011). "System model for green manufacturing", *Journal of Cleaner Production*, 19, 1553–1559.

Ahuja, I., and Khamba, J. (2007). "An evaluation of TPM implementation initiatives in an Indian manufacturing enterprise", *Journal of Quality in Maintenance Engineering*, 13(4), 338–352.

Ahuja, I., and Khamba, J. (2008). "An assessment of maintenance management initiatives in the Indian manufacturing industry", *International Journal of Technology, Policy, and Management*, 8(3), 250.

Alhouli, Y., Elhag, T., Alardhi, M., and Alazem, J. (2017). "Development of conceptual framework for ship maintenance performance measurements", *Journal of Mechanical Engineering and Automation*,7(3), 63–71.

Aljumaili, M., Tretten, P., Karim, R., and Kumar, U. (2012). "Study of aspects of data quality in eMaintenance," *Internaional Journal of COMADEM*, 15(4), 3–14.

Ameknassi, L., Aït-Kadi, D., and Rezg, N. (2016). "Integration of logistics outsourcing decisions in a green supply chain design: A stochastic multi-objective multi-period multi-product programming model", *International Journal of Production Economics*, 182, 165–184.

Amrina, E., and Vilci, A. L. (2015). "Key performance indicators for sustainable manufacturing evaluation in cement factory", *12th Global Conference on Sustainable Manufacturing*, pp. 19–23.

Amrina, E., and Yusof, S. M. (2011). "Key performance indicators for sustainable manufacturing evaluation in automotive companies", *Industrial Engineering and Engineering Management (IEEE), 2011 IEEE International Conference*, 1093–1097.

Andriulo, S., Arleo, M. A., Carlo, F. D., Gnonia, M. G., and Tucci Mario. (2015). "Effectiveness of maintenance approaches for high reliability organizations", *IFAC-PapersOnLine*, 48(3), 466–471.

Antonakakis, N., Cunado, J., Filis, G., Gabauer, D., and Gracia, F. P.. 2018. "Oil volatility, oil and gas firms and portfolio diversification", *Energy Economics*, 70(Feb), 499–515.

Arashpour, M., Bai, Y., Mena, G. A., Hadiashar, A. B., Hosseini, R., and Kalutara, P. (2017). "Optimizing decisions in advanced manufacturing of prefabricated products: Theorizing supply chain configurations in off-site construction", *Automation in Construction*, 84, pp. 146–153.

Arunraj, N. S., and Maiti, J. (2007). "Risk-based maintenance—Techniques and applications", *Journal of Hazardous Materials*, 142, pp. 653–661.

Azadeh, A., Sheikhalishahi, M., and Monshi, F. (2016). "Selecting optimum maintenance activity plans by a unique simulation-multivariate approach", *Internattional Journal of Computer Integrated Manufacturing*, 29 (2), 222–236.

Bacchetti, A., and Saccani, N.. 2012. "Spare parts classification and demand forecasting for stock control: Investigating the gap between research and practice", *Omega* 40(6), 722–737.

Bag, S. (2012). "World class procurement practices and its impact on firm performance: A selected case study of an Indian manufacturing firm", *Journal of Supply Chain Management Systems*, 1(3), 27–39.

Baidya, R., Dey, P. K., Ghosh, S. K., and Petridis, K. (2018). "Strategic maintenance technique selection using combined quality function deployment, the analytic hierarchy process and the benefit of doubt approach", *The International Journal of Advanced Manufacturing Technology*, 94(1–4), 31–44.

Baldwin, J., and Lin, Z. (2002). "Impediments to advanced manufacturing technology adoption for Canadian manufacturers", *Research Policy*, 31(8), pp. 1–18.

Bansal, P., and Roth, K. (2000). Why companies go green: A model of ecological responsiveness. *Academy of Management Journal*, 43(94), 717–736.

Beaumont, N., Schroder, R., and Sohal, A. (2002). "Do foreign-owned firms manage advanced manufacturing technology better", *International Journal of Operations and Production Management*, 22(7), pp. 759–771.

Ben-Daya, M. (2000). "You may need RCM to enhance TPM implementation", *Journal of Quality in Maintenance Engineering*, 6(2), pp. 82–85.

Ben-Daya, M., Kumar, U., and Murthy, D. N. P. (2016). *Introduction to Maintenance Engineering: Modelling, Optimization and Management*, Hoboken, United States: John Wiley & Sons.

Berntsen, M., Bøe, K. S., Jordal, T., and Molnár, P. (2018). "Determinants of oil and gas investments on the norwegian continental shelf", *Energy* 148(Apr), 904–914.

Bertling, L., Allan, R., and Eriksson, R. (2005). "A reliability-centered asset maintenance method for assessing the impact of maintenance in power distribution systems", *IEEE Transactions on Power Systems*, 21(1), pp. 75–82.

Bessant, J. (1993). "The lessons of failure: Learning to manage new manufacturing technologies", *International Journal of Technology Management*, 8(3–5), pp. 197–215.

Bhandari, J., Arzaghi, E., Abbassi, R., Garaniya, V., and Khan, F. (2016). "Dynamic risk-based maintenance for offshore processing facility", *Process Safety Progress*, 35(4), 399–406.

Bhanota, N., Raoa, P. V., and Deshmukha, S. G. (2015). "Enablers and barriers of sustainable manufacturing: Results from a survey of researchers and industry professionals", *The 22nd CIRP Conference on Life Cycle Engineering*, pp 562–567.

Bhateja, A. K., Babbar, R., Singh, S., and Sachdeva, A. (2011). "Study of green supply chain management in the Indian manufacturing industries: A literature review cum an analytical approach for the measurement of performance", *International Journal of Computational Engineering & Management (IJCEM), ISSN: 2230-7893*, 13, 84–99.

Bhuiyan, N., Gouw, G., and Yazdi, D. (2013). "Scheduling of a computer integrated manufacturing system : a simulation study", *Journal of Industrial engineering and management*, 4(4), pp 576–609.

Biswas, W., Lim, C. I. and Samyudia, Y.(2015). "Review of existing sustainability assessment methods for Malaysian palm oil production", *12th Global Conference on Sustainable Manufacturing*, pp 13–18.

Boyer, K. K., Leong, K. G., Ward, P. T., and Krajewski, L. J. (1997). "Unlocking the potential of advanced manufacturing technologies", *Journal of Operations Management*, 15(4), pp. 331–347.

Boyer Zeid, I., and Duggan, C. (2016). "Closing the advanced manufacturing talent gap", *Procedia Manufacturing*, 5, pp. 1197–1207.

Bulbul, H., Omurbek, N., Paksoy, T., and Bektaş, T. (2013). "An empirical investigation of advanced manufacturing technology investment patterns: Evidence from a developing country", *Journal of Engineering and Technology Management*, 30(2), pp. 136–156.

Caesarendra, W., Kosasih, B., KietTieu, A., Zhu, H., Moodie, C. A. S., and Zhu, Q. (2016). "Acoustic emission-based condition monitoring methods: Review and application for low speed slew bearing", *Mechanical Systems and Signal Processing*, 72–73, 134–159.

Campbell, J. D., and Reyes-Picknell, J. V. (2015). *Uptime: Strategies for Excellence in Maintenance Management* (3rd ed.). CRC Press.

Campos, M. A. L., Fernández, J. F. G., Díaz, V. G., and Márquez, A. C. (2010). *A New Maintenance Management Model Expressed in UML*, London: Taylor & Francis Group.

Canito, A., Fernandes, M., Conceição, L., Praça, I., Santos, M., Rato, R., . . . , and Marreiros, G. (2017). "An Aachitecture for proactive maintenance in the machinery industry", *Paper presented at the Ambient Intelligence– Software and Applications – 8th International Symposium on Ambient Intelligence (ISAmI 2017)*.

Cardoso, R. D. R., Edson, P. D. L., Sergio, E., and Costa, G. D. (2012). "Identifying organizational requirements for the implementation of Advanced Manufacturing Technologies (AMT)", *Journal of Manufacturing Systems*, 31(3), pp. 367–378.

Carnero, M. (2006). "An evaluation system of the setting up of predictive maintenance programmes", *Reliability Engineering and System Safety*, 91(8), 945–963.

Carnero, M. C. (2015). "Auditing model for the introduction of computerized maintenance management system", *Production Planning and Control*, 1(1), 17–41.

Carnero, M. C., and Noves, J. L. (2006). "Selection of computerized maintenance management system by means of multicriteria methods", *Production Planning & Control*, 17 (4), 335–354.

Castrillon, I. S., and Cantorna, A. I. S. (2005). "The effect of the implementation of advanced manufacturing technologies on training in the manufacturing sector", *Journal of European Industrial Training*, 29(4), 268–280.

Chang, T. H., and Wang, T. C. (2007). "Forecasting the probability of successful knowledge management by consistent fuzzy preference relations", *Expert Systems with Applications*, 32(3), 801–813.

Chang, C.-C. (2014). "Optimum preventive maintenance policies for systems subject to random working times, replacement, and minimal repair", *Computers & Industrial Engineering*, 67, 185–194.

Chemweno, P., Pintelon, L., Horenbeek, A. V., and Muchiri, P. (2015). "Development of a risk assessment selection methodology for asset maintenance decision making: An analytic network process (ANP) approach", *International Journal of Production Economics*, 170, 663–676.

Chen, I. J., and Small, M. H. (1994). "Implementing advanced manufacturing technology: an integrated planning model", *International Journal of Management Science*, 22(1), 91–103.

Chen, L., and Meng, B. (2011). "How to apply TPM in equipment management for Chinese enterprises", *Chinese Business Review*, 10(2), 137–145.

Chen, M. K., and Shih, L. H. (2007). "An empirical study of implementation of green supply chain practices in the electrical and electronic industry and their relation to organizational performances", *International Journal of Environmental Science and Technology*, 4(3), 383–394.

Chen, Z., Maiti, S., and Agapiou, A. (2017). "Evidence-based safety management in building refurbishment", *Paper presented at the Proceedings of the Doctoral Workshop in Building Asset Management*, Glasgow, UK, Association of Researchers in Construction Management (ARCOM).

Chen, I. J., and Small, M. H. (1996). "Planning for advanced manufacturing technology: A research framework", *International Journal of Operations and Production Management*, 16(5), 4–24.

Chen, Y. (2017). "Integrated and intelligent manufacturing: Perspectives and enablers", *Engineering*, 3(5), 585–588.

Chopra, A., Sachdeva, A., and Bhardwaj, A. (2016). "Productivity enhancement using reliability centered maintenance in the process industry", *International Journal of Industrial and Systems Engineering*, 23(2), 155.

Ciocci, R., and Michael, P. (2006). "Impact of environmental regulations on green electronics manufacture", *Microelectronics International: An International Journal*,23(2), 45–50.

Clement, K., and Hansen, M. (2003). "Financial incentives to improve environmental performance: A review of Nordic public sector support for SMEs", *European Environment*, 13, 34–47.

Congbo, L., Liu, F., and Wang, Q. (2010). "Planning and implementing the green manufacturing strategy: Evidences from western China", *Journal of Science and Technology Policy in China*, 1(2), 2010, 148–162.

Costa, C. A. B. E., Carnero, M. C., and Oliveira, M. D. (2012). "A multi-criteria model for auditing a predictive maintenance programme", *European Journal of Operational Research*, 217(2), 381–393.

Cronin, J. R., Smith, J. S., Gleim, M. R., Ramirez, E., and Martinez, J. D. (2011). "Green marketing strategies: An examination of stakeholders and the opportunities they present", *Journal of the Academy of Marketing Science*, 39(1), 158–174.

Croom, S. R. (2005). "The impact of E-business on supply chain management: An empirical study of key developments", *International Journal of Operations and Production Management*, 25(1), 55–73.

Dangayach, G. S., and Deshmukh, S. G. (2005). "Advanced manufacturing technology implementation-evidence from Indian SMEs", *Journal of Manufacturing Technology Management*, 16(5), 483–496.

Dangayach, G. S., Pathak, S. C., and Sharma, A. D. (2006). "Advanced manufacturing technology: A way of improving technological competitiveness", *International Journal of Global Business and Competitiveness*, 2(1), 1–8.

Dasgupta, T. (2003). "Using the six-sigma metric to measure and improve the performance of a supply chain", *Total Quality Management and Business Excellence*,14(3), 355–366

David, A.(2014). "Moving towards green and sustainable manufacturing", *International Journal of Precision Engineering and Manufacturing-Green Technology*, 1(1), 63–66.

Deif, A. M. (2011). "A system model for green manufacturing", *Advances in Production Engineering & Management*, 6(1), 27–36.

Dekker, R. (1996). "Applications of maintenance optimization models: A review and analysis", *Reliability Engineering & System Safety*, 51(3), 229–240.

Deshpande, V. S., and Modak, J. P. (2002). "Application of RCM to a medium scale industry", *Reliability Engineering & System Safety*, 77(1), 31–43.

Deshpande, V., and Modak, J. (2003). "Maintenance strategy for tilting table of rolling mill based on reliability considerations". *Reliability Engineering & System Safety*, 80(1), 1–18.

Dey, P. K., Ogunlana, S. O., and Naksuksakul, S. (2004). "Risk-based maintenance model for offshore oil and gas pipelines: A case study", *Journal of Quality in Maintenance Engineering*, 10(3), 169–183.

Diabat, A., and Govindan, K. (2011). "An analysis of the drivers affecting the implementation of green supply chain management", *Resources, Conservation and Recycling*, 55(6), 659–667.

Digalwar, A. K., Tagalpallewar, A. R., and Sunnapwar, V. K. (2016). "Green manufacturing performance measures: An empirical investigation from Indian manufacturing industries", *Measuring Business Excellence*, 17(4), 59–74.

Do, P., Voisin, A., Levrat, E., and Lung, B. (2015). "A proactive condition-based maintenance strategy with both perfect and imperfect maintenance actions", *Reliability Engineering & System Safety*, 133, 2–32.

Dubey, R., and Ali, S. S. (2015). "Exploring antecedents of extended supply chain performance measures: An insight from Indian green manufacturing practices", *Benchmarking: An International Journal*, 2(5), 752–772.

Dubey, R., Gunasekaran, A., Papadopoulos, T., Childe, S. J., Shibin, K., and Wamba, S. F. (2017). "Sustainable supply chain management: framework and further research directions", *Journal of Cleaner Production*, 142, 1119–1130.

Dubey, R., Gunasekaran, A., Papadopoulos, T., and Childe, S. J. (2015). "Green supply chain management enablers: Mixed methods research", *Sustainable Production and Consumption*, 4, 72–88.

Dunning, J. H. (2006). "Towards a new paradigm of development: Implications for the determinants of international business", *Transnational corporations*, 15(1), 173–227.

Efstathiades, A., Tassou, S. A., Antoniou, A., and Oxinos, G. (1999). "Strategic considerations in the introduction of advanced manufacturing technologies in the cypriot industry", *Technovation*, 19(2), 105–115.

Efstathiades, A., Tassou, S. A., Oxinos, G., and Antoniou, A. (2000). "Advanced manufacturing technology transfer and implementation in developing countries: The case of the Cypriot manufacturing industry", *Technovation*, 20(2), 93–102.

Ellingsen, O. (2017). "Commercialization within advanced manufacturing: Value stream mapping as a tool for efficient learning", *Procedia CIRP*, 60, 374–379.

Endrenyi, J., Aboresheid, S., Allan, R. N., Anders, G. J., Asgarpoor, S., Billinton, R., and Chowdhury, N. (2001). "The present status of maintenance strategies and the impact of maintenance on reliability", *IEEE Transactions on Power Systems*, 16(4), 638–646.

Engeler, M., Treyer, D., Zogg, D., Wegener, K., and Kunz, A. (2016). "Condition-based maintenance: Model vs. statistics a performance comparison", *Procedia CIRP*, 57, 253–258.

Espinosa, F. F., and Salinas, G. E. (2010). "Evaluación de la madurez de la función mantenimiento para implementar innovaciones suggestión", *Información Tecnológica*, 21(3), 3–12.

Fazleena Badurdeen, F., and Jawahir, I. S. (2017). "Strategies for value creation through sustainable manufacturing", *14th Global Conference on Sustainable Manufacturing, GCSM 3–5 October 2016*, Stellenbosch, South Africa, 20–27.

Feng, F-D. (2010). "Green company or green consumers: A Kantian retrospective", *International Journal of Social Economics*, 37(10), 779–782.

Fernández, J. F. G., and Márquez, A. C. (2012). *Maintenance Management in Network Utilities: Framework and Practical Implementation*, London: Springer.

Fischer, K., Besnard, F., and Bertling, L. (2012). "Reliability-centered maintenance for wind turbines based on statistical analysis and practical experience", *IEEE Transactions on Energy Conversion*, 27(1), 184–195.

Fore, S., and Mbohawa, S. (2015). "Greening manufacturing practices in a continuous process industry: Case study of a cement manufacturing company", *Journal of Engineering, Design and Technology*, 13(1), 94–121.

Fraser, K., Hvolby, H. H., and Tseng, T. L. (2015). "Maintenance management models: A study of the published literature to identify empirical evidence: A greater practical focus is needed", *International Journal of Quality & Reliability Management*, 32(6), 635–664.

Gandhi, S., Mangla, S. K., Kumar, P., and Kumar, D. (2015). "Evaluating factors in the implementation of successful green supply chain management using DEMATEL: A case study", *International Strategic Management Review*, 3(1–2), 96–109.

García-Sanz-Calcedo, J., and Gómez-Chaparro, M. (2017). "Quantitative analysis of the impact of maintenance management on the energy consumption of a hospital in Extremadura, Spain", *Sustainable Cities and Societies*, 30 (Apr), 217–222.

Garg, A., and Deshmukh, S. G. (2006). "Maintenance management: Literature review and directions", *Journal of Quality in Maintenance Engineering*, 12(3), 205–238.

Garg, A., and Deshmukh, S. G. (2009). "Flexibility in maintenance: A framework", *Global Journal of Flexible Systems Management*, 10(2), 21–33.

Geng, R., Mansouri, S. A., and Aktas, E. (2017). "The relationship between green supply chain management and performance: A meta-analysis of empiricalevidence in Asian emerging economies", *International Journal of Production Economics*, 183, 245–258.

Ghani, K. A., and Jayabalan, V. (2000). "Advanced manufacturing technology and planned organizational change", *The Journal of High Technology Management Research*, 18(1), 1–18.

Ghani, K. A., Jayabalan, V., and Sugumar, M. (2002). "Impact of advanced manufacturing technology on organizational structure", *The Journal of High Technology Management Research*, 13(2), 157–175.

Godwin, J. Udo and Ehie, Ike C. (1996). "Advanced manufacturing technologies", *International Journal of Operations & Production Management*, 16(12), 6–26.

Gosavi, A., Murray, S. L., Tirumalasetty, V. M., and Shewade, S. (2011). "A budget-sensitive approach to scheduling maintenance in a total productive maintenance (TPM) program", *Engineering Management Journal*, 23(3), 46–56.

Govindan, K., Kaliyan, M., Kannan, D., and Haq, A. (2014). "Barriers analysis for green supply chain management implementation in Indian industries using analytic hierarchy process", *International Journal of Production Economics*, 147, 555–568.

Goyal, D., Pabla, B. S., Dhami, S. S., and Lachhwani, K. (2017). "Optimization of condition-based maintenance using soft computing", *Neural Computing and Applications*, 28(Suppl 1), 829–844.

Green, K. W., and Inman, R. A. (2005). "Using a just-in-time selling strategy to strengthen supply chain linkages", *International Journal of Production Research*, 43(16), 3437–3453.

Groves, G., and Valsamakis, V. (1998). "Supplier-customer relationships and company performance", *The International Journal of Logistics Management*, 9(2), 51–63

Guck, D., Spel, J., and Stoelinga, M. (2015). "DFTCalc: Reliability centered maintenance via fault tree analysis", *Paper presented at the Formal Methods and Software Engineering*, Cham, Lecture Notes in Computer Science, Springer.

Guerry, S., and Boots, S. (2012). *Green Manufacturing – "A Roadmap to Green Manufacturing in Los Angeles: Policies, Planning, and Partnership for Quality Jobs"*, A Comprehensive Capstone Project, UCLA Luskin School of Public Affairs, Urban & Regional Planning, 62–69.

Guillén, A. J., Crespo, A., Gómez, J. F., and Sanz, M. D. (2016). "A framework for effective management of condition based maintenance programs in the context of industrial development of E-Maintenance strategies", *Computers in Industry*, 82(1), 170–185.

Gunasekaran, A., and Spalanzani, A. (2012). "Sustainability of manufacturing and services: Investigations for research and applications", *International Journal of Production Economics*, 140(1), 35–47.

Gupta, G., and Mishra, R. P. (2016). "A SWOT analysis of reliability centered maintenance framework", *Journal of Quality in Maintenance Engineering*, 22(2), 130–145.

Gupta, A., and Whitehouse, F. R. (2001). "Firms using advanced manufacturing technology management: An empirical analysis based on size", *Integrated Manufacturing Systems*, 12(5), 346–350.

Hamia, N., Muhamab, M. R., and Ebrahimb, Z. (2015). "The impact of sustainable manufacturing practices and innovation performance on economic sustainability", *12th Global Conference on Sustainable Manufacturing*, 190–195.

Hamraz, B., and Clarkson, P. J. (2015). "Industrial evaluation of FBS Linkage: A method to support engineering change management", *Journal of Engineering Design and Technology*, 26 (1–3), 24–47.

Harrison, A., and New, C. (2002). "The role of coherent supply chain strategy and performance management in achieving competitive advantage: An international survey", *Journal of the Operational Research Society*, 53(3), 263–271.

Hart, S. L. (1995). "A natural resource-based view of the firm", *Academy Management Revision*, 20(4), 986–1014.

Hayes, R. H., and Jaikumar, R. (1991). "Requirements for successful implementation of new manufacturing technologies", *Journal of Engineering and Technology Management*, 7(3-4), 169–175.

Hendrick, T. E., and Ruch, W. A., (1988). "Determining performance appraisal criteria for buyers", *Journal of Purchasing and Materials Management*, 24(2), 18–26.

Henri, J. F., and Journeault, M. (2008). "Environmental performance indicators: An empirical study of canadian manufacturing firm", *Journal of Environmental Management*, 87, 165–176.

Heo, J., Kim, M., and Lyu, J. (2014). "Implementation of reliability-centered maintenance for transmission components using particle swarm optimization", *International Journal of Electrical Power & Energy Systems*, 55, 238–245.

Heriot, K. C., and Kulkami, S. P. (2001). "The use of intermediate sourcing strategies", *Journal of Supply Chain Management*, 37(1), 18–26.

Hofmann, C., and Orr, S. (2005). "Advanced manufacturing technology adoption - the German experience", *Technovation*, 25(7), 711–724.

Hong, P., Kwon, H., and Roh, J. J. (2009). "Implementation of strategic green orientation in supply chain: An empirical study of manufacturing firms", *European Journal of Innovation Management*, 12(4), 512–532.

Horvath, A., Hendrickson, C., Lave, L., and McMichael, F. (1995). "Performance measurement for environmentally conscious manufacturing", *Manufacturing Science and Engineering*, 22, 855–860.

Huang, R., Yang, C., and Kao, C. (2012). "Assessment model for equipment risk management: Petrochemical industry cases", *Safety Science*, 50(4), 1056–1066.

Huynh, K. T., Castro, I., Barros, A., and Bérenguer, C. (2012). "Modeling age-based maintenance strategies with minimal repairs for systems subject to competing failure modes due to degradation and shocks", *European Journal of Operational Research*, 218(1), 140–151.

Hynek, J., and Janecek, V. (2013). "Issues affecting advanced manufacturing technology projects", *23rd International Conference on Flexible Automation and Intelligent Manufacturing*, 775–784.

Ikediashi, D., and Ekanem, A. M. (2015). "Outsourcing of facilities management (FM) services in public hospitals: A study on Nigeria's perspective", *Journal of Facilities Management*, 13(1), 85–102.

Ilangkumaran, M., and Kumanan, S. (2009). "Selection of maintenance policy for textile industry using hybrid multi-criteria decision-making approach", *Journal of Manufacturing Technology Management*, 20(7), 1009–1022.

Ilgin, M. A., and Gupta, S. M., (2010). ""Environmentally conscious manufacturing and product recovery (ECMPRO)": A review of the state of the art", *Journal of Environmental Management*, 91(3), 563–591.

Isa, C. R., and Foong, S. Y. (2005). "Adoption of advanced manufacturing technology (AMT) and management accounting practices: The case of manufacturing firms in Malaysia", *World Review of Science, Technology and Sustainable Development*, 2(1), 35–48.

Islam, S., Karia, N., Fauzi, F. B. A., and Soliman, M. S. M. (2017). "A review of green supply chain aspects and practices", *Management and Marketing. Challenges for the Knowledge Society*, 12(1), 12–36.

Jackson, K., Efthymiou, K., and Borton, J. (2016). "Digital manufacturing and flexible assembly technologies for reconfigurable aerospace production systems", *Procedia CIRP*, 52, 274–279.

Jaffer, M. A., Udaiappan, M., Taisum, T. K., and Srinivasan, S. (2013). "Reliability availability and maintainability study: A business perspective", *International Journal of Performability Engineering*, 9(4), 445–454.

Jain, A., Bhatti, R., and Singh, H. (2014). "Total productive maintenance (TPM) implementation practice", *International Journal of Lean Six Sigma*, 5(3), pp. 293–323.

Jain, J., Dangayach, G. S., Agarwal, G., and Banerjee, S. (2010). "Supply chain management: Literature review and some issues", *Journal of Studies on Manufacturing*, 1(1), 11–25.

Jamshidi, A., Rahimi, S. A., Ait-Kadi, D., and Ruiz, A. (2015). "A comprehensive fuzzy risk-based maintenance framework for prioritization of medical devices", *Applied Soft Computing*, 32, 322–334.

Jandali, D., and Sweis, R. (2018). "Assessment of factors affecting maintenance management of hospital buildings in Jordan", *Journal of Quality in Maintenance Engineering*, 24(1), 37–60.

Jared, R. O., Matias, J. C. M., and Vizan, A. (2017). "A method for estimating the influence of advanced manufacturing tools on the manufacturing competitiveness of aaquiladoras in the apparel industry in Central America", *Computers in Industry*, 87(1), 31–51.

Jawahir, I. S., Dillon, O. W., and Rouch, K. E., (2006). "Total life cycle considerations in product design in sustainability: A frame work for compherensive evaluation", *Trends in the Development of Machinery and Associated Technology*, Barcelona, 1–10.

Jayant, A., and Azhar, M. (2014). "Analysis of the barriers for implementing green supply chain management (GSCM) practices: An interpretive structural modeling (ISM) approach", *Procedia Engineering*, 97, 2157–2166.

Jenab, K., Moslehpour, S., and Khoury, S. (2016). "Virtual maintenance, reality, and systems: A review", *International Journal of Electrical and Computer Engineering*, 6(6), 2698–2707.

Jonge, B. D., Dijkstra, A. S., and Romeijnders, W. (2015). "Cost benefits of postponing time-based maintenance under lifetime distribution uncertainty", *Reliability Engineering & System Safety*, 140, 15–21.

Jonge, B., Teunter, Ruud, and Tinga, Tiedo. (2017). "The influence of practical factors on the benefits of condition-based maintenance over time- based maintenance", *Reliability Engineering & System Safety*, 158(1), 21–30.

Karsak, E. E., and Tolga, E. (2001). "Fuzzy multi-criteria decision-making procedure for evaluating advanced manufacturing system investments", *International Journal of Production Economics*, 69(4), 49–64.

Kaur, H., and Singla, D. J.. (2019). "MCDM evaluation of activities influencing adolescents buying decision making", *Global Journal of Accounting and Management*, 6(1), 59–68

Kaur, H., and Singla, D. J.. (2018a). "Demographic analysis of adolescents' role in family buying decision making", *PCMA Journal of Business*, 11(2), 35–49.

Kaur, H., and Singla, D. J.. (2018b). "Evaluating parameters of advertising media used by marketers to influence adolescents' buying decision making", *Indian Management Studies Journal*, 22(1), 171–188.

Keizer, M. C. A. O. P., Flapper, S. D., and Teunter, R. (2017). "Condition-based maintenance policies for systems with multiple dependent components: A review", *European Journal of Operational Research*, 261(2), 405–420.

Ketokivi, M. A., and Schroeder, R. G., (2004). "Strategic, structural contingency and institutional explanations in the adoption of innovative manufacturing processes", *Journal of Operations Management*, 22(1), 63–89.

Khamba, J. S., Singh, C. D., and Singh, H. (2013). "Exploring manufacturing competencies of a car manufacturing unit", *in Proceedings of International Conference on Advancements and Futuristic Trends in Mechanical and Materials Engineering*, in Jalandhar, 2013, pp. 88–97.

Khanchanapong, T., Prajogo, D., Sohal, A. S.,Cooper, B. K., Yeung, A. C. L., and Cheng, T. C. E. (2014). "The unique and complementary effects of manufacturing technologies and lean practices on manufacturing operational performance", *International Journal of Production Economics*, 153, 191–203.

Khorshidi, H. A., Gunawan, I., and Ibrahim, M. Y. (2016). "A value-driven approach for optimizing reliability-redundancy allocation problem in multi-state weighted k-out-of-n system", *Journal of Manufacturing Systems*, 40(part 1), 54–62.

Kilsby, P., Remenyte-Prescott, R., and Andrews, J. (2017). "A modelling approach for railway overhead line equipment asset management", *Reliability Engineering & System Safety*, 168, 326–337.

Kim, J., Ahn, Y., and Yeo, H. (2016). "A comparative study of time-based maintenance and condition-based maintenance for optimal choice of maintenance policy", *Structure and Infrastructure Engineering*, 12(12), 1525–1536.

Koc, T., and Bozdag, E. (2009). "The impact of AMT practices on firm performance in manufacturing SMEs", *Robotics and Computer-Integrated Manufacturing*, 25(2), 303–313.

Kong, D., Feng, Q., and Zhou, Y. (2016). "Local implementation for green-manufacturing technology diffusion policy in China: from the user firms' perspectives", *Journal of Cleaner Production*, 129, 113–124.

Kudroli, K. (2014). "Green supply chain management and environmental sustainability – a comparative study on global and Indian perspective", *International Journal of Conceptions on Management and Social Sciences, ISSN: 2357-278*, 2(2), 27–54.

Kotha, M. S., and Swamidass, P. M. (2000). "Strategy advanced manufacturing technology and performance: empirical evidence from US manufacturing firms", *Journal of Operations Management*, 18 pp. 257–277.

Kumar, N., Agrahari, R. P., and Roy, D. (2015). "Review of green supply chain processes", *IFAC-PapersOnLine*, 48(3), 374–381.

Kumar, S., Kumar, S., and Gahlot, P. (2012). "Green practices in Indian automobile supply chain: factors important for implementation", *Journal of information, knowledge, and research in mechanical engineering, ISSN 0975-668X*, 2(1), 156–162.

Kumar Sharma, R., and Gopal Sharma, R. (2013). "Integrating six sigma culture and TPM framework to improve manufacturing performance in SMEs", *Quality and Reliability Engineering International*, 30(5), 745–765.

Kung, F-H. (2012). "Assessing the green value chain to improve environmental performance: Evidence from Taiwan's manufacturing industry", *International Journal of Development Issues*, 11(2), 111–127.

Kusi-Sarpong, S., Sarkis, J., and Wang, X. (2016). "Assessing green supply chain practices in the Ghanaian mining industry: A framework and evaluation", *International Journal of Production Economics*, 181, 325–341.

Kusumawardhani, M., Kumar, R., and Tore, M.. 2016. "Asset integrity management: Offshore installations challenges", *Journal of Quality in. Maintenance Engineering*, 22(3), 238–251.

Labib, A. W. 1998. "World-class maintenance using a computerised maintenance management system", *Journal of Quality in. Maintenance Engineering*, 4(1), 66–75.

Lai, K., and C. W. Y. Wong (2012). "Green logistics management and performance: Some empirical evidence from chinese manufacturing exporters", *Omega*, 40, 267–282.

Lanndon, O., and Omela, O. (2015). "A proposed sustainable manufacturing strategy framework", *Business Systems and Economics*, 5(1), 87–98.

Laosirihongthong, T., and Paul, H. (2004). "Competitive manufacturing strategy: An application of quality management practices to advanced manufacturing technology implementation", *International Journal of Business Performance Management*, 6(3–4), 262–286.

Lei, X., and Sandborn, P. A. (2016). "PHM-based wind turbine maintenance optimization using real options", *International Journal of Prognostics and Health Management*, 1(1), 1–14.

Levrat, E., Iung, B., and Marquez, A. C. (2008). "E-maintenance: Review and conceptual framework", *Production Planning and Control*, 19(4), 408–429.

Li, A. Q., and Found, P. (2016). "Lean and green supply chain for the product-services system (PSS): The literature review and a conceptual framework", *Procedia CIRP*, 47, 162–167.

Li, D., and Gao, J. (2010). "Study and application of reliability-centered maintenance considering radical maintenance", *Journal of Loss Prevention in the Process Industries*, 23(5), 622–629.

Li, K., Zhang, X., and Joseph, Y. T. (2016). "Parallel machine scheduling problems in green manufacturing industry", *Journal of Manufacturing Systems*, 38, 98–106.

Li, Y. (2011). "Research on the performance measurement of green supply chain management in china. *Journal of Sustainable Development*, 4(3), 1–7.

Liao, K., and Tu, Q. (2008). "Leveraging automation and integration to improve manufacturing performance under uncertainty: An empirical study", *Journal of Manufacturing Technology Management*, 19(1), 38–51.

Liu, P., Zhou, Y., and Dillon, K. (2017). "Energy performance contract models for the diffusion of greenmanufacturing technologies in China: A stakeholder analysis from SMEs' perspective", *Energy Policy*, 106, 59–67.

Lopes, I., Senra, P., Vilarinho, S., Sá, V., Teixeira, C., Lopes, J.,Alves, A., Oliveira, J. A., and Figueiredo, M.. 2016. "Requirements specification of a computerized maintenance management system–A case study", *Procedia CIRP* 52, 268–273.

Lopez-Gamero, M. D., Molina-Azorin, J. F., and Claver-Cortes, E. (2009). "The whole relationship between environmental variables and firm performance: Competitive advantage and firm performance as mediator variables", *Journal of Environmental Management*, 90(10), 3110–3121.

Luthra, S., Garg, D., and Haleem, A. (2015). "An analysis of interactions among critical success factors to implement green supply chain management towards sustainability: An Indian perspective", *Resources Policy*, 46, 37–50.

Luthra, S., Kumar, V., Kumar, S., and Haleem, A. (2010). "Green supply chain management issues: A literature review approach", *Journal of Information, Knowledge, and Research in Mechanical Engineering, ISSN 0975-668X*, 1(1), 12–20.

Macchi, M., Márquez, A. C., Holgado, M., Fumagalli, L., and Martínez, L. B. (2009). "Value-driven engineering of E-maintenance platforms", *Journal of Manufacturing Technology Management*, 25(4), 568–598.

Machuca, J. A. D., Diaz, M. S., and Gil, M. J. A. (2004). "Adopting and implementing advanced manufacturing technology: new data on key factors from the aeronautical industry", *International Journal of Production Research*, 42(16), 3183–3202.

Madu, C. N. (2000). "Competing through maintenance strategies", *International Journal of Quality & Reliabilty Management* 17 (9), 937–949.

Maleki, H., and Yang, Y. (2017). "An uncertain programming model for preventive maintenance scheduling", *Grey Systems: Theory and Application*, 7(1), 111–122.

Manning, S., Larsen, M. M., and Bharati, P. (2015). "Global delivery models: The role of talent, speed and time zones in the global outsourcing industry", *Journal of International Business Studies*, 46(7), 850–877.

Márquez, A. C., León, P. M. D., Fernández, J. F. G., Márquez, C. P., and Campos, M. L. (2009). "The maintenance management framework: A practical view to maintenance management", *Journal of Quality in Maintenance Engineering*, 15(2), 167–178.

Maruthi, G. D., and Rashmi, R (2015). "Green manufacturing: It's tools and techniques that can be implemented in manufacturing sectors", *4th International Conference on Materials Processing and Characterization, Proceedings*, 2, 3350–3355.

McCall, J. J. (1965). "Maintenance policies for stochastically failing equipment: A survey", *Management science*, 11(2), 493–524.

McKone, K., and Weiss, E. (2002). "Guidelines for implementing predictive maintenance". *Production and Operations Management*, 11(2), 109–124.

Millen, R., and Sohal, A. S. (1998). "Planning processes for advanced manufacturing technology by large American manufacturers", *Technovation*, 18(12), 741–750.

Mishra, R. P., Kodali, R. B., Gupta, G., and Mundra, N. (2015). "Development of a framework for implementation of world-class maintenance systems using interpretive structural modeling approach", *Procedia CIRP*, 26, 424–429.

Mittal, R., Pareek, S., Singh, S., and Khair, M. A. (2011). "GREEN: RACE to compete or imagination to RIOT: A review in Indian perspective", *International Journal of Multidisplinary.Research & Advances In Engineering. (IJMRAE)*, 3(1), 1–10.

Mkandawire, B. O., Ijumba, N., and Saha, A. (2015). "Transformer risk modeling by stochastic augmentation of reliability-centered maintenance", *Electric Power Systems Research*, 119, 471–477.

Modgil, S., and Sharma, S. (2016). "Total productive maintenance, total quality management and operational performance: An empirical study of Indian pharmaceutical industry", *Journal of Quality in Maintenance Engineering*, 22(4), 353–377.

Moghaddass, R., and Ertekin, ş. (2018). "Joint optimization of ordering and maintenance with condition monitoring data", *Annals of Operations Research*, 263, 1–40.

Mohanty, R. P., Seth, D., and Mukadam, S., (2007). "Quality Dimensions of E-Commerce and their Implications", *Total Quality Management & Business Excellence*, 18(3), 219–247.

Mohanty, R. P., and Prakash, A. (2014). "Green supply chain management practices in India: An Empirical Study", *Production Planning & Control: The Management of Operations*, 25(16), 1332–1337.

Mokashi, A., Wang, J., and Vermar, A. (2002). "A study of reliability-centered maintenance in maritime operations". *Marine Policy*, 26(5), 325–335.

Monge, C. A., Rao, S. S., Gonzalez, M. E. and Sohal, A. S. (2006). "Performance measurement of AMT: A cross regional study", *Benchmarking: an International Journal*, 13(1–2), 135–146.

Mostafa, S. (2004). "Implementation of proactive maintenance in the Egyptian glass company", *Journal of Quality in Maintenance Engineering*, 10(2), 107–122.

Mostafa, S., Lee, S., Dumrak, J., Chileshe, N., and Soltan, H.. (2015). "Lean thinking for a maintenance process", *Production Manufacturing Research*, 3 (1), 236–272.

Muchiri, A. K., Ikua, B. W., Muchiri, P. N., and Irungu, P. K. (2014). "Development of a theoretical framework for evaluating maintenance practices", *International Journal of System Assurance Engineering and Management*, 8(S1), 198–207.

Muduli, K., Govindan, K., Barve, A., Kannan, D., and Geng, Y. (2013). "Role of behavioral factors in green supply chain management implementation in Indian mining industries", *Resources, Conservation and Recycling*, 76, 50–60.

Munoz, V. A., Santos, J., Viles, E. and Ormazabal, M. (2018). Manufacturing and environmental practices in the Spanish context, *Journal of Cleaner Production*, 178, 268–275.

Murthy, D., Atrens, A., and Eccleston, J. (2002). "Strategic maintenance management", *Journal of Quality in Maintenance Engineering*, 8(4), 287–305.

Natalia, I., Alfnes, E., and Thomassen, M. K. (2016). "A differentiated approach for justification of advanced manufacturing technologies", *Advances in Manufacturing*, 4(3), 257–267.

Nath, S. and Sarkar, B. (2016) Decision system framework for performance evaluation of advanced manufacturing technology under fuzzy environment, *Opsearch*, 55, 1–18.

New, S., Green, K., and Morton, B., (2000), *Buying the Environment: The* (ed.), Routledge: London, 35–53.

Ni, J., Gu, X., and Jin, X. (2015). "Preventive maintenance opportunities for large production systems", *CIRP Annals*, 64(1), 447–450.

Nunnaly, J. C. (1978), *Psychometric theory*, New York: McGraw-Hill, ISBN: 978-0-07-107088-1.

O'Brien, C. (2002). "Global manufacturing and the sustainable economy", *International Journal of Production Research*, 40(15), 3867–3877.

Okhovat, M. A., Nehzati, T., and Hosseini, S. A. (2012). "Development of world class manufacturing framework by using six-sigma, total productive maintenance and lean", *Scientific Research and Essays*, 7(50), 4230–4241.

Orji, I., and Wei, S. (2016). "A detailed calculation model for costing of green manufacturing", *Industrial Management and Data Systems*, 116(1), 65–86.

Pagell, M., Handfield, R. B., and Barber, A. E., (2000). "Effects of operational employee skills on advanced manufacturing technology performance", *Production and Operations management society*, 9(3), 22–238.

Palcic, I., Koren, R. and Buchmeister, B. (2015) Technical Innovation Concepts in Slovenian Manufacturing Companies, *Procedia Engineering*, Vol. 100, pp. 141–149.

Palencia, O. G. (2007). "Optimización integral del mantenimiento: Hacia la terotecnología de clase mundial", *Revista Clepsidra*, 3(4), 59–70.

Pandza, K., Polajnar, A., and Buchmeister, B. (2005). "Strategic management of advanced manufacturing technology", *International Journal of Advanced Manufacturing Technology*, 25(3–4), 402–408.

Parmar, V., and Shah, H. G. (2016). "A literature review on supply chain management barriers ina manufacturing organization", *International Journal of Engineering Development and Research*, 4(1), 1–17.

Pathak, S. S. (2015). "TPM Implementation to Fine-Tune Manufacturing Performance: An Indian Industrial", *International Journal of Business Quantitative Economics and Applied Management Research*, 1(8), 71–82.

Paul, I. D., Bhole, G. P., and Chaudhari, J. R. (2014). "A review on green manufacturing: It's important, methodology and its application", *3rd International Conference on Materials Processing and Characterisation*, Elsevier Ltd., 1644–1649.

Piasson, D., Bíscaro, A. A. P., Leão, F. B., and SanchesMantovani, J. R. (2016). "A new approach for reliability-centered maintenance programs in electric power distribution systems based on a multi-objective genetic algorithm", *Electric Power Systems Research*, 137, 41–50.

Perotti, S., Zorzini, M., Cagno, E., and Micheli, G. J. L. (2012). "Green supply chain practices and company performance: The case of 3PLs in Italy", *International Journal of Physical Distribution & Logistics Management*, 42(7), 640–672.

Pierskalla, W. P., and Voelker, J. A. (1976). "A survey of maintenance models: The control and surveillance of deteriorating systems", *Naval Research Logistics Quarterly*, 23(3), 353–388.

Poduval, P. S., Pramod, V. R. (2015). "Interpretive structural modeling (ISM) and its application in analyzing factors inhibiting implementation of total productive maintenance (TPM)", *International Journal of Quality & Reliability Management*, 32(3), 308–331.

Prabhakar, P. D., and Jagathy, V. P. (2013). "A new model for reliability centred maintenance in petroleum refineries", *International Journal of Scientific & Technology Research*, 2(5), 56–64.

Pramod, V., Devadasan, S., Muthu, S., Jagathyraj, V., and Dhakshina, G. (2006). "Integrating TPM and QFD for improving quality in maintenance engineering", *Journal of Quality in Maintenance Engineering*, 12(2), 1355–2511.

Pui, G., Bhandari, J., Arzaghi, E., Abbassi, R., and Garaniya, Vikram. (2017). "Risk-based maintenance of offshore managed pressure drilling (MPD) operation", *Journal of Petroleum Science and Engineering*, 159, 513–521.

Pun, K., Chin, K., Chow, M., and Lau, H. (2002). "An effectiveness-centered approach to maintenance management: A case study", *Journal of Quality in Maintenance Engineering*, 8(4), 346–368.

Qiu, Q., Cui, L., and Gao, H. (2017). "Availability and maintenance modelling for systems subject to multiple failure modes", *Computers and Industrial Engineering*, 108(C), 192–198.

Raman, P. (2014). "Green supply chain management in India - An overview", *Journal of Supply Chain Management Systems*, 3(1), 14–23.

Rao, R. V., (2009). "An improved compromise ranking method for evaluation of environmentally conscious manufacturing programs", *International Journal of Production Research*, 47(16), 4399–4412.

Rao, Y., Xu, B.-L., Jing, T., Zhang, F., and Zhao, X.-Y. (2017). "The current status and future perspectives of virtual maintenance", *Procedia Computer Science*, 107, 58–63.

Raucha, E., Dallingera, M., Dallasegaab, P., and Mattab, D. T. (2015), "Sustainability in manufacturing through distributed manufacturing systems (DMS)", *The 22nd CIRP Conference on Life Cycle Engineering*, 544–549.

Raymond, L., (2005). "Operations management and advanced manufacturing technologies in SMEs: A contingency approach", *Journal of Manufacturing Technology Management*, 16(8), 936–955.

Raymond, L., and Croteau, A. M. (2006). "Enabling the strategic development of SMEs through advanced manufacturing systems: A configurational perspective", *Industrial Management and Data Systems*, 106(7), 1012–1032.

Rehman, M. A., and Shrivastava, R. L., (2013). "Green manufacturing (GM): past, present and future (a state of art review)", *World Review of Science, Technology and Sustainable Development*, 10, 17–55.

Rehman, M. A., Shrivastava, R. R., and Shrivastava, R. L., (2013). "Validating green manufacturing (GM) framework for sustainable development in an Indian steel industry", *Universal Journal of Mechanical Engineering*, 1(2), 49–61.

Roni, M., Jabar, J., Razali, M., and Murad, M. M. (2017). "Sustainable manufacturing drivers and firm performance: Moderating effect of firm size", *International Journal of Advanced and Applied Sciences*, 4(12) 2017, 243–249.

Rosen, M. A., and Kishawy, H. A. (2012). "Sustainable manufacturing and design: Concepts, practices and needs", *Sustainability*, 2012(4), 154–174.

Rosqvist, T., Laakso, K., and Reunanen, M. (2009). "Value-driven maintenance planning for a production plant", *Reliability Engineering & System Safety*, 94(1), 97–110.

Roy, M., and Khastagir, D., (2016). "Exploring role of green management in enhancing organizational efficiency in petro-chemical industry in India", *Journal of Cleaner Production*, 121, 109–115.

Rozenfeld, H., and Nappi, V. (2015). "The incorporation of sustainability indicators into a performance measurement system", *12th Global Conference on Sustainable Manufacturing*, 7–12.

Rutherfoord, R., Blackburn, R. A., and Spence, L. J. (2000). "Environmental management and the small firm: an international comparison", *International Journal of Entrepreneurial Behaviour and Research*, 6(6), 310–326.

Sabri, S. M., Sulaiman, R., Ahmad, A., and Tang, A. Y. (2015). "A comparative study on it outsourcing models for Malaysian SMEs e-business transformation", *ARPN Journal of Engineering and Applied Sciences*, 10(23), 17863–17870.

Sahoo, T., Sarkar, P. K., and Sarka, A. K. (2014). "Maintenance optimization for critical equipment in process industries based on FMECA method", *International Journal of Engineering and Innovative Technology (IJEIT)*, 3(10), 107–112.

Salaheldin, S. I. (2007). "The impact of organizational characteristics on AMT adoption: A study of Egyptian manufacturers", *Journal of Manufacturing Technology Management*, 18(4), 443–460.

Samanta, B., Sarkar, B., and Mukherjee, S. K. (2001). "Reliability-centered maintenance (RCM) for heavy earth-moving machinery in an open cast coal mine", *CIM Bulletin*, 94, 104–108.

Sang, M. L., Kim, S. T., and Choi, D. (2012). "Green supply chain management and organizational performance", *Industrial Management & Data Systems*, 112(8), 1148–1180.

Sangwan, K. S., and Mittal, V. K. (2015). "A bibliometric analysis of green manufacturing and similar frameworks", *Management of Environmental Quality: An International Journal*, 26(4), 566–587.

Sarker, B. R., and Faiz, T. I. (2016). "Minimizing maintenance cost for offshore wind turbines following multi-level opportunistic preventive strategy", *Renewable Energy*, 85, 104–113.

Sarkis, J., and Rasheed, A. (1995). "Greening the manufacturing function", *Business Horizons*, 38(5), 17–27.

Sarkis, J., Torre, P. G., and Diaz, B. A., (2010). "Stakeholder pressure and the adoption of environmental practices: The mediating effect of training", *Journal of Operations Management*, 28(2), 163–176.

Schiederig, T., Tietze, F., and Herstatt, C., (2011), *What is Green Innovation? A Quantitative Literature Review, Working Papers / Technologies- Und Innovations Management*, Technische Universität Hamburg-Harburg, No. 63.

Schoenherr, T., and Talluri, S. (2012). "Environmental sustainability initiatives: A comparative analysis of plant efficiencies in Europe and the U.S", *Science*, 35(1), 87–108.

Seles, B. M., De Sousa Jabbour, A. B., Jabbour, C. J., and Dangelico, R. M. (2016). "The green bullwhip effect, the diffusion of green supply chain practices, and institutional pressures: Evidence from the automotive sector", *International Journal of Production Economics*, 182, 342–355.

Selim, H., Yunusoglu, M. G., and Balaman, Ş. Y. (2016). "A dynamic maintenance planning framework based on fuzzy TOPSIS and FMEA: Application in an international food company", *Quality and Reliability Engineering International*, 32(3), 795–804.

Sellappan, N., Nagarajan, D., and Palanikumar, K. (2015). "Evaluation of risk priority number (RPN) in design failure modes and effects analysis (DFMEA) using factor analysis", *International Journal of Applied Engineering Research*, 10(14), 34194–34198.

Sellitz, C. (1965). *Research methods in social relations [by] Claire Selltiz [et al.]*. New York: Holt, Rinehart and Winston.

Seth, D., and Tripathi, D. (2005). "Relationship between TQM and TPM implementation factors and business performance of manufacturing industry in Indian context", *International Journal of Quality & Reliability Management*, 22(3), 256–277.

Seth, D., and Tripathi, D. (2006). "A critical study of TQM and TPM approaches on business performance of Indian manufacturing industry", *Total Quality Management & Business Excellence*, 17(7), 811–824.

Seth, D., Shrivastava, R. L., and Shrivastava, S., (2016). "An empirical investigation of critical success factors and performance measures for green manufacturing in cement industry", *Journal of Manufacturing Technology Management*, 27(8), 1076–1101.

Seuring, S. (2011). "Supply chain management for sustainable products – insights from research applying mixed methodologies", *Business Strategy and the Environment*, 20(7), 471–484

Sezen, B., and Sibel, Y. C. (2013). "Effects of green manufacturing and eco-innovation on sustainability performance", *9th International Strategic Management Conference*, Science Direct, 99, 154–163.

Shafeek, H. (2012). "Maintenance practices in cement industry", *Asian Transactions on Engineering (ATE ISSN: 2221-4267)*, 1(6), 10–20.

Shafiee, M. (2015). "Maintenance strategy selection problem: An MCDM overview", *Journal of Quality in Maintenance Engineering*, 21(4), 378–402.

Shafiee, M., and Finkelstein, M. (2015). "An optimal age-based group maintenance policy for multi-unit degrading systems", *Reliability Engineering and System Safety*, 134, 230–238.

Shafiee, M., Patriksson, M., and Chukova, S. (2016). "An optimal age–usage maintenance strategy containing a failure penalty for application to railway tracks *Proceedings of the Institution of Mechanical Engineers, Part F: Journal of Rail and Rapid Transit*, 230(2), 407–417.

Sharma, A. D., Dangayach, G. S., and Pathak, S. C. (2008). "Implementation of advanced manufacturing technologies: Experiences of Indian manufacturing companies", *International Journal of Business and Systems Research*, 2(1), 67–85.

Sharma, R. K., Kumar, D., and Kumar, P. (2006). "Manufacturing excellence through TPM implementation: A practical analysis", *Industrial Management & Data Systems*, 106(2), 256–280.

Sherwin, D. (2000). "A review of overall models for maintenance management", *Journal of Quality in Maintenance Engineering*, 6(3), 138–164.

Sheu, S.-H., Chang, C.-C., Chen, Y.-L., and Zhang, Z. G. (2015). "Optimal preventive maintenance and repair policies for multi-state systems', *Reliability Engineering & System Safety*, 140, 78–87.

Shyjith, K., Ilangkumaran, M., and Kumanan, S. (2008). "Multi-criteria decision-making approach to evaluating optimum maintenance strategy in the textile industry", *Journal of Quality in Maintenance Engineering*, 14(4), 375–386.

Siegel, D. S., Waldman, D. A., and Youngdahl, W. E. (1997). "The Adoption of advanced manufacturing technologies: Human resource management implications", *IEEE Transactions on Engineering Management*, 44(3), 288–298.

Siemieniuch, C. E., Sinclair, M. A., and de Henshaw, M. J. C. (2015). "Global drivers, sustainable manufacturing and systems ergonomics", *Applied Ergonomics* 51(2015) 104–119.

Simpson, M., Taylor, N., and Barker, K., (2004). ""Environmental responsibility in SMEs": Does it deliver competitive advantage?", *Business Strategy and the Environment*, 13(3), 156–171.

Singh, A., Singh, B., and Dhingra, A. K., (2012). ""Drivers and barriers of green manufacturing practices": A survey of Indian industries", *International Journal of Engineering Science*, 1(1), 5–19.

Singh, C. D. (2019). "Competency and strategy parameters selection based on fuzzy based modeling for Indian automobile industries", *International Journal of Quality Engineering and Technology*, 7(4), 346–360

Singh, C. D. (2018a). "Competency and strategy formulation in automobile industry", *International Journal of Industrial and Manufacturing Engineering*, 12(6), 648–651

Singh, C. D. (2018b). "A review of competency and strategy formulation in industry", *International Journal of Applied Studies and Production Management*, 4(1), 159–165

Singh, C. D., and Khamba, J. S. (2014a). "Analysis of manufacturing competency for an automobile manufacturing unit", *International Journal of Engineering, Business and Enterprise Applications*, 9(1), June-August 2014, 44–51.

Singh, C. D., and Khamba, J. S. (2014b). "Analysis of strategic success for an automobile manufacturing unit", *International Journal of Engineering, Business and Enterprise Applications*, 9(2), June-August 2014, pp: 104–111.

Singh, C. D., and Khamba, J. S. (2014c). "Evaluation of manufacturing competency factors on performance of an automobile manufacturing unit", *International Journal for Multi-Disciplinary Engineering and Business Management*, 2(2), June-2014, 4–16.

Singh, C. D., and Khamba, J. S. (2014d). "Evaluation of strategic success factors on performance of an automobile manufacturing unit", *International Journal of Engineering Research& Management Technology*, 1(4), July-2014, 144–157.

Singh, C. D., Khamba, J. S., Singh, S., and Singh, N. (2014a). "Exploring manufacturing competencies of a tractor manufacturing unit", *International Journal of Applied Studies*, 1(1), Jan 2014, 53–62.

Singh, C. D., Singh, P., and Khamba, J. S. (2014b). "To study the role of manufacturing competency in the performance of preet tractor manufacturing unit", *International Journal for Multi-Disciplinary Engineering and Business Management*, 2(2), June-2014, 4–7

Singh, C. D., Singh, P., and Khamba, J. S. (2014c). "To study the role of manufacturing competency in the performance of sonalika tractor manufacturing unit", *International Journal of Engineering, Business and Enterprise Applications*, 8(1), March-May., 2014, 62–66

Singh, C. D., and Khamba, J. S. (2015a). "Competency strategy model analysis using SEM", *International Journal for Multi-Disciplinary Engineering and Business Management*, 3(3), July2015, 37–41.

Singh, C. D., and Khamba, J. S. (2015b). "AHP analysis of manufacturing competency and strategic success factors", *International Journal in Applied Studies and Production Management*, 1(2), May-August 2015, 357–373.

Singh, C. D., and Khamba, J. S. (2015c). "Manufacturing competency & economic effects: A review",*Journal of Emerging Trends in Engineering, Science and Technology*, 3(2), September 2015, 16–20.

Singh, C. D., and Khamba, J. S. (2015d). "Technological competency & strategic management: A review",*Journal of Emerging Trends in Engineering, Science and Technology*, 3(2), September 2015, 21–26.

Singh, C. D. and Khamba, J. S. (2015e). "Competency development through strategic management", *International Journal for Multi-Disciplinary Engineering and Business Management*, 3(3), September 2015, 129–132.

Singh, C. D., and Khamba, J. S. (2015f)."A case study of a two wheeler manufacturing unit on manufacturing competency & strategic success",*International Journal of Engineering Research in Africa (Trans Tech Publications)*, 19, October 2015, 138–155.

Singh, C. D., and Khamba, J. S. (2015g)."Structural equation modelling for manufacturing competency and strategic success factors",*International Journal of Engineering Research in Africa (Trans Tech Publications)*, 19, October 2015, 156–170.

Singh, C. D., and Khamba, J. S. (2015h). "Effect of manufacturing competency on strategic success: A case study in an agricultural manufacturing unit",*International Journal of Physical and Social Sciences*, 5(10), October 2015, 544–571.

Singh, C. D., and Khamba, J. S. (2015i). "Role of manufacturing competency in strategic success of a commercial vehicle manufacturing unit: A case study", *International Journal of Management, IT & Engineering*, 5(10), October 2015, 24–41.

Singh, C. D., Khamba, J. S., and Kaur, H. (2015). "Exploring manufacturing competency and strategic success: A review", *in Proceedings of ICPIE 2015: International Conference on Production and Industrial Engineering*, in Singapore, 2015, 1655–1658.

Singh, C. D., Khamba, J. S., Singh, R., and Singh, N. (2014d). "Exploring manufacturing competencies of a two wheeler manufacturing unit", *in Proceedings of 27th International Conference on CADCAM, Robotics and Factories of the Future 2014*, in London, 2014, 1–10.

Singh, C. D., Singh, R., and Khan, A. A. (2019). "Evaluating the strategic potential of AMT in Indian manufacturing industries", *International Journal of Management Concepts and Philosophy*, 12(1), 80–101.

Singh, C. D., and Singh, P. (2018). "Exploratory analysis of green manufacturing in the context of performance of Indian manufacturing industries", *PCMA Journal of Business*, 11(2), 72–88.

Singh, C. D., and Khamba, J. S.. (2017) "Impact of manufacturing competency on strategic success in automobile manufacturing unit", *International Journal of Industrial and Systems Engineering*, 25(3), 335–359.

Singh, R. K., Garg, S. K., Deshmukh, S. G., and Kumar, M. (2007). "Modelling of critical success factors for implementation of AMTs", *Journal of Modelling in Management*, 2(3), 232–250.

Singh, H., and Khamba, J. S. (2009). "An evaluation of AMTs utilisation in Indian industry for enhanced manufacturing performance-evidence from large and medium scale organizations", *International Journal of Indian Culture and Business Management*, 2(6), 585–601.

Singh, H., and Kumar, R. (2013). "Measuring the utilization index of advanced manufacturing technologies: A case study", *IFAC Proceedings Volumes*, 46(9), 889–904.

Singh, P. J., Mittal, V. K., and Sangwan, K. S. (2013). "Development and validation of performance measures for environmentally conscious manufacturing", *International Journal of Services and Operations Management*, 14(2), 197–220.

Sivalingam, R. (1997). "Applying best practices to maintenance: A 12 step programme for moving down the road to recovery", *Plant Engineering*, 51 (6), 120–122.

Sivapirakasam, S. P., Mathew, J., and Surianarayanan, M., (2011). "Multi-attribute decision making for green electrical discharge machining", *Expert Systems with Applications*, 38(7), 8370–8374.

Small, M. H., and Chen, I. J. (1997). "Economic and strategic justification of AMT inferences from industrial practices", *International Journal of Production Economics*, 49(5), 65–75.

Small, M. H., Yasin, M. M., and Czuchry, A. J. (2009). "Enhancing competitiveness through effective adoption and utilisation of advanced manufacturing technology: Implications and lessons learned", *International Journal of Business and Systems Research*, 3(1), 34–57.

Soda, S., Sachdeva, A., and Garg, R. K. (2016). "Implementation of green supply chain management in India: Bottlenecks and remedies", *The Electricity Journal*, 29(4), 43–50.

Sohal, A., Sarros, J., Schroder, R., and O'Neill, P. (2008). "Adoption framework for advanced manufacturing technologies", *International Journal of Production Research*, 44(24), 5225–5246.

Spector, Y. (2011). "Theory of constraint methodology: Where the constraint is the business model", *International Journal of Production Research*, 49 (11), 3387–3394.

Steurer, R., Langer, M. E., Konrad, A., and Martinuzzi, A. (2005). "Corporations, stakeholders and sustainable development: A theoretical explorations of business – Society relations", *Journal of Business Ethics*, 61(3), 263–281.

Sun, H. (2000). "Current and future patterns of using advanced manufacturing technologies", *Technovation*, 20(11), 631–641.

Teles, C. D., Ribeiro, J. L. D., and Tinoco, M. A. C. (2015). "Characterization of the adoption of environmental management practices in large Brazilian companies", *Journal of Cleaner Production*, 86, 256–264.

Thomas, A. J., Barton, R., and John, E. G. (2008). "Advanced manufacturing technology implementation: A review of benefits and a model for change", *International Journal of Productivity and Performance Management*, 57(2), 156–176.

Tooru, S. (2001). "Certification and operational performance of ISO14001", *KamipaGikyoshi*, 55(1), 52–58.

Tousley, P. C. (2010). "Maintain it and save: Why we need maintenance management programs", *Journal of Energy Engineering*, 107 (5), 64–75.

Travis, D. E., and Casinger, L.. (1997). "Five causes of and remedies for maintenance manager headaches", *Plant Engineering* 51, 144–147.

Tyagi, M., Kumar, P., and Kumar, D. (2015). "Parametric selection of alternatives to improve performance of green supply chain management system", *Procedia - Social and Behavioral Sciences*, 189, 449–457.

Udo, G. J., Ehie, I. C., and Olorunniwo, F. (1995). "Fulfilling the promises of advanced manufacturing systems", *Industrial Management*, 37(5), 23–26.

Uygun, Ö., and Dede, A. (2016). "Performance evaluation of green supply chain management using integrated fuzzy multi-criteria decision-making techniques", *Computers & Industrial Engineering*, 102, 502–511.

Upton, D. (1995). "What really makes factories flexible", *Harvard Business Review*, 74(4), 74–84.

Vamsi, K. J., Sharma, A., and Karinka, S., (2014) ."Development of a framework for green product development", *Benchmarking: An International Journal*, 2(3), 427–445.

Veshagh, A., and Li, W., (2006), "Survey of eco design and manufacturing in automotive SMEs", In *Proc. of 13th CIRP International Conference on Life Cycle Engineering, Leuven, Belgium, May 31- June 02, 2006*, 305–310.

Vintr, Z., and Valis, D. (2006). "Vehicle maintenance process optimisation using life cycle costs data and reliability-centred maintenance", In *Proceedings of the First International Conference on Maintenance Engineering*, 180–188.

Vishal, M. S., and Avinash, S. (2016). "Green supply chain management – An overview", *International Journal of Advanced Engineering and Innovative Technology (IJAEIT), ISSN No. 2348-7208, 3*(1), 1–4.

Vishnu, C., and Regikumar, V. (2016). "Reliability-based maintenance strategy selection in process plants: A case study", *Procedia Technology*, 23, 1080–1087.

Waeyenbergh, G., and Pintelon, L. (2002). "A framework for maintenance concept development", *International Journal of Production Economics*, 77(3), 299–313.

Wang, S. H., Chang, S. P. , Williams, P., Benjamin, K., and Yan-Rui, Q. (2015). "Using balanced scorecard for sustainable design centered manufacturing",*43rd Proceedings of the North American Manufacturing Research*, 1, 2015, 181–192.

Wang, W. (2012). "An overview of the recent advances in delay-time-based maintenance modelling", *Reliability Engineering & System Safety*, 106, 165–178.

Wang, Y., Deng, C., Wu, J., Wang, Y., and Xiong, Y. (2014). "A corrective maintenance scheme for engineering equipment", *Engineering Failure Analysis*, 36, 269–283.

Webster, J., and Watson, R. T., (2002). ""Analyzing the past to prepare for the future": Writing a literature review", *Management Information Systems Quarterly*, 26(2), 13–23.

Weissman, S. H., and Sekutowski, J. C. (1991). "ECM: A technology for the nineties", *AT&T Technical Journal*, November-December, 70, 24–33.

Wheeler, D., Colbert, B., and Freeman, R. E. (2003). ""Focusing on value: Reconciling corporate social responsibility," sustainability and a stakeholder approach in a network world", *Journal of General Management*, 28(3), 1–28.

Wiengarten, F., Pagell, M., and Fynes, B. (2012). "Supply chain environmental investments in dynamic industries: Comparing investment and performance differences with static industries", *International Journal of Production Economics*, 135(2), 541–551.

Wienker, M., Henderson, K., and Volkerts, J.. (2016). "The computerized maintenance management system: An essential tool for world class maintenance", *Procedia Engineering* 138, 413–420.

Wikstrom, P., Terens, L., and Kobi, H. (2000). "Reliability, availability, and maintainability (RAM) of high power variable speed drive systems (VSDS). *Record of Conference Papers". IEEE Industry Applications Society 45th Annual Petroleum and Chemical Industry Conference (Cat. No.98CH36234)*, 36(1), 231–241.

Williamson, D., and Lynch-Wood, G., (2001). "A new paradigm for SME environmental practice", *The TQM Magazine*, 13(6), 424–433.

Williamson, D., Lynch-Wood, G., and Ramsay, J., (2006). "Drivers of environmental behavior in manufacturing SMEs and the implications for CSR", *Journal of Business Ethics*, 67(3), 317–330

Woo, C., Moon, G. K., Yanghon, C., and Jae, J. R. (2015). "Suppliers' communication capability and external green integration for green and financial performance in Korean construction industry", *Journal of Cleaner Production*, 112, 1–11.

Yadav, R. N., Sarkis, R. C., and Joseph, C., (2006). "Investment justification of advanced manufacturing technology: A review", *International Journal of Services and Operations Management*, 3(1), 41–73.

Yang, W., Tavner, P. J., Crabtree, C. J., Feng, Y., and Qiu, Y. (2014). "Wind turbine condition monitoring: technical and commercial challenges", *Wind Energy*, 17(1), 673–693.

Yongfeng, Li., Tao, F., Cheng, Y., Zhang, X., and Nee, A. Y. C. (2016). "Complex networks in advanced manufacturing systems", *Journal of Manufacturing System*, 12(1), 409–421.

Yssaad, B., and Abene, A. (2015). "Rational reliability centered maintenance optimization for power distribution systems", *International Journal of Electrical Power & Energy Systems*, 73, 350–360.

Zackrisson, M., Kurdve, M., Sasha Shahbaz, S., Magnus Wiktorsson, M, Mats Winroth, M., Landström, A., Almström, P., Andersson, C., Windmark, C., Öberg, A. E., and Andreas Myrelid, A. (2017), "Sustainability performance indicators at shop floor level in large manufacturing companies", *The 24th CIRP Conference on Life Cycle Engineering*, 457–462.

Zhang, Q., Vonderembse, M. A., and Cao, M. (2006). "Achieving flexible manufacturing competence: The roles of advanced manufacturing technology and operations improvement practices", *International Journal of Operations and Production Management*, 26(6), 580–599.

Zhang, Z., and Chu, X. (2010). "A new approach for the conceptual design of product and maintenance", *International Journal of Computer Integrated Manufacturing*, 23(7), 603–618.

Zhao, B., Verma, A., and Kapp, B. (1992). "Implementation advanced manufacturing technology in organizations: a socio-technical systems analysis", *IEEE Transactions on Engineering Management*, 39(1), 9–13.

Zhou, Y., and Chauh, K. B. (2002). "Computer integrated manufacturing in China", *International Journal of Operations and Production Management*, 22(3), 271–288.

Zhu, Q., Sarkis, J., and Geng, Y. (2005). "Green supply chain management in China: Pressures, practices and performance", *International Journal of Operations & Production Management*, 25(5), 449–468.

Zhu, W., and He, Y. (2017). "Green product design in supply chains under competition", *European Journal of Operational Research*, 258(1), 165–180.

BOOKS

Kaur, H., and Singh, C. D. (2020). *Adolescents', Family and Consumer Behaviour*, Routledge Press, Taylor & Francis.

Kaur, H., Singh, C. D., and Singh, R. (2018a). *Impingement of TPM and TQM on manufacturing performance*, Munich, Germany: BookRix GmbH & Co. KG, Sonnenstraße 23, 80331.

Kaur, H., Singh, C. D., and Singh, R. (2018b). *Achieving Excellence through Green Supply Chain Management in Manufacturing Industries*, Munich, Germany: BookRix GmbH & Co. KG, Sonnenstraße 23, 80331.

Kaur, H.,Singh, C. D., and Khan, A. A. (2018c). *An Exploratory Analysis of Green Manufacturing in Indian Manufacturing Industries*, Munich, Germany: BookRix GmbH & Co. KG, Sonnenstraße 23, 80331.

Singh, C. D., and Khamba, J. S.. (2019). *Manufacturing Competency and Strategic Success in the Automobile Industry*, CRC Press, Taylor & Francis

Singh, C. D., and Kaur, H. (2018a). *Evaluating JIT initiatives in Manufacturing Industry,* Munich, Germany; BookRix GmbH & Co. KG, Sonnenstraße 23, 80331.

Singh, C. D., Kaur, H., and Khan, A. A.. (2018a). *Evaluating the Strategic Potential of AMT on performance of manufacturing industries*, Munich, Germany: BookRix GmbH & Co. KG, Sonnenstraße 23, 80331.

Singh, C. D., and Kaur, H. (2018b). *To Study the Effect of Technology Competencies On Performance of Manufacturing Industry*, Munich, Germany: BookRix GmbH & Co. KG, Sonnenstraße 23, 80331.

Singh, C. D., Kaur, H., and Khan, A. A. (2018b). *An Industry View on Turning ERP Into a Competitive Advantage*, Munich, Germany: BookRix GmbH & Co. KG, Sonnenstraße 23, 80331.

Singh, C. D., Kaur, H., and Singh, R. (2018c). *Impact of Risk Factors and Techniques in Lean Manufacturing*, Munich, Germany: BookRix GmbH & Co. KG, Sonnenstraße 23, 80331.

Singh, R., Singh, C. D., and Kaur, H. (2017a). *Impact of Six Sigma and SCM on performance of MSME's*, Germany: LAP LAMBERT Academic Publishing.

Singh, C. D., Khamba, J. S., and Singh, R.. (2017b). *Manufacturing Competency: Case Studies in Manufacturing Industries*, Germany: LAP LAMBERT Academic Publishing.

Singh, C. D., Singh, R., and Kaur, H. (2017c). *Critical Appraisal of 5S and Kaizen on Success of SMEs*, Munich, Germany: LAP LAMBERT Academic Publishing.

Singh, C. D., Singh, R., and Kaur, H. (2017d). *Enactment of Six-Sigma in Manufacturing Industry*, Germany: LAP LAMBERT Academic Publishing.

Singh, C. D., Singh, R., and Kaur, H. (2017e), *Critical Appraisal for implementation of ERP in Manufacturing Industry*, Germany: LAP LAMBERT Academic Publishing.

Singh, C. D., Singh, R., and Kaur, H. (2017f). *Analytical Study of the Perspectives for Implementation of ERP*, Germany: LAP LAMBERT Academic Publishing.

Singh, C. D., Singh, R., and Kaur, H.(2017g). *Application of Lean and JIT principles in Supply Chain Management*, Germany: LAP LAMBERT Academic Publishing.

Singh, C. D., Singh, R., and Kaur, H. (2017h). *Impact Analysis of critical risk factors and operational techniques in Supply Chain Management*, Germany: LAP LAMBERT Academic Publishing.

Singh, C. D., Singh, R., and Kaur, H. (2017i). *Appraisal of SCM in Manufacturing Industry performance*, Germany: LAP LAMBERT Academic Publishing.

Appendix A

Questionnaire

Research Work

**INVESTIGATION OF SUSTAINABLE GREEN INITIATIVES IN
PERFORMANCE OF INDIAN MANUFACTURING INDUSTRIES
THROUGH ADVANCED MANUFACTURING AND MAINTENANCE
TECHNIQUES**

By
Dr CHANDAN DEEP SINGH
ASSISTANT PROFESSOR
DEPARTMENT OF MECHANICAL ENGINEERING
PUNJABI UNIVERSITY, PATIALA
&
Dr. HARLEEN KAUR
MANAGER (HR)
DELBREC INDUSTRIES Pvt. Ltd.,
CHANDIGARH

MAILING ADDRESS
Please mail the Questionnaire to the following Address:
Dr CHANDAN DEEP SINGH
DEPARTMENT OF MECHANICAL ENGINEERING,
PUNJABI UNIVERSITY, PATIALA
PUNJAB (INDIA)

Email: chandandeep@pbi.ac.in

Organization's Name				
Organization's Address				
Respondent's Name & Designation				
Respondent's Email Address				
Respondent's Contact No./Fax No.				
i.	PRODUCTS OF THE ORGANIZATION (Please Specify)			
ii.	PRESENT TURNOVER (In Crores of Rupees)	<10 Crores	10 – 50 Crores	50 – 100 Crores	>100 Crores
iii.	NUMBER OF EMPLOYEES	<200	201 – 500	501 – 1000	>1000
iv.	MARKET SHARE	<20 %	20 – 40 %	40 – 60 %	>60 %

(Please Tick the appropriate choice)

S. No.		Not at All 1	To Some Extent 2	Reasonably Well 3	To a Great Extent 4
A	**Concurrent Engineering**				
1	Employees feel that CE is long and arduous process	1	2	3	4
2	Inadequate internal expertise that required to implement change	1	2	3	4
3	No top management willing to accept responsible as champion of CE	1	2	3	4
B	**Just In Time**				
1	Implementation requires formal approval	1	2	3	4
2	JIT does not fit well with the organization	1	2	3	4
3	Eliminated the waste by producing ZERO defects	1	2	3	4
C	**Predictive Maintenance**				
Does your organization perform the following activities concerned with Predictive maintenance					
1	Failure pattern Recognition	1	2	3	4
2	Systematic Maintenance	1	2	3	4
3	Improving Unplanned Services	1	2	3	4
D	**Computerized Report Management**				
How does your organization deal with the following activities concerned with report management?					
1	supports real time report generation of ongoing work activity	1	2	3	4
2	report generation of completed maintenance work	1	2	3	4
3	Facilitates the flow of maintenance information	1	2	3	4
E	**Computer-Aided Design**				
1	Whether your organization has an effective Design Technology Program (e.g., CAD)?	1	2	3	4
2	Whether the design program includes Aesthetics and Ergonomics of the product?	1	2	3	4
3	Does your organization track design and development program costs?	1	2	3	4
F	**Rapid Prototyping**				
1	Does RPT leads to cost and time cutting	1	2	3	4
2	RPT is too expensive	1	2	3	4

S. No.		Not at All 1	To Some Extent 2	Reasonably Well 3	To a Great Extent 4
3	RPT is too complex	1	2	3	4
G	**CNC**				
1	Whether your organization use CNC machines?	1	2	3	4
2	Does your organization prefer using robots?	1	2	3	4
3	Does your organization regularly track Production costs?	1	2	3	4
H	**Residual Life Prediction**				
1	Whether your organization prefer product testing under actual conditions?	1	2	3	4
2	Does your organization carry out lifecycle analysis of the product?	1	2	3	4
I	**Automated Storage and Retrieval System**				
1	Does your organization use computer for analysis and record keeping?	1	2	3	4
2	Whether your organization has enough warehouses for Inventory storage?	1	2	3	4
3	Does your organization have sufficient automated equipment to meet market demands?	1	2	3	4
J	**Computerized Material Management and Inventory**				
Does your organization perform the following computerized maintenance activities concerned with material management / inventory control					
1	Track the movement of spare parts affecting costs and ensure its availability when required	1	2	3	4
2	Tracking lifecycle of an asset from the original purchase date up until it gets decommissioned	1	2	3	4
3	Possess a mechanism for material and machine selection	1	2	3	4
K	**Reliability-Centred Maintenance**				
To what extent your organization performs following reliability centred maintenance planning and scheduling functions					
1	Supporting unscheduled maintenance activities	1	2	3	4
2	Prioritizing work and resources for the maintenance activities	1	2	3	4

S. No.		Not at All 1	To Some Extent 2	Reasonably Well 3	To a Great Extent 4
3	Tracking and managing backlog of the maintenance activities	1	2	3	4
L	**Automated Guided Vehicle**				
1	Are Hydraulic and Pneumatic systems are employed in your organization?	1	2	3	4
2	Are robots deployed by your organization	1	2	3	4
M	**Finite Element Analysis**				
1	Whether the organization extensively uses Finite Element Method for Analysis purposes?	1	2	3	4
2	Does your organization use simulation and modelling for analyzing designs?	1	2	3	4
N	**Resource & Asset Management**				
To what extent your organization supports following resource-management activities?					
1	Allocate tools, equipment and materials (spare parts component assembly) at proper time	1	2	3	4
2	performs real time machine monitoring and alerts	1	2	3	4
3	Keeping computerized records of assets and assemblies, such as storing manufacturer and model	1	2	3	4
O	**Manufacturing Resource Planning**				
1	Improved order cycle	1	2	3	4
2	Improved decision-making capability	1	2	3	4
3	Organizational resistance to change	1	2	3	4
P	**Product Lifecycle**				
1	Does your organization invest in quality control and inspection?	1	2	3	4
2	Does your organization use computer to analyze quality?	1	2	3	4
Q	**Preventive Maintenance**				
To what extent your organization following Preventive maintenance activities					
1	Failure Mode Effect Analysis	1	2	3	4
2	Root Cause Identification	1	2	3	4
3	Acceptance Testing	1	2	3	4

S. No.		Not at All 1	To Some Extent 2	Reasonably Well 3	To a Great Extent 4
R	**Reverse Engineering**				
1	Do you use dynamic analysis?	1	2	3	4
2	Do you use static analysis?	1	2	3	4
3	Do you use software metrics?	1	2	3	4
S	**Kaizen**				
1	Are Kaizen principles and standards employed in organization?	1	2	3	4
2	Does your organization provide kaizen training?	1	2	3	4
3	Have relationships between managers and employees improved due to kaizen?	1	2	3	4
T	**Green Supply Chain Management**				
1	Do you associate with green suppliers, or use suppliers that share sustainability commitment?	1	2	3	4
2	Do you have an organizational commitment to implementing green logistics?	1	2	3	4
3	Do you make green strategies to meet customer requirements?	1	2	3	4
U	**Economic**				
1	New market opportunities	1	2	3	4
2	Commitment from various business stakeholders	1	2	3	4
3	Industrial sectors initiatives	1	2	3	4
V	**Greenhouse Gas Reduction**				
1	Do you train your employees for environmental consciousness?	1	2	3	4
2	Do you use fuel-efficient tools and machines to make environment friendly?	1	2	3	4
3	Does your environmental policy specify your organization's sustainability initiative?	1	2	3	4
W	**Material Requirement Planning**				
1	Improved lead time	1	2	3	4
2	Improved interaction with supplier	1	2	3	4
3	Improved information accuracy	1	2	3	4
X	**Computer-Aided Inspection and Reporting**				

S. No.		Not at All 1	To Some Extent 2	Reasonably Well 3	To a Great Extent 4
1	Do inspection processes in your organization improve quality?	1	2	3	4
2	Does your organization use computer programs for inspection and reporting?	1	2	3	4
Y	**Social**				
1	Public awareness	1	2	3	4
2	Customer demand	1	2	3	4
3	Socio-cultural responsibility	1	2	3	4
Z	**Enterprise Resource Planning**				
1	Better resource utilization	1	2	3	4
2	Reduction of redundancy in database	1	2	3	4
3	Top management authority can find easily which department require attention or focus	1	2	3	4
AA	**Automated Material Handling Systems**				
1	Do you think AMHS improves yield	1	2	3	4
2	Do you think AMHS reduces damage to product	1	2	3	4
3	Do you think AMHS reduces dependence on human labour	1	2	3	4
AB	**Computer-Aided Process Planning**				
1	Does your organization have an effective process planning program?	1	2	3	4
2	Does your organization apply group technology while planning?	1	2	3	4
3	Does your organization possess a mechanism for material and machine selection?	1	2	3	4
AC	**Environment**				
1	How much priority is given to reuse, recycle or recovery of the products, parts or materials?	1	2	3	4
2	Initiatives taken to avoid the use of hazards materials or manufacturing processes which affects the environment	1	2	3	4
3	Promotion about environmental-friendly packaging in organization	1	2	3	4
AD	**Flexible Manufacturing Systems**				

S. No.		Not at All 1	To Some Extent 2	Reasonably Well 3	To a Great Extent 4
Kindly indicate the level of following for adopting FMS					
1	Increased flexibility	1	2	3	4
2	Capacity increases	1	2	3	4
3	Reduced floor space requirement	1	2	3	4
AE	**Eco-Friendly**				
1	Strategy planned for environmental awareness of consumers	1	2	3	4
2	Promotion of environmentally-friendly products by suppliers	1	2	3	4
3	Role to establish a green corporate image	1	2	3	4
AF	**5-S**				
1	Are tools, equipment and materials are managed for smooth flow?	1	2	3	4
2	Has 5-S made a noticeable contribution to a safe and healthy environment?	1	2	3	4
3	Do employees feel 5-S adds the value for customers?	1	2	3	4
AG	**Robotics**				
1	Do you think robots lead to cleaner operations?	1	2	3	4
2	Is your management open to deploying robots?	1	2	3	4
3	Does the use of robots lead to increased safety and reduced injuries?	1	2	3	4
AH	**Renewable Energy**				
1	Do you utilize more alternate energy sources?	1	2	3	4
2	Do your quality human resources provide green ideas?	1	2	3	4
3	Do you consult with environmental specialists while using new technology?	1	2	3	4
AC	**OUTPUT**				
Impact of Sustainable Green Development on following Manufacturing Performance factors in an organization, when advanced manufacturing and maintenance techniques are being employed?					
1	Production Capacity	1	2	3	4
2	Production Time	1	2	3	4

S. No.		Not at All 1	To Some Extent 2	Reasonably Well 3	To a Great Extent 4
3	Lead Time	1	2	3	4
4	Quality	1	2	3	4
5	Reliability	1	2	3	4
6	Productivity	1	2	3	4
7	Growth & Expansion	1	2	3	4
8	Competitiveness	1	2	3	4
9	Sales (Annually)	1	2	3	4
10	Profit (Annually)	1	2	3	4
11	Market Share	1	2	3	4
12	Customer Base	1	2	3	4

(Please tick the appropriate choice)

(SIGNATURE OF RESPONDENT AND SEAL OF THE ORGANIZATION)

Appendix B

Analytical Hierarchy Process Questionnaire

Sustainable Development	1 2 3 4 5 6 7 8 9	Natural Resources
	1 2 3 4 5 6 7 8 9	Green Manufacturing
	1 2 3 4 5 6 7 8 9	Waste Management
	1 2 3 4 5 6 7 8 9	Lifecycle Analysis
	1 2 3 4 5 6 7 8 9	Computer-Aided Manufacturing
	1 2 3 4 5 6 7 8 9	Automation
	1 2 3 4 5 6 7 8 9	Computer Integrated Production Management Systems
	1 2 3 4 5 6 7 8 9	Expert Systems
	1 2 3 4 5 6 7 8 9	Advanced Maintenance
	1 2 3 4 5 6 7 8 9	Computerized Maintenance Management System
Natural Resources	1 2 3 4 5 6 7 8 9	Green Manufacturing
	1 2 3 4 5 6 7 8 9	Waste Management
	1 2 3 4 5 6 7 8 9	Lifecycle Analysis
	1 2 3 4 5 6 7 8 9	Computer-Aided Manufacturing
	1 2 3 4 5 6 7 8 9	Automation
	1 2 3 4 5 6 7 8 9	Computer Integrated Production Management Systems
	1 2 3 4 5 6 7 8 9	Expert Systems
	1 2 3 4 5 6 7 8 9	Advanced Maintenance
	1 2 3 4 5 6 7 8 9	Computerized Maintenance Management System
Green Manufacturing	1 2 3 4 5 6 7 8 9	Waste Management
	1 2 3 4 5 6 7 8 9	Lifecycle Analysis
	1 2 3 4 5 6 7 8 9	Computer-Aided Manufacturing
	1 2 3 4 5 6 7 8 9	Automation
	1 2 3 4 5 6 7 8 9	Computer Integrated Production Management Systems
	1 2 3 4 5 6 7 8 9	Expert Systems
	1 2 3 4 5 6 7 8 9	Advanced Maintenance
	1 2 3 4 5 6 7 8 9	Computerized Maintenance Management System

Waste Management	1 2 3 4 5 6 7 8 9	Lifecycle Analysis
	1 2 3 4 5 6 7 8 9	Computer-Aided Manufacturing
	1 2 3 4 5 6 7 8 9	Automation
	1 2 3 4 5 6 7 8 9	Computer Integrated Production Management Systems
	1 2 3 4 5 6 7 8 9	Expert Systems
	1 2 3 4 5 6 7 8 9	Advanced Maintenance
	1 2 3 4 5 6 7 8 9	Computerized Maintenance Management System
Lifecycle Analysis	1 2 3 4 5 6 7 8 9	Computer-Aided Manufacturing
	1 2 3 4 5 6 7 8 9	Automation
	1 2 3 4 5 6 7 8 9	Computer Integrated Production Management Systems
	1 2 3 4 5 6 7 8 9	Expert Systems
	1 2 3 4 5 6 7 8 9	Advanced Maintenance
	1 2 3 4 5 6 7 8 9	Computerized Maintenance Management System
Computer-Aided Manufacturing	1 2 3 4 5 6 7 8 9	Automation
	1 2 3 4 5 6 7 8 9	Computer Integrated Production Management Systems
	1 2 3 4 5 6 7 8 9	Expert Systems
	1 2 3 4 5 6 7 8 9	Advanced Maintenance
	1 2 3 4 5 6 7 8 9	Computerized Maintenance Management System
Automation	1 2 3 4 5 6 7 8 9	Computer Integrated Production Management Systems
	1 2 3 4 5 6 7 8 9	Expert Systems
	1 2 3 4 5 6 7 8 9	Advanced Maintenance
	1 2 3 4 5 6 7 8 9	Computerized Maintenance Management System
Computer Integrated Production Management Systems	1 2 3 4 5 6 7 8 9	Expert Systems
	1 2 3 4 5 6 7 8 9	Advanced Maintenance
	1 2 3 4 5 6 7 8 9	Computerized Maintenance Management System
Expert Systems	1 2 3 4 5 6 7 8 9	Advanced Maintenance
	1 2 3 4 5 6 7 8 9	Computerized Maintenance Management System
Advanced Maintenance	1 2 3 4 5 6 7 8 9	Computerized Maintenance Management System

Index